TRIADIC COERCION

Columbia Studies in Terrorism and Irregular Warfare

COLUMBIA STUDIES IN TERRORISM
AND IRREGULAR WARFARE
Bruce Hoffman, Series Editor

This series seeks to fill a conspicuous gap in the burgeoning literature on terrorism, guerrilla warfare, and insurgency. The series adheres to the highest standards of scholarship and discourse and publishes books that elucidate the strategy, operations, means, motivations, and effects posed by terrorist, guerrilla, and insurgent organizations and movements. It thereby provides a solid and increasingly expanding foundation of knowledge on these subjects for students, established scholars, and informed reading audiences alike.

Ami Pedahzur, *The Israeli Secret Services and the Struggle Against Terrorism*
Ami Pedahzur and Arie Perliger, *Jewish Terrorism in Israel*
Lorenzo Vidino, *The New Muslim Brotherhood in the West*
Erica Chenoweth and Maria J. Stephan, *Why Civil Resistance Works: The Strategic Logic of Nonviolent Conflict*
William C. Banks, editor, *New Battlefields/Old Laws: Critical Debates on Asymmetric Warfare*
Blake W. Mobley, *Terrorism and Counterintelligence: How Terrorist Groups Elude Detection*
Jennifer Morrison Taw, *Mission Revolution: The U.S. Military and Stability Operations*
Guido W. Steinberg, *German Jihad: On the Internationalization of Islamist Terrorism*
Michael W. S. Ryan, *Decoding Al-Qaeda's Strategy: The Deep Battle Against America*
David H. Ucko and Robert Egnell, *Counterinsurgency in Crisis: Britain and the Challenges of Modern Warfare*
Bruce Hoffman and Fernando Reinares, editors, *The Evolution of the Global Terrorist Threat: From 9/11 to Osama bin Laden's Death*
Boaz Ganor, *Global Alert: The Rationality of Modern Islamist Terrorism and the Challenge to the Liberal Democratic World*
M. L. R. Smith and David Martin Jones, *The Political Impossibility of Modern Counterinsurgency: Strategic Problems, Puzzles, and Paradoxes*
Elizabeth Grimm Arsenault, *How the Gloves Came Off: Lawyers, Policy Makers, and Norms in the Debate on Torture*
Assaf Moghadam, *Nexus of Global Jihad: Understanding Cooperation Among Terrorist Actors*
Bruce Hoffman, *Inside Terrorism*, 3rd edition
Stephen Tankel, *With Us and Against Us: How America's Partners Help and Hinder the War on Terror*

Triadic Coercion

ISRAEL'S TARGETING OF STATES THAT
HOST NONSTATE ACTORS

Wendy Pearlman and Boaz Atzili

Columbia University Press
New York

Columbia University Press
Publishers Since 1893
New York   Chichester, West Sussex
cup.columbia.edu
Copyright © 2018 Columbia University Press
Paperback edition, 2019
All rights reserved

Library of Congress Cataloging-in-Publication Data
Names: Pearlman, Wendy, author. | Atzili, Boaz, author.
Title: Triadic coercion : Israel's targeting of states that host nonstate actors / Wendy Pearlman and Boaz Atzili.
Other titles: Columbia studies in terrorism and irregular warfare.
Description: New York : Columbia University Press, 2018. |
Series: Columbia studies in terrorism and irregular warfare | Includes bibliographical references and index.
Identifiers: LCCN 2018007692 | ISBN 9780231171847 (cloth) | ISBN 9780231171854 (pbk.) | ISBN 9780231548540 (e-book)
Subjects: LCSH: Non-state actors (International relations) | International relations. | Security, International. | Arab-Israeli conflict. | Israel—Foreign relations—Arab countries. | Arab countries—Foreign relations—Israel.
Classification: LCC JZ4059 .P43 2018 | DDC 956.05/4—dc23
LC record available at https://lccn.loc.gov/2018007692

Cover design: Lisa Hamm

We dedicate this book to our fathers and also to the struggle for peace and freedom in the Middle East.

Contents

Map of Israel and the Surrounding Region ix
Preface and Acknowledgments xi

1 Understanding Triadic Coercion 1

2 Israel's Use of Triadic Coercion: Sources and Historical Evolution 23

3 Egypt Since 1949: Triadic Coercion from Raids to Peace 59

4 Syria Since 1949: Triadic Coercion from Coups to Revolution 95

5 Israel and the Palestinian Authority Since 1993: Strategic Culture in Asymmetric Conflict 130

6 Lebanon Before and Since 2006: Strategic Culture at War 175

7 Triadic Coercion Beyond the Arab-Israeli Conflict 218

Conclusion 242

Notes 255
Bibliography 313
Index 351

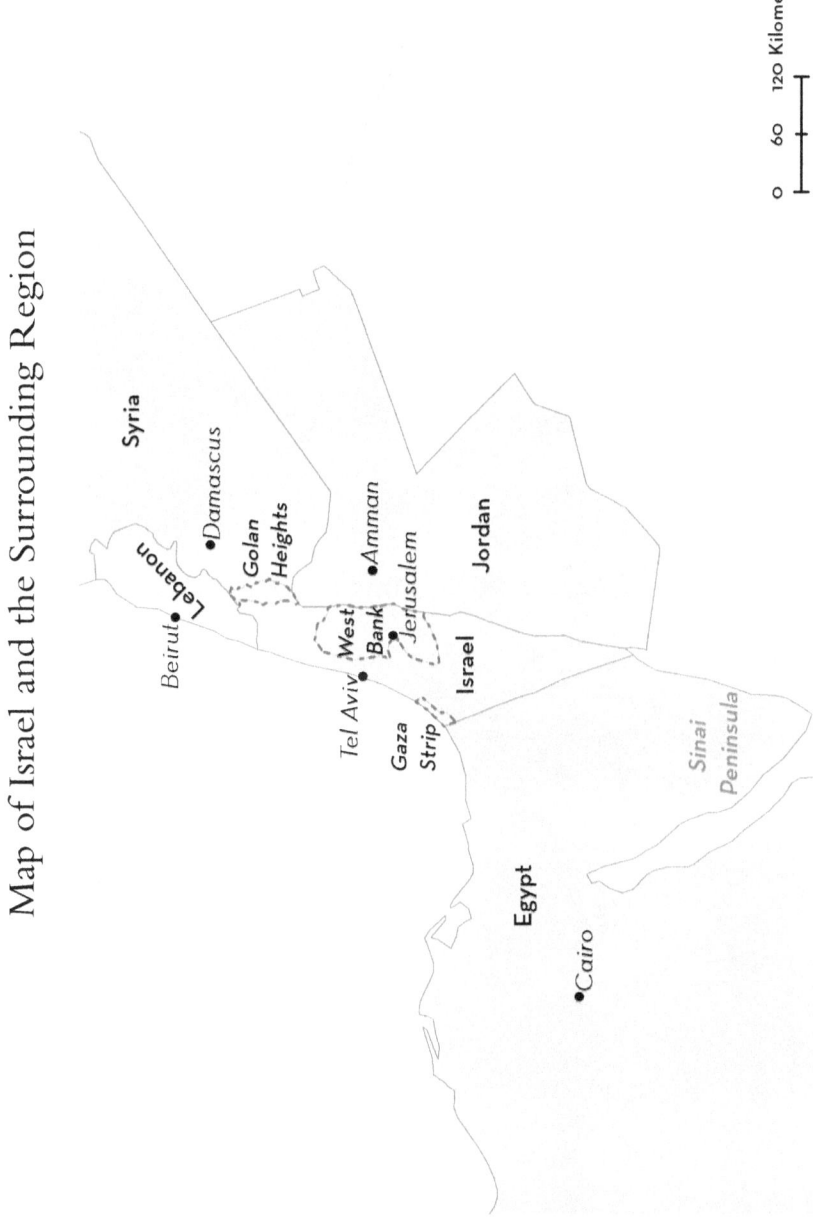

Preface and Acknowledgments

This project's roots were planted at Harvard's John F. Kennedy School of Government's Belfer Center for Science and International Affairs, where we had postdoctoral fellowships in 2007–2008. Having offices across the hallway from each other, we had many conversations about the still-fresh 2006 War between Israel and Hezbollah. We shared a deep dismay about the vast destruction and loss of life, and were particularly alarmed by the scope of Israel's bombardment of Lebanon. What began as a normative concern about excessive use of force spurred our attention to an intellectual puzzle about its targeting. Why would Israel pound Lebanon, a famously weak state, to demand that it block the actions of Hezbollah, a famously strong nonstate actor?

To answer these questions, we delved into both theory and history. Building on work on deterrence, intrastate conflict, and other dynamics of warfare, we crafted an analytical framework and developed generalizable hypotheses about the causes and effects of states' use or threat of force to coerce other states to stop attacks by nonstate actors. We then investigated these dynamics across the rich seventy-year trajectory of the Arab-Israeli conflict. Researching the foundations of Israel's security decision-making and thinking from statehood to the present, we discovered that its approach to fighting nonstate actors was not uniform. Israel had not always targeted host states in the demand that they "take responsibility" for stopping nonstate actors on their soil. Even when it employed this policy, it did not do so in precisely the same way over time or space. Seeking to explain these shifts on the part of Israel in these three-actor conflicts, we were struck by how developments in its strategic culture went far in accounting for variation and, in particular, for what appeared to be its increasingly aggressive actions in recent years.

We also threw ourselves into the study of Arab states that Israel charged with harboring violent nonstate actors. We examined their governing regimes, with particular interest in regime origins, internal compositions, institutional structures, and connections to society. We were attentive to the complex relationships between host regimes and nonstate actors, noting how they could range from patronage to hostility. We saw that these relationships were typically driven less by regimes' claimed ideological commitments to armed struggle against Israel than they were by concern for their own political survival. In this context, we were drawn to a consistent pattern: only regimes that were strong, in terms of both cohesion and capacity, had the ability to determine when raison d'état demanded that they assert control over nonstate actors and then do what was needed to impose that control. This pattern had direct implications for Israel's strategy of using military pressure against host states to force them to act against nonstate actors. Such a strategy, history showed us, was bound to fail when that host's regime was weak.

The product of this multistranded research is this book on what we came to call "triadic coercion." We set out to study this topic with as much scholarly objectivity as possible in the belief that social scientific analysis of the empirical record was the best way to make inferences about causes and effects and thereby derive both academic conclusions and policy recommendations. At the same time, we have not lost sight of the moral intensity of the competing commitments that imbue every aspect of the Arab-Israeli conflict. In beginning our research with the wake of the 1948 War, we do so with attentiveness to the momentousness of that war itself as an historic justice or injustice, depending on one's point of view. We acknowledge that even the most seemingly simple terms that we employ in this book might be deeply contested. We understand that the violence that we refer to with such dry terms as "attacks," "reprisals," "retaliation raids," and "operations" are not simply events to be modeled and counted but actions that can obliterate lives, destroy families, terrorize or dehumanize entire communities, and rob individuals of their most basic rights to life and physical security. Similarly, the "nonstate actors" in our story are not simply nuisances for state sovereignty and border security. For some they are terrorist groups deliberately killing civilians. For others they are the legitimate representatives of dispossessed peoples struggling for liberation. For the sake of consistency, we refer to the main actors that we examine by the names that they call themselves. When we use Israel's chosen name for its army, the Israel Defense Forces, we do so with sensitivity to those who view it as a force of aggression and occupation rather than defense.

As this book was many years in the making, the list of people to whom we owe gratitude is similarly long. We are thankful to the Belfer Center for the intellectual environment it provided us as newly minted PhDs. We could not have predicted that our casual chats would spawn an article and then an academic monograph but are grateful for institutes like Belfer and others that offer academics the time, resources, and community to explore new ideas and follow them to wherever they lead.

In the years since then many others helped us make this project better than we could have made it alone. Early in this project several scholars offered feedback on what became our first write-up about what we then called "triadic deterrence," an article in the journal *Security Studies*. We thank Jeff Colgan, Erica Chenoweth, Christopher Day, Patrick Thaddeus Jackson, Amir Lupovici, Joseph Olmert, and Janice Stein for valuable comments and suggestions during that stage. We are particularly grateful to Zeev Maoz, who offered us early advice and encouragement and made his datasets available for our use.

As we worked on this project over the course of years, we presented parts of it at workshops and talks at Northwestern University, American University, and the University of Chicago, and the annual conferences of the International Studies Association and Association of Israeli Studies. At each event we were lucky to gather feedback from engaged readers and listeners, all of which left important imprints on this work.

We are grateful to our institutions, American University and Northwestern University, for the multiple forms of support they gave us, from library services to time to commit to writing. We consider ourselves fortunate to be able to call these universities home. In addition, we express special thanks to American's SIS Research, especially Shannon Looney and Holly Bennett Christiansen, for funding and expert organizational help in sponsoring a daylong "book incubator" to discuss an early draft of the complete manuscript. We owe gratitude to Dima Adamsky, Ariel Ahram, Jon

Caverley, Keith Darden, Miles Kahler, Austin Long, and Jeremy Pressman for participating in this workshop. Their insights and brainstorming were invaluable in shaping and improving the project. Similarly, we thank two anonymous readers solicited by Columbia University Press for their comments.

Throughout the process of producing this book, we benefitted from research assistance from students at both American University and Northwestern University. For that, we owe gratitude to Laura Bosco, Jiajie He, Min Jung Kim, Karen Saunders, Jeffrey Bilik, Alli Divine, Clara Clymer, John Quigley, and Tova Yampolsky. We could not have asked for a better team. We thank the dedicated staff at Columbia University Press, and especially Caelyn Cobb and Miriam Grossman, for shepherding the manuscript from submission to fruition.

Lastly, we owe a great debt to our families and friends. Wendy gives special thanks to her partner, Peter Cole, and her grandmother, Margaret Pearlman. Boaz thanks his son, Tomer, daughter, Melanie, and wife, Orit. These and others dear to our hearts not only bore the burden of the countless months in which we were buried in our books and computer screens but also endured occasional lectures on the concept of strategic culture or now-forgotten skirmishes from the 1950s. For us, their patience and good cheer are proof of all that is good in human nature.

We dedicate this book to our fathers. Wendy's father, Michael Pearlman, passed away just a few weeks before we finished this book manuscript. She misses him tremendously but is grateful for what she learned from his love of history, passion for scholarship, tremendous wit, and inspiring humility. He taught her to try to keep things in perspective and be grateful for her immense good fortune in being able to study for a living. As he used to say, "it sure beats a real job." Boaz's father, Avraham Atzili, was wounded at the altar of triadic coercion, though he might not know that this was the larger context in which a bullet hit his leg. Beyond this event, Avraham, always the intellectual and the historian, instilled in his son curiosity about the past and a desire to improve the future.

TRIADIC COERCION

CHAPTER 1

Understanding Triadic Coercion

> We will make no distinction between the terrorists who committed these acts and those who harbor them.
>
> —GEORGE W. BUSH, SEPTEMBER 11, 2001

Barely had the Twin Towers fallen on September 11 when U.S. president George W. Bush announced that he held accountable not only the al-Qaeda network that flew the planes but also the state in which that organization was based. "The Taliban must act and act immediately," he warned the governing authorities of Afghanistan. "They will hand over the terrorists or they will share in their fate."[1] Bush's declarations were reflective of a general trend in the post–Cold War era. Though an increasing number of conflicts involve states and nonstate actors, states often have difficulty fighting such groups due to their small size, secretive structures, lack of visible assets, and sometimes extremist ideologies. Given these circumstances, some analysts conclude that states cannot deter nonstate actors directly and instead should aim to coerce the states that host them.

We call such a strategy "triadic coercion," wherein one state uses military threats and/or punishments against another state to deter it from aiding or abetting attacks by nonstate actors from within its territory or to compel it to stop such violence.[2] According to Idean Salehyan, 55 percent of the 291 rebel groups that were known to be fighting against states between 1951 and 1999 used the territory of a neighboring state as a sanctuary or a base for attacks.[3] Facing such attacks, governments then and now have responded by using force or threats against the states that willingly or unwillingly played the role of host. The United States has continually pressured Pakistan to crack down on the Afghan Taliban and Haqqani networks.[4] Turkey has engaged Iraq, Syria, and Iran in its struggle against the Kurdistan Workers' Party.[5] India has repeatedly warned Pakistan to end complicity with Kashmiri separatists.[6] Sudan attacked Chad to force it to cease support for Darfurian rebels.[7] Nicaragua's Sandinista government pressured Honduras and Costa Rica to stop harboring Contra rebels.[8] Triadic coercion, thus, has been entwined with some of the most pressing conflicts in the contemporary international system.

Extending our earlier work,[9] this book explores triadic coercion through scrutiny of nearly seventy years of Israeli history. For the entirety of its existence, Israel has engaged in strategies of triadic coercion against neighboring Arab states in an effort to end violence and border violations by nonstate actors from those states. Some might argue that this particularly intensive history renders Israel a unique case not suitable for generalizable insight. By contrast, we posit that the very heightened character of Israel's conflicts with nonstate actors and host states offers a natural laboratory for evaluating triadic coercion as a strategy. Furthermore, it presents a wealth of within-case variation for causal inference. Our *longue durée* examination of these rises and falls in Israel's triadic conflicts makes patterns visible that might be difficult to detect elsewhere.

Two main questions drive our research. First, we investigate the conditions under which triadic coercion is likely to succeed. Traditional discussions of interstate conflict assume that the greater a state's power relative to the state that it seeks to coerce, the more likely coercion is to succeed. The coercer state should thus prefer its adversary to be weak. We argue that triadic coercion turns this logic on its head. For the host state to act effectively against a nonstate actor on its soil, it requires internal political cohesion and institutional capacity. The host state's executive decision-making must be sufficiently consolidated to recognize the national security interest in averting another state's coercive assaults. It likewise must possess the competencies to design measures against the nonstate actor and the domestic clout to implement such policies even if they are unpopular. Strong regimes possess these means, whereas weak ones do not. As a result, we argue, triadic coercion can only succeed when directed against a host state with at least a minimum level of regime strength. Triadic coercion strategies against weak hosts are unlikely to suppress nonstate actor violence, regardless of the military power that the coercer state projects.

Our second major query builds on the first. If triadic coercion is only effective against strong regimes, why do states frequently employ it against weak ones? We attribute such actions to strategic culture. A state's system of beliefs, values, and practices can elevate the use of coercive force as an appropriate response—and host states as appropriate targets—independent of the efficacy of those choices. Politicians, public opinion, media, and military leaders might contribute to rhetoric, attitudes, images, and analogies that crystalize this strategic culture. Under these circumstances, national security decision-making elite, and perhaps even the social and political environment at large, encourage triadic coercion on the basis of conviction rather than calculation, and due to a utility that is intrinsic rather than instrumental. The outcome is increased use of the strategy, even when conditions for success are absent.

In investigating these questions, we adopt an approach of "analytical eclecticism": a selective integration of concepts, logics, and mechanisms that stem from separate paradigms as needed to address different aspects of the substantive problem under consideration.[10] Our analysis of the sources of triadic coercion policy in Israel's early years uses a mix of arguments, ranging from a straightforward realist orientation to a more liberal emphasis on domestic politics. Noting that such rationalist lenses fail to explain the persistence over time of policies when they are unlikely to be effective, we find greater explanatory value in an alternative perspective. Our study of the sources of triadic coercion in more recent years thus adopts a constructivist sensitivity to the ways in which collective perceptions, beliefs, and culture are crucial for understanding strategic choices. Employing this varied approach, this introductory chapter elaborates on these arguments, lays out an analytical framework for evaluating them, and discusses the broader contribution of this research.

Triadic Coercion

Triadic conflicts occur when a nonstate actor that is geographically based in a "host" state attacks a second state. The attacked state plays what we identify as the role of the "coercer" when it carries out threats or military operations that attempt to persuade the host to prevent the nonstate actor's attacks (see figure 1.1).

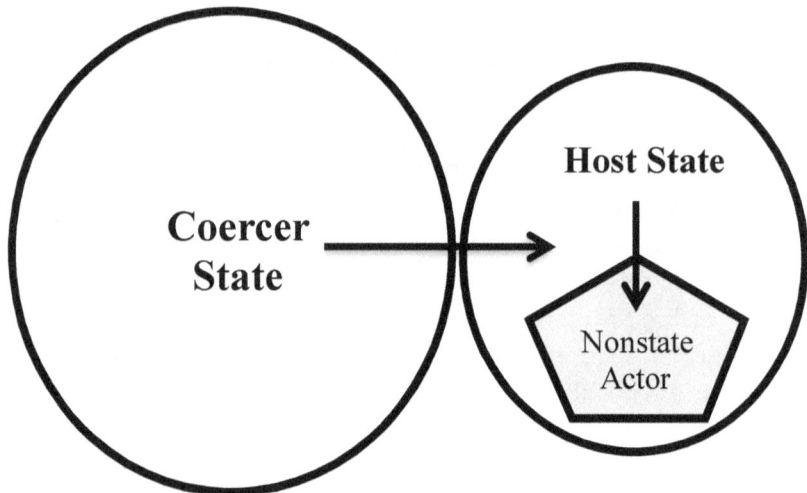

Figure 1.1 Triadic coercion.

Conflicts often become triadic when coercer states conclude that they are unable to resolve their disputes with nonstate actors using bilateral strategies targeting those actors directly. Among such bilateral strategies, a coercer state might attempt to defeat the nonstate actor or render it inoperable by targeting its fighters and assets. Such an approach is often termed "brute force."[11] If unable to defeat the nonstate actor with brute force, the state might seek to use various kinds of deterrence. The state might attempt "deterrence by denial," through which it seeks to minimize nonstate actors' attacks by preventing their effective execution. Approximating regular defense strategies, deterrence by denial may involve gathering intelligence, erecting physical barriers, or engaging in diplomatic cooperation to enlist the host state's help.[12] Alternatively, a state might pursue "deterrence by punishment." The state then uses threats or applies force to demonstrate to the nonstate actor that the costs of aggression outweigh its benefits. Though a rational actor might cease attacks, many analysts doubt that nonstate actors would necessarily do so. Some posit that militant groups are motivated by extremist ideologies that state leaders simply cannot affect. Even if terrorism is judged to be a strategic rather than fanatical choice,[13] the rationales of groups that employ it may entail preferences, calculations, and decision-making processes that are distinct from those of states. This makes it more difficult for states to communicate threats in a way that will coerce nonstate actors, undermining the prospects that nonstate actors will behave as the logic of deterrence assumes.[14]

Nonstate actors are also well positioned to withstand deterrence by punishment due to their organizational characteristics. Small size and secretive structures may allow them to elude state intelligence. Nonstate actors typically lack valuable assets to threaten and are unlikely to have a territorial "return address" against which to retaliate.[15] Paradoxically, the asymmetry of these conflicts might thus work to the detriment of states. The balance of motivation thus may favor the nonstate actor—whose very survival is at stake—even if the balance of power favors the state.[16] Some propose that the nonstate actor might not even have an interest in averting harsh retaliation. According to that logic, nonstate actors might in fact welcome punishment in the belief that it will increase popular sympathy for their cause.[17]

Given these difficulties surrounding direct deterrence by punishment, a state seeking to defeat a nonstate actor might instead pursue "indirect deterrence." Such a strategy, Jeffrey Knopf explains, is "not aimed at the attackers themselves but at third parties whose action can affect the likelihood that a potential attacker can or will carry out an assault."[18] Those third parties are typically other states. As nonstate actors do not enjoy their own sovereignty, they must be based within the territory of some state. In addition to territorial safe haven, these groups often seek material assistance, which states are best positioned to supply. Recognizing this, some argue that the principal way for states to fight violent nonstate actors is via the states from which they operate or obtain support.[19]

We focus on "coercer states" that employ this strategy of triadic coercion against "host states" on whose territory nonstate actors are based. We recognize that states can aid insurgent or terrorist groups in ways other than hosting them. However, as Daniel Byman writes, physical haven is "perhaps the most important form of support" that states can provide.[20] Unlike other types of sponsorship that entail significant resources, any state can be a host state simply by virtue of possessing territory. Investigation of triadic coercion against host states is thus potentially applicable to a large universe of cases.

Triadic coercion against host states entails a mix of two strategic logics. It seeks deterrence by invoking threat of punishment, or limited strikes that suggest the possibility of harsher punishment, to dissuade host states from enabling nonstate actors' violence. It also entails "compellence" to force the host state to reverse some actions, such as assisting the nonstate actor, or begin taking new actions, such as repressing the nonstate actor or impeding its free movement.[21]

Conventional wisdom about the difficulty of combatting nonstate actors suggests that a coercer state is rational to target deterrence and compellence at host states instead.[22] Keren Fraiman, for example, argues that "placing the onus of containing violent groups back on the states that host them is an attractive and a potentially efficacious strategy."[23] Still, triadic coercion is far from easy. Byman notes: "Support for terrorism can be exceptionally difficult to stop. Sponsors often anticipate the punishment that they may receive for backing terrorists and nevertheless choose to provide support, believing they can endure or avoid the pain. . . . Military strikes—particularly limited ones—often backfire."[24]

Jonathan Shimshoni concurs. Scrutinizing some of the same empirical material that we do, he concludes that a state's attempts to coerce a host state are likely to fail if that host is either sufficiently strong to confront the coercer or too weak or sympathetic to the target group to act against it.[25] Shimshoni introduces this observation in the final pages of his study and does not have a chance to develop it into a set of general arguments, no less evaluate them systemically across time and space. Taking up where Shimshoni left off, we craft a study centered on two questions: Under what conditions can triadic coercion succeed? Why do states pursue it even when those conditions do not hold?

Outcomes: Under What Conditions Can Triadic Coercion Succeed?

We conceptualize triadic coercion outcomes along a spectrum, assuming the point of view and goals of the coercer state (see figure 1.2).

At one extreme, complete success is achieved when the coercer's actions toward the host state causes it to take actions that result in total cessation of the nonstate actor's belligerence. At the other extreme, triadic coercion is counterproductive when the coercer's actions toward the host state cause it to take actions that intensify the nonstate actor's belligerence. Midway between these poles, triadic coercion can be viewed as irrelevant when the coercer's attempts to pressure the host state have no effect on the nonstate actor. On the continuum from irrelevance to counterproductivity

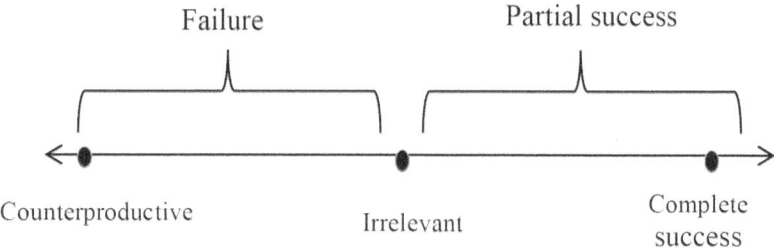

Figure 1.2 Spectrum of triadic coercion outcomes.

are different levels of strategic failure that result in increasingly greater threats to the coercer. On the continuum from irrelevance to complete success are outcomes of partial success that offer increasingly greater benefits for the coercer.

To predict the likely outcomes of triadic coercion, one must understand interstate and intrastate dynamics, which operate at three levels (see figure 1.3).

Figure 1.3 presents a decision tree that details the logic of the argument elaborated and evaluated throughout this book. Again, this tree assumes the point of view of the coercer state. The first level is the issue of greatest salience in interstate relations: balance of power. If the coercer state cannot muster the political or military resources to communicate credible threats against the host state, triadic coercion is likely to fail. In most cases, it will not even be attempted.

The schema's second level concerns the host state's predisposition toward the nonstate actor's use of violence. All things being equal, "defiant" host states support nonstate attacks and "cooperative" hosts oppose them. States may be defiant or cooperative for a variety of reasons, including their own foreign policy goals, ideological orientation, domestic public opinion, or pressures to maintain a ruling coalition of key elites. We consider a predisposition in favor or against aiding nonstate actors to exist in advance of triadic coercion and regardless of its use.

Practitioners and scholars devote considerable attention to host states' predispositions. As we show in the Israeli case, decision-makers sometimes never move beyond the question of whether host states are defiant or cooperative. Similarly, key academic studies construct detailed typologies of host-states' orientations toward nonstate violence. For example, Paul Pillar notes that a host state's relationship to a terrorist group might be one of

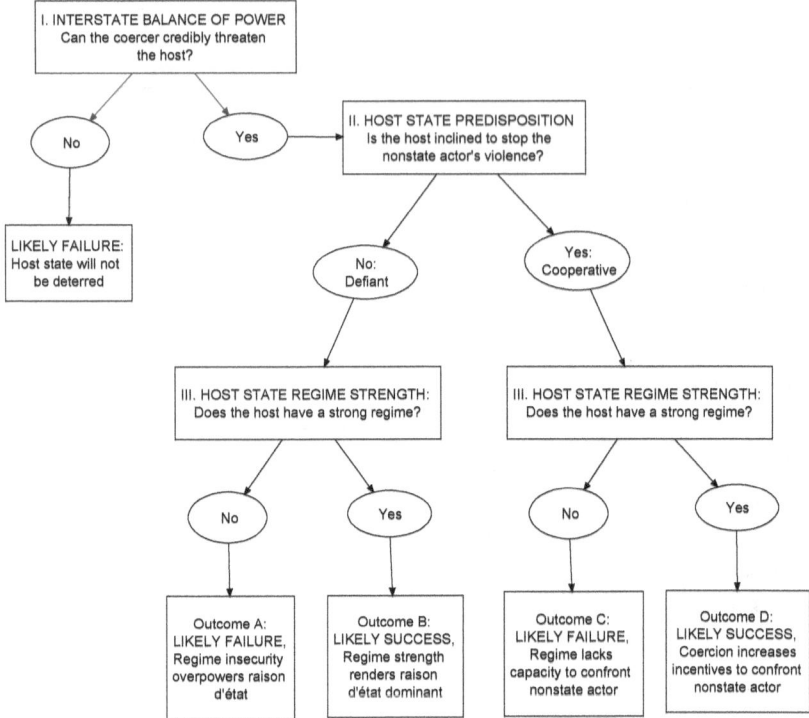

Figure 1.3 Explaining triadic coercion outcomes.

sponsor, enabler, or cooperator.[26] Byman elaborates a spectrum of six types of state sponsors: (1) strong supporters that offer both intense commitment and significant resources, (2) weak supporters that are committed yet lack resources, (3) lukewarm supporters that do little to advance groups directly, (4) antagonistic supporters that offer assistance with the aim of controlling or weakening a group, (5) passive supporters that turn a blind eye to groups, and (6) unwilling supporters that, too weak to stop groups, are more victims than supporters of terrorism.[27]

While helpful, successful triadic coercion does not depend primarily on such distinctions. Rather, the more significant determinant of triadic coercion outcomes is the third level in Figure 1.3: the strength of the host state's regime. Here the emphasis on "regime," rather than "state," is deliberate. A state is a set of governing institutions and practices with administrative, judicial, rule-making, and coercive powers. A regime refers to who it is that controls those institutions and how they use them to rule. Though the lines between "state strength" and "regime strength" can be blurred in practice,[28] we focus on the latter, because it assumes a measure of the former. It is difficult for a system of rule to be effective unless the institutions through which rule is exercised are effective. At the same time, focusing on regimes goes beyond institutional elements to take into account political dimensions such as relations among governmental elites and between those elites and society.[29] Regime strength is thus a more dynamic element that better captures the variability that we observe in empirical cases of conflict. Within a given country, regimes might rise, fall, and change, even if the overarching strength of state institutions does not. This comes to the fore in the modern Middle East, where revolutions and coups d'état have brought swift shifts in political systems.

We conceptualize regime strength as the product of two components: cohesion and capacity. Cohesion is the degree to which a regime acts as if it were a unitary entity. We measure cohesion qualitatively by assessing the degree to which institutions, a unifying ideology, and/or authoritative leadership integrate political elites, consolidate decision-making power, and create command and control throughout the state apparatus.[30] In a cohesive regime, the forces assisting cooperative behavior exceed the forces encouraging competitive or antagonistic behavior. Under such conditions, leaders are able to direct human and material resources authoritatively. In a fragmented regime, by contrast, a proliferation of actors has the autonomy to act upon divergent preferences.

Cohesion in a composite political entity such as a regime must be evaluated rather than assumed because decision-making in such entities is fundamentally different than decision-making by individuals.[31] It is not simply a matter of ranking preferred outcomes, recognizing constraints, and selecting the most efficacious option. In armed confrontations, therefore, strategy cannot be automatically derived from the logic of strategic action with an adversary. Instead, it is produced through processes of internal bargaining and structured by the institutionalization of procedures for regulating interelite conflict. The more internal rivals submit to the same political rules, the more cohesive the regime, and the less it must resort to force to implement policy.[32]

Coercive strikes threaten the national sovereignty and security of the host state. The more cohesive the regime, the more it can prioritize such state interests and act as triadic coercion demands.[33] Conversely, if a regime lacks effective mechanisms to regulate interelite conflict and produce coherent policy, it will be unable to behave as a rational actor attuned to credible external threats. Rather, competing political elites will prioritize their own survival vis-à-vis their rivals over the well-being of their state vis-à-vis other states. Steven David observes, "Since the dominant goal of Third World leaders is to stay in power, they will sometimes protect themselves at the expense of the interests of the state."[34] In a regime where decision-making power is fragmented and nonstate actors enjoy popular support, political leaders or aspirants will have few incentives to engage in costly confrontations, regardless of the consequences for the state as a whole. When an armed nonstate actor is a valuable ally to one or another rival faction, elites are even less likely to suppress it, regardless of raison d'état.

The second element of regime strength is capacity, which, building on Doug McAdam, Sidney Tarrow, and Charles Tilly, we define as the "degree of control that state agents exercise over persons, activities, and resources within their government's territorial jurisdiction."[35] We measure capacity qualitatively by assessing its robustness in three domains: institutional, territorial, and social. Institutional capacity, synonymous with what Michael Mann terms "infrastructural power,"[36] is a regime's command of the bureaucratic, coercive, and executive apparatuses necessary to harness resources, enforce policies, and carry out such tasks as extracting revenue, providing public goods, and maintaining order.[37] Such capacity enables a regime to exercise control over space, as captured in Max Weber's definition of a state as an institution successfully claiming a monopoly on the legitimate use of violence within a given territory.[38] Capacity also empowers the regime to project power over people, such that it can rise above or harness the power of social forces, rather than be controlled by them. This authority vis-à-vis society is facilitated by political legitimacy, in the sense of the population's acceptance of the appropriateness of the regime's rule and deference to its laws. Without legitimacy, a regime must muster greater resources to impose its authority through force and against the active impediment of organized challenges.[39]

Like cohesion, a host state's regime capacity crucially mediates the effectiveness of triadic coercion targeted against it. High-capacity regimes possess control over military and police forces, a judicial system, and other state apparatuses. Should a coercer's threats persuade the host that it is in the host's interest to restrict nonstate challengers, the host is able to do so.

Low-capacity regimes, by contrast, are not able to prevent nonstate actors from exploiting ungoverned spaces, exercising operational autonomy on the host's soil, establishing headquarters, storing and transporting weapons, training cadres, and planning and executing attacks. The nonstate actor's armed capabilities and popular base might even be greater than those of the regime. Without institutional, territorial, and social capacity, government agents will have difficulty mustering the resources necessary to confront such a group, or perhaps even to enter areas where the nonstate actor is based, without exercising violence or considerable political acumen.

Host states' strong or weak regimes combine with their "defiant" or "cooperative" predisposition toward the coercer state to produce the four predicted outcomes identified at the bottom of figure 1.3. Triadic coercion is likely to fail when targeted against regimes that are defiant but weak (Outcome A). Engrossed in internal divisions and lacking authority over social forces, politicians are prone to value their own survival over the state's national security. The coercer's threats and strikes are unlikely to alter those incentives, and will thus be irrelevant. They might even create crises that intensify divisions rather than cooperation among elites, in which case triadic coercion backfires. Where political rivalries dominate, competing aspirants might form alliances with nonstate actors to harness their popularity or military power. To the degree that outside pressure enflames domestic political turmoil, it can counterproductively expand opportunities and flows of resources for nonstate violence.

By contrast, triadic coercion is likely to succeed against regimes that are defiant but strong (Outcome B), though not militarily stronger than the coercer. Under such conditions, a regime is sufficiently coherent to enact a unified policy, sufficiently secure to take unpopular political decisions, and sufficiently capable to confront the nonstate actor and compel it to cease attacks. It thus has the means to put raison d'état before domestic politics. Such a host supports violence against the coercer but has the internal cohesion to recognize when the costs of the coercer's retaliation outweigh the benefits of its alliance with the nonstate actor. Triadic coercion will thus push it to deploy its political and military competencies to constrain the nonstate actor's autonomy. As the regime remains hostile to the coercer, it might search for less costly means of defying it, such as supporting nonstate actors' activities in a third country. It might even challenge the coercer state directly. If it does, however, it will be according to its own initiative and timing. It will not allow the nonstate actor to drag it into confrontations that do not suit its interests.

When triadic coercion is targeted against a weak regime, it is likely to fail even if that regime is predisposed to be "cooperative" (Outcome C). A coercer's threats are of little consequence for the motivations of such a host, as they already align with the coercer's wishes. Nevertheless, the host state is unable to mobilize the political or physical capacity to thwart the nonstate actor's violence. The coercer's threats will not increase these capacities, and might instead degrade them. If they do, coercive measures counterproductively reduce the host state's ability to act now and in the future. They can also provoke more radical action by the nonstate actor, which can exploit the opportunities generated by collapsing constraints.[40]

Finally, triadic coercion is likely to succeed when targeted against a regime that is both cooperative and strong (Outcome D). Such a host is predisposed to oppose nonstate actors, but the incentives in favor of permitting them might outweigh those in favor of taking steps to confront them. A coercer's threats and punishments can shift those calculations by warning the host of the serious consequences of continued toleration. As a strong regime, it can coherently respond to changed incentives. It enjoys the domestic political cohesion to recognize that its vital national security interests lie in averting threats or strikes by a more powerful state, which demands acting against nonstate actors on its territory. It enjoys the infrastructural capacity to translate this recognition into effective action.

Once coerced to act against a nonstate actor, a host state's actions might take various forms. It can try to move the nonstate actor to the territory of a third party or impose new border controls to prevent the nonstate actor from carrying out attacks. It can end its financial, political, and/or rhetorical support for the nonstate actor; impede its access to supplies; or arrest, prosecute, or imprison its members. More radically, it can kill members of the nonstate actor or destroy it as an organization. A host regime must be politically and materially strong to undertake these measures because they typically entail domestic costs. It is not uncommon for a host regime to be hostile to a nonstate actor while segments of its own population support it.[41] Under these circumstances, host states face contradictory pressures: from the outside, military pressure to block the nonstate challenger, and from the inside, political pressure to enable it. The stronger the regime, the more secure it will be domestically, and the more the external pressure will outweigh the internal one.[42]

In sum, regime strength is a necessary condition for the success of triadic coercion, regardless of the host state's predisposition toward defiance or cooperation. A coherent and capable regime has both the incentives and the tools to suppress nonstate violence. A regime lacking in cohesion and capacity cannot stop such activity, even if triadic coercion convinces it that it is in its own interest to do so.

Causes: What Strategic Thinking Drives Triadic Coercion?

In an analysis of triadic conflicts similar to ours, David Carter identifies what he calls "the compellence dilemma."[43] Carter argues that coercer states will resist using harsh punishments against host states due to concerns that those punishments will reduce the host's capacity in the future. Though this expectation is rational, the empirical record shows that coercer states often fail to act accordingly. Despite the reasons to expect triadic coercion to succeed only against strong host regimes, states sometimes employ it against weak ones. For example, white minority governments in Rhodesia (1965–1980) and South Africa (1979–1990) regularly engaged in cross-border raids against neighboring countries such as Mozambique, Zambia, and Zimbabwe with the aim of disrupting rebel activities and coercing those states to abandon their support for black nationalist groups.[44] While South Africa focused on these states' antiapartheid stances, little evidence suggests that it paid much attention to the strength of their regimes. Cross-border insurgency against South Africa thus continued, despite severe blows to its neighbors.[45] Similarly, in both 1996 and 1998, Rwanda invaded Zaire to force it to cease offering safe haven to Rwandan Hutu rebels. Given its fragmentation and weak territorial capacity under both Mubutu Sese Seko and Joseph Kabila, successive Congolese regimes were unable to prevent these rebel sanctuaries.[46]

If triadic coercion is unlikely to succeed against weak regimes, why do coercer states nevertheless employ it against hosts such as these? Extant research suggests various explanations, yet none is sufficient. Fighting nonstate actors is, in Lawrence of Arabia's famous words on counterinsurgency, "messy and slow, like eating soup with a knife."[47] In directing threats and strikes at host states instead, a coercer state shifts the terms of conflict from the bewildering terrain of asymmetric warfare to the more straightforward parameters of interstate conflict. The coercer state might assume that the host, like all states, seeks to protect its sovereignty, territory, and citizenry. The host state might be willing to absorb heavy costs when its core national interests are at stake but will be less willing to do so for the interests of a nonstate actor. The coercer is thus reasonable to assume, as does traditional deterrence theory, that its efforts to coerce the host state will be effective as long as the coercer enjoys power preeminence and clearly communicates credible threats.[48] The stronger the coercer relative to the state it seeks to coerce, deterrence theory assumes, the greater its likelihood of coercing compliance.

This strategic logic is sound for many state-to-state conflicts. Yet even the mightiest of strikes against a host state will not compel it to change its behavior when it lacks the material and institutional capacity to implement the coercer's demands or lacks the internal cohesion to withstand domestic pushback against unpopular decisions. The success of triadic coercion is thus not determined by balance of power alone. Paradoxically, the coerced state needs a minimum level of strength to be effectively coerced. That the coercer is stronger than the host state, therefore, does not itself explain why it is rational to choose triadic coercion against a weak host.

An alternative explanation for the strategic logic of triadic coercion against weak states is that coercion itself can provide the powerful impetus for hosts to invest in strengthening their regimes. According to this thinking, external pressure can shift not only a host regime's interests from defiance to compliance but also incentivize it to build institutions and centralize political control, creating the conditions that render triadic coercion more effective over time. Faced with threats to vital security concerns, host regimes might therefore muster the authority to confront nonstate actors that they previously had not. In addition, coercion by an external foe might bring fractured host societies to "rally 'round the flag,"[49] pushing elites and masses to resolve their internal conflicts and forge the unity to thwart imminent dangers.

This reasoning is plausible, yet it confuses the increased patriotism and solidarity that nations experience under threat with deeper forms of political consolidation. As Lewis Coser argues, external conflict tends to unite a group, yet whether it also results in centralization depends on both the group's preexisting degree of consensus and the nature of the conflict.[50] Coser's argument suggests two lessons for triadic coercion. First, one must understand the internal structure and politics of a host regime prior to the onset of coercion in order to understand how that host is likely to react once such action ensues. Regimes that do not possess some measure of cohesion and capacity prior to the implementation of coercive measures are unlikely to create such regime assets once punishments are imposed. Second, different kinds of conflict carry different likelihoods of impelling a regime to centralize or a polity to unify. Research suggests that nonterritorial threats have less impact on state building than territorial threats.[51] Though triadic coercion might entail temporary occupation, it rarely threatens annexation, which is the peril most likely to induce robust state building.[52] Triadic coercion itself is thus unlikely to cause a host regime to grow in strength.

Offering a new explanation for states' engagement in triadic coercion, we propose that some states that use that policy are guided not by strategic calculations as much as a particular strategic culture. Colin Gray defines strategic culture as "the persisting (though not eternal) socially transmitted ideas, attitudes, traditions, habits of mind, and preferred methods of operation that are more or less specific to a particular geographically based security community that has had a necessarily unique historical experience."[53] Some theorists view strategic culture as a system of beliefs that is durable over time,[54] while others emphasize how it varies with shifting circumstances.[55] Some conceive of it as a broad conceptual framework or "national style" that envelops preferences, assumptions, and outlooks.[56] Others instead concentrate on how cultural tendencies infuse such realms as military innovation,[57] integration of technology,[58] doctrine,[59] and intelligence.[60] These and other works teach us that strategic beliefs are deeply imbedded in states' collective experiences and interpretations, and that they can lead to different security imperatives and strategies.[61] Of particular interest in this culturist approach is Amir Lupovici's conceptualization of deterrence as "ontological security," meaning that elites and publics may view deterrence as essential to their self-identity. Beyond physical risk, therefore, threats to a state's deterrence posture might destabilize a nation's very perception of itself.[62]

Synthesizing these works, we examine strategic culture empirically through two main components: decision-making processes and ideas. In probing both elements, we show how strategic culture infuses a state's understanding of the "logic of appropriateness," in James March and Johan Olsen's sense of guides for behavior that are grounded more in socially constructed norms and identities than in interests.[63] Directed by notions of appropriateness, security decision-makers may adopt certain military responses to threats because they perceive them to be right or just. Strategic culture also shapes decision-making on the basis of what March and Olsen label the "logic of consequences," or rational action guided by the calculation of expected returns from alternative choices. Applied to states, rational choice theory regards governments as self-interested entities that optimize gains and minimize costs by obtaining information, forming beliefs on that basis, and then choosing the most beneficial course of action.[64] Theories of strategic culture remind us that this process of rational calculation is embedded in a social context. Pre-existing ideas and attitudes affect how actors form preferences, define interests, weigh costs to benefits, perceive new events, forecast the future, and gauge expected probabilities.[65]

Attention to strategic culture can enhance our understanding of when, why, and how states use triadic coercion. In targeting military threats and punishments against hosts of nonstate actors rather than the nonstate actor itself, a state might be undertaking what it perceives to follow the logic of appropriateness. Strategic culture can uphold a set of collectively held, historically developed beliefs, attitudes, and practices that lead decision-makers to regard punishing host states as the best response to violence from nonstate actors. Under such circumstances, the coercer state regards punitive action to be fitting on moral, rather than instrumental grounds. Such reasoning can come into play in interstate war, but it is especially likely in struggles against violent nonstate actors, given their relatively greater tendency to target civilians and thus provoke popular indignation.

When decision-making processes and ideas favor it, states can regard triadic coercion, a seemingly severe and resolute military response to a threat, as a goal in and of itself. Various state and social institutions can play a role in generating, diffusing, and enforcing attitudes and beliefs that support that orientation. Such a strategic culture can be ingrained in an education system and enshrined in national symbols, rituals, and discourse. It can also infuse the security establishment and agencies of foreign policy-making with particular ways of thinking about how to achieve security. Even when careful military intelligence is gathered, strategic culture affects how decision-makers interpret it and what signals they privilege or discount. It affects the questions that analysts do or do not ask about the information before them, the questions that policy-makers do or do not ask analysts, and the questions that the public does or does not ask of policy-makers.

Though strategic culture is not divorced from cost-benefit calculations, it is not a simple product of utilitarian reasoning. A culturally infused endorsement of triadic coercion thus merits theorization and empirical scrutiny in its own right. In seeking to explain states' efforts to fight nonstate actors by targeting host states, even under conditions when they are unlikely to be effective, scholars ought not underestimate the role of strategic culture.

Contributions and Implications

Triadic coercion has not received sufficient scholarly attention in part because it has fallen through the cracks of two security literatures. On the one hand, deterrence theory has traditionally focused on bilateral state conflicts, with the assumption that one state's ability to deter challenges from another depends on its relative power superiority, the clarity of its signaling of preferences, and its reputation for credibly following through on threats.[66] Later "waves" of scholarship have integrated attention to targeted states' material ability to endure retaliation, the political costs of their acquiescence to threats, and the effects of leaders' cognitive psychology on their choices.[67] Since the Cold War, a fourth wave of scholarship has named various types of "complex deterrence" that expand attention to actors and circumstances that have emerged in the contemporary era.[68]

On the other hand, scholarship on insurgency examines how states' internal strength affects their relations to nonstate actors on their soil. Weak states provide fertile ground for rebel groups in general and transnational insurgents in particular.[69] Strong states are less likely to allow violent nonstate actors to take root and are more capable of uprooting them should they do so. By contrast, when a state is too weak to win the population over from rebels, its counterinsurgency against militant groups is prone to fail.[70] The presence of such militant groups in one state in turn increases the probability that it will engage in militarized disputes with other states.[71] These relationships help explain the frequency of hostilities involving nonstate actors, the states that they target, and the weak states that host them. However, it leaves us to wonder about the conditions under which coercive measures against host states bring them to curtail nonstate actors' violence.

Thus, literature on deterrence tends not to consider how the strength of the host regime conditions deterrent policies. Literature on insurgency continually highlights the issue of state weakness yet does not sufficiently investigate the impact of that weakness on interstate deterrence or coercion. This book bridges that gap. In doing so, we build on studies that address how the strength of states, regimes, and governments, as well as leaders' relative autonomy from society, affect foreign policy strategies.[72] We also learn from Steven David's theory of "omnibalancing," which proposes how state weakness makes domestic threats loom larger than external dangers in leaders' decision calculus.[73]

Our arguments about the role of host regime strength in mediating the effects of triadic coercion have direct policy implications. Our analysis suggests that it is not fruitful for a state to carry out triadic coercion against a regime with weak cohesion and capacities. It is even less helpful for a state to hit the pillars of an already weak regime. Such policies reduce the host regime's ability to cope with nonstate actors, and can even render it weaker than the nonstate actor itself. Rather than striking a weak host state, a coercer state would be wiser to help strengthen it by aiding its institution building. Even when the host state is not friendly, diplomacy and conciliatory measures are a preferable alternative to war.

Our analysis of the role of strategic culture in influencing states' embrace of triadic coercion also carries policy implications. Strategic culture can shape a coercer state's decision-making in ways that produce results that are suboptimal, or even counterproductive, for its own security. Awareness of these relationships should encourage citizens and policy-makers to examine critically the ideas and beliefs that they bring to designing triadic coercion policies. Such examination might reveal that some strategic thinking that people take for granted might not be a rational response to current imperatives but rather an outcome of habitual assumptions and cognitive blind spots. When that is the case, leaders and publics would be well advised to rethink, and ultimately to eschew, triadic coercion.

Research Methodology and Chapter Outline

In evaluating our hypotheses, we employ three primary methods of empirical analysis. First, within each chapter, we use within-case process tracing, carefully mapping out the ideas, relationships, and mechanisms that led actors to take the courses of action that they did. These chapters delve into variation over time in each country. Thus, we examine Egypt preceding and after the rise of Gamal Abdel Nasser's charismatic legitimacy, Syria from the early years of Ba'ath rule through the consolidation of Hafez al-Assad's authoritarian control, the Palestinian Authority over the full course of its development as a self-governing apparatus, and Lebanon from the start of Palestinian cross-border activity in the 1960s to the most recent Israeli confrontations with Hezbollah. Dedicating a chapter to each of these internally varied cases enables us to examine triadic coercion under a diverse set of circumstances and to trace change across decades.

Second, in juxtaposing these chapters against each other, we compare the sources and consequences of Israeli triadic coercion policies among cases. This comparison allows us to examine the consequences of similar policies in both similar and different situations across time and space, offering another layer of validity for evaluation of our hypotheses. For example, in comparing triadic coercion against relatively strong regimes in both post-1956 Egypt and post-1970 Syria, we are able to verify that host states' cohesion and capacity enabled even defiant regimes to comply with Israel's demand to stop cross-border attacks. Conversely, in comparing triadic coercion against weak regimes in early 1950s Egypt, late 1960s Syria, post-1990s Lebanon, and the Palestinian Authority, we show how governments characterized by weak institutions and internal political fragmentation proved unable to act against nonstate actors, regardless of their disposition toward Israel. In these and many other junctures throughout the book, comparison of similar and different cases of triadic coercion confirms our predicted outcomes. It also provides insight about the mechanisms that drive outcomes, beyond that possible from analysis of any single case.

Third, we explore two "shadow cases" by briefly examining both the causes and consequences of India's and Turkey's policies toward neighboring states that host or assist hostile nonstate actors. This inquiry serves as a "plausibility probe," designed to explore how our concepts and arguments travel beyond the Arab-Israeli arena. Though preliminary, the comparative analysis confirms our arguments both about the role of host regime strength in mediating triadic coercion effects and the role of strategic culture in shaping states' likelihoods of carrying out triadic coercion in the first place.

In carrying out these three forms of analysis, we utilize a wealth of secondary sources and a range of primary sources, such as official documents and newspapers articles, augmented by several interviews in Israel. Chapter 2 introduces our conceptualization of strategic culture and shows how, in the Israeli case, both security decision-making processes and ideas have entrenched a "cult of the offensive" as well as an anti-intellectual ethos that discourages the military from reevaluating those tenets. The chapter then examines and explains the historical evolution of Israel's adoption of triadic coercion, distinguishing between three eras. Triadic coercion emerged in the 1950s as a reaction to nonstate actors' border violations after other strategies floundered or sparked international outcry. Some Israeli leaders advocated triadic coercion not only due to its perceived effectiveness but also as a means for serving wholly distinct strategic or institutional objectives. From the 1956 Suez War through the mid-1990s, Israel adopted a more tailored, nuanced application of triadic coercion. It thus targeted host states that actively assisted nonstate attacks on Israel but spared hosts that did not. We explore this period through a brief overview of Israel's policies vis-à-vis nonstate actors operating from Jordan. Since the mid-1990s, a changing security environment has brought Israel's traditional security concepts into crisis. Security elites have turned to their inherited strategic culture for guidance in how to respond to nonstate actors. The outcome has been the hardening of a less discriminating, more aggressive policy of triadic coercion as Israel's modus operandi. Israeli decision-makers have increasingly come to embrace triadic coercion nearly as a matter of principle, even in the face of evidence suggesting its ineffectiveness.

Chapters 3 and 4 explore the consequences of triadic coercion policies by respectively comparing Israel's triadic coercion against Egypt and Syria since 1949. In both cases, the main nonstate violators of Israel's borders were Palestinian groups. Our comparison of these cases thus holds constant both the coercer state (Israel) and the identity of the relevant nonstate actor, allowing us to focus on host regime strength. In both Egypt and Syria, regimes were initially weak in both cohesion and capacity. Host state authorities were hence unable to act against nonstate actors on their soil and sometimes deferred to domestic political motivations to support such actors. After coups in the 1950s and 1970s, respectively, new regimes in both states consolidated institutional capacities and centralized authority. This rendered each more able and willing to put state interests above parochial pressures. Israel's attempts to prevent attacks by nonstate actors by threatening and punishing Egypt and Syria were unsuccessful when they were governed by weak regimes but proved increasingly effective as each regime became stronger. This situation largely held until the mass uprisings of 2011, after which each state lost ability to assert territorial control and authority over social forces. These new conditions created novel opportunities for nonstate actors and renewed old challenges for Israel's use of triadic coercion.

Chapters 5 and 6 sustain this analysis of the effects of triadic coercion but also turn greater attention to the causes of the persistent use of this policy choice. Exploring Israel's relations with the Palestinian Authority and Lebanon, respectively, these chapters attribute Israel's use of triadic coercion to the development of a strategic culture that upholds the appropriateness of threatening or punishing states that host violent nonstate actors. In these cases, Israel aimed threats and strikes against regimes that were feeble, fragmented, and, at some junctures, hardly stronger than the nonstate actors that they "hosted." Nevertheless, Israel increasingly defended triadic coercion on the grounds that it was morally justified, if not imperative. Israel asserted that these regimes *should* act as responsible sovereigns; it did not soundly assess that they *could*. Triadic coercion thus evolved to represent an article of faith and conviction as much as a calculated strategy. Pounding host states stood nearly as an end in itself.

Chapter 7 probes the applicability of our arguments beyond the Arab-Israeli conflict through brief examination of two cases that, like Israel, have faced long-lasting conflicts in which nonstate actors launch raids from bases in other states. First, India's battle against Kashmiri separatist movements has compelled it to respond to Pakistan. Second, Turkey's struggle against the Kurdistan Workers' Party (PKK) has brought it into conflict with the states of Iraq, Syria, and Iran. When either India or Turkey used triadic coercion, the outcomes corroborate our arguments: It worked against strong regimes but failed against weak ones. Nevertheless, such usage has been rare. While both countries have engaged in triadic conflicts, they have resisted engaging in triadic coercion. We attribute this to their respective strategic cultures, which differ from that of Israel insofar as they have traditionally emphasized defensive postures, caution, and an aversion to excessive force.

The concluding chapter recaps our book's findings and considers their implications for theory development and policy. Coercive strikes against a weak regime risk sparking spirals of escalation that only further undermine the coercer state's security. Counterintuitively, when facing states that host violent nonstate actors, a strong enemy might not always be worse than a weak one. States that advocate policies to the contrary might be acting less upon the strategic logic of connecting means to ends than upon socially ingrained beliefs and practices. To the degree that such a culture can be identified, interrogated, and changed, new—and perhaps better—ways of ensuring peace and security might become possible.

CHAPTER 2

Israel's Use of Triadic Coercion

Sources and Historical Evolution

Great Britain relinquished its Mandate for Palestine to the United Nations in 1947, after which the UN General Assembly approved a resolution to partition Palestine into Arab and Jewish states. The Jewish community accepted the plan; Palestinian leaders and Arab states, believing that the Zionist project was usurping Palestinians' rightful homeland, rejected it. Communal violence began; with it, fear and expulsions began forcing the flight of Palestinian refugees. After Israel declared statehood in May 1948, Arab states' intervention transformed the conflict into an interstate war. The war drew to a close during the first half of 1949, when Israel signed armistice agreements with Egypt, Jordan, Syria, and Lebanon. These agreements did not establish recognized international borders but rather Armistice Demarcation Lines (ADLs). According to those lines, Israel extended over approximately 78 percent of mandatory Palestine, or 50 percent more territory than allotted by the UN partition plan. Egypt assumed control of the Gaza Strip, the five-by-twenty-eight-mile swath of land on the southern Mediterranean Coast. Jordan maintained control of East Jerusalem and the area on the West Bank of the Jordan River, which it officially annexed in April 1950.

Israel emerged through and into war, and security concerns thus became a formative dimension of its strategic culture. We begin this chapter by describing the two primary components of that strategic culture: decision-making processes and ideas. We show how both have combined to effect a propensity to swift and severe use of force against adversaries as well as an anti-intellectualist aversion to rethinking assumptions about the appropriateness of military solutions.

We then turn to the history of Israel's policies toward nonstate actors' cross-border violations, distinguishing between three periods. First, from 1949 to the 1956 Suez War, Israel adopted various strategies to combat border infiltrations and attacks from nonstate actors, adapting them in response to operational failures, international rebuke, and other pressures. Along the way, Israel shifted from targeting reprisal raids directly at perpetrators to targeting civilian communities, and finally to targeting the states in which those nonstate actors were based. While some Israeli politicians criticized harsh retaliation, others embraced it as a strategy for building deterrence, enhancing the army's combat skills, or even provoking the war that they perceived to be inevitable. For the most part, neither hardline nor dovish leaders considered whether a host state was predisposed to defy or cooperate with its demands. Nor did they take into account that state's regime strength. In terms of the decision-making chart presented in chapter 1, Israel remained at the first level. It concerned itself only with questions of the interstate balance of power and Israel's ability to inflict punishing force against a rival.

Second, from 1956 through the mid-1990s, Israel adopted greater nuance in its application of triadic coercion, developing especially the distinction between defiant and cooperative regimes. When Israel perceived host states as complicit in nonstate actors' violence, it struck fiercely at those states; when it perceived host states as victims that did not support violence, it instead aimed reprisals at nonstate actors directly. To illustrate this distinction, we explore Israel's policies toward Jordan, which it regarded as a mostly cooperative regime.

Third, the period since the 1990s, which witnessed the increased importance of asymmetric threats, undermined the relevance of Israel's inherited security concept, which had been designed for conventional interstate threats. Nevertheless, an anti-intellectual ethos in the military discouraged reconsideration of the engrained "cult of the offensive." Israel continued to take an aggressive approach to deterrence in general and an undifferentiated, moralistic application of triadic coercion in particular. Israel's strategic culture intensified belief in the appropriateness of holding host states accountable for nonstate actors, without regard for the strength of their regimes and the role of regime strength in mediating the effectiveness of such strategies.

Conceptualizing Israel's Strategic Culture

Israel's strategic culture is the product of both the institutional arrangements that structure decision-making processes and the ideas and assumptions that influence the content of those decisions. We examine both elements in turn.

Decision-Making Processes

We use the term "decision-making processes" to refer to both formally codified laws and institutions and informal customs and tendencies that pattern who makes security-related decisions and how. In Israel, key in this regard is the military's sweeping influence over security matters. Although the Israel Defense Forces (IDF) has historically followed government orders even when it disagrees with them,[1] its relations with the government have developed into what Yoram Peri terms a "civil-military partnership" rather than strict civilian control.[2] Brief and vague laws fail to define the IDF's place in the chain of command or its exact relationship to either the prime minister or civilian minister of defense. Government leaders' effective power vis-à-vis the military is thus often driven by their own personalities, not by formal frameworks.[3] The lack of effective parliamentary oversight of the military further increases its effective autonomy.[4]

Bureaucratically, the security establishment, which includes both military and civilian sectors, dominates other government ministries, especially the Ministry of Foreign Affairs. The latter lacks the budget, institutional capacity, and personnel to challenge the Ministry of Defense seriously on security or foreign policy issues. The defense minister's policy positions are more influential in cabinet discussions than those of the minister of foreign affairs.[5] Beyond this, the tendency of IDF officers to "parachute" into civilian government and civilian security positions on their retirement further integrates military thinking and culture into state realms that are not formally military.[6]

There is no countervailing force offsetting the military's preeminence on security issues. The IDF's Planning Branch completely dominates strategic planning; no other institution approximates its level of expertise or technological and bureaucratic resources. Therefore, though the army does not control the decision to go to war, it determines strategic goals once war has begun.[7] In peacetime, the IDF is typically the only body presenting the cabinet with strategic options. After repeated recommendations for the need for a civilian institutional counterweight, the Israeli National Security Council was established in 1999. The council produces position papers and offers consulting to the government but lacks budget, staff, or authority to execute serious planning functions. It has yet to acquire a "seat at the table" for significant security decision-making.[8] The military dominates in the realm of intelligence as well. Though the IDF's intelligence division shares responsibilities with the Mossad (Israel's national intelligence agency) and the Shin Bet (the internal security service), its resources and influence far eclipse those of its civilian counterparts. It has sole responsibility for preparing Israel's annual "National Intelligence Estimate," which lays out the country's main strategic and security challenges and proposes ways to tackle them.[9]

As important as the military's influence on security policy is its own organizational approach to decision-making. Scholars have described the IDF's ethos as "weak intellectualism" or even "anti-intellectualism."[10] The army has historically regarded grand concepts and abstract discussions as useless and has instead extolled "no-nonsense" talk that is direct and to the point (*dugri* or *tachlis*), being a "doer" (*bitsuist*) rather than an armchair thinker, tinkering and resourcefulness (*tushia*), and improvisation in the field (*iltur*).[11] Critics charge that this emphasis on practice over theory has discouraged deep thinking, even when conditions demand self-reflection.[12]

The IDF's ethos has become embedded in its organizational structure. Military command and control are notably decentralized, allowing low levels of command broad discretion in the field. Orders are often conveyed orally, and field commanders enjoy a high degree of autonomy.[13] The IDF's antiplanning bias has infused national security decision-making at large,[14] leaving it highly personalized, politicized, reactive, ad hoc, and unsystematic.[15] The result, Gil-li Vardi writes, has been habitual "sacrifice [of] both political and military long-term and medium-term considerations in favor of a superficial, short-termed satisfaction of [the IDF's] drive for action."[16]

This ethos, cemented in institutions, reinforces Israel's strategic culture and its bias toward severe force against any perceived threat.

Ideas

We use the term "ideas" to encompass Israel's dominant assumptions about its security environment and its principles about how to respond to security threats. Though Israel did not have an official written military doctrine until 2015, an unofficial doctrine crystalized in the 1950s. Sometimes called Israel's "national security concept" (*tfisat habitachon haleumi*),[17] it emphasizes collective perception of constant threat from a hostile environment. In the words of David Ben-Gurion, Israel is "a small island surrounded by a great Arab ocean."[18] Compounding this, Israel long perceived itself as acutely vulnerable before what it saw as Arab states' strengths. Materially, it cannot compete with their oil wealth. Demographically, the combined population of the Arab states that fought Israel in 1948 totaled more than 33 million.[19] Even after mass immigration, Israel's Jewish population in 1952 reached only 1.4 million.[20] Strategically, Israel lacked territorial depth, with the majority of its population living in a narrow coastal strip.[21]

Given its perception of existential threat vis-à-vis an Arab world that does not accept its legitimacy, Israel has held to the notion that it has "no choice" but to face adversaries in repeated war.[22] For decades after 1948, most decision-makers believed that Israel could not permanently dissuade Arab states to relinquish their hope to undo the loss of Palestine. They hence argued that Israel must prepare for "rounds" of wars that Arab states would inevitably launch against Israel.[23] In triumphing repeatedly in such rounds, Israel could exhaust its enemies and eventually force them to acquiesce to Israel's existence.[24]

Since the 1950s, Israel has operationalized its national security concept through three core elements, dubbed the "national security triangle."[25] The first element, battlefield decision (*hachra'a*), reflects the belief that, given the strategic, economic, and diplomatic disadvantages of drawn-out confrontations, Israel must win military encounters as swiftly and definitively as possible. For this reason, the IDF developed an operational strategy of blitzkrieg: a preemptive or quick counterattack, based on rapid mobilization, concentration of forces, maneuver warfare, and moving fighting to enemy territory. The triangle's second element, early warning (*hatra'a*), enables initiation of such speedy action and prevention of surprise attacks. The third element, deterrence (*harta'a*), is essential for avoiding wars in the first place. Israel seeks "immediate deterrence," which dissuades adversaries already contemplating attack by threatening dire responses should these enemies cross implicit or explicit "red lines."[26] Israel also pursues "general deterrence" in the sense of anticipating and preventing potential threats. Finally, Israel endeavors to achieve "cumulative deterrence."[27] Should adversaries not be deterred from particular actions, cumulative deterrence demands that Israel carry out severe reprisals to remind enemies of Israel's refusal to surrender and its ability to inflict pain. Over time, this logic holds, such shows of power should persuade adversaries to make peace.[28]

The three corners of the national security triangle have never been equal. Swift, decisive defeat of the enemy has been considered key for "basic security" (*bitachon bsisi*), or protection from major threats to sovereignty, as well as smaller, periodic attacks to provide "current security" (*bitachon shotef*). In what some have dubbed the IDF's "cult of the offensive,"[29] Israel's army has developed a penchant for preemptive strikes and commando feats. Israel has often proceeded as if defense alone were not an option.[30] In the twenty-first century, at least one rationale for the army's support for major, seemingly defensive measures such as the West Bank separation wall and the Arrow missile defense system appears to be the perception that they will expand the IDF's offensive room for maneuver. As a 2015 "IDF Strategy" document explains, the top priority is "protection that permits the continuous use of military force both for defense and for attack."[31] Similarly, Israel has often taken an offensive approach to deterrence. At least until the 1990s, Israeli strategists largely assumed deterrence to be a result of successful battlefield decisions. That is, the more Israel won wars, the more it believed that it would discourage enemies from engaging in them.[32]

A Sum Greater Than Its Parts: Strategic Culture

Decision-making processes and the ideas fueling those decisions have interacted with and reinforced each other to produce a unique strategic culture that is more encompassing than the influences feeding into it.

Strategic culture is the glue cementing the other elements of Israel's security landscape.

In Israel, strategic culture has institutionalized a system of relationships, beliefs, values, and behaviors that elevate military force against all perceived security threats.[33] This culture has become engrained in manifold aspects of public life, including patterns of political competition; school curricula; media discourse; and national monuments, myths, and holidays.[34] Strategic culture is reinforced in the military's own approach to training, promotion, and relations with both the government and society.[35] It is no less rooted in the rhetoric and approaches of civilian political leaders; when they argue that it is vital to "do something" in reacting to a threat, that something is, by default, military action.[36] This strategic culture has remained largely impervious to changing conditions.[37] In Vardi's words, it has defined some patterns of action as "indisputable truths" and set some practices "in stone, even if new realities prove them obsolete."[38] It is within this strategic cultural context that Israel has approached triadic coercion.

Development of Triadic Coercion, 1949–1956

Infiltrations

During the course of the 1948 War, nearly 60 percent of Palestinian Arabs, approximately 700,000–760,000 out of a total population of 1.3 million, were made refugees.[39] Many settled in camps near the new armistice borders. In 1949, thousands illegally crossed Israel's border, a phenomenon that Israelis called "infiltrations." Infiltrations rose to a peak of 16,000 in 1952 and declined to several thousand by 1956.[40]

Benny Morris finds that less than 10 percent of infiltrations from 1949 to 1953 were politically motivated.[41] The remainder were refugees' individual attempts to return to their former lands in order cultivate fields, graze livestock, fish, obtain goods, visit family members, engage in minor theft or smuggling, pass between the Gaza Strip and West Bank, or resettle in what had become Israel. Though the overwhelming majority of infiltrations were nonviolent, a small number targeted Israelis with killings, robbery, sabotage, or planting landmines at roads and buildings.[42] Scholars disagree about precisely how many were violent and the damage they caused.[43] Figure 2.1 uses Zeev Maoz's dataset, the most comprehensive and

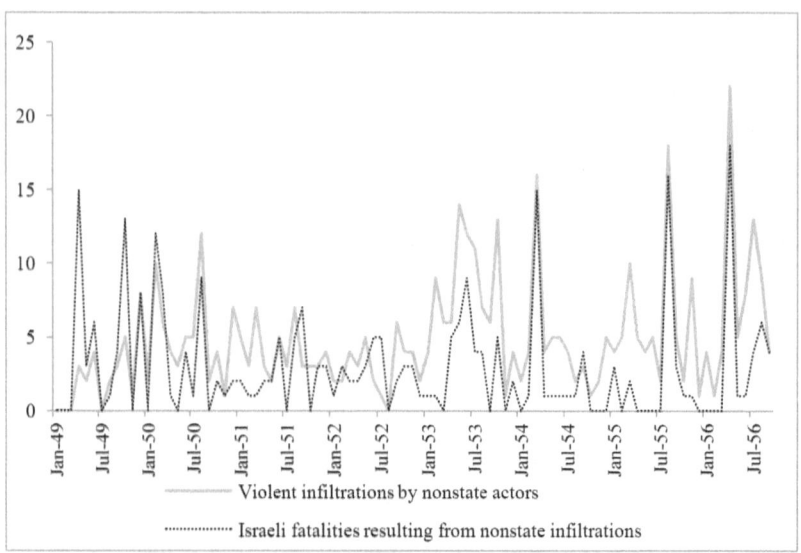

Figure 2.1 Attacks by Arab nonstate actors and resulting Israeli fatalities, January 1949–September 1956.
Source: Zeev Maoz, "Arab Nonstate Aggression and Israeli Limited Uses of Force" dataset, *The Quantitative History of the Arab-Israeli Conflict*, available at http://vanity.dss.ucdavis.edu/~maoz/arabisrhost.htm.

accurate available, to show violent acts perpetrated by nonstate actors infiltrating Israel from a neighboring state from 1949 until the eve of the 1956 Suez War.[44] Figure 2.1 suggests no discernible pattern, with the exception of a relative lull in 1952.

Israeli Responses

Israel took various actions against infiltrations. It filed complaints with UN Mixed Armistice Commissions to urge Arab states to curb cross-border activity.[45] As these typically resulted in inconclusive investigations,[46] Israel also invested in a program of "territorial defense" that used barbed wire fences, mines, and armed guards to protect towns, villages, and farms. The focus on safeguarding settled communities, however, could not guarantee safety for those traveling or working fields outside them. In 1949 Israel thus established a dedicated paramilitary unit under police command called the Border Police (*Mishmar Hagvul*).[47] Both the IDF and the Border

Police carried out patrols and ambushes along the borders. They laid mines and booby traps and expelled infiltrators or fired at them under a policy of shoot-to-kill.[48] These actions killed between 2,700 and 5,000 would-be infiltrators between 1949 and 1956, most before 1952.[49]

Nevertheless, border violations continued, resulting in costly theft and sabotage. Violations also generated fear among citizens, especially new immigrants residing near the armistice lines.[50] Ben-Gurion expressed great concern over "the hysteria prevailing in the border settlements" and the need for Israel to take military action to "boost their morale."[51] The government feared that infiltrations would drive border residents to abandon peripheral areas and cluster in the center of the country. Such demographic movement would undermine Israel's claim to border lands and perhaps encourage more infiltrations.[52]

Against this backdrop, Israel also carried out reprisal raids across its borders. Chief of Staff Moshe Dayan explained the rationale for this policy: "We cannot safeguard every water pipe against explosives or every tree against uprooting. We cannot prevent the murder of orchard workers or a sleeping family. But we can exact a high price for our blood, a price that an Arab community, Arab army, Arab regimes will not consider worth paying."[53] Figure 2.2 presents Israeli cross-border retaliation raids, defined as any violent cross-border activity by Israeli regular or paramilitary forces into its neighbors' territories. The chart also displays the total known Arab fatalities in which those raids resulted.[54]

Israel's retaliation raids between 1949 and 1956 can be divided into three distinct phases. From 1949 to July 1953 retaliation raids were relatively contained, in terms of the size of the military units that conducted them and the casualties that they inflicted.[55] They typically responded to a particular attack by directly targeting those believed to be its perpetrators. When intelligence was unable to identify the perpetrators, the IDF aimed raids at the village or refugee camp from which the attack had appeared to emanate.[56]

That strategy served multiple functions, as the minutes from a Ministry of Foreign Affairs meeting documented with reference to Jordan:

> [Prime Minister Moshe] Sharett explained that the policy of reprisals does not spring merely from a desire for revenge but rather from considerations of the General Staff: (1) When intelligence reports indicate that certain villages are serving as jumping-off points for

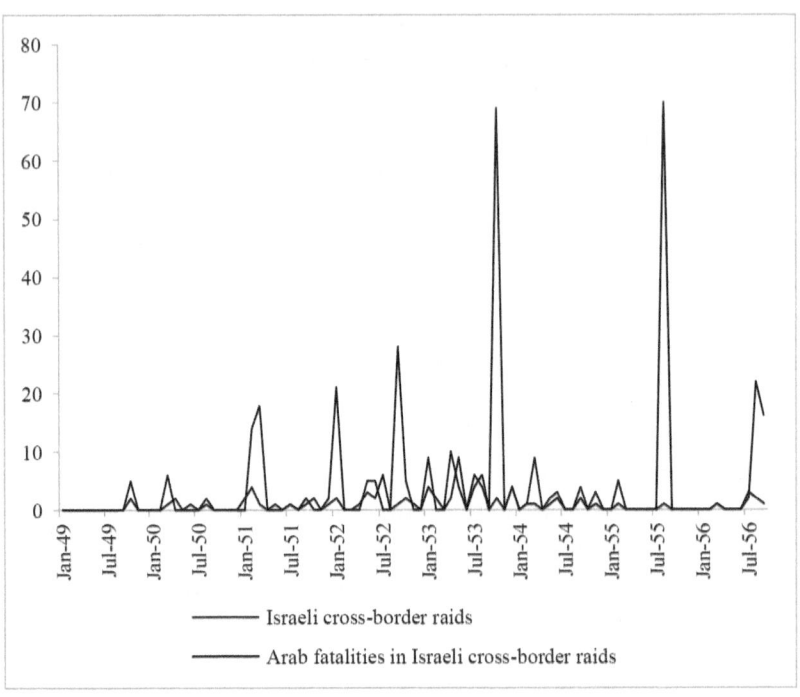

Figure 2.2 Israeli cross-border raids and resulting Arab fatalities, January 1949–September 1956.
Source: Maoz, "Arab Nonstate Aggression" dataset.

attacks, Israel retaliates by attacking one village in order to deter the others. (2) Retaliation spurs the Jordanian government to take action. (3) Retaliation lifts the morale of the residents of border settlements and encourages them to stay put. (4). Retaliation raises the morale of the army, which cannot sit idly by and watch the Jordanians make a mockery of the country. Those who favor reprisals do not assert that they constitute a solution to the problem, but only that there is a need to react when matters reach such a pitch that the frontier and the settlements along it are wide open to attack.[57]

Reprisals satisfied the "need to react," as Israel's strategic culture demanded. Yet they did not appear to improve border security. Evaluating eighty-five raids through the end of 1953, the IDF's General Staff judged forty-one to be unqualified failures and six to be partially successful in achieving their operational goals.[58] A British diplomat agreed, noting, "The Israeli policy has been a total failure. They have failed to discourage the infiltrators, have offended the western powers, and through the action of the latter have given aid and comfort to the Jordanians."[59]

Many of Israel's difficulties were operational problems, whose roots lay in the demobilization of Israel's army after the 1948 War.[60] In 1949, Ben-Gurion dismantled the most effective branch of Israel's army at that time, the Palmach, because most of its officers were affiliated with a rival political party.[61] The post-1948 military thus became dominated by officers who had served in the British Army's Jewish Brigade. The IDF gained the appearance of a conventional military with uniforms, drills, and a formal hierarchy. The cost for this transformation, however, was that infantry units were considerably less skilled in combat, night navigation, and tactical initiative, which had been Palmach strengths.

These shortcomings came to light in early reprisal raids. IDF troops failed in their attempts to uproot a small Syrian company in Tel Mutilla in 1951 or find their way in the dark in the West Bank village of Falame in 1953.[62] Ben-Gurion and Dayan realized that an army incapable of such small-scale missions would be unable to repel a large-scale invasion, no less launch an offensive assault. With this background, some came to endorse reprisals, and especially attacks on hostile states' military installations, as exercises that could help improve the IDF's readiness, performance, and morale.[63]

Against this backdrop, Israeli raids took a new form from July to October of 1953. The IDF created a special commando unit named Unit 101. Under the leadership of Colonel Ariel Sharon, the force began conducting retaliation raids across Israel's borders.[64] Privileging improvisation and initiative, Unit 101 used guerrilla techniques such as night field craft, silent infiltrations, and hand-to-hand combat.[65] To enhance the element of surprise, it did not direct reprisals at the believed source of infiltration. Rather, the IDF prepared a list of potential targets, such as villages known to be hubs for infiltrators. Commanders would choose targets, and the prime minister or minister of defense would authorize them.[66] Trained rigorously, Unit 101 fighters largely avoided the operational blunders of the prior period.[67]

Israel thus shifted from narrow, directed retaliations against perpetrators to operations that intended to "send a message" by punishing broader communities. It reasoned that these raids would force civilians to complain to the appropriate authorities, who would then curb infiltrations. Dayan explained, "If we try to search for that Arab [who planted mines] it has no value. But if we harass the nearby village . . . then the population there comes out against the [infiltrators] . . . and the Egyptian government and the Transjordanian government are [driven] to prevent such incidents, because their prestige is [assailed]."[68]

Retaliation policy shifted again after October 1953, when a Palestinian infiltrator killed three Israelis in the town of Yahud. In response, Unit 101, with paratroopers' support, attacked the West Bank village of Qibya. It detonated forty-five houses, most with the residents still inside,[69] killing sixty-nine Palestinians. The United States, Britain, and France sponsored a UN Security Council resolution that declared the raid "prejudicial to chances of peaceful settlement."[70] The United States called on Israel to try those responsible for Qibya and ensure such raids never recurred. Britain expressed horror at the attack and declared that it showed Israel's purported desire for peace to be "empty and meaningless."[71] In Israel, Foreign Minister Moshe Sharett used the UN resolution to rebuke Ben-Gurion and to argue that retaliation raids were causing the state severe diplomatic fallout.[72]

This widespread criticism spurred Israel to undertake a dramatic change toward triadic coercion. Rather than targeting infiltrators directly or civilian communities indiscriminately, it began to aim reprisals at the states from whence infiltrations came.[73] Effective December 1953, a new IDF operational directive specified five tenets for implementing this strategy:

A. Confrontation will be open and there will be no camouflaging or blurring the identity of the perpetrators.
B. Arab villages will not be needlessly attacked, and injury to unarmed civilians, women and children will be avoided.
C. The principle of cleaving to the place and method of the crime—is revoked. We shall hit the enemy where and how we choose, even if the objective does not exactly match the enemy's crime.
D. The speed of the operation is decisive—the reaction must be as quick as possible and as soon as possible after the crime.
E. The targets chosen [for attack] will be crucial objectives: military centers, [military] camps, police [stations], National Guards concentrations deep behind [enemy lines], the attack upon which will be as painful as possible.[74]

Intensifying the scale of reprisals, Israel thus began to target military and police installations. "These strikes [in the Arab countries] are not acts of revenge," Dayan said about the new approach. "If that government does not control its residents and prevent them from hurting Israel, the Israeli forces will devastate its own country."[75] The UN representative in the Armistice Committee, Lieutenant-General E. L. M Burns, observed that, according to Israel's perspective: "It was the responsibility of the government's party to the General Armistice Agreements to prevent anyone from the territory under their control from crossing the Armistice Demarcation Lines. If an Arab government failed to do that, it was more than just inefficiency and negligence; it meant that the government concerned condoned and secretly favored such action against Israel."[76]

State security targets were better fortified and guarded than civilian communities and striking them required larger troop formations and heavier weapons. The IDF thus upgraded Unit 101 to become Paratroop Battalion 202. Dayan, though not originally a supporter of Unit 101, came to recognize its utility as a way to transform the IDF into an army more capable of tackling serious strategic threats. Edward Luttwak and Dan Horowitz explain, "Just as the small Unit 101 had been used to reinvigorate the larger paratroop unit, Dayan hoped to use the new paratroop battalion as a morale-builder and tactical school for the mass of the infantry."[77]

Sharon assumed command of the new battalion, bringing Unit 101's methods of training and combat as well as its military culture, which was based on daring initiatives, grueling field training, and minimal hierarchy. Through joint training and operations with other military divisions, the small elite unit gradually instilled a new set of skills and its particular esprit de corps throughout the IDF. This not only enhanced the fighting characteristics that became the Israeli army's source of pride for decades thereafter; it also further engrained the "cult of the offensive" as a core principle in Israel's strategic culture.

As the new tool of triadic coercion, paratroop units conducted more than forty retaliation raids against Jordanian, Egyptian, or Syrian installations from 1953 to 1956. As targeted armies became more adept at resisting these raids, the IDF escalated accordingly, leading to increased Arab and Israeli casualties.[78] Ultimately, triadic coercion did not succeed significantly more than had the previous strategies.[79] Yitzhak Rabin, then chief of the IDF's Northern Command, noted by 1956 that "reprisal raids . . . proved ineffective in dealing with the problem of terrorism."[80] Dayan wrote that there was a consensus in the IDF command that "the present system needed revision."[81] Meanwhile, in the political sphere, the "dovish" Sharett (minister of foreign affairs from May 1948 to June 1956; prime minister from January 1954 to November 1955) undertook continued efforts to limit harsh reprisal policies.[82]

If retaliation were an effective deterrent, we would expect to see a significant drop in violent infiltrations following Israeli raids. Furthermore, the length of these lulls in infiltrations would roughly correspond to the severity of Israeli attacks, as measured by the number of Arab fatalities. Figure 2.3, depicting monthly accounts of Arab deaths in Israeli retaliation raids and of violent infiltrations by Arab actors, does not suggest such patterns.

These trends show an immediate, short-term drop in violent infiltrations following especially bloody Israeli retaliatory strikes, such as the October 1953 raid in Qibya and August 1955 raid in the Gaza Strip. However, upticks in infiltrations following each of these low points suggest that such retaliations did not achieve long-term deterrence.[83] A Pearson linear-correlation test finds no correlation between the severity of Israeli raids (measured in Arab fatalities) and a decrease in Arab violent infiltrations in either the short or long term. Performance of this test with a two-month lag yields a correlation of $-.094$ while a one-year lag yields a correlation of $-.013$.[84]

The fact that raids had no measurable effect in deterring infiltrations in the 1950s suggests that triadic coercion did not succeed. Why then did Israel adopt and sustain it? Israeli adoption of triadic coercion was the outcome of a process of trial and error through which decision-makers gradually came to believe that the best way to fight infiltrations, while also averting criticism about civilian casualties, was to convince Arab states that it was in their interests to prevent infiltrations.[85] Still, not all Israeli elites completely agreed on this point. Some political and military figures viewed triadic coercion as a means toward achieving long-term cumulative deterrence. As Doron Almog summarized this position, Israel sought to create a "victory bank" in which every retaliatory raid was another deposit toward the ultimate goal of forcing Arab states to acquiesce to Israel's existence.[86] In Dayan's words, "Indirectly, the retaliation raids serve as a demonstration of the Arab-Israeli balance of power. . . . The raids force the

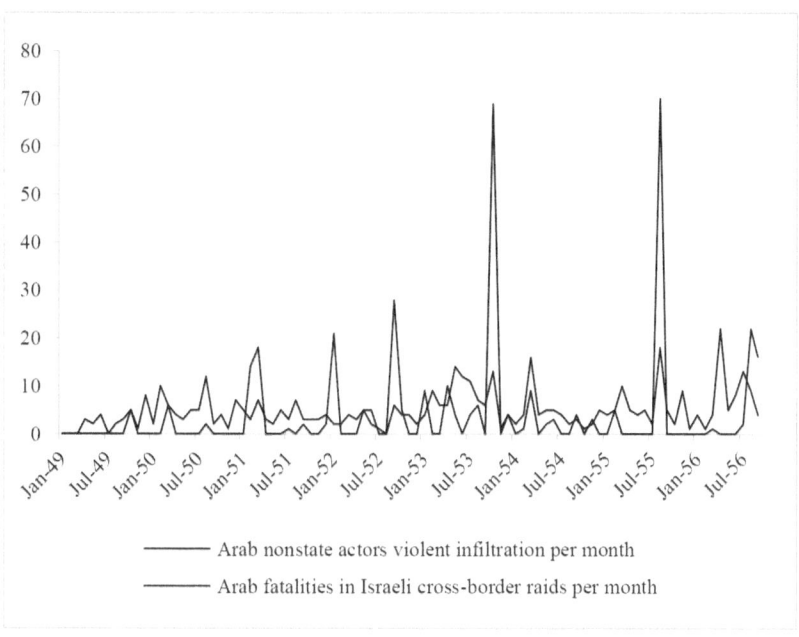

Figure 2.3 Arab infiltrations and fatalities from Israeli raids, January 1949–September 1956.
Source: Maoz, "Arab Nonstate Aggression" dataset.

Arabs to ask themselves from time to time: Is destroying Israel a realistic plan, or shall we give it up?"[87]

Other Israeli leaders went further, implying that the goal of triadic coercion was not to avert the next war with Arab states but actually to hasten it on terms favorable to Israel. This was the position of the Israeli camp identified at the time as "activists," in the sense that they endorsed the most offense-driven ideas of Israel's strategic culture. Convinced that Arab states would inevitably pursue another war, such leaders supported aggressive retaliation against infiltrations to bait Arab states into war at a time and under conditions of Israel's choosing.[88] In this understanding, reprisals were not a means of specific deterrence in the sense of preventing immediate threats as much as an instrument of escalation toward a larger, decisive battle. A clear victory in such a battle, supporters of this approach believed, would enhance Israel's cumulative deterrence, if not coerce its neighbors to accept peace based on the territorial status quo.

A major problem impeded this vision: The IDF of the early 1950s did not have the capacity to win a "second round" against Arab armies. Retaliation raids provided a means through which that army could continue training and gain battle experience. Neither the IDF command nor Ben-Gurion originally understood triadic coercion to serve this purpose. Rather, they stumbled upon it in searching for a solution to the problem of infiltrations. With time, leading forces in Israeli security decision-making came to appreciate triadic coercion as a tool to rekindle a fighting culture in the heart of the army. In upgrading Unit 101 to a battalion, that is what they sought to do.

In summary, Israel's powerful security apparatus tried various methods to combat nonstate actors' cross-border attacks in the 1950s. It started with defensive and limited diplomatic efforts, then moved to retaliation raids directed against infiltrators or their immediate bases, and then embraced reprisals on civilian targets unrelated to the particular infiltration being avenged. Finally, Israeli decision-makers decided to aim operations against the host states' military and police, launching the practice of triadic coercion. Security elites endorsed triadic coercion for various reasons, not all of them directly tied to its success at constraining infiltrations and attacks. Regardless of its rationales, this approach gradually became institutionalized in both political and military decision-making. The institutionalization of triadic coercion helped ingrain in Israeli strategic culture a belief in the utility and appropriateness of holding states accountable for the actions of nonstate actors. Once it chose triadic coercion, Israel repeatedly sought to "speak loudly and periodically use a big stick."[89] In doing so, it focused on only one factor: Israel's combat skills and ability to impose costs on the states from which infiltrations emanated. Decision-makers assumed that sufficiently high costs would compel the targeted state to stop border violations. They made no effort to consider the political, material, or institutional constraints of the targeted regimes. In terms of the decision tree that we introduced in chapter 1, Israel did not move past the first, most rudimentary question about interstate balance of power (see figure 2.4).

Triadic Coercion, 1956–1990

Israel's approach to triadic coercion became more nuanced during the period ranging from the aftermath of the Suez War of 1956 through the

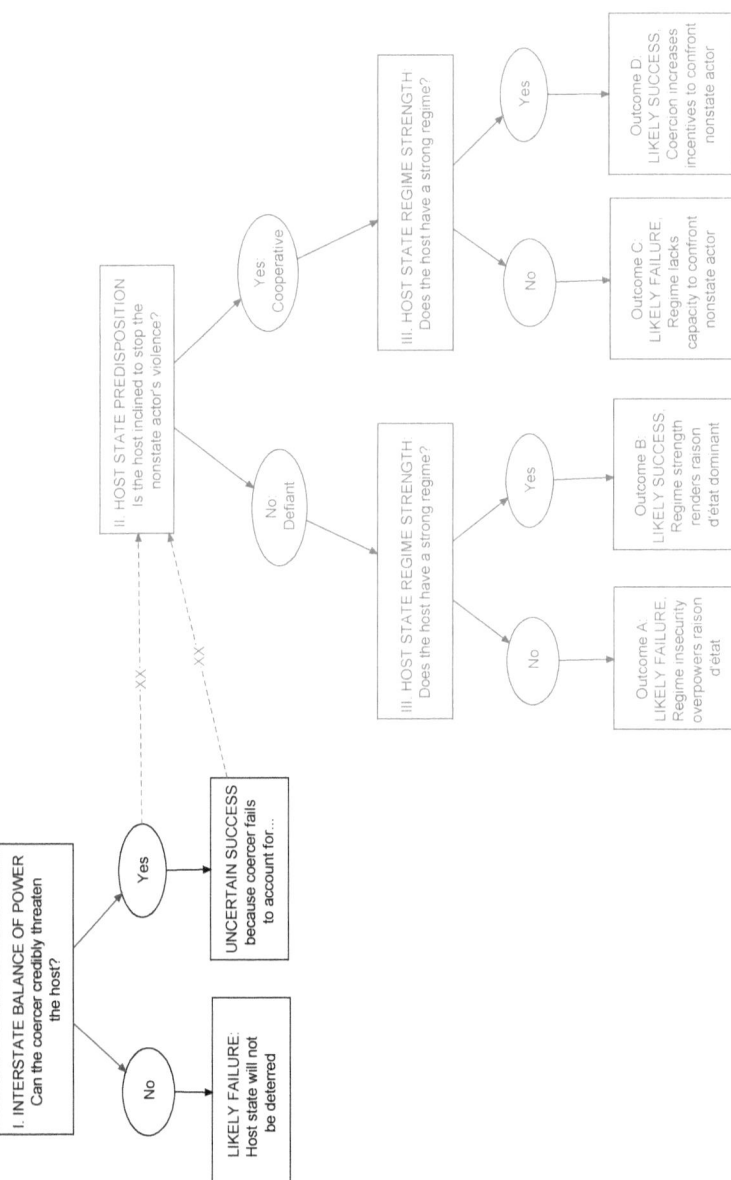

Figure 2.4 Triadic coercion decision-making, 1949–1956.

early 1990s. Following Menachem Klein, we call Israel's approach to triadic coercion in this era "the Rabin Doctrine,"[90] named after Chief of Staff Yitzhak Rabin (1964–1967). This was not a proper doctrine but a focused concept that guided operationalization of triadic coercion during these decades, which, as is elaborated in chapter 3, saw the emergence of Palestinian guerrilla groups and their intensified cross-border operations. The Rabin Doctrine held that Israel should vary its responses to nonstate actors according to what Israel perceived to be the stance of the state in which those nonstate actors were based. If the host state actively encouraged nonstate actors' violence, Israel would aim its threats and punitive strikes at that state. If the state did not encourage nonstate actors, or in fact opposed them, Israel would forego triadic coercion and instead target the nonstate actor directly. In terms of the triadic coercion decision chart, the Rabin Doctrine moved from considerations about interstate balance of power to questions about host states' predispositions toward complying with Israel's dictates (see figure 2.5).

Rabin explained his doctrine by distinguishing Syria, which he viewed as complicit in attacks by Palestinian groups, from Jordan and Lebanon, which he considered to be victims of the militants that carved out bases on their soil. He elaborated in an April 1967 interview: "Israel's response to Jordan and Lebanon is appropriate only for states that are not interested in terrorist attacks launched against their will. With Syria the problem is different, because the regime is supporting the terrorists. Therefore, the essence of the response to Syria must be different. . . . Since the Syrian regime is behind the acts of terrorism, it had better take measures to curb these actions, and the sooner, the better."[91]

Not all security elites agreed with the Rabin Doctrine. Some, including Intelligence Branch Director Aharon Yariv and Mossad Director Meir Amit, thought that the approach was too belligerent toward Syria and might lead to escalation. Other generals opposed it as too lenient toward Jordan and Lebanon. The ruling Mapai and Ahdut Haavoda parties supported Rabin's policy. Ben-Gurion and Dayan's breakaway Rafi Party called for a more hawkish line.[92] Debate notwithstanding, the Rabin Doctrine became Israel's approach to triadic conflicts from 1956 until the 1990s. The chief of staff's sweeping power over security decision-making aided this institutionalization.

In adopting Rabin's logic, political and military decision-makers made a necessary distinction between nonstate actors and host states and also

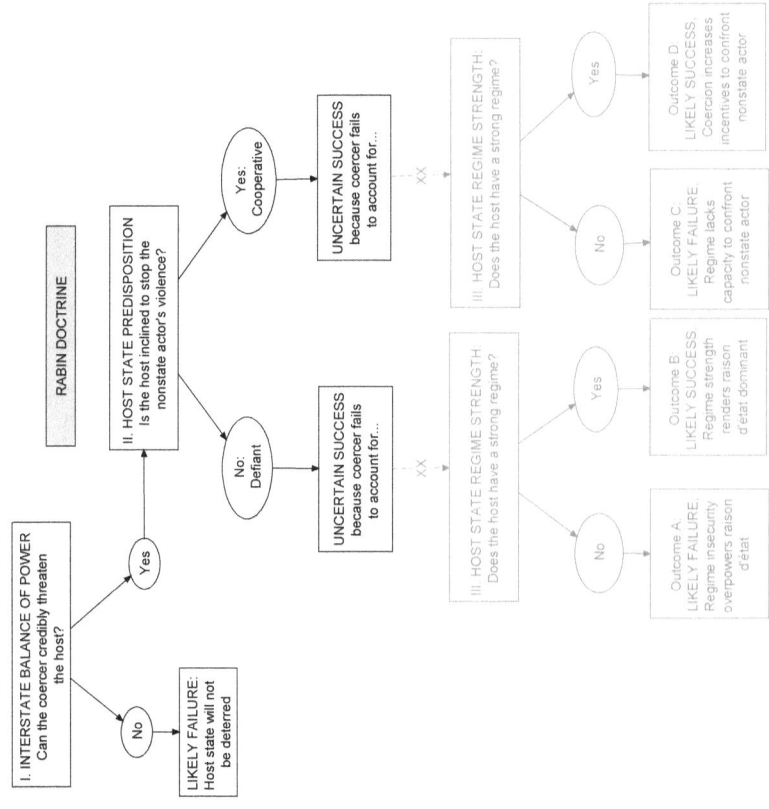

Figure 2.5 Triadic coercion, 1956–1990.

between defiant and compliant host states. Implicitly, they assumed that there was no need for coercion to alter the calculations of a host state whose preferences already aligned with those of Israel. While important, host states' predispositions represented only the first step of the multistep decision-making process demanded by triadic situations. In not moving to the next step, Israeli leaders failed to take into account host regimes' strength. They thus ignored how a host's level of cohesion and capacity mediated its ability to curb nonstate actors' activity, regardless of its wishes to do so.

Triadic Coercion, the Rabin Doctrine, and Jordan

Subsequent chapters examine the implementation of these policies in Egypt, Syria, and Lebanon. To complete that regional portrait, we illustrate the Rabin Doctrine's impact on Israel's triadic conflict with Jordan. This conflict was largely contained between 1949 and 1970, a period that saw the Hashemite monarchy beleaguered by multiple sources of regime weakness.

The first element of regime weakness was capacity. The Transjordan Mandate was created in 1921, when Great Britain installed Abdullah, the son of the Hashemite emir of Mecca, as king of what had been a peripheral area of the Ottoman Empire. Under colonial rule, state-building centered largely on the use of generous British subsidies to co-opt the territory's tribes and merchant elite with side payments, tax exemptions, and jobs in the Jordanian army, which was dubbed the Arab Legion and served under British commanders.[93] This political strategy, yielding a monarchical coalition more than strong institutions, might have been sufficient for a small population. However, the 1948 War remade Jordan territorially by precipitating its annexation of the West Bank, and demographically by adding some 900,000 Palestinians (400,000 of whom were refugees) to the preexisting Transjordanian population of 400,000.[94] This transformation of society generated not only new cleavages and tensions but also tremendous economic strain. With shortages of water and arable land as well as very limited industry, unemployment soared. For its economic survival, Jordan came to rely even further on British and other external aid, which totaled more than half of all official revenues from 1949 to 1956.[95]

Beyond these deficiencies in capacity, the Hashemite regime also faced serious challenges to its cohesion. Given the regime's annexation of the

West Bank and its overtures toward Israel, many Palestinians viewed the monarchy as not only treasonous but, in Kamal Salibi's words, "chiefly responsible for the plight of their people."[96] Against this backdrop, a Palestinian gunman assassinated Abdullah in 1951. While the assassination of a head of state could generate political crisis under any political system, it was especially dire in Jordan because Abdullah's son quickly abdicated power due to schizophrenia. This left his grandson, Hussein, to become king at the age of sixteen.

Tensions continued between the inexperienced monarch and his Palestinian subjects, who obtained citizenship but were denied proportionate representation in government.[97] Opposition to the throne intensified as Nasser's rise in Egypt inspired enthusiasm for pan-Arabist, anti-imperialist challenges to conservative regimes throughout the Middle East. By the md-1950s, parties espousing Arab nationalism, communism, or Ba'athism, as well as labor unions, students, and other civil society groups, were agitating for greater democratic checks on the monarchy and an end to British control of the Arab Legion. Street demonstrations grew and then escalated in the wake of rigged elections and Hussein's consideration of membership in the pro-Western Baghdad Pact.[98] As the army suppressed riots and loyalist-led governments resigned, boiling public pressure forced Hussein to dismiss the British heads of the Arab Legion and appoint an Arab nationalist-leaning chief of staff.[99] The 1956 elections brought oppositionists to power, and, the following year, oppositionist army officers encircled the palace and then attempted a coup d'état. Declaring a state of emergency, Hussein requested U.S. aid, which came in an immediate $10-million grant and the dispatching of the Sixth Fleet to the eastern Mediterranean.[100] He also proclaimed martial law, suspended the parliament, dissolved political parties, arrested oppositionists en masse, and purged critics from the army.[101]

The crackdown salvaged the regime from a crisis from within, but threats continued from without. Egypt and Syria broadcast a stream of anti-Hussein propaganda, and both sent funds to support antiregime activities in the West Bank.[102] In 1958, a coup overthrew the Hashemite monarchy in Iraq, which was headed by Hussein's cousin Faisal. The British ambassador at the time commented, "Not a single foreign observer in Amman outside the British Embassy believed that, even with British and American help, the Jordanian monarchy had a chance of surviving."[103] That the monarchy nevertheless survived was due in part to the loyalty of the army, recruited largely from East Bank tribes. It was also crucially enabled by tens of millions of dollars in annual U.S. aid. Hussein used that aid to expand his support base through development of the economy and distribution of welfare benefits, and also to build a coercive apparatus to monitor and repress would-be dissenters.[104] Though this helped solidify the Jordanian regime's cohesion and capacity over the years, both elements of regime strength remained tentative and crucially reliant on external rents.

It was in this political context that King Hussein maintained a mixed predisposition toward Israel. As Clinton Bailey explains, his stance was "moderate as a precaution against being destroyed by its western neighbor, but hostile as a precaution against being overthrown by the Palestinians."[105] In Bailey's view, the history of Jordan from 1949 to 1971 is defined by the regime's attempt to balance between these two competing pressures.

As an organized force, the Palestinian national movement remained incipient through the early 1960s. In 1964, the Arab League established the Palestine Liberation Organization (PLO). In 1965, the Fatah movement carried out its first cross-border guerrilla operations, spurring the development of what would become dozens of different groups of fedayeen, or guerrilla fighters. In 1969, the PLO became the umbrella organization for the national movement's many factions. Fatah, the largest faction, assumed leadership. Jordan took various measures to restrict the fedayeen and prevent their cross-border attacks. Jordanian security forces clashed with Palestinian guerrillas, confiscated weapons caches, arrested activists and leaders, seized explosives, and temporarily closed the PLO headquarters in Jerusalem. By 1967, it had detained or imprisoned more than half of Fatah's fighting force.[106] Jordan's main motivations for taking these steps were twofold: Israel's demonstrations of power in 1956 and 1967 and, more importantly, the challenge that Palestinian groups posed to the Hashemite regime itself.

Israeli decision-makers keenly followed Jordan's stance and reasoned that it was not fruitful to punish a regime predisposed against Palestinian militancy. When confronting cross-border strikes from Jordan, Israel therefore departed from its post-1953 norm of attacking host states and largely returned to the earlier approach of targeting nonstate groups directly.[107] Exemplifying this changed approach was Israel's most severe raid on Jordanian soil between the 1956 and 1967 wars. In November 1965 a vehicle hit a landmine and exploded in Israel near the border with Jordan. The IDF responded with a massive raid on the West Bank village of Samu', from which Israel believed the attackers had hailed and received aid.[108] A large infantry force, including an armored brigade and heavy artillery, detonated some 118 houses and other buildings.[109] In accordance with the Rabin Doctrine, Israel did not target its coercion against the regime. In this case, it instead targeted civilians supportive of Fatah. Even Jordan's defense minister reported, "The enemy's goal was to blow up homes thought to be Fatah bases near the cease-fire lines."[110] Nevertheless, Jordanian troops rushed to the scene, and the ensuing battle left fifteen Jordanian soldiers dead and thirty-four injured, in addition to five civilians killed and six wounded.[111] Israeli forces also shot down a Jordanian aircraft, killing the pilot, who happened to be the king's personal friend.[112]

The raid sparked unprecedented antiregime protest in Jordan. Thousands of Palestinians joined demonstrations, strikes, and riots across the West Bank calling for the king's overthrow. The regime suppressed protest at the cost of more than a dozen protestors killed or injured, well over one hundred arrested, some ten days of curfew in major cities, and a troop presence on the streets for nearly a month.[113] Having directly and repeatedly reported to Israel his extensive efforts to suppress Palestinian militancy, Hussein felt personally betrayed by Israel's aggression and saw it as evidence that Israel was bent on full-scale war to seize the West Bank, "whether or not Jordan entered the fray." Moshe Shemesh thus judges the Samu' raid to be the turning point that launched Jordan on the path toward its May 1967 mutual defense treaty with Egypt and subsequent participation in the war with Israel.[114] Avi Shlaim agrees that, for Israel's purposes, the raid was "a terrible blunder."[115]

The raid's backfire exposed two enduring flaws in Israel's use of triadic coercion, even as rendered more nuanced by the "Rabin Doctrine": Israel's insufficient attention to the weakness of targeted host regimes and its strategic culture's valorization of disproportionate force. Driven by a strategic culture upholding severe force and blinded to the domestic politics of host states, Israel, in Shlaim's words, "exacted an eye for an eyelash, but this time it exacted it from the wrong Arab party."[116] Rabin was adamant that the raid had aimed to punish nonstate actors and their supporters and not, in his words, "to arrive at a confrontation with Jordan or to humiliate Hussein."[117] Nonetheless, it resulted in precisely the latter. In Shlaim's assessment, Samu' exposed Jordan's "military weakness and fragility" as well as the huge "rift" between the monarchy and its Palestinian subjects.[118]

Had Israel been more attentive to the precariousness of the king's domestic position, it might have realized that an operation that massive, even if not aimed directly at regime targets, would have destabilizing consequences. As Hussein himself said, it "created a devastating effect in Jordan."[119]

The 1967 War resulted in Israel's occupation of the West Bank and the flight of another approximately 140,000 Palestinian refugees to Jordan's East Bank.[120] As the defeated Arab states retreated, the emboldened fedayeen seized the initiative against Israel. Palestinian attacks on Israeli targets intensified in 1968, numbering seventy-eight attacks in its first three months alone.[121] Israel continued to view them through the lens of the Rabin Doctrine and its assessment of Jordan as a cooperative state. When Israel carried out a large-scale raid in March 1968, therefore, it aimed at the East Bank village of Karameh, where several Palestinian factions had bases. Acting on early intelligence, Palestinian and Jordanian forces ambushed Israeli troops. Fierce combat claimed the lives of 33 Israeli soldiers, 84 Jordanian soldiers, and 151 Palestinian fighters.[122]

As in Samu', Israel's target in Karameh was a nonstate actor, not Jordanian assets. Also as in Samu', the raid backfired. The 1967 rout had weakened Arab regimes vis-à-vis their own societies, reducing the legitimacy and political capital with which they had once restricted Palestinian activity on their soil. The fedayeen transformed the defeat of states into an opportunity for nonstate actors and soon won popular praise as the only force continuing to stand up to Israel.[123] Karameh intensified these dynamics, and in its wake the Palestinian resistance movement rose "like a phoenix out of ashes" to reap "a harvest of hero-worship."[124] Dozens of new guerrilla groups formed, and recruits to Fatah skyrocketed.[125]

The Arabic press, once reluctant to acknowledge Fatah, now published its communiqués with enthusiasm.[126] Leaders were pressured to ease restrictions on the fedayeen to divert popular criticism of their defeat in the war, recuperate their credibility, and prove commitment to the Palestinian cause. The shift was especially dramatic in Jordan, where popular pressures made it politically costly to continue prior measures against nonstate actors.[127] Hussein was even compelled to say, famously, "We have come to the point now where we are all fedayeen."[128] Despite this rhetoric, however, the regime's basic predisposition remained unchanged. It did not actively support Palestinians' militant activity but simply lacked the political or institutional capacity to oppose it. As such, armed Palestinian activists moved into refugee camps and towns, and carved out semi-autonomous areas near the border. They thereby increased their ability to attack the Israeli-controlled West Bank.[129]

Judging Jordan to be cooperative, Israel continued to direct its reprisals at nonstate actors. It increased its strikes on guerrilla bases in the Jordan Valley and even launched assaults in the suburbs of Amman.[130] These strikes did not curtail nonstate actors' attacks as much as erode the monarchy's legitimacy. Shlaim writes, "The harder Israel struck at the Fedayeen, the more popular the latter became in Jordan, and the greater was the threat they posed to the Hashemite regime."[131] When Hussein finally turned forcefully against the fedayeen it was due not to Israeli military coercion but to the political challenge posed by Palestinian militancy. In the years after Karameh, the guerrillas continued to expand their armed presence in Jordanian cities. They erected roadblocks, clashed with police and military, and kidnapped diplomats. More radical Palestinian organizations, such as the Popular Front for the Liberation of Palestine (PFLP), advocated overthrowing the monarchy.[132] On September 1, 1970, security forces foiled an attempt to assassinate the king, which they traced to the PFLP.

The following week, the PFLP hijacked three airplanes and landed them on a Jordanian airstrip that they declared liberated territory. The king demanded immediate release of the aircraft and passengers. The PFLP evacuated the passengers but ignited the planes. The king declared martial law, and the already restive Jordanian army launched a twelve-day onslaught on PLO bases. Though the PLO and Jordan reached a ceasefire, the army continued a "creeping offensive" against Palestinian forces until it liquidated them from Jordanian territory in July 1971. These events, recalled as "Black September" or the "Jordanian civil war," forced the PLO to relocate its headquarters to Lebanon, where it remained until 1982.[133]

The Rabin Doctrine dominated Israel's approach to triadic coercion into the 1990s. Israel viewed Lebanon, like Jordan, as predisposed to cooperate against nonstate actors. It therefore did not directly punish the government for attacks emanating from its soil. Though it continued to conduct raids in these two countries, it targeted nonstate actors, not state installations. By contrast, it regarded Syria as accountable for groups operating from Syrian territory and punished it accordingly. In terms of our triadic coercion decision tree, Israel's military-dominated decision-making advanced to the second level of considering host states' predispositions. It did not move to the third level and address host state regime strength. Acting on an impoverished understanding of its adversaries' domestic politics, Israel thus neglected the fuller range of motivations and constraints that shape states' relationships to nonstate actors.

Triadic Coercion since 1990

Shift in Israel's Strategic Thinking

The 1990s constitute the beginning of the third period in Israel's triadic coercion evolution. For the first forty years of statehood, Israel's national security concept centered on battlefield decision, early warning, and deterrence. As General Israel Tal said in 1977, "Israel's military thought, to this date, is little more than a series of footnotes to the doctrine which crystallized in the fifties."[134]

By the early 1990s, however, many Israeli elites realized that this doctrine had become out of sync with security conditions. Israel's main security challenges were no longer conventional state armies but irregular forces. For such threats, "battlefield decision" was not effective, and blitzkrieg-style rapid campaigns were inappropriate. Though the IDF had been facing nonstate adversaries for years, Israeli security thinkers did not focus on them.[135] Only 3 percent of the articles published between 1948 and 2000 in *Maarachot*, the IDF's premier professional journal, focused on low-intensity conflict of the kind that involves nonstate actors.[136] Had there been significant debate on these topics prior to the 1990s, the pages of *Maarachot* would have featured it. Relatedly, Israeli strategists realized that their achievement of unambiguous military victory in large-scale war was not effectively deterring nonstate actors. Though this disjuncture was apparent in the wake of the 1967 War, Israeli military elites did not systematically address it for another thirty years.[137]

Israel's strategic culture contributed to the long delay in recognizing the need to update its security thinking. The domination of decision-making by the IDF or by its former officers in government positions limited opportunities for serious critique of military approaches to security problems. The military's own anti-intellectual tradition further discouraged it from stopping to take stock of fundamental assumptions or to ask big, paradigm-shifting questions about the country's strategic environment.[138] Brigadier General Arie Shalev reported that, in his six years as head of the research division of the IDF's intelligence branch, he never participated in discussions of the IDF's operational concept.[139] Retired Brigadier-General Shimon Naveh regards that silence as a kind of denial of reality:

> Since the logical roots of the operational doctrine of preemptive offensive lay in the siege mentality and the strategic circumstances that preceded the 1967 War, it seems only natural that the decisive victory and the ensuing profound territorial changes should have led the country's military and political leadership to re-examine the validity of the traditional concepts. Yet, neither this re-examination nor any attempt to re-interpret the new strategic reality took place. To the contrary, unable to resist the addictive temptations of success, the captains of Israel's strategy became ever-more obsessed with the magical formula of combining a preemptive approach with the operational method of offensive armoured manoeuvre.[140]

The Rabin Doctrine notwithstanding, it was not until the 1990s that Israeli security thinking and practice saw a significant increase in attention to low-intensity conflict, nonstate actors, deterrence, and, in this context, triadic coercion. Some civilian academics urged this rethinking.[141] Given the military's structural power, however, two military institutions were most influential in spearheading the shift. First, the IDF's Training and Doctrine Division (TOHAD) published several publications on counterinsurgency starting in 1996. Of particular influence was *Haimut Hamugbal* (Limited conflict), a 2001 booklet of insights from historic cases of asymmetric conflict. Integrated into the IDF's training manuals,[142] the publication came to stand as the General Staff's unofficial counterinsurgency doctrine.[143] Second, the Operation Theory Research Institute (OTRI, or Maltam), an internal IDF think tank, disseminated ideas about reforming strategic and operational concepts through a series of officers' seminars. It influenced high-ranking commanders and the IDF as a whole, especially when General Moshe Yaalon was chief of staff from 2002 to 2005.[144] Though the institute was later criticized and dismantled, its ideas remained influential.[145]

Among the questions that this new thinking addressed was what ought to be Israel's military objective in an era in which battlefield victories did not necessarily bring security. By the early 2000s the IDF arrived at an answer that Dima Adamsky calls a "new Israeli deterrence paradigm."[146]

Israel's traditional security concept understood deterrence as a by-product of victory in war and a means for achieving security. The new thinking regarded deterrence as a goal in itself. This shift was on display in the August 2015 "IDF Strategy" document, the closest Israel had come to adopting a formal written doctrine. In it, the General Staff presented four "principles of the national security doctrine":

A. **Maintenance of extended periods of security calm** to enable the development of society, science, and the economy, as well as to improve Israel's preparedness for times of emergency and war.
B. **Creation of regional deterrence,** as well as deterrence against elements that could generate threats, through the maintenance of a strong and relevant military force, and the resolve to operate the full might of this force when needed.
C. **During routine times**—The application, deepening, and maintenance of deterrence through force-building and the creation of a credible threat in accordance with the willingness and readiness to use military force. At the same time, the coordinated operation of all of Israel's defense organizations for the purpose of damaging the enemy's capabilities and force-building.
D. **In times of emergency and war**—A speedy removal of the threat, while minimizing the damage to the state of Israel and enhancing Israel's regional deterrence.[147]

Three of these principles point directly to deterrence, indicating its enhanced importance as something of a replacement for "battlefield decision." In this new paradigm, deterrence has two operational components. First, "deterrence operations," which are large-scale offensives aimed at demonstrating Israel's superior technological and intelligence capacity, and thereby convincing enemies of the futility of challenging it. In Israel's thinking, examples of deterrence operations included Accountability (1993) and Grapes of Wrath (1996) in Lebanon, and Cast Lead (2008–2009), Pillar of Defense (2012), and Protective Edge (2014) in the Gaza Strip. Second, "operations between wars" (*mivtzaim bein milhamot*, or *mabams*) are periodic missions intended to demonstrate Israel's prowess and thereby extend the interval of time between deterrence operations.[148] These missions are on a smaller scale, often using aircraft or special forces beyond the boundaries of the state. Examples include Israel's bombing of what it believed to be an incipient Syrian nuclear reactor in 2007 and Israel's destruction of Hezbollah weapon convoys in Syria in 2016 and in Sudan in 2012.[149]

The "IDF Strategy" document does not explicitly discuss what should be the appropriate targets of deterrence. Implicitly, however, the security establishment's approach since the 1990s has focused on what it calls the "leverages approach" (*torat hamenofim*). In Adamsky's words, this entails "influencing non-state entities through a third actor, usually state patrons of terrorist proxies."[150] The leverages approach has thus been effectively equivalent to triadic coercion. Unclassified materials do not offer many specifics about how security elites understand "levers" to work and under what conditions. Rather, as in the past, practice has driven theory, not vice versa. This practice came to light in the first stages of the second Palestinian Intifada when, as the then IDF commander of the northern West Bank said, Israel's idea was to "create a steady and continuous pressure on the Palestinian Authority so that it will fight [anti-Israeli] terrorism."[151] He explained that the idea of leveraging was that "through the application . . . of force, the Palestinian system would be convinced to act, whether because it was deterred or because it understood that it would be better for its interests."[152]

Israel's increasing embrace of triadic coercion has not been a simple response to circumstances. The particular way that security elites have conceptualized and implemented triadic coercion has also been conditioned by a set of collectively held, historically developed beliefs, attitudes, and practices. Facing a crisis in long taken-for-granted concepts and methods, Israeli security elites have looked to their strategic culture for a repertoire from which to draw solutions. In the 1990s and 2000s, this strategic culture has shaped Israel's approach to triadic coercion in four main ways.

*Belief in the Inherent Rather Than Instrumental Utility
of Actions in Pursuit of Deterrence*

Throughout most of its history, Israel adopted deterrence as a means to achieve specific goals, such as increasing the state's security or convincing its foes to accept its existence. Since the 1990s, however, Israel has increasingly adopted "deterrence operations" that seem to laud military action taken in pursuit of deterrence, independent of whether they in fact achieve deterrence. The shift in Israel's discourse and behavior came to the fore with two bombing campaigns in Lebanon in the 1990s, Operation Accountability and Operation Grapes of Wrath, as well as in its operations against the second Intifada after the year 2000. In these cases, Israel was intensely concerned about any appearance of weakness and expressed a conviction that severe shows of force were needed to demonstrate strength, nearly for its own sake. That is, officials came to celebrate the intensity of strikes taken in pursuit of deterrence more than they critically evaluated the real effectiveness of those actions in establishing deterrence. In championing extreme military force, elites revealed less and less concern about the need to explain, either in their internal deliberations or public communications, how such actions realized political or security goals. Military action gradually became a goal in and of itself.

In Israel's strategic culture, there was thus a blurring between asserting a deterrent posture and actually achieving deterrence. This development suggested the extent to which Israel's decision-making was the product of an inherited esteem for severe force rather than a rational response to pressing circumstances. Israelis' faith that preponderant military strikes generated deterrence seemed impervious to evidence to the contrary. Rather than rethink the utility of blunt coercion, decision-makers redefined what constituted utility. Punishing the enemy became necessary because it was necessary to punish the enemy, not because it caused the enemy to change its thinking or behavior.[153]

Lack of Nuance or Differentiation

In the United States and elsewhere, strategists and scholars have increasingly invoked the notion of "tailored deterrence" to argue for adapting the character and emphasis of deterrence policies to address "fundamental differences in the perceptions and resulting decision calculus of specific adversaries in specific circumstances."[154] The "IDF Strategy" document endorsed this idea in theory, stating, "Deterrence must be specific and adapted to each enemy; it must be based on an ongoing analysis of the enemy's characteristics, considerations, capabilities, identity, and decision-making processes."[155] In practice, however, Israel has done less and less "tailoring" of deterrence over time.

Guided by the Rabin Doctrine for decades, decision-makers distinguished between defiant and cooperative host states but did not take into account the strength of the host regimes. Since the 1990s, as many non-state actors have grown more powerful vis-à-vis host states, inattention to host regime strength has become an increasingly deleterious blind spot. At the same time, Israel's use of military might against weak host states has reached heights of sustained, devastating intensity unknown during earlier eras. In targeting triadic coercion against the Palestinian Authority and Lebanon, Israel has advocated blanket coercion without meaningful consideration of either the particular nature of the actors that it faces or the contextual conditions rendering each situation unique. Israeli security decision-makers seem to assume, as a matter of fact, that the greater physical pressure and destruction Israel brings on the host state, the more it will compel these hosts to act against nonstate actors.

Israeli strategists also exhibit a lack of nuance in their failure to distinguish between deterrence (or coercive diplomacy more broadly) and mere brute force. Security elites often refer to deterrence operations with the expression "mowing the grass," meaning brute force to degrade enemies' capabilities to challenge Israel.[156] As a metaphor, "mowing the grass" reveals how Israel views its adversaries. Grass has neither feelings nor intelligence. Nor can it be deterred. As long as grass is alive, it is biologically destined to grow; the only thing that can limit that growth is periodically taking a blade to shorten it. In using this analogy, Israel's security establishment seems to suggest that its enemies are similarly undeterrable and their belligerence inevitable. It does not seriously consider their motivations or the possibility that they may respond to incentives other than violence. What Israel has presented as operations seeking deterrence hence actually negate the idea of deterrence in either the immediate or cumulative sense. Efraim Inbar and Eitan Shamir explain that Israel's logic in "mowing the grass" is to show restraint in absorbing a certain number of attacks and then launching mass-scale offensives both to destroy foes' capabilities and "have a temporary deterrent effect in order to create periods of quiet along its borders."[157] Yet what kind of deterrence has Israel achieved if it has needed to embark on three wars—or "deterrence operations"—in six years, as it did against Gaza between 2008 and 2014?

The lack of distinction either among different targets of coercion or between deterrence and brute force reflects the extremes that Israel's strategic culture has reached in the twenty-first century. The IDF's unnuanced approach demonstrates a new ethos that prioritizes acting over thinking about how, why, and under what circumstances any course of action might actually increase Israel's security. Serious exploration of nonmilitary options, while never paramount in Israeli strategic culture, have all but disappeared. Pounding the enemy has thus become the solution to every problem, regardless of the type of enemy or the nature of the problem.

Targeting Enemy Consciousness

Increasingly since the 1990s, Israel has given marked attention to the need for military operations to produce messages, symbols, and images that will convince adversaries that Israel is invincible and that challenging it will result in utter devastation. It is not atypical for counterinsurgency to consider psychological dimensions. Yet while Western notions of "winning hearts and minds" imply a positive effort to earn sympathy and support among insurgents' social bases,[158] Israel has emphasized a negative approach, centered on causing fear and surrender.[159] As the IDF's training manual, updated in 2000, expresses it, the goal of operations in low-intensity conflict is not to acquire territory or to vanquish the enemy but "to achieve a change of consciousness in an adversary's society by an extended process of wearing the adversary down."[160]

The 2015 "IDF Strategy" document devotes significant attention to enemy consciousness (*todaah*), discussing it multiple times in a range of contexts.[161] As a tool for achieving deterrence, it maintains the centrality of "consciousness operations," designed to demonstrate Israel's ability to take risks, inflict harm, and reach challengers wherever they might hide.[162] A "consciousness operation" is the Israeli version of American "shock and awe" but with the objective of increasing deterrence rather than achieving decisive victory. According to IDF strategist Shmuel Nir, consciousness operations aim to change enemies' images of both current and future realities by altering their perceptions, evaluations, positions, and decisions.[163] Should an adversary continue to defy Israel's harsh military posture, Israel must apply even harsher force to convince it to acquiesce, at least for a while.[164]

This idea—that when force fails to achieve deterrence in the present, greater force will achieve its success in the future—appears consistent with the logic of "cumulative deterrence."[165] Yet it effectively allows leaders to defer indefinitely critical assessment of how their strategies actually affect adversaries' calculations. Instead of specifying and proving the mechanisms by which military punishment changes foes' behavior, leaders hide behind vague metaphors about "burning" lessons into enemy psyches. Both decision-makers and the public are therefore absolved of the need to scrutinize and reevaluate the assumptions that undergird their choices.

Parallel to the focus on adversaries' perceptions, the IDF has devoted growing attention to the use of propaganda (*hasbara*) to shape attitudes both among Israelis at home and key audiences abroad.[166] The 2015 "IDF Strategy" document devotes a complete section to this topic, in addition to other frequent references to the need to create, maintain, and promote belief in the legitimacy of the military's actions.[167]

Logic of Appropriateness

Finally, Israel's belief that it is justified in using military might, even disproportionately, is deeply rooted in its historic sense of existential vulnerability, or "siege mentality."[168] While this conviction has infused Israel's strategic culture since before statehood, it has taken on a more sweeping, moralistic tone over time. Indeed, the rationale guiding military actions has increasingly shifted from that of the "logic of consequences" (rational action calculating expected returns from alternative choices) to the "logic of appropriateness" (whereby action seeks to fulfill social norms about what is good and proper).[169] Applied to triadic coercion, Israel's understanding of appropriateness posits that host states are morally culpable for nonstate actors on their soil, and Israel is thus morally justified in holding those states accountable when those nonstate actors carry out attacks. Israeli decision-makers have not ignored the strategic utility of targeting host states. Yet utility is no longer the only, or perhaps even the primary, rationale for triadic coercion. Rather, triadic coercion is considered legitimate and necessary, regardless of its effects.

Emphasis on the appropriateness and inherent utility of triadic coercion, together with the lack of nuance in advocating destructive power to reshape adversaries' consciousness, has combined to effect a deterioration in the strategic sophistication of Israel's decision-making. In terms of figure 2.4, Israel has regressed to asking only the first question in the triadic coercion decision tree. It no longer considers the second question about host state willingness, which had been the core of the Rabin Doctrine, much less the third question about host strength, which we find to be definitive in determining triadic coercion outcomes.

Conclusion

This chapter provides the essential background explaining Israel's understanding and practice of triadic coercion. A constellation of decision-making processes and ideas has shaped the unique strategic culture within which Israel views threats and has made and implemented decisions to address them. In this context, Israel's use of triadic coercion evolved in three eras.

From 1949 until the 1956 Suez War, Israel's approach to threats from nonstate actors underwent a process of trial and error as it adjusted various strategies and assessed their efficacy for achieving multiple military and political objectives. Israel thus moved from defensive and diplomatic measures to military reprisals across its borders. It first targeted raids against areas from which it believed infiltrators to originate and then shifted to punishing communities believed to be hostile. When the latter strategy garnered criticism, Israel began striking installations of the state hosting nonstate infiltrators. Israeli leaders believed that such use of triadic coercion would not only force neighboring states to prevent border violations but perhaps also build cumulative deterrence, train the army for future wars, or even hasten such a war on terms that favored Israel.

From 1956 until the mid-1990s, Israel continued to apply triadic coercion, but with greater nuance. Guided by Rabin, it targeted coercion against host states perceived to support nonstate actors' attacks and aimed coercion directly at nonstate actors when the state did not support such activity. This showed Israel's attention to the important distinction between states predisposed to cooperate with Israel or defy it. Nevertheless, Israel largely failed to consider host regimes' strength. Israel's experience with Jordan in this period was formative of this policy; its limited success is instructive of the problems of triadic coercion against weak regimes, even when they share an interest in preventing nonstate actors' attacks.

The 1990s ushered in a crisis in Israel's security concept as strategists realized that many key assumptions about their strategic environment were no longer valid. In this context, Israel turned attention to low-intensity conflict and deterrence. The bulk of Israeli history confirms the assumption of mainstream deterrence theory, that state leaders choose actions vis-à-vis other states on the basis of their expected utility for advancing strategic goals. By the 1990s, however, Israel's approach to deterrence took on new dimensions. It became intensely concerned about any perceived weakening of its deterrent posture and, correspondingly, developed a compulsion to reassert that posture for its own sake and not only as a vehicle for achieving security. Military and strategic elites increasingly came to uphold triadic coercion as an effective method in this regard.

Attention to strategic culture helps explain both this rise of triadic coercion and particularities in its design and implementation. In the Israeli case, these particularities include a focus on the inherent utility and moral righteousness of military strikes, lack of nuance in their targeting and application, and a drive to sear the "consciousness" of the enemy with the lesson that Israel repays threats with destructive force. Culturally constructed assumptions about its neighbors' invariable hostility have blinded Israeli security decision-makers to differences in the preferences, capabilities, and incentives of various Arab regimes. If nonstate actors attack from a neighboring state, Israeli leaders nearly automatically perceive that as exposing the host state's willful complicity in violence. The IDF's traditional anti-intellectualism has infused this continued embrace of inherited tendencies toward brute force. In a strategic culture that favors doing over deep thinking and long-term planning, sticking with old assumptions has been easier than questioning them.

The Israeli military's ongoing application of severe force, even in the quest for deterrence, shows that its "cult of the offensive" remains operative. By the mid-1990s, the security apparatus realized that "battlefield decision" was unobtainable against nonstate threats. Nevertheless, IDF actions still seem to seek such an outcome. As nonstate actors like Hamas and Hezbollah have been difficult to pinpoint and defeat, Israel has embraced targeting host state infrastructures as a natural alternative. Israel possesses the means to identify and destroy such targets; doing so produces the immediately visible results that decades of idolizing offensive measures have brought Israeli decision-makers and citizens to want and expect. Defensive or diplomatic action might achieve better results in providing security to Israeli citizens, with less bloodshed. According to the norms of

Israel's strategic culture, however, defensive and nonmilitary actions are not regarded as the "doing something" that the army, media, and public demand. Attacks by nonstate actors require a response. Striking the states that host them offers a satisfying one, whether or not it actually makes Israel more secure.

CHAPTER 3

Egypt Since 1949

Triadic Coercion from Raids to Peace

The Egypt-Israel Armistice Agreement of February 1949 recognized a 250-kilometer Armistice Demarcation Line (ADL) that prohibited crossings between the two countries.[1] Throughout the decades that followed, however, both nonstate and state forces traversed from Egyptian-controlled territory into Israel, and Israel in turn launched raids into Egypt in an attempt to end such infractions. Many studies have recognized, as we do, that Israel's efforts to deter border violations largely failed before 1954, appear to have counterproductively increased attacks from 1954 to 1956, and then achieved dramatic success with the 1956 Suez War. Thereafter, the border remained strikingly quiet for eleven years. Zeev Maoz's dataset illustrates these patterns (see figure 3.1).

Figure 3.1 should be viewed with two caveats. First, these data rely on reported incidents that occurred in southern Israel. Although responsibility and place of origin cannot be definitively established, it is assumed that these border crossings most likely emanated from Egypt or the Egypt-controlled Gaza Strip. Second, the fatalities tally for the year 1956 does not include October and November, when the Suez War occurred. Inclusion would otherwise skew the pattern significantly.

Scholars offer different explanations of these trends. Avner Yaniv argues that Israel initially favored an approach to the Egyptian border that combined diplomacy, defense, and alliance with a great power. When border

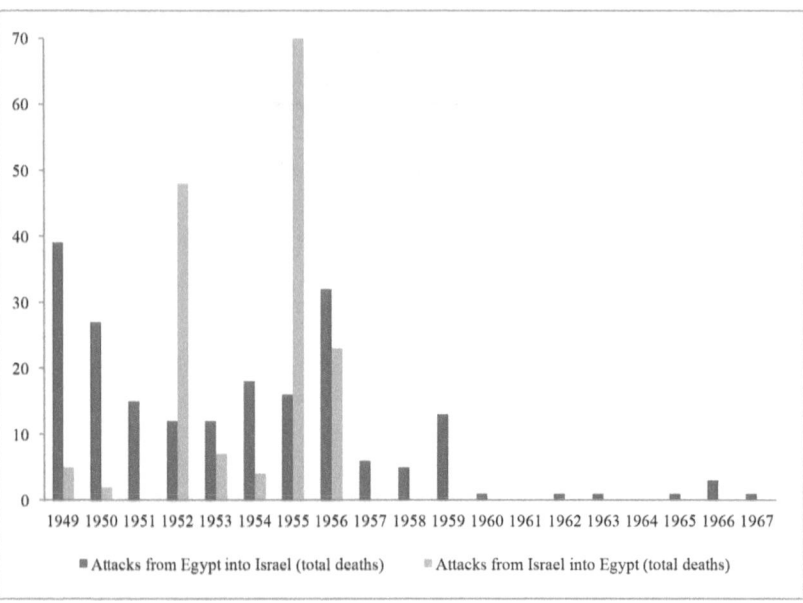

Figure 3.1 Attacks into southern Israel and Israeli raids in Egypt, January 1949–1967.
Source: Zeev Maoz, "Arab Nonstate Aggression and Israeli Limited Uses of Force" dataset, *The Quantitative History of the Arab-Israeli Conflict*, available at http://vanity.dss.ucdavis.edu/~maoz/arabisrhost.htm.

violations continued, Israel shifted to deterrence by punishment, often wielding deliberately disproportional force. Domestic political pressures, as well as Israel's aversion to tension with great powers, served as some brake on that use of force. Yaniv concludes that this searching for the right approach came to an end with the Suez War, which created effective deterrence. In taking part in the tripartite invasion of Egypt, the war replaced Israel's prior hesitancy with a new image of its army as "a gigantic harpoon, a powerful and pointed instrument of massive punishment."[2]

By contrast, Maoz concludes that Israel's security policies reflected flawed decision-making, political mismanagement, and a tendency toward excessive force that consistently fueled escalation. He argues that, in carrying out reprisals against Egypt in the 1950s, Israeli "activist" elites never sought deterrence. Rather, they wanted to create tension that could serve as a pretext for a direct confrontation that Israel otherwise refrained from initiating due to fear of international censure. Maoz recognizes that the Israel-Egypt border was "notoriously quiet" during the ten years after the

Sinai campaign, but he sees this as an "unintended" side effect of a war that failed to achieve its primary aims.[3]

While both Yaniv and Maoz examine Israel's security policy in general, others concentrate on Israeli-Egyptian interactions. Jonathan Shimshoni argues that Egypt's attitude toward the border before 1954 was one of relative neglect. Egypt subsequently became belligerent due to the externalization of Gamal Abdel Nasser's search for legitimacy, not because of his response to Israeli actions specifically. Only after Israel's "astounding victory" of 1956 was Israel able to force a change in Egypt's calculations.[4] Invoking Lawrence Freedman's concept of "internalized deterrence,"[5] Shimshoni conceives of deterrence as a learning process. He argues that Egypt defied Israeli coercion before 1956 because Israel's threats were not perceived as credible, and Israel had yet to convince Egypt otherwise. Like Shimshoni, Elli Lieberman holds that the "balance of motivations" in Israel's disputes with Egypt favored Israel. Border hostilities posed a vital challenge to Israel's security yet offered Egypt only marginal gain. In Lieberman's view, Israel's retaliation nevertheless failed because cycles of violence "played nicely into the Egyptian strategy to claim its leadership role in the Arab world."[6] The Suez War transformed this situation by generating an Israeli military reputation that thereafter deterred Egypt, despite continued political pressures to adopt a more confrontational stance.[7]

These varied explanations contribute to our understanding of tensions on the Israel-Egypt demarcation line. Nonetheless, they remain incomplete. In prioritizing interstate dynamics, all of these analyses fail to distinguish between host states and nonstate actors as two distinct parties and thus miss how their multifaceted relations conditioned the success of Israeli coercion. Benny Morris's historical account of Israel's border conflicts is an exception in bringing these distinctions to the forefront. Nonetheless, his aim is to establish the empirical record, not theorize causality or derive arguments with generalizable implications.[8]

With those broader analytical aims, we consider four periods in the triadic conflict between Israel, Egypt, and nonstate actors. During the first period, from 1949 to 1954, the triadic conflict was one in which the coercer (Israel) credibly threatened the host (Egypt), whose predisposition toward nonstate actors (Palestinian infiltrators) ranged from passive neglect to active opposition. Israel's credible threats increased Egypt's motivations to act against infiltrations, but Egypt lacked ability to do so due to the weakness of its two successive regimes. As a result, triadic coercion was largely irrelevant.

The second period begins with Nasser's assumption of power in 1954 and his incipient consolidation of a new regime. Still yet to develop institutional capacity and political capital, Nasser's regime evidenced an intermediate level of regime strength. Israel's 1955 raid on Gaza was sufficiently punishing to alter Nasser's calculations, yet not strong enough to convince him to ignore the domestic pressures on him. Under these middling conditions, coercion backfired. The government in Cairo eclipsed nonstate actors, undertook its own sponsorship of cross-border assaults, and became the main challenger in a bilateral conflict with Israel, waged partially through asymmetrical means.

Only after the 1956 Suez War, at which point the third period begins, was Israel's triadic coercion against Egypt successful. Israel's invasion of Egypt was a much more significant show of force than the reprisal raids of prior years. At the same time, the invasion tremendously boosted Nasser's status, giving him regional and domestic standing with which he fortified a strong regime. This markedly increased regime strength enabled the host state to act on its predisposition to restrict nonstate actors. The government in Cairo thus imposed controls on Palestinian actors, preventing them from breeching the border. Triadic coercion held strong for decades, unaffected by Israel and Egypt's engagement in three more regular wars.

Israeli triadic coercion against Egypt ended with the 1979 peace agreement between the two countries. However, we consider a fourth period, occurring since the 2011 Egyptian uprising, to illustrate points of both continuity with and difference from the past. As Egypt's regime became unsettled in 2011, its police presence in the Sinai Peninsula weakened. Aggrieved local residents, criminal elements, and jihadist groups found new opportunities to carry out attacks on both Israeli and Egyptian state targets. This confirmed the relationship that we theorize between regime weakness and nonstate violence. Israel's response to such violence, however, reflected a changed attitude toward its southern neighbor. Since 2003, the regime in Cairo has clearly demonstrated its predisposition to cooperate with Israel in asserting control over the border. This marked an evolution from triadic conflict to bilateral collaboration. Still, such collaboration is not irreversible. The future of triadic coercion on the Israel-Egypt frontier remains pendant on the nature of nonstate actor threats, the still-unclear strength of the Egyptian regime, and Israel's willingness to avoid actions that counterproductively escalate tension.

Background: Infiltrations and Reprisals, 1949–1956

During the 1948 War, about 210,000 Palestinian refugees fled to the Gaza Strip, joining 100,000 indigenous inhabitants in the 140-square-mile territory. Falling under Egypt's de facto trusteeship, Gaza became one of the poorest and most overcrowded places in the world.[9] Against a backdrop of misery and dispossession, thousands of Palestinians illicitly crossed the ADL into Israel. At first Israel and Egypt shared an interest in avoiding hostilities, and the border was relatively quiet.[10] As infiltrations increased, the United Nations Truce Supervision Organization (UNTSO) responsible for monitoring the ADL recommended cooperative measures, including joint patrols, negotiation of a local commanders' agreement, erection of a barbed-wire obstacle, and outposts and patrols staffed by regular Egyptian and Israeli troops.[11] UNTSO's chief of staff believed that such measures could reduce infiltrations to a mere "occasional nuisance," not more than "a kind of thieving which Israel must probably regard as inevitable," as long as "there were vast numbers of poverty-stricken refugees on its border."[12] Another UN officer concurred, noting that "it is naturally difficult to prevent people living on a bare subsistence level, and too often below it, from crossing lines beyond which they hope to find a few blades of grass for their hungry sheep, or a few dry twigs for fuel."[13]

Israel regarded infiltrations as intolerable threats, which it was justified to combat with force.[14] According to Michael Oren, Israel launched its first raid on the Gaza Strip in October 1950 in response to infiltrators' shooting of two Israeli soldiers. He reports that Israel carried out another eleven "small-scale raids" during the first months of 1952.[15] Barry Blechman instead registers the first Israeli reprisal raid in June 1950, and four others through August 1954.[16] He reports that all were directed at civilian targets, in line with the pre-1953 strategy discussed in chapter 2. Israel carried out one small incursion against a military target in Gaza in April 1954. Thereafter, it intensified reprisals and targeted them exclusively at military installations (see table 3.1).

This strategy of triadic coercion did not stem the tide of infiltrations, which increased through 1956 (see figure 3.1). Throughout this time, Israel repeatedly accused Egyptian authorities of instigating, encouraging, aiding, or failing to prevent infiltrations.[17] Commander E. H. Hutchison, military

TABLE 3.1
Israeli raids into the Gaza Strip

	Reprisals (civilian targets)	Reprisals (military targets)	Arab casualties (killed/total)
1949	0	0	0
1950	1	0	3/5
1951	1	0	1/12
1952	1	0	Unknown
1953	1	0	20/82
1954	1	1	4/7
1955	0	5	87/179
1956	0	8	196/345

Source: Barry M. Blechman, "Consequences of Israeli Reprisals: An Assessment," PhD diss., Georgetown University, 1971, 73–74, 88.

observer and chairman of the Mixed Armistice Commission, wrote that Israel justified retaliation on the theory that "the 'infiltrator,' in nearly every case, was paid by some Arab 'higher-up' to go into Israel and steal, or attack the inhabitants."[18] The Commission's UN Representative E. L. M. Burns noted that, whenever an Arab government failed to prevent a crossing from territory under its control, Israelis argued that "it was more than just inefficiency and negligence; it was evidence that meant that the government concerned condoned and secretly favored such action against Israel."[19]

Israel's view was erroneous. With the exception of the period between 1955 and 1956, the main engine of infiltrations lay outside the Egyptian government's control. Before 1955 Egypt may have secretly used some infiltrations for sabotage and intelligence gathering.[20] However, most scholars believe that Egyptian authorities wanted to avoid antagonizing Israel lest it renew war.[21] Ehud Yaari articulates this view in one of the first analyses of Egyptian state documents that Israel captured in the 1956 war. His conclusion is emphatic: "Without exception, the Egyptian documents in my possession point to a consistent Egyptian policy of blocking infiltration, and orders in this spirit, which were delivered from the higher echelons of the local government."[22] He finds that infiltrations, far from resulting from governmental directive, were initiated by local Palestinian "strongmen, sometimes as a moneymaking enterprise."[23]

Ilana Feldman provides a more recent investigation based on the United Nations archives and other Egyptian and Israeli documents. She finds that Egypt responded harshly to any Palestinian attempt to cross the border, prioritizing avoidance of conflict with Israel to such an extent that it sometimes put its own government in peril.[24] As early as October 1949, Egyptian officials met with Palestinian village leaders (*mukhtars*) in Gaza to seek help in enforcing this tough line. Army officer Abdullah Sharqawi opened the meeting with a statement in which he explained, "We expect from the people that they . . . will not cross the armistice line under any circumstances." His warning to the Palestinians was equally clear. "From now on," he said, "each mukhtar will be considered responsible for any incident that occurs in his area and is required to present the perpetrator or he will be taken himself."[25]

Regime Weakness and Nonstate Autonomy, 1949–1954

What explains the continuation of nonstate actors' infiltrations from the Gaza Strip despite Israel's clear communication of its demands that Egypt stop them and Egypt's predisposition to cooperate with those demands? We attribute this outcome to the weakness of the Egyptian regime. This weakness stemmed from the legacy of the colonial era and the corrupt, fraught rule of King Farouk in the early 1950s. The king arbitrarily dismissed cabinets, and an ineffectual parliament changed power repeatedly.[26] In this context of extreme government instability, political factions competed with each other by adopting more and more assertive stances on the Palestine question.[27] The beleaguered monarchy defended itself from its critics by doing the same.[28] Even had Egyptian governments been willing to adopt the controversial policy of deferring to Israeli pressures on the border, its institutions would have been too feeble to implement them.

This regime weakness left Egypt without the cohesion or capacity to stop nonstate actors' border violations, even when it wished to do so. As Oren writes, "Though Egypt's official policy in the strip was to stop infiltration, lest it elicit an armed Israeli response for which the Egyptian army was not prepared, strong measures to block all infiltrators proved to be politically as well as physically impossible."[29] A key element of the regime's deficient capacities was its lack of full territorial control. The 1949 armistice agreement prevented Egypt from deploying regular army units in the

Gaza Strip.[30] It thus depended on the single company stationed there as well as locally recruited police.[31] If state presence in Gaza was inadequate, hostility and distrust between Palestinian refugees and their Egyptian governors was overabundant.[32] A British visitor to Gaza noted that Palestinians "speak with the utmost bitterness of the Egyptians and the Arab states," suggesting that they, even more than Israel, were their true enemies. In turn, local Egyptian officials spoke "with equal contempt and hatred of the Palestinian Arabs."[33] In this context, Egypt struggled to assert its authority over its Palestinian residents. It faced difficulty in penetrating Gazan society as was necessary in order to gather information about illegal border crossings and thereby preempt them.

Egyptian citizens' resentment of their government was also mounting. Most saw politicians, who typically hailed from a small elite, as ineffectual, corrupt, complicit with colonialism, and indifferent to the plight of the poor masses. Popular discontent with the regime's role in the disaster of 1948 further compounded dissatisfaction with the status quo. In this context of ferment, the Muslim Brotherhood movement assassinated the prime minister in 1948. By 1951 guerrilla bands were clashing with British Army units in the country. When British forces attacked an Egyptian police station in January 1952, riots erupted that left hundreds of establishments burned and hundreds of individuals killed or injured.[34] The political leadership all but collapsed as civil unrest persisted for another six months.

On July 23, 1952, nine young military men calling themselves "the Committee of the Free Officers' Movement" ousted King Farouk and seized control of the government. They announced the formation of the Revolutionary Command Council (RCC) to administer the country. The RCC took preliminary steps to enact an ambitious vision to transform Egypt's society and economy.[35] Within months, it passed laws to raise minimum wages, reduce work hours, increase spending on education, establish rent controls, construct affordable housing, and guarantee government employment for university graduates. Yet, at this early stage, it possessed neither the cohesion nor the capacity to implement these measures fully.[36] In terms of cohesion, the RCC's reforms challenged the vested interests of the old, aristocratic ruling classes, and it therefore had to break the power of that elite before it could carry out reforms. The RCC thus quickly instituted land reform that dramatically limited and requisitioned landholdings.[37] Redistribution of these lands upheld the RCC's vision of social justice while also creating a constituency among the agrarian population and eliminating large landlords as a political force. Further neutralizing the elite, the RCC abolished aristocratic titles, tried political leaders on accusations of corruption, and decreed that anyone who held office between 1946 and 1952 was ineligible to hold it again. In January 1953 it banned all political parties, sequestered their funds, and declared that the RCC would rule for a three-year transition period. Cementing the end of the old order, it then abolished the monarchy and proclaimed Egypt to be a republic.

In addition to marginalizing the aristocracy, the RCC addressed challenges from grassroots social forces. In August 1952 more than ten thousand textile workers went on a strike that became violent when workers attacked and seized the factory. The RCC sent troops that killed several workers, injured scores, arrested hundreds, and, in Peter Mansfield's words, "made bitter enemies of the political left within a month after the revolution."[38] Facing criticisms from the press, the ruling junta levied new restrictions on freedom of expression and initiated its own publicity campaign to legitimize its rule and denounce its rivals.[39] The RCC also undertook a campaign to cultivate new supporters. Early in 1953 the RCC launched the Liberation Rally as a mass-based political party that aspired to develop linkages to society, especially key sectors like workers and students. While these steps went far in silencing or co-opting opposition, the most powerful movement in the country, the Muslim Brotherhood, remained independent. As it became increasingly bold in demonstrating against the junta, the RCC ordered it dissolved and banned in 1954.[40]

Beyond political challenges, the RCC inherited an insolvent state and faced ongoing dire economic problems. World demand for cotton plummeted in 1952, leaving Egypt unable to sell surplus stocks.[41] As was common throughout the developing world in this era, the RCC launched a project in state-led economic growth. It developed plans for infrastructure development, capital mobilization, and sponsorship of large works.[42] It issued laws encouraging foreign and domestic private investment, made increased capital available for entrepreneurs, began several significant joint ventures with firms, and moved forward with plans to electrify the Aswan Dam.[43] All of these initiatives required major financial outlays but did not reap immediate profits. In consequence, GNP per capita remained flat through 1953.[44]

The most acute problem sapping the strength of the new regime, however, was the fierce power struggle within its own ranks.[45] The RCC chose

Major-General Mohammed Naguib to serve as its chairman and subsequently as prime minister and president of the republic. RCC members believed that Naguib, a revered hero of the 1948 War, could increase the coup's legitimacy in the eyes of the army and masses. Nonetheless, Lieutenant-Colonel Gamal Abdel Nasser, who served as vice-premier and minister of the interior, was the real power within the RCC. Naguib, a generation older than most members of the Free Officers' Movement, advocated a return to popularly elected civilian government. While the bulk of the officer corps supported that position,[46] most RCC members supported Nasser and his preference for continued autocratic military rule. Naguib possessed unparalleled admiration from Egyptians. Nasser, in turn, controlled institutional resources that he used to construct his own power base. He tightened his grip on the armed forces by dismissing suspect officers, used the Ministry of the Interior to eliminate civilian rivals, and maneuvered media organizations and the Liberation Rally to fortify his linkages with different sectors of society.[47] Animosity deepened between the two leaders as rival camps formed around them.

These multiple challenges rendered the RCC a weak regime. Rather than demonstrating political cohesion, it was racked by internal divisions. Far from exercising authority over social forces, it was engaged in a multifronted struggle to impose its rule. The RCC seized a state beleaguered by institutional deficiencies, economic crisis, and a long history of mismanagement—legacies that needed years to rectify. Under these conditions, its top priority was consolidating power and implementing economic and social reform. It neither wished, nor could afford, to divert resources from these projects to the task of controlling Palestinian nonstate actors, no matter how forcefully Israel demanded it.[48] In Keith Wheelock's assessment, the new government in Cairo not only "wanted to avoid open fighting along the border" but also regarded the entire question of Palestine to be a lower priority than the Suez or Sudan.[49] Indeed, until 1955, Egypt was arguably less antagonistic toward Israel than were other Arab states.[50]

In this context, infiltrations continued. Israel denounced Egypt for failing to stop them. Between November 1951 and October 1952, Israel registered with the Mixed Armistice Commission no less than 321 complaints about crossings into its territory.[51] After a brief respite in the immediate wake of the coup, Israel intensified its reprisal policy again in late 1952.[52] Israeli raids into Gaza killed five in January 1953, twenty in

August 1953, and twelve in July 1954. In August 1954 raids killed ten Egyptian soldiers and destroyed Gaza's water tower.[53] Israel's use of force was so severe that the U.S. State Department expressed concern. Apart from raids, Israel articulated threats in public forums and diplomatic channels. Israeli troops penetrated Egyptian territory and left leaflets warning against further violations of the demarcation line.[54] In clandestine talks in 1954, Prime Minister Sharett informed Egypt of Israel's impending retaliation.[55]

There is hence little chance that Egypt could have failed to understand Israel's "signals" that demanded Egypt to cease aiding or abetting nonstate actors' infiltrations. Israel's threats were exceedingly clear and absolutely central to Egypt's relations with Israel.[56] In coordination talks on border management, Egyptian officers repeatedly told their Israeli counterparts that they were doing their utmost to stem infiltrations. Indeed, after a Palestinian raid on an Israeli bus in the Negev killed eleven, Egypt secretly appealed to Israel to avoid retaliation.[57]

In terms of our triadic conflict decision tree, the coercer credibly threatened the host state, which was predisposed to cooperate in order to avoid conflict. Nevertheless, infiltrations reached a new peak from January 1953 to mid-1954.[58] The weakness of the Egyptian regime contributed to this outcome in several ways. First, as the RCC was consumed with pressing domestic imperatives, Gaza was a low priority. Its attitude toward Palestinians under its rule was one of general disinterest.[59] Given its limited resources and multiple, urgent challenges, the government could invest only a minimum of time, effort, and funds in governing Gaza and policing the border.

Second, the Free Officers did not automatically command the deference of Egyptians, let alone Palestinians who already regarded Egyptian authorities with suspicion. The government thus had to balance its desire to avoid antagonizing Israel with the very real pressure of Egyptians' and Palestinians' demands for action. The latter intensified as Israeli raids further enflamed indignation and restlessness.[60] As conditions deteriorated in 1954 and early 1955, demands for stronger retaliation came from Gazans, the Egyptian public, and the Egyptian army alike.[61] Egyptian authorities' efforts, focused on blocking infiltrations, did not resolve the crisis of mounting discontent.[62]

Third, when Israeli pressure did force the RCC to turn its attention to Gaza, the limitations of its ability to project power became apparent. From 1953 to 1955, authorities carried out various measures to prevent infiltrations, including arresting infiltrators and imprisoning them for long sentences, coercing village leaders to identify infiltrators, withholding food aid from suspects, erecting watch towers, and eventually ordering troops to "shoot to kill" in response to movements in border areas after dusk.[63] Still, these and other actions remained insufficient to assert meaningful control over Gaza or stem the powerful motivations that propelled infiltrations.

The government then attempted another strategy. Given restrictions on stationing its own troops on the border, Egypt created a new paramilitary formation, the Civil Guard, in 1953. Later renamed the Palestine Border Guard, it was a Palestinian force under Egyptian supervision. This unit's objectives were to strengthen Egyptian control over refugee camps, neutralize Palestinian agitation, and thwart actions that would provoke Israeli strikes.[64] Far from curbing infiltrations, however, the Palestine Border Guard sometimes aided or participated in them.[65] In a July 1954 memorandum, Egypt's chief of intelligence in Gaza, Colonel Mustapha Hafez, noted that while "the main purpose of placing armed forces along the armistice line is to prevent infiltration . . . entrusting Palestinian soldiers with this task will not further that aim, because they encourage infiltration and repeatedly conduct attacks."[66] Yezid Sayigh agrees that, facing the challenge of stopping infiltrations, the Border Guard proved "inadequate or unwilling for the task."[67]

Fourth, the Egyptian regime's weakness was apparent in its inability to impose its dictates on its own personnel in Gaza. Analyzing captured Egyptian documents, Yaari judges that Egypt's main challenges vis-à-vis infiltrations were ineffective authority over Gaza and "mishaps, sometimes deliberate, perpetrated by lower-level echelons, in whose hands rested the authority to implement official policy."[68] Indeed, Colonel Hafez may himself have embodied that problem. Israel alleged that captured infiltrators confessed that Hafez had ordered their mission.[69] Explaining the inconsistency between those confessions and Hafez's memos, Yaari speculates that Hafez may have sponsored some raids while opposing those not under his supervision, or he may have permitted some violence in a bid to increase his own credibility among the Palestinians on whose cooperation he depended. Alternatively, he might have been less than fully honest in his reporting to his superiors. Regardless, Hafez's actions suggest a degree of autonomy and discretion on the part of authorities on the ground, and thus their ability to diverge from Cairo's policy preferences.

A 1954 Israeli Military Intelligence report confirmed this problem. "The Egyptian Army generally makes efforts to prevent infiltration," it noted. "But . . . the authorities' line is not carried out."[70] UN representative Burns similarly judged that some of the Egyptian army's actions that resulted in the most border friction were likely undertaken by "hotheads," "irresponsible" lower-ranking soldiers, or juniors who "exceeded their instructions."[71]

The upshot was that Egypt's failure to stop infiltrations in the years 1952–1954 was due to a lack of regime cohesion and capacity, not to a defiant predisposition toward Israel. Even Moshe Dayan admitted as much, remarking in 1953, "The problems along the border with Egypt are not the fruits of Egyptian Government plots but a fruit of its neglect, especially in the Gaza Strip area, where Egyptian rule is weak and the refugee problem is going from bad to worse."[72] Though the RCC transformed the Egyptian regime, it did not immediately strengthen it. It wanted to uphold Egyptian raison d'état vis-à-vis Israeli triadic coercion but did not wield the institutional fortitude or political legitimacy that this required. Under these conditions, Israeli attempts at deterrence and compellence were irrelevant. Egypt was unable to respond in the way Israel wished—or even in the way it wished.

A Stronger Regime Eclipses Nonstate Actors, Mid-1954–1956

This situation shifted in 1954, as the Egyptian regime surmounted some of its political challenges and entered a new stage of consolidation. The first step on that path was Nasser's triumph over Naguib. Nasser gradually cemented his own power base by arresting or purging the president's supporters and isolating him within the RCC. In February 1954 Naguib responded by announcing his resignation. Street protests erupted in demand of his reinstatement, dramatically demonstrating his "tremendous popularity among the masses."[73] Under popular pressure, Nasser returned Naguib to the presidency but rendered it effectively ceremonial. Nasser assumed the posts of prime minister and RCC chairman himself, thereby becoming the country's key decision-maker.

Nasser then turned attention to the only organized challenge to his rule: the Muslim Brotherhood.[74] He denounced the group in the media and persecuted its leadership. This prodded the Brotherhood's split into two camps, one advocating accommodation with the regime and the other calling for violence against it.[75] In October 1954 a failed attempt to assassinate Nasser sparked an outpouring of support. It gave him a pretext to carry out a "systematic pulverization" of the Muslim Brotherhood. Thereafter, show trial prosecutions, executions, and the arrests of thousands of members drove the organization underground. Nasser then took care of the last obstacle to his unopposed rule, President Naguib. The RCC accused Naguib of involvement in the assassination attempt and placed him under house arrest. In November 1954 Nasser became president of Egypt.

These events marked the growing consolidation of the Egyptian regime, which in turn affected conditions on the border. The second half of 1954 registered a decline in infiltrations, which Yaari believes were likely attributable to the "stabilization of Nasser's position."[76] Yet stabilization did not automatically increase the regime's institutional capacity and political autonomy. In Anouar Abdel-Malek's words, this "was a period of searching, of groping."[77] Though GNP recovered slightly from 1954 to 1956,[78] economic woes were the government's greatest preoccupation. As Abdel-Malek writes, "at the heart of everything was the economic problem."[79] Beyond this, the bureaucracy's ability to project power over space and population remained far from complete.[80] This was evident in civil violence in Egypt, which rose from eight events in 1950 to a peak of thirty-three events in 1954, before dropping to just two events in 1955.[81] Finally, in terms of symbolic power, the Nasser of this era was not yet the towering leader he later became. Even his ideology was embryonic; indeed, in Wheelock's classic book on Nasser, the chapter on this era is titled "Prelude to Nasserism."[82]

Nasser's regime was thus stronger in terms of cohesion yet remained weak in terms of capacity, particularly as related to territorial control, institutional competencies, and authority over social forces. This mixed and inconsistent level of regime strength affected the country's posture toward Israel, which was likewise mixed and inconsistent. On the one hand, Nasser had no appetite for a war for which he was not prepared.[83] As he told an interviewer in April 1954, "With Israel, a battle would indefinitely postpone internal reform, and the government has said that reform was the key foundations to its *raison d'etre*."[84] In a January 1955 interview, he reiterated, "We do not want to start any conflict. War has no place in the reconstructive policy which we have designed."[85] The leadership in Cairo was thus predisposed to maintain quiet on the Gaza-Israel border. The stronger it became, the more it was able to impose that preference. Thus when Israel carried out a bloody raid on the al-Bureij refugee camp in August, Palestinian civilians launched riotous demonstrations demanding that Egypt supply them with weapons.[86] This time, Egyptian authorities responded by arresting about fifty demonstrators and enforcing a thirteen-hour-per-day curfew on areas of Gaza.[87] The following month, authorities interned two hundred Gazans whom they believed might carry out incursions.[88]

Though the regime was thus predisposed to cooperate with Israel in avoiding conflict, its ongoing political weakness generated incentives for it to act defiantly. The RCC had established its rule by force. By mid-1955 the regime was "groping" for alternative ways to foster legitimacy. The most promising resource, apart from the president's personal charisma, was an assertive foreign policy.[89] Thus, weaknesses in Nasser's domestic power helped propel him to embrace external sources of power and prestige.[90] Over the course of 1954 he increasingly invested in his stature as an international champion of anti-imperialism, nonalignment, Arab nationalism, and Palestinian liberation. This pursuit of regional and Third World leadership "required" or "created the need" for a more aggressive stance toward Israel.[91] The need to outmaneuver the Muslim Brotherhood did likewise. The Brotherhood advocated war to avenge the loss of Palestine; as long as it retained popular influence, Nasser could not afford to act in ways that the Brotherhood could denounce as weak or conciliatory.[92] The Nasser regime was not completely solidified, and competition with the Brotherhood pushed it toward a more defiant stance vis-à-vis Israel than its own understanding of national interests recommended.

Such was the backdrop for a dramatic escalation of hostilities in 1955. That January and February, Egyptian forces, both formal military units and irregular actors, carried out several ambushes and killings targeting Israeli civilians or military posts.[93] On February 23, guerrillas from Gaza even reached the suburbs of Tel Aviv, where they killed an Israeli civilian.[94] The attack occurred days after David Ben-Gurion began a new tenure as minister of defense,[95] and he ordered Dayan to retaliate.

On the night of February 28, Israel's Unit 101 carried out a massive raid near Gaza City in which it killed thirty-seven Egyptian soldiers and two Palestinian civilians and wounded another thirty soldiers and two civilians.[96] The Mixed Armistice Commission reported: "A force of the Israeli Army estimated at two platoons strength, crossed the Armistice

Demarcation Line east of Gaza, advanced more than three kilometres inside Egyptian-controlled territory, and, using mortars, anti-tank projectiles, handgrenades, Bangalore torpedoes and heavy explosives charges, attacked an Egyptian military camp, the Gaza Stationmaster's house and a concrete water-pump house supplying part of the Gaza area."[97]

The raid was an act of triadic coercion, avenging nonstate actors by targeting the state from whence they came. Ariel Sharon, who ordered the assault, described it as having "struck at the heart of the Egyptian military institution in Gaza."[98] The logic driving this targeting is subject to debate. Some argue that Israel was straightforwardly seeking to prevent further border violations.[99] Others insist that its aim was "provocation and escalation."[100] Regardless, the raid instigated an unmistakable shift in Egypt's policy. Nasser called the Gaza raid a "turning point," a phrase prominently featured in several histories of the event.[101] Morris expresses it succinctly: "Before the raid, there was no confrontational policy of harassment and guerrilla warfare. Afterwards, there clearly was."[102]

Why did the raid have that effect? A common view holds that Israeli reprisals humiliated Nasser, provoked him to retaliate, and thus sparked an escalatory spiral.[103] Contesting this interpretation, Shimshoni argues that Egypt became more militant due to political and geostrategic interests independent of Israeli actions.[104] Our theory of triadic coercion offers an alternative explanation. The weakness of the Egyptian regime served as an intervening variable conditioning the effect of reprisals on state interests and calculations. The coercer's threats were sufficiently punishing to provoke the host state, yet insufficiently punishing to convince it that the costs of defying coercion were too high to bear. At the same time, the host regime was increasingly capable of organizing its own use of force, yet did not have the strength to flout domestic demands.

In other words, Nasser's regime lacked the cohesion and capacity to suppress or ignore domestic political pressures that demanded that it act more defiantly toward Israel. Israel's aggression intensified those pressures in several ways. First, the raid outraged Palestinians. While Gazans had long demanded action to aid their return to their former homes,[105] the Gaza attack caused unprecedented popular uproar. The next morning, violent demonstrations spread throughout the Strip. Crowds burned UN food storage facilities, stoned trucks transporting Egyptian soldiers, besieged state officers visiting the wounded in hospital, attacked border monitors' headquarters, and stormed both the governor's office and homes of UN officials.[106] Throughout the riotous events, which some Gazans would call an *intifada*,[107] demonstrators repeated a key demand: weapons to use against Israel. Abu Iyad, a future founder of the Fatah movement, recalled witnessing these events as a young man in Gaza: "The Israeli raid on Gaza . . . gave rise to a surge of anger among Palestinians, indignant at the Egyptian army's passivity and inability to defend the population or counterattack on the same scale. Throngs of demonstrators swarmed through the streets of Gaza demanding arms. Palestinian students in Cairo organized strikes and demonstrations, publicly calling for the downfall of the regime."[108] The unrest became so intense that Nasser met with the protesting students. They presented him with several demands, including "obligatory military training for Palestinians to enable them to defend themselves." According to Abu Iyad, Nasser hesitated but then promised to comply.[109] Later that month Nasser made his first personal visit to Gaza since 1948.[110]

Second, the raid intensified the Egyptian army's demands for militancy. For months, Nasser had refused the armed forces' requests for upgraded equipment on the grounds that funds were needed for social and economic development instead. Western powers had communicated to Nasser what he believed was a promise that the border would remain quiet. "The raid proved that there were no assurances," Nasser later said. "So I myself decided . . . that we must have arms."[111] As the army was Nasser's main base of support, he could not ignore its discontent for long.[112] He was aware that, just as the army's indignation about the 1948 disaster contributed to propelling the overthrow of the monarchy, so could its resentment about being restrained at the border foster a revolt against him.[113]

Third, Nasser faced pressures resulting from Middle East regional politics. Just four days before the Gaza raid, Iraq, Iran, Turkey, and Pakistan signed the Baghdad Pact, an anti-Soviet treaty sponsored by the United States and Britain. The pact enhanced Iraq's military capability and claims for regional leadership while undermining Egypt's bid for the same.[114] Nasser actively denounced the Baghdad Pact, signed an alternative military defense pact with Syria, and reached a mutual-aid agreement with Saudi Arabia.[115] That April, Nasser gained international attention and accolades when he attended the Conference of the Nonaligned Movement in Bandung, Indonesia, as head of the Arab delegations.[116] He reportedly made such a "decisive contribution" to the conference that one analyst labeled him "the hero of Bandung."[117] Concern about this international image was probably insufficient to cause Nasser to confront Israel, given his awareness of the risks entailed. In dramatically escalating hostilities, however, the Gaza raid aggravated pressure on Nasser to act consistently with the reputation that he was cultivating. The raid made it more difficult for him to remain passive or to acquiesce to Israel's wishes by cracking down on infiltrators.

This combination of social, military, and political pressures prompted Nasser to respond to Israel's escalation with an escalation of his own. Nasser ordered a dramatic increase of military forces to Gaza, which led directly to mining, shelling, and ambushing of Israeli patrols. Four months after the Gaza raid, Nasser also increased the military budget by over 50 percent: the single largest jump in yearly defense outlays until 1970.[118] Appropriations for the military surpassed those for development and welfare programs, which had received the largest share in the prior national budget.[119] This new prioritization of military needs helped satisfy restive voices in the armed forces, raising morale within their ranks as well as increasing the public confidence that they enjoyed.[120]

In addition, Egypt activated a new military unit named the Fedayeen. This was a commando unit adjunct to the Egyptian army consisting of Palestinians from Gaza, trained by Egyptian officers, with the aim of infiltrating and attacking Israel.[121] The Fedayeen unit was a hybrid between a nonstate actor and an arm of a state. Its formation marked a shift in Nasser's stance toward Israel from one of quiet but effective nonbelligerence to active defiance. In sponsoring infiltrations, the government in Cairo eclipsed nonstate actors and itself became the main challenger in cross-border antagonism against Israel. The Fedayeen began operations in August 1955, with a series of raids that caused twenty Israeli casualties.[122] Israel ratcheted up its retaliations in response. During 1955–1956 it executed at least nine raids on Egyptian military installations, inflicting heavy Egyptian losses. These included assaults on Khan Younis that resulted in thirty-five Egyptian dead, on al-Sabha that resulted in fifty Egyptians killed and forty captured, on an Egyptian police post at El Kuntilla, where five Egyptians were killed and thirty captured, and on Gaza City that killed fifty-nine.[123] Israel registered complaints with the UN Security Council, attributing the unprecedented "succession of new and serious outbreaks of violence" to the deliberate policy of the Egyptian government. Israel also voiced threats. The military spokesman warned, "It should be clear that if the Egyptian authorities in Gaza continue in their games, and to the previous sin of failing to stop the infiltration add the crime of instigating provocative operations, they will create a 'complication' that Israel does not desire. Responsibility for such development will lie with them."[124]

Far from creating deterrence, Israel's escalating violence only hardened Nasser's stance. Rhetoric from Cairo became more bellicose. In August 1955 Nasser declared, "Egypt has decided to dispatch her heroes, the disciples of Pharaoh and the sons of Islam and they will cleanse the land of Palestine. . . . There will be no peace on Israel's border because we demand vengeance, and vengeance is Israel's death."[125] Meanwhile, the Fedayeen continued attacks, including an assault on an Israeli wedding in March 1956, attacks that killed twelve Israeli citizens in one week that April, and engagement in exchanges of artillery on the border.[126] Violent incidents with political motives emanating from Egyptian-controlled territory increased from a rate of about twenty to forty per year from 1949 to 1952 to fifty to sixty per year from 1953 to 1956.[127]

By summer 1955, Dayan wrote, the explosive pattern of Arab and Israeli violence had "snowballed" to produce an "eve-of-war atmosphere."[128] Egypt's engagement in cross-border aggression provoked reprisals that directly undermined Egyptian national security. Nevertheless, sponsorship of the Fedayeen was a rational choice in terms of Nasser's need to address domestic political pressures. By formalizing the guerrilla force Nasser wrested control of infiltrations that he had been unable to stop and thus were likely to persist, whether he intervened or not. He thereby satiated calls for action against Israel while also circumscribing them within a modicum of institutional bounds. For Mansfield, the Fedayeen thus "achieved the supremely important purpose for Nasser of staving off demands for an immediate all-out war with Israel which he knew would be disastrous."[129] Had he commanded a stronger regime, Nasser might have been able to ignore, silence, or mollify those restive demands. Given the regime's still young and transitional character, however, the president judged that his best alternative was to engage in some escalation in the service of avoiding a more far-reaching conflagration.

Nasser's regime grew stronger as his months in power passed. By fall 1955, however, his efforts to obtain military aid from Western powers had failed to bear fruit. In consequence, Nasser instead signed an arms deal with the Soviet Union, by way of Czechoslovakia. This deal supplied Egypt with weapons systems that were qualitatively and quantitatively beyond any other in the Middle East.[130] Egypt acquired tanks, armored personnel carriers, mobile antitank guns, Howitzers, artillery pieces, anti-aircraft guns, jet fighters, transport planes, radar installations, Skori destroyers, minesweepers, torpedo boats, and submarines as well as ammunition, spare parts, vehicles, small arms, and other general equipment.[131] Especially alarming for Israel was that Egypt also acquired jet bombers that could reach heights that Israel's jets could not.[132] The arms deal was a game-changer in the Egyptian-Israeli balance of power. It effectively neutralized what Israeli strategists long assumed was Israel's main advantage: superior manpower due to military education and training.[133] Furthermore, the arms deal gave Nasser a jolt of support at home, and especially with the army.[134]

By the end of 1955, Nasser's leadership had made the Free Officers Executive, in P. J. Vatikiotis's words, "the most effective ruling elite in the Arab Middle East."[135] Egypt, moreover, was rising in stature over its regional rivals.[136] It was against this backdrop that, in July 1956, the United States, Britain, and the World Bank withdrew their offer to aid construction of a High Dam at Aswan, the cornerstone of Nasser's development plans. Shortly after, Nasser announced nationalization of the Suez Canal Company. He demanded that British troops leave the base in Suez that they had occupied since 1882. Watching Nasser's shocking boldness, many in the Israeli leadership were convinced that it was just a matter of time before tension with Egypt erupted into full-fledged war. They judged that it was better to fight that war earlier rather than later.[137]

A Strong Regime Restricts Nonstate Actors, 1956–1979

In late October 1956, Israel joined Britain and France in instigating a war to return the Suez Canal to British control. During the war, Israel occupied the Gaza Strip and Sinai Peninsula for six months. In joining the invasion, Israel aspired to topple Nasser's regime, gain additional territory, or, at the very least, coerce a peace agreement with Egypt. Its objective was not to deter cross-border attacks by nonstate actors. Yet, as figure 3.1 shows, a sharp decrease in those attacks was an outcome of the war. This change occurred without any formal agreement between Israel and Egypt or any significant change in the conditions endured by Palestinian refugees in Gaza.

Israel's pressure on Egypt was effective in stopping nonstate actors' border violations due to two factors. First, Israel, as the coercer state, made a dramatic and credible threat against the host state. This unambiguously demonstrated that the balance of power favored the coercer. Though Israel did not eliminate Egypt's hopes of someday defeating Israel, its ability to seize territory through a blitzkrieg assault sent a message that this was impossible in the foreseeable future. Consequently, in speech after speech, Nasser declared that Arabs would strike to erase the injustice of 1948 and avenge the conspiracy of 1956—but not before the time was right.[138] He thereby acknowledged that Egypt was unready to undertake war with Israel and would not allow Palestinian infiltrations to drag it into one prematurely.

Second, the war ushered in a palpable increase in the strength of the Egyptian regime. Israel's projection of military might would not have reduced Palestinian infiltrations were it not accompanied by this shift in Nasser's own stature, popularity, and institutional consolidation. For Egypt, the Suez War was a military loss but a political victory. Arab publics hailed Nasser as a brave leader who foiled the ambitions of three imperialist powers and forced their withdrawal.[139] In Walter Laqueur's estimation, a hero's aura gave Nasser "almost unlimited credit in his own country and throughout the Arab world."[140] Thereafter he would continue to win admiration through a stunning blend of charisma, myth-making, and an ability to unify publics behind an ideology of state-led development and Arab and Egyptian nationalism.

The new strength of Nasser's regime was rooted in its cohesion and capacity. Cohesion was centered in the person of Nasser and the bureaucratic organs that he commanded. As Vatikiotis observes, "internal consolidation of power by Nasser was by no means complete with his triumph over Naguib and the Muslim Brethren." Rather, foreign policy developments in the crucial two-year period of 1955–1957 tipped the scales to solidify his towering political role.[141] In June 1953 the RCC had declared that it would rule for a three-year transition period. When that expired in 1956, Nasser was elected president. A plebiscite approved a new constitution that granted the president extraordinary powers and rendered the legislature little more than a rubber stamp for his initiatives.

Thereafter, Nasser's regime underwent an authoritarian centralization whose logic, as Roger Owen describes it, was "to destroy those that it cannot control, and to remake and reorder those that it can."[142] The 1956 constitution established the National Union to replace the Liberation Rally as a single mass organization in which all citizens were deemed members.

In the years that followed Nasser used the National Union, succeeded by the Arab Socialist Union in 1962, as a tool of popular integration and mobilization, and of marginalization of would-be opponents.[143] Just as the new ruling party sought to channel all political activity though its auspices, so did the 1957 creation of the General Federation of Egyptian Trade Unions give the state a monopoly on all issues of labor organization and representation. In similar fashion, the state extended its control over both existing professional associations and new parallel corporatist associations that it created for students, women, peasants, and other social groups. Supporting these institutions in penetrating, monitoring, and steering society was a vast coercive apparatus. Expanded internal security agencies, endowed with broader powers, carried out surveillance and punishment of would-be political challengers, effectively crushing dissent and eliminating the president's rivals.

These institutional developments produced a highly cohesive regime capable of acting as if it were a unitary entity exercising command and control throughout the state apparatus. Nasser stood at the summit of this regime as, to quote Vatikiotis, "the supreme, unchallengeable authority."[144] Concurring with that judgment, R. Hrair Dekmejian traces the evolution of the Egyptian regime from the phase of military dictatorship, during which the RCC ruled by force, through the early years of Nasser's leadership, when he governed by charismatic authority. He concludes that the period after the mid-1950s was when Nasser's legitimacy became "routinized."[145]

This consolidation of political cohesion further bolstered the other pillar of regime strength: capacity. Even as Nasser continued to stir support through direct communication with the masses and skilled management of the elite, he also made sweeping investments in institution building and socioeconomic restructuring.[146] A boon of economic resources enabled state agents to exercise greater control over persons, activities, and resources than in any prior era of Egyptian history. The Suez conflict itself offered a significant fiscal boost, as removal of colonial claims on the canal transferred to the Egyptian government capital that it had previously been denied.

Nasser used his new budgetary power to magnify economic measures that the RCC had introduced but not been able to implement fully. Extending the 1952 land reform law, subsequent reforms in 1958, 1961, and 1969 further reduced the maximum amount of land that any individual could possess. In 1956–1957, Nasser pushed forward with a program nationalizing foreign banks and commercial enterprises and subsequently private Egyptian businesses.[147] By the 1960s the state controlled most industry, import, transport, finance, and trade,[148] a domination that enabled ambitious state-led development. New governmental economic and planning councils led the design and implementation of a series of five-year development plans. Their immediate harvest was positive: steady growth in both per capita income and GNP, with the latter rising by 8.7 percent in 1963–1964.[149] The state was both an engine and a beneficiary of growth, as increased direct taxation and revenues from public enterprises filtered into state coffers.[150] Government expenditure as a percentage of GNP, increasing from 18.3 percent to 55.7 percent in 1970,[151] extended education, health, and other welfare services throughout society. These measures registered dramatic improvements in indicators ranging from the numbers of hospital beds per capita to rates of children in school to the number of villages with clean drinking water.[152] Another large portion of the state budget was defense expenditures, which rose from $211 million in 1958 to $425.5 million in 1966. In these years Egypt's budget was more than those of Iraq, Syria, and Jordan combined.[153]

Parallel to the intensification of state infrastructural power was a ballooning of the state's human and bureaucratic capacity. Propelled by a 1961 decree guaranteeing government employment for all university graduates, the number of civilian public employees increased from 350,000 in 1951–1952 to more than 1 million in 1965–1966. The number of military personnel increased from 80,000 in 1955–1956 to 180,000 in 1966, not including 90,000 paramilitary police. Eventually this inflated state proved a wasteful economic burden. During this phase of Nasser's rise, however, it marked a transformative increase in state and regime capacity.

By the 1960s the Egyptian regime was vastly stronger than its former self. Other Arab leaders opposed Nasser's hegemony, yet they were constrained by his immense popularity among their own populations as well as the developing world at large.[154] Nasser's regional status gave him more room to maneuver and less need to justify his policies, including those related to Israel. This directly affected Egypt's policy toward the border. During its brief occupation of Gaza in 1956, Israel carried out massive arrests and executions that effectively broke the Fedayeen contingent. It was reasonable to expect Egypt to reestablish the force after Israel's withdrawal.

Nasser not only did not do so but also actively prevented Palestinians from reestablishing the Fedayeen themselves.[155] To avoid unnecessary clashes with Israel, he authorized the deployment to Gaza of only a police force, not military forces. Egypt reestablished the Palestinian Border Guards, but deep in the Sinai Peninsula, far from the Israeli border. Stationed in Sinai, the Guards served little purpose beyond offering Palestinian youth jobs and an outlet for frustration. It played no role in aiding infiltrations as it had before the Suez War.[156]

At the same time that Egypt curtailed opportunities for challenging the Israeli border, it solidified its authority over civilian life in Gaza. Feldman notes that Nasser extended to Gaza some of the same broad governmental agenda that it was enacting in Egypt. Leveraging improved cohesion and capacity, the regime expanded not only civil administration and social services in its Palestinian territory but also the ubiquitous presence of security services empowered to gather information on residents and regulate their political expression and organization.[157] Feldman writes that the regime in Cairo, still wary of security concerns in Gaza, thus used its improved strength to monitor the area:

> To address the range of threats they identified in Gaza, Egyptian administrators established an extensive police force with expansive authority and jurisdiction. Few moments in life were beyond the scrutiny of the security establishment . . . and few techniques of control were off-limits to police. One obvious effect of these multiple techniques deployed in a wide array of sites was that security personnel exercised a high degree of control over people's lives, their actions, and their relationships.[158]

Palestinians, meanwhile, were increasingly impatient with the stalemate with Israel. They formed some forty clandestine groups from 1959 to 1963.[159] In Beirut in 1956, George Habbash and Wadi Haddad founded the Arab Nationalist Movement (ANM) to call for Arab unity and the liberation of Palestine. At the University of Cairo a young Yasser Arafat argued that Palestinians should not rely on Arab states but instead wage their own guerrilla war to liberate their homeland. Arafat and others formalized their group as the Palestine Liberation Movement, or Fatah. This revival of an independent Palestinian national movement put pressure on Nasser to honor his own rhetoric about defying Israel. Militant stances by the newly formed Ba'athist regimes in Baghdad and Damascus did likewise.

Still, Nasser remained cautious. He walked a tightrope between appearing to lead Arab commitment to Palestine, on the one hand, and doing everything possible to prevent nonstate military activity, on the other. With these goals, he led the 1964 Arab Summit in authorizing Ahmed Shuqayri, a personal devotee of Nasser and the Arab League's Palestinian delegate, to establish an entity to represent the Palestinian people. Shuqayri founded the Palestine Liberation Organization (PLO). Nasser arguably sought a mechanism that would satisfy some Palestinian demands yet contain them within the bounds of Egyptian interests.[160] Solidifying his sway over the PLO, he granted it a base in Cairo as well as institutional and monetary support. Simultaneously Nasser cultivated his influence over the ANM and thereby steered it to obey Egypt's wish to avoid military engagement with Israel.

Nasser acquiesced to the creation of the Palestinian Liberation Army (PLA) as the PLO's military wing. Consistent with his wish to check nonstate militarism, however, he demanded that the PLA be integrated into the Unified Arab Command, the Arab League's military coordination mechanism led by Egypt's chief of staff. Nasser further limited the PLA's autonomy by establishing a base for its contingents that he could monitor and control. In these ways Egypt refused to give Palestinian commanders meaningful authority over either the PLA's military operations or its day-to-day functioning.[161] Beyond this, Nasser debilitated the PLA by ensuring that it received armaments that were outdated, of dubious quality, and limited in supply.[162] Fearing that a large Palestinian army would instigate strikes on Israel, Nasser rejected Palestinians' appeals for mandatory enlistment of Gazans and limited the number of Palestinians from outside Egypt who were allowed to join.[163] Sayigh concludes, "The Egyptian command strove consistently to deny the PLA the means to provoke Israel, directly and indirectly, and in that manner sought to contain the potentially destabilizing force."[164]

Egypt thus used its sway over the PLO, PLA, and ANM to block them from acting as nonstate engines of hostilities against Israel, at least from Egypt's own territory. However, Fatah did not defer to Nasser personally, ideologically, economically, or strategically. It thus posed a threat to state interests that the president would not tolerate. On New Year's Day 1965

Fatah carried out its debut attack in Israel, launching a new era in the struggle of the Palestinian fedayeen, a term that thenceforth came to refer not to the Egyptian-sponsored military contingent but to Palestinian nonstate guerrilla fighters. In subsequent years, Fatah carried out dozens more attacks from Jordan, Lebanon, and Syria, including by planting landmines and bombing pipelines, water pumps, warehouses, and roads.[165]

Egypt was vigilant in stopping Fatah from launching attacks from its territory. It gathered intelligence on Fatah, detained its members, and hampered its activities.[166] Nasser accused Fatah of trying to drag him into war and discredited it by suggesting that it was, successively, a front for the Muslim Brotherhood, a proxy of Saudi Arabia, and an agent of the U.S. Central Intelligence Agency. Under Nasser's leadership Arab Summit meetings denounced guerrilla actions on the grounds that they achieved little beyond provoking Israeli retaliation. Nasser's hostility toward Fatah tempered somewhat as the organization came to attract popular support throughout the Arab world. Nevertheless he remained adamant in opposing Fatah's attacks from across Egypt's border and in monitoring Fatah supporters and activists on Egypt's soil.[167] Nasser may have been content to see Israel retaliate against Syria, Jordan, and Lebanon, yet he would not allow Palestinian groups give Israel the excuse to do the same against Egypt.[168]

Israel's use of coercive threats to compel quiet on the border thus proved effective once they were targeted against an Egyptian regime that was politically, socially, and bureaucratically strong enough to act in accordance with them. Egypt continued preventing nonstate actor violence over the border after the 1967 war. Nasser's popularity held, despite the enormity of the defeat, as demonstrated by the tens of thousands of Egyptians who went into the streets to implore him not to resign. Dekmejian argues that the Egyptian regime's survival of such a trouncing was evidence of "a degree of internal legitimacy and stability uncommon in the world of developing nations." That Nasser also permitted space for dissent and questioning during that national emergency was an even greater "demonstration of system strength."[169]

Regime strength empowered the president to recalculate state interests in the aftermath of defeat. Thereafter, Egypt's main preoccupation vis-à-vis Israel shifted from liberation of Palestine to recovery of the Sinai Peninsula. From 1967 to 1970 Egypt engaged in a "War of Attrition" across the Suez. Still, it continued to prohibit Palestinian nonstate actors from launching attacks from Egyptian soil. After Nasser's death, Anwar Sadat inherited the strong state institutions that Nasser had built. This enabled Egypt to continue to bar Palestinian action through such tumultuous events as another war with Israel in 1973, Sadat's visit to Jerusalem in 1977, the subsequent negotiations with Israel, and the signing of the Camp David Accords in 1979. The peace treaty, in turn, ended the need for military coercion in general, and triadic coercion in particular, as pillars of the Israel-Egypt relationship.

From Triadic Conflict to Bilateral Cooperation: Militants in the Sinai since 2011

Despite challenges over the decades, Nasser's successors, Anwar Sadat and Hosni Mubarak, generally sustained the strength of the regime that he established and likewise the government's ability to assert authority over nonstate actors challenging Israel from its territory. These conditions held until 2011, when a mass popular uprising forced Mubarak to resign and set the country on a tumultuous path characterized by domestic conflict and instability. With political competitors focused on the struggle for power in Cairo, Sinai increasingly became "lawless" and "chaotic."[170]

Islamist extremist organizations based in the Sinai, affiliated with al-Qaeda or, later, the Islamic State in Iraq and Syria (ISIS), targeted the vast majority of their attacks within Egyptian territory. The Tahrir Institute for Middle East Policy counted 1,700 attacks by these organizations from 2013 to September 2017. According to the Egyptian government, nearly a thousand Egyptian security personnel were killed in terrorist attacks throughout Egypt during this period, most in Sinai or by Sinai-based groups.[171] In addition to this violence, between 2011 and 2017 militants also targeted numerous attacks across the Israeli-Egyptian border. In consequence, as one journalist observed in 2011, "What was Israel's quietest border for many years has, over the past few months, turned into the deadliest one."[172] Cross-border violence peaked in 2012, when groups in Sinai launched eleven attacks on Israel, six involving rockets and five entailing physical breaches of the border.[173] Incidents declined thereafter, with an average of only one violent border violation occurring annually between 2012 and 2017, resulting in only one Israeli fatality in total.[174]

These patterns in the rise and fall of nonstate actor violence from Sinai revealed both continuity and change in triadic conflict across the

Israeli-Egyptian border. As in the past, conflict dynamics demonstrated the importance of host regime strength in mediating nonstate actors' cross-border violence. In contrast to the past, these patterns suggested that bilateral cooperation and defensive measures could prove more effective than triadic coercion in combatting that violence. As long as Sinai residents remained alienated from the state, and insurgency continued, however, the danger of renewed cross-border conflagration persisted.

The conditions that gave rise to nonstate violence in Egypt's Sinai Peninsula confirm scholarly findings that state weakness creates both grievances that facilitate rebellion and opportunities to act upon those grievances.[175] Even as Nasser, Sadat, and Mubarak built strong regimes, the presence of those regimes in Sinai arguably remained weak relative to their presence in other parts of the country. This had a social dimension, as the area's independent Bedouin tribes are culturally and socially distinct from the majority of Egypt's population. The peninsula's incomplete integration with the rest of Egypt is also a product of political history. Sinai was under Israeli occupation from 1967 to 1982, and the Egyptian government continues to suspect residents of being prone to collaborate with Israeli state or commercial interests. Egyptian law thus prohibited Sinai Bedouin from owning land on the grounds that they might sell it to Israelis. In addition, the state denied citizenship to nearly a fifth of the Bedouin population and excluded all Bedouin from mandatory military conscription, joining police or military academies, or holding key governorate-level posts.[176] This discrimination, in addition to general poverty and neglect, created a reservoir of discontent with the Egyptian state. In this context, Islamist extremists established a presence in the area as early as the 1980s. Illicit economic activity, aided by Sinai's border location between the Suez Canal, Gaza Strip, and Israel, had been a prominent feature of the area since the late 1990s as well.[177]

Socially, legally, historically, and geographically, therefore, Sinai was a prime place for nonstate actors. Such actors' turn to violence since 2011, however, was also a product of fluctuations in the strength of the regime in Cairo. During the early days of the uprising, Mubarak took desperate measures to cling to power, including deliberately sowing chaos by withdrawing police from streets and freeing some 17,000 prisoners.[178] Some former prisoners made their way to Sinai, where they joined with local tribes and formed criminal gangs.[179] Full law enforcement eventually returned to most of Egypt, except in the Sinai, where residents forced the police to withdraw by attacking them with guns and grenades.[180]

The security vacuum in the Sinai grew after Mubarak resigned and the Supreme Council of the Armed Forces (SCAF) assumed power. During the sixteen fraught months in which Egypt's highest military body ruled the country, the government's stance toward Sinai resembled that of "an absentee landlord." As the area came to take on a semiautonomous, lawless character, extremist groups proliferated. Some Bedouin groups transmuted into armed militias and moved from their traditional homes to new jihadist-type camps. Others acted less out of ideology than opportunism and sold their services to militants from elsewhere.[181] Trafficking of drugs, humans, and arms increased exponentially. Smuggling was bolstered by auspicious conditions in neighboring areas, such as tunnels dug into Gaza with the tightening of the blockade there after 2007. With Libya's descent into civil war in 2011 and the flourishing of the arms market there, increasingly heavy and sophisticated weapons trickled into Sinai.[182] In this context, nonstate actors, some believed to be linked to al-Qaeda, perpetrated suicide attacks, bombings, shootings, and other attacks on Egyptian infrastructural, civilian, police, and military targets.[183] Militants also conducted more than a dozen bombings of the pipeline transporting natural gas from Egypt to Israel.[184]

After an August 2011 attack on both Egyptian and Israeli forces, the Egyptian army launched Operation Eagle, its first major military campaign into Sinai since 1979, with the goal of crushing terrorism.[185] Nevertheless, violence and lawlessness in the Sinai continued. Meanwhile, the regime in Cairo wavered between transition to electoral democracy and new and old forms of authoritarianism. Parliamentary elections beginning in November 2011 and presidential elections in June 2012 brought the Muslim Brotherhood to power for another tumultuous year. While sustaining the army's security approach to the Sinai, President Mohammed Morsi also undertook some nonmilitary measures, including signaling concern for Bedouin socioeconomic grievances, using mediators to engage in talks with armed groups, and lifting some restrictions on movement to and from Gaza.[186]

Pledging to pursue and eliminate terrorists, the Egyptian army launched a second major campaign, Operation Eagle II, later renamed Operation Sinai, in August 2012.[187] While the army claimed some successes in arresting militants and destroying tunnels, it did not resolve the political problem of freely maneuvering nonstate actors. That would have required a strong regime with the cohesion and capacity both to impose law and to make some progress in addressing the underlying causes of violence. In its absence, what emerged in Sinai was "an uneasy, unofficial, status quo agreement" in which the security apparatus ceased military campaigns as long as militants halted attacks.[188]

Morsi faced difficulties in imposing his regime authority in Cairo no less than in Sinai. The Brotherhood-led government faced opposition from the bureaucratic and judicial elements of Egypt's "deep state" as well as protests from popular forces criticizing its rule as exclusionary, unaccountable, incompetent, and even sectarian.[189] A grassroots campaign collected millions of signatures against Morsi and then rallied millions to the streets demanding his resignation. On July 3, the military removed the government, arrested Morsi, suspended the constitution, and assumed power. Brotherhood supporters formed a protest camp in Cairo demanding Morsi's reinstatement. The military laid siege to the camp, killing an estimated six hundred to one thousand people. It subsequently banned the Brotherhood and arrested tens of thousands of citizens on trumped-up charges.[190]

The conflict between the military and the Brotherhood distracted the government from governing. As attention shifted from the Sinai, attacks on security forces there increased "exponentially" in the wake of Morsi's ouster.[191] July saw eighty-six attacks, nine times that of any month since 2010. Total attacks dropped to forty-six in August, after which they became lesser in number but greater in deadly impact, suggesting greater planning and coordination.[192] What was once "endemic violence" thus "spiraled into something like an insurgency."[193]

Egypt's military, by far the most powerful institution in the country, assumed responsibility for confronting this insurgency. The armed forces boasted internal cohesion, social prestige, strong ties to the United States, an economic empire in diverse sectors, and networks in the bureaucracy and local government.[194] Moreover, Commander-in-Chief Abdel Fattah el-Sisi gained popularity across society, at least initially. After a year in which a veritable cult of personality emerged around Sisi,[195] he easily won presidential elections in May 2014. That October the government imposed a curfew and state of emergency in parts of Sinai. It greatly increased troop presence in the area, carried out mass arrests and killings of militants, cleared a fourteen-kilometer "buffer zone" between Sinai and the Gaza Strip, and continued destroying smuggling tunnels from Gaza.[196]

Still, the insurgency in Sinai continued. In November 2014, Ansar Bait al-Maqdis, the most capable and powerful of the many Islamist groups active in Sinai, pledged allegiance to the Islamic State and renamed itself "Sinai Province."[197] By then the group had wrested control of nearly one third of Sinai's villages, rendering entire sections of the peninsula inaccessible to the army.[198] Between the coup in Cairo in July 2013 and 2017, violent nonstate actors in the Sinai killed hundreds of soldiers and police in raids against checkpoints and bases. In 2015, ISIS claimed responsibility for downing a Russian plane over Sinai.[199]

Some of this violence spilled across the border into Israel. The most severe incident, occurring on August 2011, was a multipronged attack in which militants fired at police and civilians on the Israeli side of the border and then entered Israel, ambushed a bus, and used firearms, explosives, and a rocket-propelled grenade against security forces that rushed to the scene. The attack left eight Israelis, five Egyptian soldiers, and ten attackers dead. In what Israel described as an accident that occurred in a hot pursuit of the assailants, Israeli troops shot and killed several more Egyptian soldiers. Those casualties triggered heated demonstrations near the Israeli embassy in Cairo and a diplomatic crisis between Israel and Egypt.[200]

Given the tenuous strength of Egypt's governmental authority in the Sinai as well as continued violence inside the peninsula, one might have expected more attacks across the Israeli border. That this was not the case was due, at least in part, to the actions of the other party in the triadic conflict: Israel. Eschewing the triadic coercion it had used in the past against Egypt (and continued to use against other host states), Israel instead invested in several defensive measures. First, it constructed a border fence, complete with cameras and other surveillance technology, spanning nearly the entire length of its border with Egypt, from Rafah to Eilat.[201] Second, Israel significantly increased its troop deployment along the same border.[202] Third, Israel increased its intelligence gathering effort around its southern border and in the Sinai, establishing a special unit of Shin Bet, the Israeli internal security service, for this assignment.[203] Fourth, Israel deployed the Iron Dome antiballistic missile system to intercept rockets at key points, especially near Eilat.[204] These measures represented an unprecedented emphasis on defensive, as opposed to coercive, measures. Defense Minister Moshe

Ya'alon's discourse reflected this orientation when he responded to a 2013 rocket attack with a tone markedly different from the belligerence advocated in prior triadic conflicts, saying "Sinai militants will strike again. But Iron Dome will keep south Israel safe."[205]

Apart from defensive actions, Israel also showed a shift away from triadic coercion by making significant efforts to cooperate with Egypt to work jointly against nonstate actors. Israel actively transmitted intelligence to Egyptian forces to aid their antiterror campaign, including by revealing the location, capabilities, and plans of nonstate threats.[206] In addition, it is believed that, on several occasions, such as in August 2013 and February 2017, Israel obtained Egyptian military consent before it used armed drones to strike Sinai militants. Various sources, including Sinai militants, testified to this drone use, though neither Israel nor Egypt confirmed it.[207] Revealing an even greater degree of Israeli-Egyptian cooperation, Israel agreed to the deployment of the Egyptian military in the peninsula. The 1979 peace agreement explicitly curtailed the Egyptian army's presence in the eastern Sinai and completely prohibited its deployment in central and western Sinai, near the Israeli border. Against those stipulations, and despite concerns about larger strategic implications—namely how demilitarization helped maintain peace between the two nations—Israel repeatedly agreed to Egyptian troop deployments in the Sinai after 2011. As of 2014 these forces included Apache attack helicopters and ten military battalions, including a tank battalion.[208]

What explains Israel's turn away from triadic coercion, and indeed coercion in general, in this case? Amos Harel and Avi Issacharoff attribute this shift to strategic rationality, noting in the wake of a 2012 attack that there was "no place against which Israel can retaliate" and "no one to send the message to, even indirectly."[209] We disagree with this assessment. The lack of a credible and capable "return address" had not prevented Israel from embarking on triadic coercion operations in the past. What had changed, we propose, is how Israel had come to view Egypt through the prism of its strategic culture. The peace agreement between Israel and Egypt led Israeli decision-makers to exclude Egypt from the category of actors to which it would almost automatically apply triadic coercion. In other words, the strategic culture that considers triadic coercion to be the best Israeli response, regardless of the opponent it faces, did not apply to these attacks from Sinai. Instead, Israel pitted the risk of nonstate attacks from Sinai against the risk of a renewed confrontation with its largest and militarily strongest neighbor.[210] As Zack Gold observes, "At a strategic level, Israel is significantly more concerned about the maintenance of the Egypt-Israel Peace treaty. A trickling of rockets is a threat, but returning to a state of war with Egypt . . . would completely change Israel's strategic calculus and military posture."[211]

Compared to the risk of war with Egypt, attacks from the Islamic State affiliates in Sinai were not a serious threat. As Defense Minister Avigdor Liberman said in 2017, these attacks were merely "annoying" and "hindersome."[212] By 2014 Israeli officials and observers described Israel's security cooperation with Sisi's regime as "exceed[ing] all expectations" and "at its zenith."[213] In 2016 Israel re-opened its Cairo embassy, and Egypt appointed, for the first time since 2011, an ambassador to Israel.[214] In July of that year Egypt's foreign minister, Sameh Shoukry, made a rare public visit to Israel and met with Prime Minister Benjamin Netanyahu.[215] In adopting this noncoercive approach, Israel was guided by its strong belief that the Sisi regime was predisposed to cooperation. That stood in contrast to its view of the Morsi government. When a rocket landed in Eilat during Morsi's tenure, Netanyahu responded aggressively, threatening "We will strike at those who attack us."[216]

Our analysis suggests the erroneousness of this exclusive focus on perceptions of the host state's predisposition toward Israel, in neglect of its regime strength. In this regard, Egypt might have been similarly misguided in thinking that sheer military force, rather than a deeper kind of political cohesion and capacity, could effectively bring an end to violence by nonstate actors on Egyptian soil. Fundamentally, Egypt seemed to hold that using tanks and troops was the best strategy against insurgents in Sinai. Some critics argued that the Egyptian government instead needed to develop a strategy of asymmetric counterinsurgency built on local intelligence and cooperation with residents.[217] Military measures alone do not end lawlessness and insurgency fueled by deep-seated socioeconomic grievances, decades of government neglect, and mutual hostility between state and society.[218] At the least, the government needed to avoid increasing the resentment of Sinai residents, as would be caused by punishing the innocent. Yet many of Egypt's tactics—from the killing and harsh interrogation of uninvolved civilians to the demolishing of homes and agricultural lands in the creation of a border buffer zone—did precisely that.[219]

As earlier eras of Egyptian history demonstrated, regime strength entails more than a monopoly on violence. It is grounded in internal political cohesion and the state's capacity to govern society though legal, bureaucratic, and other means. The application of brute force can hinder rather than substantiate such strength. Hence, some analysts predicted that Egypt's heavy-handed military tactics would ultimately backfire and add "fuel to Bedouin militancy."[220]

Conclusion

We have identified four periods in Israel's triadic conflict with Egypt. During the first period, from 1949 to 1954, Israel gradually adopted triadic coercion, but that strategy proved ineffective for deterring nonstate border violations. Egypt was ruled by very different regimes under King Farouk and during the first two years after the Free Officers' coup. Nevertheless, these regimes were similar in the two characteristics pertinent for triadic coercion: both shared a predisposition toward preventing nonstate actors from antagonizing Israel from its territory and both were too weak to translate that preference into effective policy. Lacking internal political cohesion and institutional capacity, Egyptian governments in this era did not wield the policing power or authority over social forces in the Gaza Strip necessary to fulfill Israel's demands that it control the nonstate actors under its rule.

During the second period, from mid-1954 through the 1956 Suez War, the effects of Israel's triadic coercion moved from irrelevance to counterproductivity. Israel's 1955 raid on Gaza, exercising theretofore unprecedented severity, spurred Palestinian civilians and Egyptian military officers to demand retaliation. Egypt's response to the crisis was conditioned by its intermediary, transitional level of regime strength. Nasser did not yet possess the political or institutional fortitude to neutralize domestic pressures. His regime did, however, possess sufficient capacity to sidestep Palestinian groups by undertaking a new strategy altogether. The state thus initiated its own guerrilla force that assumed leadership of irregular attacks on Israel. Given Nasser's balance of domestic political resources and constraints, Israel's strikes transformed a situation of triadic coercion into bilateral interstate confrontation. Far from deterrence, the outcome was an escalatory spiral across the Egypt-Israel demarcation line.

It was only during third period, beginning after the 1956 war, that Israel's triadic coercion could be deemed successful. Nasser's political victory in the Suez War, along with the sweeping domestic reforms he instituted thereafter, gave his regime the strength that it previously lacked. At the same time, Israel's demonstrated military power increased Nasser's incentives to prevent nonstate actors from embroiling him in a confrontation that he knew he could not win. The result was a striking shift in the effectiveness of triadic coercion. During the years 1956–1967, the border between Israel and Egypt, and especially along the Gaza Strip, was relatively quiet. Never again would Egypt allow nonstate actors to attack Israel from its territory, despite the resumption of conventional interstate fighting in the 1967 and 1973 wars and the 1967–1970 War of Attrition.

Israel's favorable balance of power versus Egypt was a necessary, yet insufficient, component for triadic coercion. Before the 1955 Gaza raid, Egypt had the will to restrain Palestinians' infiltrations but lacked capacity to do so due to the regime's domestic crises and overall institutional and political weakness. Between 1955 and the Suez War, the same internal constraints contributed to Nasser's support for infiltrations, even though doing so meant goading a more powerful adversary. The Suez War was a turning point in regime strength and, thereby, triadic coercion outcomes. In the war's aftermath, Israel no longer needed to issue explicit threats to Egypt. Nasser was well aware of Israeli raids in Jordan, Lebanon, and Syria, where nonstate actors' border attacks continued. After Suez, however, Nasser was able to use his new political and institutional power to curb nonstate actors in Egypt. He was both deterred from aiding the fedayeen and compelled to take active steps to prevent their attacks of Israel. This shift would not have been possible if not for the significant increase in the strength of the Egyptian regime.

This regime strength held through both of Nasser's successors and helped make possible the peace accord between Israel and Egypt in 1979. However, a fourth period of triadic coercion began in 2011 after a mass uprising forced Hosni Mubarak from his thirty-year presidency. Developments in this period confirm the continued importance of regime strength or weakness but also highlight shifts in Israeli-Egyptian relations. Against a backdrop of intense struggle between elements of the old political system and newly mobilized groups seeking to transform it, the regime in Cairo showed new signs of fragility. Its authority over the peripheral Sinai Peninsula weakened in turn. Some Sinai Bedouin tribes, long alienated by poverty and neglect, took up arms, and new extremist groups proliferated. The result, a surge of violence against the Egyptian state and across the border against Israel, echoed familiar patterns in the relationship between regime weakness and nonstate actors' insurgency. Facing an Egypt with which it had been at peace for nearly forty years, however, Israel responded in ways very different than it had when facing an Egypt that it regarded as strictly an adversary. Israel combined defensive measures with cooperation with Egypt as a way to combat these cross-border incursions. As of 2018, this strategy, eschewing coercion, has proven effective in reducing violations of the Israeli-Egyptian border, even as violence inside Sinai itself remains ongoing.

Over nearly seventy years, the triadic conflict on Israel's southern border has thus witnessed dramatic change. In the 1950s, Israel advocated greater and greater military force to compel a weak Egyptian regime to do what it was institutionally and politically unable to do. By the 2000s, Israel and Egypt were engaged in a military and intelligence collaboration to fight nonstate actors that both shared a desire to defeat. What continued to elude both Israel and Egypt alike, however, was a fuller embrace of nonmilitary and defensive solutions better attuned to addressing the political and socioeconomic problems that gave rise to those nonstate actors in the first place.

CHAPTER 4

Syria Since 1949

Triadic Coercion from Coups to Revolution

This chapter analyzes four distinct phases shaping the consequences of Israel's use of triadic coercion against Syria. From 1949 to 1962, the Syrian regime lacked cohesion and capacity, rendering it a potentially hospitable host for nonstate actors. Unlike in the Gaza Strip, however, there was not a large, destitute refugee population living directly on Syria's border with Israel. Available information thus affirms that infiltrations by individuals and groups were limited.[1] While the relationship between Israel and Syria remained bilateral during this period, Syria's turbulent politics—apparent in a succession of unstable, short-lived governments—laid the foundation for regime weakness that would mediate the effects of triadic coercion during the next phase.

That second period began with the Ba'ath Party-led coup of 1963, after which Syria became a key supporter of the rising Palestinian guerrilla movement. This support was a manifestation not only of Ba'ath ideology but also of regime weakness. Internal factionalism, unconstrained by unifying state institutions, drove competing Syrian political elites to provide nonstate actors with unprecedented support, access to resources, and operational autonomy. As nonstate attacks soared, Israel undertook triadic coercion and demanded that the government in Damascus take responsibility for securing the border. Triadic coercion failed, however, because the host regime lacked the cohesion and capacity to end nonstate actors' attacks, even if doing so served Syria's own national security interests.

The role of regime weakness in generating incentives and opportunities for nonstate militancy came to a dramatic halt after 1970, when Hafez al-Assad seized power and established a strong authoritarian regime. In this third period, Assad had both a will to avoid confrontation with Israel and the cohesion and capacity to enforce it. In this context, Israel's credible threats successfully pushed Syria to prohibit nonstate attacks from Syria, even as it encouraged them from other states. Triadic coercion would not have yielded such results had the host regime not had the political cohesion to recognize that securing the border served its national interests and the infrastructural capacity to translate those preferences into action.

Successful triadic coercion against Syria was sustained through interstate war in 1973, the 1975–1990 Lebanese civil war, and the 1985 birth of a new nonstate actor, Hezbollah, in Syria-dominated Lebanon. Conditions changed in the final period that we examine, beginning with Syrians' 2011 uprising against the Assad regime. The subsequent escalation of violence and collapse of regime authority in many parts of the country opened new opportunities for nonstate actors, including on the Syria-Israel border. As of this writing, the various rebel and militia groups active in Syria have not aimed significant attacks at Israel. Nonetheless, their proliferation in the context of a severely weakened state and regime warn of complications that could affect future triadic relations.

Foundations of Border Friction, 1949–1962

Unlike on Israel's border with Egypt, the main source of friction on the Israeli-Syrian border after 1948 was not triadic conflict involving Palestinians' infiltrations but bilateral conflict centered on rival claims to land and water rights.[2] Whereas Israel upheld the original demarcation between the Palestine and Syria Mandates, Syria endorsed the truce lines drawn when fighting ended in 1949.[3] As a compromise, the 1949 armistice agreement designated contested areas as a demilitarized zone (DMZ) where, until a final settlement was reached, the UN Mixed Armistice Commission would prevent entry of any military or paramilitary force. Arguing that it had sovereignty over the DMZ, except for the freedom to deploy armed forces, Israel repeatedly attempted to cultivate farmland in the territory. It also carried out attacks on Arab villages to force their inhabitants to flee.[4] Israeli farmers frequently carried out these activities under guard of armed police, and sometimes military personnel and vehicles. Syria accused Israel of illegally seeking to annex territory and often responded with gunfire. Israel responded with gunfire of its own, or with threats of more intense reprisals.[5]

Israel's and Syria's conflicting claims to Lakes Huleh and Tiberias followed a similar pattern. Whereas Syria asserted that Anglo-French Agreements from the 1920s gave it full fishing and navigation rights, Israel claimed sovereignty and deployed armed boats to forbid Syria from using these waters without its consent. It also carried out raids on Arab villages, provoking Syrian gunfire and periodically leading to exchanges of fire and to casualties. Ben-Gurion ordered harsh action,[6] including major assaults on Syrian communities and positions in December 1955 and March 1962.[7]

Compounding tension, in 1951 Israel began efforts to drain Lake Huleh and the surrounding swamps in an effort to expand access to agricultural lands. In 1953 Israel cut into the DMZ near the lake to build a canal to divert waters from the Jordan River.[8] Deferring to Syrian and international censure, Israel suspended the canal project. It later resumed it but modified the project to circumvent the DMZ. Syrian and Arab League opposition only intensified, however, as it became apparent that Israel was pumping water not only for an electrical power plant but also to irrigate the Negev. They protested that this usage would severely reduce water available to Arab states, while simultaneously strengthening Israel's capacity to absorb new immigrants.[9]

This interstate tension colored Israel's perceptions of the Syrian border and Syria-based nonstate actors. Though infiltrations by Palestinian civilians were of much lesser scale than across other borders, Israel still tended to view those violations as part of Syria's larger rejection of Israel. General Mordechai Makleff, Israel's chief of staff in the mid-1950s, later recognized that this was erroneous, remarking, "We mistakenly regarded every infiltrator as a *fida'iyyun* [guerrilla fighters] and saw [infiltration] as a deliberate action."[10] Israel developed a view of Syrians as vicious, if not "barbaric," after incidents such as the 1954 capture of four Israeli soldiers in Syria on an espionage mission, leading to one soldier's execution.[11] Israel considered Syria's enmity to be particularly threatening because Syria could shell Israeli targets from the topographical advantage of the Golan Heights.

Israel's perception of Syria's defiant predisposition was unsubstantiated. There is little evidence that Syrian officials deliberately aided or abetted nonstate actors' activities against Israel in these years. The closest Syria came to such involvement was the Deuxième Bureau, a division of Syrian intelligence, and its creation of a "Palestinian unit" in which Palestinian refugees served as operatives under Syrian officers. Although the unit originally carried out some espionage missions in Israel, commanding officers appeared to have suspended those missions in the early 1950s. The Palestinian unit is not believed to have ever carried out violence inside Israel.[12]

Furthermore, the Palestinian unit's operations do not appear to have been endorsed by the government. Rather they seem to have been the private initiative of particular commanders, such as Colonel Abd al-Hamid Sarraj.[13] That Sarraj could act with autonomy was indicative of the weak cohesion and capacity of the governments ruling Syria in this era. The Syrian state that gained independence from France in 1946 rested on "the most rudimentary" liberal institutions and a "fragile legitimacy." It was a conservative parliamentary system in which politics was largely limited to the elite families who had been locally powerful in Ottoman times or became active in the independence struggle. Typically scions of the landed aristocracy or urban merchant class, this old generation of political leaders was prone to infighting and disregard of constitutional principles. They tended to see the state as little more than a source of patronage.[14]

The already-tenuous cohesion of this system was shaken by two sets of challenges. First, foreign and regional events, foremost the loss of Arab Palestine in the 1948 War, deeply discredited the old regime and all associated with it. The army blamed incompetent and corrupt civilian politicians for what it regarded as a disgrace. Second, Syria underwent tremendous socioeconomic change, as expansion of education, population growth, industrialization, and other transformations swelled the ranks of the educated middle classes. Mechanized agriculture hastened erosion of traditional landlord-peasant relations, spurring the politicization of the peasantry and formation of a movement for land reform.[15] As new social groups found inherited economic, political, and social structures unable to accommodate their demands and aspirations, they were increasingly attracted to radical ideologies and calls for revolutionary change. These new political trends grew both in the form of opposition political parties and within the army, where many youths from poor or religious minority communities sought social mobility.

This class conflict and ideological ferment set the stage for a series of unstable governments. Military officers staged three coups in 1949. The last of these brought to power Colonel Adib Shishakli, who suspended parliament and established a dictatorial presidency until he was overthrown by another military coup in 1954. Upheavals not only produced weak governments but also undermined the cohesion and capacity of the military itself. Officers were divided along personal, sectarian, and other lines. Patrick Seale writes that, by the time of Shishakli's ouster, Syria's army was "without a chief able to impose himself on the whole officer corps." By 1957, he adds, "petty rivalries and political enmities had reduced the Syrian army to a number of competing factions, each fearing the other more than any outside force ... each unit operated like a private army."[16]

The restoration of parliamentary rule in 1954 did little to strengthen the institutional capacity or internal cohesion of the Syrian state or its successive governments. Rather, the late 1950s witnessed the intensification of another layer of regime instability in the form of fierce interstate competition over and through Syria. Arab nationalist Egypt and pro-Western Iraq both sought to win Syria's allegiance in pursuit of political supremacy in the Arab world. Further afield, Great Britain and France likewise jostled for greater influence in the country, while the United States and Soviet Union each tried to bring Syria to its side of the Cold War. These multiple external rivalries played out in Syria in feuding media and propaganda campaigns, panic-inducing rumors, real foreign plots, and inflows of pressure, funds, and even weapons for or against different Syrian factions. The weakness of Syrian governments created space for these external struggles, which in turn further undermined regime cohesion and capacity.[17]

Though Syria's conflict with Israel was almost exclusively bilateral in this era, regime weakness affected hostilities in ways that previsioned later triadic dynamics. Weak Syrian leaders, unable to satisfy pressures at home, had extra impetus to adopt defiant stances toward Israel as compensation. In 1951, for example, the Syrian army opened fire on an Israeli patrol and killed seven policemen. When Syria did not issue an apology, Israel's Foreign Ministry concluded that the killings "were committed by order of the Syrian government, which, for reasons originating in its own internal weakness, is interested in 'heating up' the border and thus gaining the sympathies of the army and public opinion."[18] Moshe Maoz judges that, likewise in the late 1950s, insecure Syrian governments sustained bellicose rhetoric, shooting incidents, and adamancy on water issues "to divert Syrians' attention from their internal problems." Syrian leaders were wary of waging war on Israel directly, but did not shy from engaging in verbal threats, "mostly for domestic consumption."[19]

Domestic pressures also infused Syrian politicians' foreign policy stances. Nasser inspired tremendous popularity in Syria, which accentuated Syrian citizens' hostility toward both their own traditional Western-oriented elites and Western powers' maneuvers to enlist Syria in an anti-Soviet alliance. Against this backdrop, Syria signed a defense treaty with Egypt in October 1955. That alliance affected Israel's use of coercive force on the border. In December 1955 Israel attacked several Syrian army positions with land forces, air patrols, and troops landing by boat. The conflagration, dubbed Operation Kinneret, resulted in one hundred Syrian and sixteen Israeli casualties. Israel claimed that the raid was retaliation for Syrian harassment of Israeli fishing boats. UN observers and Ben-Gurion himself, however, suggested that Israel's real motivation was to warn Syria against moving toward Nasser.[20] Of as much concern was Syria's 1954 arms deals with Czechoslovakia, and later with the Soviet Union, making it the first Arab state to conclude such deals.[21]

Meanwhile, Syrian politics continued to grow more ideologically radical. The Ba'ath Party, a revolutionary movement committed to Arab unity and socialism, grew in prominence. The Ba'ath succeeded in attracting a social base among rural, provincial, and minority youth. It did not, however, build a cohesive structure or effective leadership. The party had initially begun as a loose network of local cells. Though it claimed to have developed a pyramidal structure, in practice it was plagued by factionalism unchecked by any meaningful central administration or clear institutionalized relations among its local branches.[22]

Other rival movements, including the Nasserists and communists, competed with the Ba'ath by claiming greater opposition to Israel and commitment to Palestinian liberation.[23] By 1957, in Seale's words, "Syria was on the verge of disintegration as an organized political community. Not only was there no general agreement on the rules governing political behavior but, worse still, many Syrians had lost confidence in the future of their country as an independent entity."[24] It was against that backdrop that, in 1958, the army and the Ba'ath Party pursued Syria's union with Egypt. This gave rise to a new political entity, the United Arab Republic (UAR). Nasser dominated the union, marginalizing Syrians and appointing Egyptians to control Syria's government and economy. Discontent accumulated until 1961, when a secessionist coup in Damascus brought about the UAR's collapse.

The next tumultuous nineteen months left Syrian politics even more divided. Right-leaning elites returned to power and undid the social reforms that Nasser had instituted. They were subsequently overthrown by another military revolt that reinstated the same policies. Meanwhile, during the existence of the UAR, Nasser had taken steps to undercut the Ba'ath, further weakening its institutional structure. That, followed by internal disputes provoked by the UAR's failure, effectively split the movement into disparate factions. In this context, Ba'athist military officers remained more capable of collective action than any other political force. This, in Raymond Hinnebusch's assessment, was testimony of "the regime's complete demoralization" and the "utter collapse of established authority in Syria."[25]

The first fifteen years following the 1948 War thus did not witness major nonstate violence from Syria against Israel. Correspondingly, this period did not register any significant use of triadic coercion by Israel. However, developments during this era set the stage for subsequent transformations in triadic conflict. The extreme vulnerability and turnover of successive Syrian governments, in tandem with the development of revolutionary movements calling for stronger opposition to Israel, was the backdrop for the establishment of a new regime in Damascus in 1963. This regime would not only transform the course of Syria's history but also instigate a dramatic escalation in triadic conflict.

Instability and Defiance Under the Ba'ath, 1963–1970

In March 1963, a faction of the Ba'ath Party seized control of the government. At its head were young military officers who had come together in the Military Committee as early as 1959 and consolidated after the collapse of the UAR. Many were from religious minorities and from rural, lower-middle-class backgrounds.[26] They represented just small groups within the military and commanded neither an effective party apparatus nor a popular following.[27]

The new leadership declared commitment to the armed struggle of emerging Palestinian groups, most notably the Fatah movement forming underground at the time. During an era in which Jordan, Lebanon, and Egypt thwarted the fedayeen, Syria became their most important state ally.

Air Force Commander Hafez al-Assad, prominent in the coup, reportedly quipped, "It was in Syria that the lungs of the Resistance were filled with oxygen."[28] In the early 1960s, sympathetic army officers allowed Fatah to use training camps in Syria.[29] When Fatah carried out its debut operation in 1965, it was under Syrian directives.[30] Thereafter, the regime offered commandos training and arms. It allowed Fatah to organize and distribute publications on Syrian soil as well as receive, transport, and store weapons shipments in Syria. Syria's military and intelligence services offered support, and its media publicized Fatah's announcements and lauded its exploits.[31]

The Syrian regime's endorsement of nonstate militancy was rooted both in national grievances and Ba'ath principles, which held that avant-garde guerrilla groups should lead a popular war of liberation against Israel.[32] "The Palestinian movement was a centerpiece of Ba'thist ideology," David Lesh writes. "It was almost a sacred duty to support the Palestinian cause."[33] Nevertheless, Syria's support for Palestinian guerrillas was not determined by ideology alone. It was also conditioned by the regime's own lack of cohesion and capacity. In the Egyptian case, regime weakness reduced the government's ability to restrict the fedayeen. In Syria, weakness played the additional roles of increasing government elites' incentives for supporting guerrilla activity and of expanding opportunities for guerrillas to operate. More specifically, Syrian regime weakness contributed to nonstate actor violence in three ways.

First, the regime's weakness vis-à-vis its own society led Ba'athist officers to champion the fedayeen, at least in part, in the hope of offsetting domestic woes. Officers' origins in somewhat peripheral communities alienated them from urban folk and the Sunni majority.[34] The Ba'ath undertook sweeping policies of nationalization, land reform, and other restructuring of the economy, which angered traditional landlords and the powerful business class.[35] In parallel, their secular pan-Arabism offended many pious Muslims. Economic deterioration accentuated domestic discontent. Political uncertainty not only scared away domestic and foreign investment but also encouraged the transfer of capital out of the country.[36]

The regime's reforms, especially in the agricultural sector, were too piecemeal to stop the economic decline.[37] Its institutional capacity was likewise too deficient to offset these woes; the coup leaders had inherited weak governmental institutions from the prior system and then weakened them further through sweeping purges of personnel. This combination of social and economic instability fueled street demonstrations, strikes, union militancy, and emigration. In this context, support for the Palestinian struggle, guaranteed to be popular and emotive, was a vehicle for placating public opinion. A strong stance toward Israel helped, in Mark Tessler's words, "put domestic critics on the defensive, deflect public attention from local grievances, and above all enhance the Ba'ath Party's legitimacy."[38]

Second, Syria's weakness in regional politics encouraged some elites to embrace the fedayeen as a political resource in contests with other states. This weakness was primarily vis-à-vis Israel. According to Seale, Ba'ath leaders "were looking for relief from the frustrations of impotence . . . they could not contemplate surrendering to Israel, but neither could they match it in conventional battle. The guerrillas seemed to offer an honorable way out."[39] Support for the fedayeen also offered a tool that Ba'athists could use to compete with Nasser, their main rival in the pan-Arab arena. Syrian leaders had pressed Nasser to expand guerrilla operations against Israel as early as 1958.[40] Nasser, prioritizing Egyptian national interests, refused. After Egypt sponsored the establishment of the PLO, Syria embraced Fatah as a counterweight. Both the Ba'ath and Fatah viewed the PLO as an "envelope" created by Arab states, with the intension of confining the Palestinian struggle rather than advancing it. In supporting Palestinian commandos, Ba'athist leaders demonstrated their uncompromising militancy, challenged Nasser's reluctance, and cast doubt on Egypt's claim to leadership of the Arab world.[41] In the words of one Syrian official, the guerrillas enabled the Ba'ath to "rub Nasir's nose in the mud of Palestine."[42]

Third, the Ba'ath's internal divisions contributed to generating both encouragement and resources for Palestinian militancy. In 1962 the Ba'ath Party leadership formed two rival camps: the Qutri faction, which favored orientation toward Syria as a nation-state and came to identify with and support the party's Regional Command organ, and the Qaumi faction, which upheld a pan-Arab perspective and instead supported the party's National Command.[43] This rivalry both undermined party order and contributed to hostilities on the border. A 1966 Regional Command memo charged National Command leaders with deliberately stoking tensions with Israel in order to divert forces loyal to its rival, labeling that ploy no less than "artificial creation (of a state of emergency) aimed at destroying the party."[44] Though the Qutri faction eventually succeeded in asserting its will in reorganizing the party, the factional rivalry played out in other institutional realms, such as the Ba'ath Military Committee.[45]

Beyond these factions, the Ba'ath were also torn by more general divisions between military and civilian, young and old, rural and urban, moderate and radical, upper- and lower-middle class, and members of religious minorities and the Sunni majority. Even party members from similar rural, minority backgrounds were split along regional and familial lines. No less acute than internal conflicts based on ideology and identity were those driven by personal ambitions and jealousies.[46] Contending Ba'athists pursued different approaches to domestic crises, which in turn pulled the ruling coalition in incompatible directions.[47] The regime lacked the experience and institutionalization to enforce legitimate procedures for regulating these divisions and for shepherding all relevant actors to accept a binding decision-making process. Rather, the party was caught in a "vicious circle," in which internal fragmentation weakened institution-building, and weak institutions prompted fragmenting behavior.[48] Even the secretary of the Ba'ath Military Organizational Bureau recognized these problems:

> The foundations on which the organisation was based were aimed not so much at belief in the Party but, unfortunately, at the protection of the organisation's leaders. . . . If we were to examine the organisation of any section, we would find that it was set up by the section secretary, who [at the same time] is commander of that unit, *according to his personal, political, regional or sectarian inclinations.* . . . Afterwards they became submerged in . . . a fierce struggle for power, which created a weakness of discipline and education in the Party, and subsequently [resulted in] a lack and loss of unity in thought, spirit and orientation.[49]

That individual power-holders faced few constraints in acting on their own preferences, was simultaneously an indicator, a product, and a reinforcer of Syria's regime weakness. In turn, it critically shaped Syria's relations with nonstate actors. The regime's aid to the fedayeen was neither formal nor official. Rather, leaders tended to undertake their own personal initiatives to assist Palestinian groups. For example, Military Intelligence Chief Ahmed Suwydani autonomously developed channels of regime assistance to Fatah. Only after he set in motion his own plans to support the guerrillas did he obtain approval from either his superiors or Arafat.[50] Similarly, Assad appeared to act on his own compulsion when he granted Fatah two training bases and helped it obtain arms from China. He took those steps without the knowledge of then Syrian president, Amin al-Hafiz.[51]

Ultimately, the Syrian regime did not exercise the authority necessary to regulate, restrict, or subordinate political elites to a coherent state policy. As Volker Perthes summarizes, Ba'ath leaders never "managed to establish more than a feeble measure of political and social control."[52] This and other sources of regime and state weakness contributed to Syria's support for the Palestinian guerrilla movement, which in turn facilitated escalation of attacks. From Fatah's January 1965 launch until the internal Ba'ath coup of February 1966, the Syrian regime aided or allowed fedayeen to carry out thirty-eight attacks.[53]

During these years, many Israeli officials viewed Fatah as no more than a "Syrian puppet organization."[54] Some charged that Israeli commanders' casting of blame on the regime in Damascus went beyond military logistics to become an emotionally laden antipathy, which some dubbed Israel's "Syrian syndrome."[55] As the military secretary to Prime Minister Levi Eshkol reflected, "Syrian syndrome afflicted everyone who ever served on the northern command lines. We loved to hate them."[56] The Israeli press and public opinion shared this orientation,[57] in part because holding the host state responsible for nonstate actors provided a satisfying solution to the perplexing problem of asymmetric threats. "A state with a capital and a government and an army could be related to," Tom Segev explained. "The still nascent Palestinian organizations were more elusive."[58]

For Chief of Staff Yitzhak Rabin, the argument that Israel should respond to Palestinian raids by attacking Ba'ath regime targets was an expression of the larger Rabin Doctrine, the principle that Israel should tailor strategies toward host regimes based on what it perceived to be their defiant or cooperative predisposition toward Israel. "The response to Syria's actions should be targeted against the terrorist operations and against the regime," Rabin explained. "In essence, the Syria problem involves clashes with the ruling power. In this sense, the situation can be compared to relations which [were] obtained between Israel and Egypt in 1955–56."[59]

The Syrian and Egyptian situations were indeed comparable. In both cases, Israel sought to punish host states for the activity of nonstate actors, and in both cases this coercion failed because it aggravated domestic political pressures that pushed weak regimes toward greater militancy. In pledging to weaken the Ba'ath government, Israel did not consider how that government's very lack of cohesion and capacity contributed to motivating support for guerrilla activity. Coercion was ineffective because it did not and could not alter those domestic incentives. Rather, it exacerbated the regime's vulnerability and its need to derive legitimacy wherever possible, including through championing the Palestinian cause. Israel missed these political complexities because it misunderstood the relationship between Syria and Palestinian commandos, which was not one of master and puppet but rather two parties maneuvering to advance their respective interests.[60] In failing to note the unique strategic logic of triadic coercion, Israel did not appreciate that its reprisals against Syria could backfire due to the weakness of the Syrian regime.

Israeli coercion did not reduce Syria's backing for Fatah. On the contrary, this support reached particular heights after February 1966,[61] when left-wing officers launched a successful coup and established what became known as the "neo-Ba'ath" government. The neo-Ba'ath's radical stances further polarized the leadership from society and thereby ushered in an even more acute stage of regime weakness. Interelite strife intensified, including a struggle between neo-Ba'athists and leaders from other political movements, contention between neo-Ba'athists and right-leaning interests, and rivalries among the neo-Ba'ath themselves.[62] Foremost among these was the multifaceted enmity between Salah Jadid, Ba'ath Party assistant secretary-general and former army chief of staff, and Hafez al-Assad, minister of defense and commander of the air force. Jadid maintained influence over a large part of the officer corps through his supporters in the Military Bureau and other personal contacts. Assad controlled a large contingent of officers, many of whom he had personally appointed.[63] Jadid loyalists in the Regional Command argued that Syria should embrace radical change, which they saw as a needed departure from the conservatism of other Arab states. Assad, by contrast, believed that Syrian Ba'athists should temper their goals in line with the region's dominant political climate.[64]

Given the dearth of institutionalized procedures for resolving interelite disputes, individual leaders mobilized factional bases of support against each other.[65] The result, to quote Seale, was that the neo-Ba'ath regime was "the most extreme Syria had ever known, rash abroad, radical at home, engulfing the country in war."[66] In this context, it is believed that Syrian leaders supported Palestinian groups in carrying out seventy-five attacks on Israel during the fifteen months between the neo-Ba'ath coup and May 15, 1967.[67] Many of these were launched from Jordan by Fatah operatives who had entered from Syria. When Jordan and Lebanon enforced various measures against Palestinian militant activity from their soil in 1966, Syria remained Fatah's sole reliable base.[68] Tracking this activity in parallel with intraregime politics, Yaacov Bar-Siman-Tov shows that nonstate attacks on Israel from Syria increased during periods in which the Jadid-Assad conflict was particularly intense and declined when that rivalry was more contained.[69] This pattern demonstrates the role of regime weakness in facilitating and encouraging nonstate groups' operations.

The conflict between Israel, Syria, and the Palestinians accelerated as Fatah gained military skill and boldness in the late 1960s. Fatah quadrupled attacks from March to April 1967,[70] amassing new popularity that pressured other Palestinian groups to join the armed struggle or be left behind.[71] Against this backdrop, the Israel-Syria confrontation escalated dramatically on April 7. Syria fired on an Israeli tractor in the demilitarized zone, Israel returned fire, and Syria responded with shelling. The Israeli air force then escalated to a theretofore unprecedented step and downed six Syrian jets. For the first time, it flew all the way to Damascus. Although these hostilities reflected state-to-state hostilities, Israel did not differentiate between such clashes and those with nonstate actors. In the weeks that followed, Israeli officials indicated that they held Syria responsible for guerrilla strikes and would punish the regime again if Palestinian activity continued. Prime Minister Eshkol repeated the promise of reprisals against the Syrian state. Rabin went further, threatening to overthrow the Ba'ath regime.[72]

Such threats directly contradicted what we argue to be the logic of effective triadic coercion. Israeli officials proposed to weaken an enemy state as a strategy for stopping nonstate operations across its borders, ignoring how that state's regime weakness was integral to its support for nonstate actors in the first place. Indeed, regime weakness was the context in which Syrian officials pressured Egypt to offer bolder support for the Palestinian cause as well.[73] In doing so, Ba'ath leaders showed that they were more attuned to the political benefits of supporting fedayeen than to the potentially much larger risks of conflict with Israel. These risks were especially grave because Syria's army, devastated by purges and distracted by politics, was in no condition for combat. In consequence, in Seale's words, "Syria escalated from weakness" and "Israel was able in response to escalate from strength."[74]

While the causes of the 1967 War are many and contested,[75] these rising hostilities on the Syrian-Israeli border were a key contributor to the environment of regional tension that precipitated war.[76] Israel's victory in 1967 projected overwhelming military power. While the defeat showed Arab states the dire costs of war with Israel, it also sapped their political latitude for restricting Palestinian commandos. Arab publics lauded the fedayeen as the only force still fighting Israel. State leaders had little choice but to endorse the guerrillas if they were to placate popular criticism and demonstrate their continued commitment to Palestine. This allowed commandos to expand their bases in Syria, Lebanon, and Jordan. New commando groups formed, and large numbers of recruits joined, especially after the 1968 battle of Karameh (see chapter 2).

In Syria, the 1967 defeat inflamed rifts among elites. They traded blame for Israel's occupation of Syria's Golan Heights and advanced distinct strategies for recovering the territory. This overlapped with and contributed to intensification of the rivalry between Jadid and Assad. Jadid's "leftist" wing, grounded in the party apparatus, called for radical socioeconomic reforms, a stricter alliance with communist and socialist countries, and maintenance of the Syrian army as an ideological force. Assad's "realist" camp, based in the military, prioritized military rebuilding and economic growth over social revolution. It endorsed cooperation with the business class and conservative as well as revolutionary Arab regimes.[77] Jadid and Assad likewise diverged in their strategies toward Israel. Rejecting other Arab regimes as defeatist and reactionary, Jadid argued that Syria must deepen support for the Palestinian fedayeen as the pillar of a popular war of liberation against Israel. For Assad, Israel's show of force in 1967 proved that guerrillas' strikes led only to devastating retaliation. In this context, he criticized Jadid for privileging the party at the expense of the army, and upheld the latter as the real guarantor of the national interest. Assad insisted that Palestinian groups be subordinated to army control lest they continue to give Israel a pretext to attack. He argued that Syria should maintain calm on its borders while it worked with other Arab states on rebuilding an effective, unified military front.[78] When Assad pushed to have the army assume greater authority over the fedayeen, however, Jadid rallied his supporters in the Regional Party Congress to reject this and others of Assad's demands.[79]

The war generally undermined support for radical stances in the military and society and thereby shifted power toward Assad.[80] Nevertheless, the Ba'ath Regional Command remained loyal to Jadid, which denied the regime the cohesion it needed to translate the popular mood into the policies that the balance of power with Israel recommended. Rather, the period from fall 1968 through fall 1970 was one of "dualism" in Syria, which saw regime power split between the two rivals.[81] Interelite rivalry distracted authorities' attention from Palestinian groups, which exploited the opportunity to increase their presence on the border.[82] These power struggles also gave leaders incentives to continue using Palestinians as a source of leverage against each other. Regardless of their actual beliefs, Ba'ath aspirants benefited politically by claiming that they supported the Palestinian struggle more than their rivals did.

Against this backdrop, Syria continued to train, aid, and shelter Fatah and other Palestinian factions. In addition, in 1968, the Ba'ath Party voted to create its own Palestinian guerrilla squad, which the Jadid faction subsequently activated under the name Sa'iqa (Thunderbolt). In taking this step, Jadid was arguably motivated by antagonism against Assad at least as much as against Israel. Assad, in turn, pursued his own strategies against the wishes of the Jadid faction, such as initiating military cooperation with Iraq in 1969. Jadid responded by augmenting Sa'iqa as his "private army" against the regular army under Assad's control.[83] Assad reacted by placing Sa'iqa's training and supplies under the military establishment. He also marshaled his connections to the Syria-based brigades of the PLA and maneuvered them against Palestinian guerrillas that answered to Jadid.[84] The result of this "tug of war" between Ba'ath Party activists and the Syrian army was that both invested in Palestinian armed groups and in the process increased their size and military power as nonstate challenges to Israel.[85] In this context, the number of violent incidents against Israel from Syrian territory soared from 25 in 1968 to 276 in 1969 and to 454 in 1970. While it is not clear how many of these were conducted by Palestinian groups, it can be presumed that they increased with the overall volume of attacks.[86]

In February 1969, Israel responded to fedayeen operations with retaliatory air raids against Fatah camps near Damascus. Blaming Jadid for those incidents, Assad launched a limited coup. When this failed to remove Jadid from the Ba'ath Regional Command, Assad continued plotting to that end.[87] He chipped away at one of Jadid's key sources of leverage by issuing special regulations to constrain the scope of guerrillas' activities in Syria and subordinating them to surveillance by the Ministry of Defense, with himself at its head.[88] Advocating regulation of nonstate actors, Assad argued that Syria should focus on rebuilding its own army and preparing for conventional war.[89] He sought to make this strategy effective by restraining the army from initiating attacks and by trying to wrestle authority over Sa'iqa from his rival.[90]

Assad's actions amounted to compliance with Israel's triadic coercion within the limited arena of state action that he controlled. This compliance did not emanate from a cooperative predisposition toward Israel. It was motivated by awareness of the risks of conflict and an understanding of what was needed to avert it. Nonetheless, he lacked power outside his base in the armed forces. Israel's coercive strikes thus effectively compelled Syria to thwart Palestinian operations where Assad was strong but were not fully effective because Assad exercised control within only one fragment of the divided Syrian regime. Should Assad manage to take the reins of the state and unify it under his authority, this partial triadic coercion could become complete.

Regime Cohesion and Supremacy of National Interests, 1970–2000

This is what came to pass. As Syrian Ba'athists struggled with each other, the Palestinian fedayeen had come to approximate a state within a state in Jordan. As explained in chapter 2, Jordanian king Hussein launched an onslaught on Palestinian bases in 1970 that became known as "Black September." Jadid sent two to three hundred Syrian tanks into Jordan to assist the fedayeen. Assad refused to dispatch the air force to provide the requisite cover. As a consequence, Jordanian planes attacked the exposed Syrian armor. Jordan destroyed nearly half of Syria's tanks, caused some six hundred casualties, and forced Syrian forces to withdraw after just two days.[91]

The aborted intervention was disastrous for Syria. Though the action was seemingly irrational from the viewpoint of state interest, it can be understood in terms of Syria's fragmented regime. Jadid intervened in Jordan at least in part to assert his power vis-à-vis Assad.[92] Assad refused to intervene to assert his own power vis-à-vis Jadid.[93] Assad was also heeding Israeli coercion. When Jadid dispatched tanks to Jordan, Israel responded by sending two brigades into the Golan. It warned air strikes if Syria did not withdraw. Syria's contradictory response to Israeli threats was thus a product of its internal turmoil.[94] It was also a turning point that brought that turmoil to the brink.

Another turning point in regional politics came two weeks later, when Nasser, whose powerful presence had shaped the entire region for fifteen years, died of a heart attack. Assad seized upon the moment of change to argue that the time had come for Syria to reevaluate the costs of provoking Israel. "It would be better to refrain in the future from all gratuitous acts of provocation which the enemy could use as a pretext to challenge the Syrian Army and force upon it a battle which it is in no position to undertake," he said in an extraordinary statement to the Ba'ath Party National Congress that October.[95] He accused Sa'iqa of not only inviting Israel's retaliation but also interfering in the business of the Syrian state. Jadid's faction struck back by denouncing Assad's "defeatism" and calling to remove Assad as minister of defense. Assad then made what was to be the final blow in his rivalry with Jadid. On November 12 he took over the government in a bloodless coup. He ordered the arrest of Jadid and his allies, and in March 1971 was himself inaugurated president.

What Assad labeled his "Corrective Movement" was not simply another turnover in an interminably weak regime. It was the culmination of Assad's work to consolidate personal power since 1967. Since that juncture, he had steadily extended his grip on the army, slowly integrated the party's paramilitary organizations into the regular forces under his command, and replaced rivals in the military with his loyalists.[96] More fundamentally, the prior seven years of Ba'ath rule had brought about a gradual process of stabilization and institutionalization in the Syrian state apparatus. As a result, Hinnebusch judges, "The state whose helm Assad inherited was a far sturdier structure than the fragile entity the Ba'ath had seized in 1963."[97]

The Ba'athist regime grew still sturdier under Assad's authoritarian rule. This regime's increased cohesion was apparent in a concentration of decision-making power in the person of the president. This was so pronounced that some dubbed the system a "presidential monarchy."[98] Assad held the offices of president and secretary-general of the Ba'ath Party. He wielded direct personal control over the armed forces, appointing and dismissing officers of any rank. Syria maintained the façade of a constitution, an elected parliament, and a handful of permitted political parties. Yet there was no doubt that it was the president who exercised final say over all decisions and throughout the entire state apparatus.

Top political and military figures advised the president, but they rarely contested his choices and did not have autonomous bases of power to challenge his authority. Assad ensured their acquiescence, as well as their stake in the regime's survival, by granting them leeway in using their positions to enrich themselves illicitly. He also reserved top spots, particularly in the security apparatus, for trusted individuals from his own Alawite community. Their loyalty to the system was solidified by disproportionate privileges and fears of popular vengeance should they lose them.[99] The outcome was the cohesion at the regime's upper echelons of, Hinnebusch writes, a "consensual team whose solidarity was rooted in a common interest in protecting the legitimacy, resources, capabilities, and territorial integrity of the state—in a word, raison d'état."[100]

Growing cohesion was reflected not only in the allegiance of elites but also in the institutions with which the authoritarian regime penetrated society. Populist welfare policies extended vital services to the countryside and offered subsidies that helped alleviate poverty. This won new support for the regime, especially among the rural and urban working classes that the Ba'ath claimed as its base. At the same time, the avowedly socialist regime increased space for the private sector from the 1980s onward, earning the political allegiance of the predominately Sunni merchant class in exchange for greater freedom to make profits. With time, this would give rise to collusive networks between business and regime figures,[101] making the bourgeoisie "a fourth pillar of support" for Assad rule.[102]

The regime's domination of the economy went far in balancing conflicting social forces and building a cross-sectarian coalition.[103] Other political stratagems and structures did likewise. The Ba'ath Party, established in the 1973 constitution as the ruling party of state, operated through thousands of cells and branch offices across the country. Acting as an instrument of local surveillance and control, it coopted millions with the professional and economic privileges of membership. Assad expanded the Ba'ath Party as a vehicle for deepening his influence, tying individuals to the regime, and marginalizing other political trends. In consequence, party membership tripled from 1971 to 1974, doubled between 1974 and 1981, and again tripled from 1981 to 1992. The Ba'ath Party claimed a larger percentage of the adult Syrian population than did the Communist Party in the Soviet Union at its height.[104] A network of corporatist and mass organizations linked workers, peasants, women, students, and other groups to the party and to the regime, enabling the government both to enlist and keep tabs on society, sector by sector.

Backing up these structures of control was a pervasive coercive apparatus in which overlapping security agencies, along with a network of undercover informants, operated an "Orwellian system of surveillance."[105] By the early 1990s, some estimated that there was one security agent for every 240 citizens and that internal intelligence absorbed nearly a third of the military budget.[106] The Emergency Law, instituted in 1963, gave these security agencies sweeping powers to censor; restrict citizens' movement and assembly; seize property; and arrest, interrogate, and detain anyone on nearly any pretext. Their chilling presence throughout society and the state went far in curtailing criticism and opposition.

Those who dared to rebel were met with severe consequences. Such was the lesson of the period from 1976 to 1982 when some civic and professional associations began agitating for human rights and the Muslim Brotherhood carried out a campaign of violence against regime targets. Authorities responded by indiscriminately killing, imprisoning, or otherwise "disappearing" tens of thousands of citizens. When Brotherhood militants led an insurrection in the city of Hama in 1982, Assad responded with a scorched earth assault that flattened the city and left tens of thousands of dead, warning generations of the consequences of challenging the regime. Assad sent another such message the following year, when his brother Rifaat made a bid to power while the president was incapacitated due to illness. Returning to health, Assad countered these maneuvers by sending his brother into exile and purging his supporters. Thereafter, he instituted additional legal safeguards and further rearranged security and military units to ensure that no subsequent coup attempts could threaten the presidency.[107]

By the mid-1980s, Assad had, in Hanna Batatu's words, "turned round his finger, outwitted, divided, marginalized, silenced, or crushed all rival or opposition forces."[108] The Assad regime was not only cohesive but also increasingly capable. Economically, liberalization of measures imposed by prior Ba'ath governments revitalized the private sector and encouraged foreign investment. Contrary to previous governments' fiery pledges to export revolution, Assad reconciled with conservative Arab oil exporters and attracted their investment and aid. This timing was fortuitous, as annual foreign assistance rose from $50 million in 1973 to $600 million in the wake of the oil boom.[109] Remittances from Syrian migrants to the Gulf also increased during this period, as did Syria's own oil production. Revenue from oil exports, surging tenfold between 1973 and 1974 alone, enabled the regime to undertake large development projects and redouble investment in education.[110] The result of this transformation, according to UN figures, was a leap in in Syria's annual GDP growth from an average of 3.6 percent from 1963 to 1970 to 10 percent from 1970 to 1979.[111]

Economic recovery helped fund an increasingly robust state apparatus. The number of nonmilitary public employees grew from 24,000 in the early 1950s to 473,285 by 1983.[112] As in Egypt, the ballooning of the state would ultimately prove an unsustainable economic burden. During the first decade of Assad rule, however, it enhanced the regime's capacity in terms of the overall breadth and complexity of its bureaucracy and its ability to exert social, political, economic, and coercive influence across society. The inflated state also aided regime cohesion, insofar as it rendered a large swath of the population dependent on the favor of those in power for its livelihood.

A final dimension of the regime's increased capacity was military. Under Assad, the Syrian army underwent a military buildup greater than that of any other army in the region.[113] Bolstered by considerable Soviet aid, Syrian military expenditures increased from $268 million in 1965 to $427 million in 1971, $1,100 million in 1976, $2,018 million in 1979, and $3,186 million in 1980. The human and material strength of the Syrian army similarly grew from a force with 60,500 troops, 430 tanks, and 150 combat planes in 1968 to 135,000 troops, 2,000 tanks, and 330 planes in 1973 to some 350,000 soldiers, 3,600 tanks, and 500 planes in 1982.[114] By the mid-1980s, the Syrian air force was the largest in the Arab world, and its military's arsenal included long-range anti-aircraft missiles, shore-to-sea missiles, and long- and short-range ground-to-ground missiles.[115] Assad sought to ensure that the quality of his supplies matched its quantity by obtaining advanced equipment and training from the Soviet Union. He sealed that alliance with a "Friendship and Cooperation" treaty in 1980.

These processes of centralization of power, institutionalization of social control, and expansion of state apparatuses gave Assad's regime the cohesion to define realistic foreign policy goals and the capacity to pursue them. This tendency was redoubled by Assad's own patient, passionless personality as a man who, Batatu wrote in the 1990s, "appears to rate ideas in terms of their political utility" and for whom "pragmatism forms the warp and woof of his mind and conduct."[116] The outcome, Hinnebusch concluded, was that Assad's Syria acted exactly as one would expect of a "rational actor,"[117] if not a "tough Machiavellian" ready to do whatever necessary to defend his regime.[118] Assad thus abandoned "the messianic goal of liberating Palestine" and focused instead on winning back the Golan, which

Israel annexed in 1981.[119] He also understood that downgrading support for the Palestinian cause, in deed if not always in word, was the price to be paid for acquiring benefits, such as aid from the same wealthy Arab monarchies that his Ba'ath predecessors had deplored as puppets of the West.[120]

Enhanced regime strength empowered Assad to restrain the fedayeen in ways that heeded both Israel's warnings and the paramount goal of Syrian national security. Yezid Sayigh describes how Assad used his centralized rule to require PLO groups to acquire permission before holding rallies, issuing publications, or recruiting Syrian nationals. The same enlarged intelligence apparatus that exerted control over Syrian civilians turned its expanded capacities on Palestinians. Syrian agents took advantage of unfettered access to refugee camps and guerrilla facilities. Military Intelligence's "National Bureau of Guerrilla Control" required guerrillas to obtain passes in order to travel and to submit advance information about any operations against Israel, including details such as the names of participants.[121]

The severity of these restrictions came to the fore in July 1971 when Syrian authorities prevented Fatah forces from crossing into northern Jordan to aid their comrades cornered by the Jordanian army's final assault.[122] These restrictions were similarly pronounced when authorities confiscated a major arms shipment from Algeria to Fatah in 1971, sending a sharp message that Syria's territory could no longer be taken for granted as a transport route.[123] Facing greater restrictions from Syria and other strong Arab states, some Palestinian groups shifted from cross-border strikes to international acts of violence, such as plane hijacking and covert operations in Europe. The mainstream of the PLO established a new base in Lebanon, where the state was too weak to prevent it from again developing into something akin to a state-within-a-state.

Apart from restricting the fedayeen, Assad directly manipulated elements within the Palestinian movement. Not only were two-thirds of the PLA's troops based in Syria by 1973, but Assad also maneuvered to control its officer corps, thereby solidifying "Syrian domination" of the PLO's official military forces.[124] Having earlier put Sa'iqa facilities under army guard, he continued both to bolster the group as a counterweight to Fatah and to subordinate it by appointing his own loyalists to its command.[125] The Syrian president sustained a similar relationship with the Popular Front for the Liberation of Palestine-General Command, a Palestinian militant organization that was based in Syria and whose leader, Ahmed Jibril, reputedly did little without Assad's approval. At later junctures, Assad would also attempt to cultivate alliances with other PLO factions, such as the Popular Front for the Liberation of Palestine and the Democratic Front for the Liberation of Palestine, and likewise push them against the PLO's Fatah-affiliated leadership. Batatu sees in these maneuvers a "coincidence of the interests of Assad and those of Israel," insofar as both "shared the common ground of opposing the independent will of the Palestinian people that Arafat personified."[126]

In this context of increased Syrian regime cohesion and capacity, Israeli military strikes achieved the triadic coercion that had previously eluded them. Between August 1970 and the October 1973 War, Israel conducted twenty-four incursions into Syria, mostly targeting Syrian armed forces and Palestinian training camps.[127] Following Palestinian militants' killing of Israeli athletes at the 1972 Munich Olympics, Israel retaliated by bombing Lebanon and Syria with the largest air strikes since 1967. Echoing the strategy of prior decades, an Israeli officer explained, "the message is directed not only to the terrorists but also to the countries that harbor them."[128] Unlike prior decades, however, the central decision-maker in Damascus had the consolidated authority to receive the message and the capacity to act on it. Exercising political and military muscle, Assad quickly ordered guerrillas away from the border.[129]

January 1973 saw another clash near the Golan, during which Israel shot down thirteen Syrian fighter jets. Although Israel was concerned that Syria was rebuilding its army with Soviet aid, its escalation, Maoz writes, "was essentially aimed at forcing Damascus to curb or stop the Palestinian *fida'yi* actions."[130] It was successful. Thereafter, the Syrian army prohibited PLO groups from entering the border area or from carrying out operations into Israeli-occupied territory without prior approval.[131] Syria's relationship to the fedayeen turned a new page. Bard O'Neill summarizes: "By the spring of 1973, the [fedayeen's] general situation in terms of sanctuary and freedom of movement was not good. Though the guerrillas were still present in Syria, they were closely monitored and restricted by the government. Moreover, operations across the Syrian border and infiltration into Lebanon and Syria were reduced to insignificance."[132]

Syria hence shifted from being the commandos' main backer in the mid-1960s to a constraint on their armed activity a decade later. This shift cannot be attributed to Israeli military prowess alone. Prior to 1967, Israel retaliated against both Palestinian raids and Syrian shelling with increasingly severe assaults, yet was unsuccessful in deterring the host regime's support of nonstate actors' attacks. Israel unambiguously demonstrated its military superiority in the 1967 war and the three years that followed, yet coercion likewise continued to fail. Only after 1970 did Israeli strikes on Syria propel it to stop guerrilla groups. What changed was not Israel's actions but the strength of Syria's regime.

Comparing the situation before and after Assad's coup illustrates three mechanisms by which host regime strength mediates the effectiveness of triadic coercion. First, Assad's strengthening of state institutions increased his ability to restrict nonstate actors. In prior years, domestic volatility, intra-elite rivalries, and fragmented institutions generated opportunities for the fedayeen to acquire resources and operational autonomy. Regime consolidation curtailed internal power struggles and thereby closed these doors to the Palestinian groups seeking support. It also redoubled the army's capacity to enforce the restrictions that the authoritarian president endorsed.

Second, the stability of Assad's regime empowered it to act on controversial issues. After 1963, Syrian society's discontent, economic instability, and capital flight reached crisis proportions. Under these conditions, Ba'ath elites welcomed the Palestinian struggle as a political resource with which to deflect and dampen domestic criticism. Under Assad, authorities no longer needed the fedayeen as a political diversion. On the contrary, growing credibility at home enabled the regime to restrict the Palestinian struggle, despite the importance of that struggle with the Syrian population and the regime's own continued claims of ideological commitment to the liberation of Palestine.

Finally, regime strength enabled Assad's Syria to act in ways closer to the assumptions of realist international relations theory. Gone were the days in which every Ba'ath official acted on private interests, using the Palestinians to outmaneuver his rivals at grave risk for the Syrian state. Centralization of power rendered Syria more akin to a unitary actor with a brutally utilitarian decision-making calculus. Responding to both deterrence and compellence, he supported Palestinian operations from Lebanon and elsewhere but banned them from the Golan Heights. Given his and public opinion's support for the Palestinian struggle, he did not turn against it completely.[133] "Asad would not prevent anyone going off to fight Israel,"

Seale concluded, "but in Syria at least any such operation had to be firmly controlled and subordinated to national policy."[134]

The Assad regime thus continued to prevent fedayeen raids from the Golan Heights into Israel, despite Syria's joining forces with Egypt in another conventional war against Israel in 1973. Despite the initial success of the Syrian campaign, its subsequent defeat in the war again laid bare the exiting balance of power in the Middle East. At the same time, Assad's propaganda machine portrayed the war as a daring challenge of Israel, and thereby used it to "magnify" the president as a victorious combatant and father figure safeguarding the nation's dignity.[135] Thereafter, Assad continued to act as triadic coercion demanded. Israeli military leaders acknowledged this, as chief of staff Lieutenant General Moshe Levi expressed in a 1985 interview:

> I think that the better way to act against terrorism that originates in other countries is through the rulers of those countries. I think this is very well demonstrated along our border with Syria. In other words, beyond the framework of relations between us and the Syrians—and the Syrians, unfortunately, are not sympathetic toward us—the local regime shoulders its responsibility to prevent terrorism from that country's soil. The Syrians have observed this very carefully for 11 years now, and despite all sorts of other actions which serve to highlight the Syrian hostility toward us, these, nevertheless, do not prevent the Syrians from doing whatever is required to prevent terrorism against us from inside Syria.[136]

For Levi, the absence of nonstate attacks from Syrian territory was evidence of the success of triadic coercion. While accurate, his remarks failed to note the condition that enabled that outcome: regime strength. That Damascus came to shoulder "its responsibility to prevent terrorism" was not simply a matter of choice. It was also an outcome of its increased domestic political cohesion and infrastructural capacity.

Assad's preoccupation with averting Israeli strikes on his own territory did not discourage him from aiding nonstate attacks on Israel from other states' territories, as he judged beneficial for his or Syria's national interests. Such actions are consistent with our arguments about triadic coercion. Strong regimes that are predisposed to defiance but nonetheless deterred from directly hosting nonstate violence might seek alternative ways to act on that predisposition without incurring retaliation from the coercer state. From 1975 to 1990, Syria's actions in this regard came primarily to the fore in its entanglement in Lebanon's tumultuous civil war. What began as a standoff between leftist challengers and rightist defenders of Lebanon's sectarian political system, complicated by the PLO's armed presence in the country, descended into overlapping intersectarian, intrasectarian, and regional wars. The up-and-down fighting was an arena not only for Lebanese factions but also for Syria and Israel, which challenged each other in part through their support for or opposition to different nonstate actors. In the war's initial months, Syria's goal was to terminate the conflict, lest unrest invite Israel's intervention or a partition of Lebanon resulting in an Israel-allied Christian state. To that end, Assad attempted to mediate among warring parties and then interfered militarily using Palestinian groups under his control. In 1976, Syria, contrary to its prior loyalties, directly deployed some thirty thousand troops to side with the Maronite Phalange militia against the alliance of Lebanese leftists and PLO groups. In doing so, Syria's goals went beyond a ceasefire to aim at political and military hegemony in Lebanon.[137] Attempting to enforce a ceasefire aligned with those interests, Syria dispatched both its army and its Palestinian proxies, Sa'iqa and the PLA.[138] Syria thus showed that it continued to view nonstate actors as tools. Its primary goal was not Palestinian liberation, however, but Syrian national interests as Assad defined them.

The 1976 intervention laid the foundation for what became a Syrian occupation or domination of Lebanon that lasted until 2005. The multiparty character of the civil war complicated entanglements between Syria, nonstate actors, and Israeli coercion. This was made even more complex by the Middle East peace process coming underway at the same time. In this context, Syria's policies toward Palestinian nonstate actors were guided by two inverse logics. On the one hand, Syria promoted militancy with the goal of blocking political or diplomatic efforts that might marginalize Syria and its claims to the Golan. From the mid-1970s, Arafat and the mainstream Fatah-PLO leadership made political overtures and outreach to the United States and conciliatory Egyptian president Anwar Sadat. Assad used Palestinian factions under his influence to disrupt those political efforts.[139] He is also believed to be implicated in the assassinations of PLO representatives and Palestinian groups' international operations.[140] Syrian involvement in such tactics led the United States to designate Syria as a state sponsor of terrorism in 1979.

On the other hand, at the same time that Syria used nonstate actors in other states to obstruct peace initiatives with Israel, it also obstructed attacks that might give Israel a pretext to invade Lebanon. It thereby sought to avoid provoking Israel to carry out actions that would lead it, or its Lebanese allies, to obtain control over territory on Syria's border. However, Palestinian factions were many, diverse, and answered to various powers beside Syria. They thus continued to carry out attacks on Israel in international arenas or from South Lebanon. These included a 1978 operation in which commandos infiltrated Israel, hijacked a bus, and triggered a standoff that killed thirty-eight Israeli civilians. In retaliation, Israel carried out a one-week invasion of Lebanon that left about 1,100 Lebanese and Palestinian dead,[141] and as many as 250,000 displaced.[142] The UN deployed peacekeepers to enforce a cessation of hostilities, but violence continued from both sides of the border.[143] In 1981, another escalation in cross-border clashes between Israel and Palestinian organizations brought an American-mediated indirect ceasefire agreement, which lasted almost a year.[144]

In Israel a Likud government assumed office in 1977 and began preparing an offensive to drive the PLO from its border with Lebanon. In June 1982, the Palestinian Abu Nidal organization provided the impetus when it shot the Israeli ambassador in London. Israel responded by sending some seventy-eight thousand troops to invade Lebanon. Given Syria's military domination of Lebanon, Israel understood its operations to be a confrontation with Syria as much as with the PLO itself.[145] Israeli troops encircled Beirut, a massive show of military might that sent a powerful message to Syria. In Batatu's telling, Assad recognized that Syria had little chance of successfully confronting an Israeli force with command of the air and other material advantages. It was thus on "cool calculation of the interests of his army that he sedulously refused to be drawn into an all-out encounter with [the Israelis]" and instead "abandoned the Palestinians to their fate."[146] As Assad himself reportedly explained, "This war is not my war."[147] Israel and Syria nevertheless came to blows as Israeli forces advanced toward the Beirut-Damascus Highway, during which time the Israeli air force destroyed the Syrian air-defense system in the Bekaa Valley and downed more than eighty Syrian airplanes. On the ground, however, Syrian armored forces held their fire.[148] After three months of siege and bombardment of Beirut, the PLO abandoned its base in Lebanon and relocated to Tunisia. Israel's occupation of southern Lebanon would last until May 2000.

Thereafter, Assad continued to consolidate his control over Lebanon. Aware that Israel held him responsible for guerrilla attacks from Lebanon, Assad ordered some Palestinian fighters to relinquish weapons and halt operations.[149] At the same time, he continued to combat Arafat's pursuit of inclusion in a Middle East peace process. Assad supported an anti-Arafat rebellion within Fatah in Lebanon in 1983.[150] When Arafat survived and regained a presence in Lebanon, Assad challenged him by aiding the Shiite Lebanese movement Amal in attacking Palestinian refugee camps in Lebanon, resulting in the three-year siege known as the "War of the Camps." Apart from general antipathy toward Fatah, Assad and Amal shared the concern that the PLO's re-emergence in the South would give Israel a pretext to extend its occupation, if not intensify reprisals.[151]

Meanwhile, Syria became increasingly implicated in nonstate actors' terror attacks abroad. In the mid-1980s Syria was believed to have played a role in the hijacking of a TWA flight to Beirut, Abu Nidal's shooting attacks in the Vienna and Rome airports, the bombing of a TWA airliner over Greece, the bombing of a club in West Berlin, and attempts to bomb El-Al airliners in London and Madrid.[152] As the U.S. State Department concluded, "Damascus utilizes these groups to attack or intimidate enemies and opponents and to exert its influence in the region. Yet at the same time, it can disavow knowledge of their operations."[153] In embracing terror, Syria was challenging Israel. Yet it was simultaneously heeding Israeli coercion, insofar as it pursued covert strategies for which it could plausibly deny responsibility. Involvement in operations based abroad allowed Syria to support nonstate actors' violence without inviting the direct retaliation likely to follow attacks launched from Syrian soil.[154]

Though Israel did not carry out triadic coercion against Syria for these actions, Western governments levied punishments. Several countries ruptured diplomatic ties with Damascus and the United States and the European Economic Community imposed economic sanctions.[155] Assad's regime had the decision-making cohesion to recognize harm to Syrian national interests as well as the capacity to command a swift change of policy when he deemed appropriate. He thus responded to this diplomatic pressure and stopped using his own operatives for clandestine international attacks on civilians in 1986.[156]

The 1970s and 1980s thus saw Syria undertake a mix of policies toward nonstate violence against Israel. Assad allied with Arafat but also went to extreme lengths to try to depose him. He offered vital support and shelter to hardline Palestinian factions but also directly challenged them.[157] Underlying these seeming contradictions was a brutally consistent logic: Syria's national priorities came first. Syria would support armed groups but, deterred by threat of Israeli retaliation, would not allow them to attack across Syria's own border or otherwise jeopardize its vital interests.[158]

After 1993, the start of the Oslo peace process opened a new front of triadic coercion when Israel accused the newly created Palestinian National Authority of abetting attacks by Palestinian militants from the Palestinian territories (see chapter 5). Syria was a player in these dynamics. It denounced Oslo and supported Palestinian groups that did likewise. It thus allowed Hamas, Palestine Islamic Jihad, the Popular Front for the Liberation of Palestine, and the Popular Front for the Liberation of Palestine-General Command to maintain headquarters, hold conferences, and operate communications on Syrian soil.[159] While Syria did not openly admit to aiding these groups, it resisted pressure to act against their leaders.

At the same time, beginning in the early 1990s, Syria began a series of direct and indirect negotiations toward its own agreement with Israel. These were focused on Israel's withdrawal from Syrian territory occupied in 1967 in exchange for peace and recognition. Analysts largely agreed that Syria did not view its support for violent nonstate actors as antithetical to peace talks. Rather, it saw this support as essential in order to extract concessions from Israel and prevent it from concluding any settlement that did not meet Syria's basic demands.[160] It nevertheless continued to prevent groups from attacking Israel from Syria's own soil.

Meanwhile, a new group had emerged that would replace Palestinians as the primary nonstate actor in the triadic relationship between Israel and Syria. In the early 1980s, some Amal members and other Shiite Lebanese formed the Hezbollah movement. Syria had facilitated Iran's arming and training of Amal and would do so to an even larger extent with Hezbollah.[161] Chapter 6 explores the subsequent development of Israel's complex triadic coercion involving Hezbollah and Lebanon. For Syria, however, support for Hezbollah served a similar function to support for Palestinian groups. In aiding the Lebanese nonstate actor, a strong Assad regime warned Israel of Syria's power to challenge and disrupt political or military situations contrary to its interests.[162] "We want the Golan and we will not surrender on that," a confidant to the Syrian president later told the International Crisis Group. "Hezbollah is our best card to guarantee our interests. . . . It is our trump card to pressure Israel."[163]

Continuation and Crisis Under Bashar: Triadic Conflicts since 2000

Israel-Syria peace negotiations under U.S. stewardship gained unprecedented momentum toward conclusion of an agreement in early 2000, only to collapse in failure in March. That June, Hafez al-Assad died, and his thirty-four-year-old son, Bashar, assumed the presidency. Though the regime's cohesion and capacity remained, Bashar did not personally embody the tested power that his father had. As Perthes wrote in 2004, Bashar "is still seen as the heir to, rather than the builder of, the strong authoritarian state he presides over, and he still has to prove his strength."[164]

The transition from Hafez's iron grip to Bashar's more tentative rule had two implications for triadic conflict with Israel. First, it gave nonstate actors a greater degree of autonomy than they previously had. Damascus retained significant influence over Hezbollah due to its preponderant power over Lebanese politics until 2005 and its control over the land route through which the movement obtained weapons from Iran. Nevertheless, some cited a "new equation in the power relationship" between Syria and Hezbollah, especially given the latter's increased political prestige and territorial control after Israel's withdrawal from South Lebanon in May 2000 (discussed in chapter 6).[165] When Hezbollah resumed military activity against Israel after September 2000, it did so on its own initiative, not Syrian orders. Bashar did not intervene to curtail Hezbollah, stating that it was neither Syria's role nor within its power to stop them. "We keep explaining that we do not direct or control Hizballah activity, and make no decisions whatsoever in these matters. . . . We have no responsibility for any activity it carries out," he told *Der Spiegel* in 2001.[166]

Second, the young president's less solid footing generated new incentives for him to champion nonstate actors' militancy with the goal of boosting his own legitimacy. Assad thus chose rhetoric that cultivated his image as a defender of resistance against Israel, distinct from other Arab heads of state, who he implied were quiescent before American dictates. Perthes dubbed Assad's strategy a "calculated populism" that aimed to win popularity among youth as a source of political leverage at home and abroad.[167] Observers concluded that Assad was seeking to take advantage of nonstate militancy from Lebanon and the Palestinian territories to demonstrate his responsiveness to Arab public opinion and "promote both his own status and Syria's regional prestige."[168] At the same time he repeatedly signaled his interest in resuming talks with Israel that could lead to a return of the Golan. Assad's ability to launch a bold initiative toward a peace process, however, was constrained by the still insecure state of his rule.[169] Regime weakness thus both curbed Assad's ability to make diplomatic outreach and increased his need to support nonstate actors.

Israel's response to border violations from Syria-supported organizations varied in accord with their intensity and Israel's own changes in government. Syria generally responded to Israeli actions with tough announcements but no military action.[170] Under U.S. pressure after September 11 and the subsequent "War on Terror," Syria took limited steps such as closing some Palestinian groups' media offices and, reportedly, helping persuade Hamas and Islamic Jihad to agree to a ceasefire with Israel in 2003.[171] That year, Israeli planes struck a camp near Damascus, which Israel charged was a training base for Palestinian militants. This was not triadic coercion because it did not aim at the assets of a host state. Still, a strike near the Syrian capital was an understood challenge. Syrian officials announced that they were capable of avenging the raid but opted to "exercise restraint" and instead filed a complaint with the UN Security Council.[172] Restraint aside, Syria did not fully comply with Israeli and American demands that it end support for Palestinian militants and deny them shelter inside Syria. To do so, the International Crisis Group reasoned, "would in [Syrian officials'] eyes be a humiliating capitulation." It would also relinquish Syria's principle source of leverage in any eventual negotiations with Israel. Furthermore, in a reversal of the assumptions of triadic coercion, maintaining ties to nonstate actors was useful for Syria to deter Israel from attacking it.[173]

For these reasons, Assad, in addition to expressing support for hardline Palestinian groups, continued to allow their leaders to reside in Syria, organize conferences, and even hold press conferences in governmental venues.[174] Israel and the United States continued to accuse Assad of involvement in terrorist financing and aiding arms shipments to militants in the

West Bank and Gaza Strip.[175] At the same time, the limits of Syria's power over Hezbollah became apparent. When Assad urged restraint for fear of being punished by the United States after September 11, Hezbollah averted the constraint by carrying out attacks without informing Syria in advance.[176] Then, in 2005, mass demonstrations in Lebanon forced Syria to end nearly three decades of hegemonic presence there (see chapter 6). This further curtailed Syria's direct power over Hezbollah as well as Israel's inclination to hold Damascus responsible for attacks emanating from Lebanon.[177]

The incomplete success of triadic coercion—where Syria did not allow nonstate actors to attack Israel from its own territory but supported them from elsewhere—continued to hold as long as the regime in Damascus remained fairly strong. Yet as Albert Hourani presciently wrote in his 1986 forward to Seale's account of interstate competition in Syria in the 1950s, "It would be rash to prophesy . . . that the apparent strength of the regime would be real and lasting, and that Syria would never again become a body over which others struggled."[178] Regime strength began to collapse with the uprisings that swept the Arab world in early 2011. When nonviolent protests erupted across Syria, Assad pledged to fight them with whatever means necessary. Should creating tension on the Israeli border offer such a means, Assad's regime might consider that too. Rami Makhluf, Assad's cousin and the country's most powerful business tycoon, eluded to such possibilities when he told the *New York Times* in early May 2011, "If there is no stability here, there is no way there will be stability in Israel. . . . Don't put a lot of pressure on the president, don't push Syria to do anything it is not happy to do."[179]

A few days later, on the anniversary of the start of the 1948 War, Palestinian refugees in Lebanon, Syria, and Gaza marched to their respective borders with Israel. These young activists had connected online, inspired in part by the regional spirit of civil resistance.[180] Those in Syria also appeared to act with encouragement and aid from the Syrian state.[181] They breached the border and moved toward the village of Majdal Shams in the Golan Heights. There they threw stones at Israeli troops, who opened fire and killed thirteen people.[182] The following month, on the anniversary of the 1967 War, Palestinians from Syria again attempted to scale the fence at the Golan, during which Israeli forces shot and killed twenty-three. In Itamar Rabinovich's opinion, those events "were clearly not a spontaneous

Palestinian act but a measure taken, or at least supported, by a beleaguered regime."[183]

The Assad regime became more beleaguered as the Syrian's popular uprising militarized and the government lost control over swaths of the country, including along the border with Israel. Between 2012 and 2015, the war in Syria gave rise to several dozen clashes with Israel. These took three major forms. First, stray bullets or mortar shells occasionally landed on the Israeli side of the border and drones or jets entered Israeli airspace.[184] Israel's response to such projectiles was usually restrained, though it did not hesitate to shoot down aircraft. These actions aimed at asserting territorial sovereignty while not escalating hostilities or becoming a party to the Syrian conflict.[185]

Second, on a few occasions, fire from the Syrian side of the border resulted, deliberately or not, in Israeli casualties. Under these circumstances Israel launched strong reprisals, such as when it bombed nine Syrian military targets after a Syrian explosive killed a teenager in the Golan.[186] Here Israel sought to send the message that Israeli fatalities were a red line not to be crossed. In attempting to use triadic coercion in these situations, Israel was replicating a strategy that had been effective against a strong Syrian regime since the early 1970s. After 2011, however, the regime of Bashar al-Assad no longer had the cohesion or capacity that Bashar's father had wielded for three decades. The likelihood was thus exceedingly slim that Israeli pressure on Assad would compel him to assert control over nonstate actors near the Israeli border. A regime rejected by large swaths of its own population and unable to hold its country together was simply too weak to act according to the demands of its state adversary next door. In targeting retaliation at the Syrian state, Israel thus again demonstrated its chronic oversight: a lack of attention to host regime strength as the crucial factor mediating the effectiveness of triadic coercion.

Third, and most gravely, Israel carried out several missile and air strikes on Hezbollah interests in Syria. Though some were unclaimed or had disputed targets, most aimed at weapons caches. In January 2015 Israel carried out an attack on Quneitra in the Syrian Golan, reportedly targeting lower-level Hezbollah fighters. Instead, among the six people it killed were Hezbollah commanders, the son of Hezbollah's late military leader, and an Iranian general.[187] Hezbollah retaliated with rockets that killed two Israeli soldiers in the Golan, after which both Israel and Hezbollah signaled that they did not seek further escalation.[188] This incident was emblematic of how Israel's triadic relationship with Syria and Hezbollah was evolving into a direct bilateral relationship with Hezbollah in which the Assad regime was an increasingly irrelevant player. Far from territory under a cohesive and capable host state, southern Syria offered "near-anarchic conditions" that some analysts believed Hezbollah and other nonstate actors might utilize against Israel. Phillip Smyth explained: "Before Syria's brutal civil war, it was Hafez and Bashar al-Assad who used Lebanon, and often Hezbollah, as a front to exact their military goals against Israel. Now the tables have turned, and it is Hezbollah and its masters in Tehran who can choose areas of Syria to use against Israel."[189]

These developments continued as the regime in Damascus continued to weaken. In March 2015, the United Nations reported that half the Syrian population had been displaced, some 80 percent lived in poverty, and economic losses topped $202 billion, or 383 percent of the prewar GDP.[190] In July 2015, Assad publicly admitted that his army was suffering shortages of manpower,[191] a vital incapacity that invited intensified foreign interventions either to collapse that regime or to salvage it. In this context Hezbollah became increasingly present on the ground in Syria, and some read its maneuvers as seeking to establish a new front with Israel that would stretch contiguously from Lebanon to the southern tip of the Golan.[192] New nonstate actors that emerged in the context of the Syrian war, some affiliated with Salafi extremism, posed still other questions about Assad's ability to impose state sovereignty on the border. As of this writing, the war in and over Syria remains tumultuous and highly uncertain. Yet one thing is predictable: to the degree that the Syrian regime remains weak and beleaguered, Israel ought not target coercion against that state in the belief that military threats and pressure will somehow bring it to control nonstate actors on its territory.

Conclusion

Investigation of the Syrian case, in conjunction with analysis of Egypt in chapter 3, illustrates how the dynamics of triadic coercion differ from conventional state-to-state encounters. In Syria, as in Egypt, a weak regime not only limited authorities' abilities to act against nonstate actors within their borders but also generated domestic motivations for supporting such actors. In this context, Israel's attempts to prevent nonstate actors' attacks by punishing host states did not have the desired effect. At some times, retaliation was irrelevant because host regimes' weakness forced them to prioritize domestic concerns over external pressures. At other times, retaliation was counterproductive because it only further weakened the regime's political and physical capacity. As host regimes institutionalized legitimate, central authority, however, they became both more able and more willing to act in ways that put their own state interests above all else.

Syria illustrates these patterns. Before the 1963 Ba'ath coup, the Israel-Syria conflict was primarily bilateral and centered on conflicting claims to land and water rights. From 1963 to 1970, the Ba'ath regime in Damascus actively aided Palestinian guerrilla groups, but its motivations for doing so stemmed largely from the domestic realm, including its internal problems and rivalries. Israeli threats and strikes had little deterrent effect on a regime beleaguered by economic crisis, social unrest, and interelite divisions. As the regime consolidated institutionally and politically under Assad, Syria obtained both the cohesion and the capacity to restrict guerrilla forces. Israeli coercion showed Assad that support of nonstate actors was, in Daniel Byman's words, a "two-edged sword": It allowed him to sustain ideological opposition to Israel but also carried the risk of provoking a potentially disastrous escalation. Assad's challenge, like Nasser before him, was hence "to control as well as exploit the Palestinian cause."[193] For Assad, the solution was to support, sometimes covertly, nonstate actors' attacks on Israel from other territories while barring them from attacking from Syria. Triadic coercion was thus successful in this period, though not fully. Israel achieved its primary goal of constraining nonstate attacks across the borders of the targeted host state. However, the coercer did not prevent a host, predisposed to defiance, from supporting nonstate actors' operations elsewhere.

The regime in Damascus, as that in Cairo, came under dramatic threat in 2011 when its own population launched mass protests demanding its ouster. As the regime's cohesion and capacity weakened, its political authority and territorial control did likewise. Bashar al-Assad's ongoing war for survival was the context in which nonstate actors established unprecedented autonomy in areas in which state sovereignty had collapsed. These groups have not, as of this writing, targeted significant attacks on Israel. Should they do so, it would be unwise for Israel to direct retaliation against the beleaguered Syrian government. If it came to do so, it would not be acting upon lessons from prior triadic coercion successes and failures as much as assumptions and preconceptions detached from that historical record. The next chapters explore how such a strategic culture encouraging triadic coercion hardened toward the end of the twentieth century, and with what consequences.

CHAPTER 5

Israel and the Palestinian Authority Since 1993

Strategic Culture in Asymmetric Conflict

Many factors, from the grassroots Intifada that began in the Occupied Territories in 1987 to the U.S.-led Gulf War against Iraq, pushed Israel and the PLO to seek a negotiated settlement in the early 1990s. In September 1993, the parties ratified the Oslo Accords and agreed to engage in negotiations toward the conclusion of a peace settlement by May 1999. As a part of these commitments, Israel recognized the PLO and transferred control of parts of the West Bank and Gaza Strip to a new Palestinian self-governing apparatus, the Palestinian National Authority (PA).

The PA is distinct from the other host states that we investigate. First, the PA has never been a sovereign state. It was an outgrowth of Palestinian revolutionary groups and the PLO—the same entities that played the role of nonstate actor in the triadic conflicts examined in prior chapters. The PA's interconnections with Fatah, embodied in Yasser Arafat's simultaneous leadership of Fatah, the PLO, and the PA, further blurred the lines between government and movement. These overlaps complicate our analysis of the PA as a host to nonstate actors rather than as a nonstate actor itself. It also complicates assessment of the PA's cooperative or defiant predispositions, as the Palestinian leadership straddled the gap between partner to a peace process with Israel and engine of a struggle for self-determination yet to be achieved. Finally, the hybrid character of the PA complicates evaluations of its strength or weakness as a regime. Its cohesion and capacity were fundamentally limited with respect to territorial control and institutional competencies. Yet it remained more powerful than other opposition groups operating in the Palestinian territories, which enabled it to repress them at times.

We wrestle with these complications, as have both Palestinians and Israelis since 1993. Applying our concept of triadic coercion, we treat the PA as a host regime because it endeavored to act as an internationally recognized government and was treated by Israel as the constituted authority responsible for security in areas it administered. On this basis, Israel sometimes used threats and force against the PA to deter it from abetting violence by nonstate militants or to compel it to act against them. Critics of these policies charge that Israel may have had tactical successes but did not achieve its strategic goals.[1] Some attribute the strategic failure to Israel's focus on the conflict's military-security dimensions at the expense of its political dimensions.[2] Others assign the blame to Israel's reliance on severe repression in the face of the second Intifada that began in 2000.[3]

Our analysis resonates with these points but also shows how the ineffectiveness of Israel's policies was the predictable outcome of triadic coercion applied against weak regimes. More than in chapters 3 and 4, however, we go beyond examination of the effects of triadic coercion and devote greater scrutiny to the ideas and decision-making processes that drive a coercer state's use of triadic coercion in the first place. We adopt that focus in this chapter because Israel's triadic conflict with the PA represents a turning point in the development of strategic culture. Increasingly in the late 1990s, and especially since the start of the second Intifada, Israel's drive to punish host states for the actions of nonstate actors demonstrated a shift from the "logic of consequences" toward a "logic of appropriateness." That is, the rationale propelling Israel's use of triadic coercion appeared to be based less in strategic calculations about the utility of alternative choices for reducing adversaries' attacks than in a moralistic conviction about the intrinsic value of actions in pursuit of deterrence, independent of their actual impact. Additionally, Israel revealed a lack of nuance in identifying the targets of coercion, blurring important distinctions among actors into a monolithic obsession with "enemy consciousness."[4] These beliefs had influenced Israeli policies before the 1990s, and utilitarian calculations did not completely disappear thereafter. Yet never before had strategic culture, as opposed to strategic rationality, become so prominent in Israeli political discourse and military behavior.

We probe the sources and effects of this strategic culture in Israel's triadic conflict with the PA, distinguishing between four periods. From 1993–1995, Israel did not use triadic coercion as a strategy against the PA. Labor Party governments committed to the peace process generally regarded the PA's predisposition as cooperative, not defiant. It thereby obtained a high level of partnership with a host regime against nonstate actors. Nevertheless, Israel's attitude shifted as militant groups began carrying out suicide bombings in 1994, laying the foundations for subsequent changes.

The second period begins with a record rise of suicide bombings in 1996, when the Israeli government turned to "closure" policies limiting Palestinian freedom of movement and other threats to compel the PA to act against nonstate actors. This use of triadic coercion did not entail military force but did impose costs that pushed the Palestinian leadership to crack down on opposition groups. This was an instance of triadic coercion success critically enabled by a Palestinian public opinion hopeful that the peace process would deliver statehood. As public opinion lost that optimism, however, the likelihood of sustaining triadic coercion dwindled.

During the third period, from 1996–1999, a new Likud government came to view the PA as a foe. That view intensified when PA police officers turned weapons against Israel during events sometimes referred to as the "tunnel clashes." Thereafter, a sense of betrayal and outrage came to infuse Israeli leaders' assessment of the PA's complicity in violence. In this context, Israel appeared to elevate retaliation in pursuit of deterrence to a goal in and of itself, rather than a means for increasing national security.

These ideas intensified during the final period, ensuing after the Camp David II summit and the militarization of Palestinians' popular uprising. Israel's endorsement of harsh punishments against the PA were fueled by indignation with what it perceived as Arafat's duplicity and the conviction that Israel must prove its strength and restore its "deterrent posture." The second Intifada hardened these assumptions and attitudes—that lost triadic coercion must be restored with preponderant shows of force—as pillars of Israel's strategic culture. That strategic culture continued to shape Israel's policies after Arafat's death and Mahmoud Abbas's election as PA president in 2005.

This chapter traces this history in six parts. The first begins by giving an overview of trends in Israeli and Palestinian violence and some of the complexities of the PA as a host regime. The next four sections, respectively, examine four periods in Israel's triadic relations with the PA. The final section concludes with a discussion about the empirical and analytical significance of this case. Throughout this chapter we give particular attention to Israel's strategic culture and the critical junctures, namely the 1996 tunnel crisis and the 2000 start of the second Intifada, where we see a crystallization of its contribution to a severe, forceful, and moralistic endorsement of triadic coercion.

Triadic Relations with a Nonstate Host

The Oslo process yielded both historic breakthroughs and acts of bad faith. Israel redeployed from parts of the West Bank and Gaza Strip and recognized the PA as a new self-governing apparatus in those areas. Yet it also imposed new restrictions on Palestinian freedom of movement, confiscated tens of thousands of acres for settlement expansion, doubled its settler population by the year 2000, and paved approximately 250 miles of bypass roads in the West Bank and Gaza Strip for exclusive Israeli use.[5] Israel carried out interim withdrawals in a limited and unilateral way, giving credence to critics who charged that Oslo was a vehicle for denying Palestinians sovereignty more than granting it.[6]

The PLO renounced violence, recognized Israel, and coordinated security, economic, and other matters with its former enemy on a nearly daily basis. Nonetheless, Palestinians' acts of violence claimed more Israeli lives during the six-year period after the Oslo Accords (258) than before it (160).[7] The number of Palestinians killed by Israelis, however, continued to dwarf the number of Israelis killed by Palestinians (see figure 5.1).

From the signing of the Oslo "Declaration of Principles" in 1993 until the start of the second Intifada in 2000, Palestinians carried out 149 lethal and nonlethal armed acts against Israel. Of these, 67 were perpetrated by unidentified suspects, and 66 were claimed by the Hamas movement or, to a lesser extent, Islamic Jihad. About one-third of the latter were suicide attacks (see table 5.1).

Established in Gaza in the 1980s, Hamas and Islamic Jihad were not members of the PLO. They professed Islamist ideologies different from the PLO's secular nationalism. They swore opposition to the Oslo process and boycotted the PA, which they viewed as an Israeli instrument and a traitor to the Palestinian cause. When these Islamist groups carried out attacks

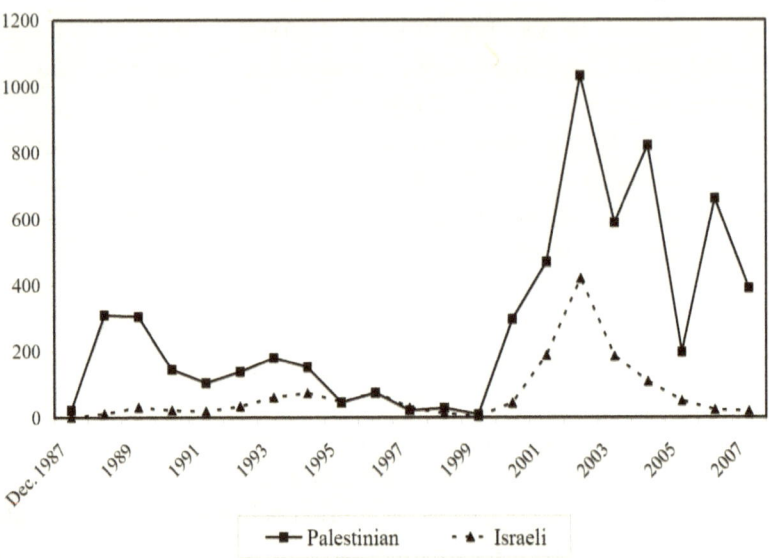

Figure 5.1 Israeli and Palestinian fatalities from the beginning of the first Intifada through 2008.
Source: B'Tselem: The Israeli Information Center for Human Rights in the Occupied Territories.

against Israel, they did so not only autonomously of the official Palestinian leadership but also as a challenge to it. They thereby generated a triadic conflict in which Palestinian opposition groups were the nonstate actors, the PA played the role of host government, and Israel again acted as coercer state.

This triadic conflict differed from others in the Israeli experience. As the entity governing Palestinian population centers in the West Bank and Gaza Strip, the PA could be considered a host regime. Yet it was not a state. The Oslo Accords did not mention Palestinian statehood, and Rabin's government remarked on several occasions that it did not support the creation of a Palestinian state.[8] In the absence of sovereignty, Palestinian politics after 1993 retained the contours and modalities of a self-determination movement, and one with a long history of political fragmentation.[9] Consequently the Palestinian leadership had to balance its interest in confronting internal challengers and external threats with its still elusive goal of attaining statehood. Moreover, the PA's power vis-à-vis non-PA militants and opposition groups rested on relations of bargaining rather than on imposition of decisions backed by "a monopoly of the legitimate use of physical force

TABLE 5.1
Suicide attacks, September 13, 1993–December 31, 2006

Year	Attacks in Israel (in West Bank/ Gaza Strip)	Killed (Injured)	Group responsible
Sept. 13–Dec. 31, 1993	0 (3)	0 (1)	Hamas (2); Islamic Jihad (1)
1994	4 (1)	38 (145)	Hamas (4); Islamic Jihad (1)
1995	3 (2)	37 (153)	Hamas (2); Islamic Jihad (2); Unidentified (1)
1996	4 (0)	57 (216)	Hamas (3); Islamic Jihad (1)
1997	3 (0)	24 (410)	Hamas (2); Unknown (1)
1998	1 (1)	3 (28)	Islamic Jihad (1); Unknown (1)
1999	0 (0)	0	——
Jan. 1–Sept. 28, 2000	0 (0)	0	——
Sept. 29–Dec. 31, 2000	1 (1)	0 (6)	Islamic Jihad (2)
2001	23 (6)	87 (1,061)	Hamas (16); Islamic Jihad (8); Joint (2); Unidentified (2)
2002	41 (6)	217 (1,604)	Hamas (11); Islamic Jihad (11); Al-Aqsa Martyrs Brigade (20); PFLP (3); Unidentified (2)
2003	17 (6)	137 (740)	Hamas (9); Islamic Jihad (4); Al-Aqsa Martyrs Brigade (3); PFLP (1); Joint (3); Unidentified (2)
2004	6 (7)	54 (311)	Hamas (1); Al-Aqsa Martyrs Brigade (4); PFLP (2); Joint (4); Unidentified (1)

(continued)

TABLE 5.1 (continued)

Year	Attacks in Israel (in West Bank/ Gaza Strip)	Killed (Injured)	Group responsible
2005	5 (8)	31 (241)	Hamas (3); Islamic Jihad (6); Al-Aqsa Martyrs Brigade (1); Unidentified (3)
2006	3 (5)	16 (76)	Hamas (1); Islamic Jihad (3); Al-Aqsa Martyrs Brigade (1); Joint (1); Unidentified (2)

Source: Mohammed Hafez, "Palestinian Violent Events Database," Naval Postgraduate School, Monterey, Calif. Collected between 2004 and 2006 with a grant from the U.S. Institute of Peace.

within a given territory."[10] Further complicating this situation, the PA was itself inextricably intertwined with nonstate actors that had pioneered armed struggle against Israel, namely the PLO (the recognized representative of the Palestinian people) and Fatah (the faction that had historically led the PLO). That Arafat stood at the head of all three bodies blurred the lines between them.[11]

In this context, both the PA and its Palestinian rivals were guided and constrained by public opinion. Our study of Egypt and Syria identified periods of regime strength that allowed both Nasser and Assad to act autonomously from their citizenry and carry out unpopular policies. While such independence is possible in a state with a strong regime, it is unlikely in a national movement, where the ultimate source of power lies in the ability to claim to represent a people and their cause. Israel's triadic coercion policies usually underestimated the importance of public opinion as a key arbiter in Palestinian politics. Palestinian organizations vying for power rarely did. In general, Palestinian support for violence decreased as confidence in the peace process increased, and vice versa.[12]

Compounding the complexity of politics in a factionalized movement was the difficulty of deciphering the true calculations of its leader. Facing Arafat, Israelis wavered between hope and distrust. The PA president insisted that he was doing his utmost to fulfill his commitment to stop violence but lacked the capacity to eliminate it completely. Most Israelis doubted his honesty.¹³ They judged that Arafat took measures against Islamist opposition groups at some times, but, at other times, he implicitly or explicitly gave them a "green light" to carry out attacks.¹⁴ According to this view, Arafat was not committed to peace as much as hedging his bets. If he calculated it to be expedient, he turned a blind eye to militant groups, feigned ignorance, and then tried to exploit their violence for political gain. For Israel, the uncertainty surrounding the Palestinian leaders' intentions created questions regarding the optimal approach to triadic conflict: should Israel support the PA as a partner and pressure it to take action against non-state actors or should it circumvent Arafat and instead undertake its own unilateral efforts against violent groups?

Debates about the sincerity of Arafat's commitment to fighting terror frequently focused on the person of the Palestinian leader. This overestimated Arafat's power. Fundamental regime weakness limited his impact as an individual, regardless of his predispositions. It consistently mediated the effectiveness of Israel's policies toward the PA in general and of triadic coercion in particular.

From Bilateral Partnership to Triadic Coercion, 1993–1996

The first years of the Oslo peace process saw a gradual shift in Israel's strategy in its triadic conflict with the PA. From 1993 until February 1996, Labor governments under Yitzhak Rabin and Shimon Peres attempted to cooperate with the PA leadership while directly combatting violence from non-PA groups.¹⁵ Rabin's initial approach was encapsulated in his famous declaration, "We have to fight terror as if there were no peace talks, and we have to pursue peace as if there were no terror."¹⁶ On the one hand, Israel facilitated the establishment of a PA security apparatus that it hoped, in Daniel Byman's words, would serve as "an arm of Israel's police and intelligence services."¹⁷ Israel thus placed onto the PA the primary onus of blocking any threats to Israeli security from territories that the PA administered. As Rabin declared, "The fundamental responsibility for preventing the coordination of . . . suicide operations . . . belongs to the Palestinian Authority."¹⁸

On the other hand, Israel reserved the autonomy to fight Palestinian militants on its own. In areas under its control, Israel made arrests, imposed curfews, demolished houses, and carried out other measures that led some to judge that the basic structure of the occupation was unchanged, if not even reinforced.[19] Israel conducted violent interrogations of detainees that human rights groups judged to be torture.[20] It also carried out assassinations, such as that of Islamic Jihad secretary general Fathi Shiqaqi in 1995 and explosives expert Yahya Ayyash in 1996. Israel also imposed "closure," or restrictions on the movement of people and goods into, out of, and between the West Bank, Gaza Strip, and East Jerusalem and into Israel proper.[21] Closure varied in severity from checkpoints that obstructed travel and the requirement of permits to enter Israel to "total closure," or sealing off of Palestinian communities after attacks. PA territories were under total closure for nearly one-third of each year between 1993 and 1996, resulting in devastating economic losses.[22]

Beyond this, the Labor government also used the promise of peace dividends to incentivize Arafat to crack down on militant groups. Using a similar logic, it withheld those dividends, such as by halting or delaying territorial withdrawals, after militants' attacks. For example, Rabin postponed the scheduled opening of a "free passage" between Gaza and Jericho after a Hamas attack in August 1994, saying that Palestinian self-rule would not be expanded until the PA made "a serious effort" to curb such attacks.[23] He also suspended talks with Arafat after Hamas's October 1994 kidnapping of Israeli corporal Nachson Wachsman.[24] Though Israel was not applying triadic coercion in these instances, its strategy followed a similar logic insofar as it assumed that pressure on the Palestinian government was the key to stopping opposition groups. Israel acted on the belief that Arafat's PA had the cohesion and capacity to impose its will on any Palestinian actor. This neglected the PA's weakness as a regime as well as how that weakness affected militants' violence against Israel.

The first element of the PA's weak capacity was its lack of territorial control. Israel redeployed from Jericho and parts of Gaza in 1994. In September 1995 the Taba Agreement (Oslo II) mandated Israel's further redeployment from Palestinian towns and villages in the West Bank. It divided that territory into Area "A," under the PA's civilian and security oversight; Area "B," in which security matters were under joint Palestinian-Israeli control; and Area "C," where security matters were under full Israeli control. By mid-2000, however, the PA controlled only the 17.2 percent of the West Bank that was in Area A as well as only 66–80 percent of the Gaza Strip. The West Bank territory under full or partial PA control was comprised of 227 noncontiguous areas, most of which were smaller than two square kilometers and separated by Israeli checkpoints. The PA's territories in the Gaza Strip were divided into three enclaves that Israel could isolate from each other.[25]

Incomplete control over territory limited both the PA's ability to fight militant groups and its incentives to do so. In December 1995, PA and Hamas leaders held talks in Cairo and reached an understanding by which Hamas agreed to allow the PA to continue with peace negotiations and the PA agreed to not forcibly disarm Hamas. According to Boaz Ganor, the PA demanded that Hamas not carry out attacks from Area A but made no such demands with regard to Area B and Area C.[26] Israel saw this as duplicitous, as it meant that Arafat would ignore Hamas's recruitment, fundraising, and leadership in PA-controlled areas as long as cells launched attacks from elsewhere. From the PA's perspective, however, such geographical distinctions were reasonable. As one PA official reportedly said, "We see it as sufficient to oblige Hamas not to embarrass the PA, which is responsible for security in the areas it has received."[27] From this perspective, if Israel wanted the PA to bear the burden of policing all of the Palestinian territories, then it should transfer them to its oversight. Yet as long as the PA's territorial control remained truncated, it considered Israel's security expectations to be unrealistic.

The second element of the PA's weak capacity was institutional. Though establishment of the PA was an institutional advance for the movement of a stateless people, its capacities remained severely limited for a regime expected to carry out state-like functions. Moreover, anti-Oslo violence started even before the PA began its process of institutional development. Hamas and Islamic Jihad attempted four suicide bombings in 1993, though all failed.[28] In February 1994, Jewish settler Baruch Goldstein opened fire in Hebron's Ibrahimi Mosque, killing 29 Palestinian worshippers and wounding 150.[29] In April 1994, Hamas carried out its first lethal bus bombing inside Israel, claiming that it was to avenge Goldstein's killings. The cycle of Israeli-Palestinian violence had thus already taken off before the PA was created by the May 1994 "Gaza-Jericho Agreement," and Arafat returned to Palestinian soil two months later. Thereafter, violence continued to outpace the PA's development of institutional competencies. When Wachsman was kidnapped in October 1994, for example, Rabin insisted that the PA locate him. The PA "cracked down hard" by arresting Hamas leaders and blocking Hamas demonstrations.[30] Though it demonstrated the will to comply with Israeli dictates, the PA lacked the capacity to do so effectively. It was hence the better-prepared Shin Bet, acting on the ground in the West Bank, that ultimately uncovered Wachsman's whereabouts.

Facing these developments, Israel did not always distinguish between the limits of the PA's capacity and what many Israeli security leaders saw as the limits of its cooperative predisposition. They suggested that PA security forces, given their own organic linkages to society, possessed significant ability to gather the most crucial resource for counterterrorism: intelligence. They criticized the PA for failing to act on that information or to forward it to Israel. More gravely, it accused the PA of failing to act on intelligence that Israel relayed to it.[31] The PA, for its part, insisted that its security services were still new and untrained, and that it needed time to build. It also noted that many of its efforts were to no avail. In 1995 the PA arrested hundreds of Islamist militants, confiscated arms held by citizens, and disarmed suspect police officers—yet attacks continued.[32] For example, the PA carried out dozens of raids to capture Yahya Ayyash but was unable to uncover his hiding place in Gaza.[33]

Another aspect of the PA's weak institutional capacity was the fact that real authority in the PA, like the PLO, was concentrated in the person of Arafat more than institutionalized in law.[34] This was compounded by Arafat's use of tactics of "divide and rule," most notably by his creation of eleven ambiguously defined police and intelligence forces and his appointment of rival elites as commanders. The result was a PA characterized by infighting at various levels and a personalization of power on top.[35] The limits of this substitute for strong institutions would become apparent in the second Intifada.

A final element of the PA's weak capacity was social. The Palestinian self-governing apparatus gained authority over social forces due to its constitution as a political entity grounded in Palestinian society and legitimated by presidential and parliamentary elections in 1996. Nonetheless, Palestinians' support for Arafat's gamble on the peace process was ultimately based on hopes that it would deliver statehood and economic recovery. Neither expectation was fulfilled. Rather, Israel's continued control over Palestinian land, water, and movement, in addition to new restrictions on labor in Israel, caused further economic decline. Unemployment soared from 7 percent before 1993 to 20 percent thereafter, and up to 60 percent when Israel imposed total closure.[36] Closure resulted in annual economic losses of 11 to 18 percent of GNP in the West Bank and 31 to 40 percent in the Gaza

Strip, according to World Bank estimates.[37] By the year 2000, per capita income levels were about 10 percent below what they were before the peace process began. At least 20 percent of the population was below the poverty line.[38]

Against this backdrop, new sources of socioeconomic tension within Palestinian society were all the more vexing for ordinary people. PA-granted monopolies and Israel-awarded passage through checkpoints increased the gap between haves and have-nots. Many of those raised under occupation felt alienated by PLO personnel returning from exile, sometimes dubbed "Tunisians."[39] Arafat used various means to elicit deference to his rule despite popular discontent. However, some of those tactics entrenched institutional vulnerabilities that would undermine the PA's regime capacity over the long run. Sweeping neopatrimonial distribution of jobs and benefits helped secure loyalists and co-opt critics but also wasted revenues and created resentment of corruption.[40] Intimidation and repression curtailed some opposition. But human rights groups decried grossly unfair trials, torture of detainees, deaths in custody, and rushed executions.[41]

Many Palestinians voiced disappointment that their decades of grassroots activism and sacrifices yielded a regime that was as authoritarian and unaccountable as others in the region. Israel was aware of PA corruption and abuses; it controlled a large portion of PA funds and arguably diverted them to Arafat purposefully so he could use them as necessary to control violence and marginalize Hamas.[42] Rabin famously remarked that Arafat would be more effective than Israel in fighting terrorism because he would not be burdened, as the Israeli government was, by a Supreme Court or the Israeli Association for Human Rights. Israel's stance aided the short-term consolidation of the PA. In prioritizing security over democracy and good governance, however, Israel became complicit in the PA's flaws and vulnerabilities.

In addition to its weak institutional, territorial, and social capacities, the PA lacked internal cohesion.[43] Hamas's creation of a network of social services and reputation for honesty made it a formidable opposition force, and its rejectionism increased its appeal among those who opposed the peace process.[44] Apart from competition with Hamas, Fatah also suffered its own internal divisions, often depicted as a split between the "old guard" of returnee PLO elites and a "young guard" who had been raised in the Occupied Territories and served at the forefront of the first Intifada, but who had not been rewarded with power within the PA.[45] As the peace process wore on, these younger aspirants criticized the futility of continued negotiations under the existent framework. Many were associated with the loose network of grassroots activists called Tanzim ("Organization"), informally headed by West Bank Fatah secretary-general Marwan Barghouti.[46]

These political splits complicated the PA's ability to act against opposition groups, and likewise complicated Israel's ability to differentiate between government and opposition actors. The political system authorized by Oslo was premised upon Islamist groups' marginalization, if not their elimination. For Hamas and Islamic Jihad, therefore, the Oslo Accords were not only a treasonous surrender but also a threat to their political existence.[47] In that context, carrying out attacks on Israel was both Islamists' way of rejecting negotiations and a way of warning the PA not to destroy them.[48] Triadic coercion against the PA did not alter these motivations. Israel pressured the PA to suppress Hamas. Paradoxically, that suppression encouraged Hamas to attack Israel as a means of fighting the PA. The communiqués that Hamas and the Islamic Jihad issued after suicide bombings were directed to the PA explicitly, threatening it not to collaborate with Israel by arresting their cadres and attacking their institutions.[49]

Triadic coercion could perhaps influence Hamas's Gaza-based leadership; living under the PA and aware of society's longing for calm, these leaders were susceptible to Israeli pressure on Arafat that resulted in Arafat's pressure on Hamas. However, triadic coercion did not have such direct impact on Hamas leaders based in Jordan and Syria.[50] The latter controlled the movement's financial resources, decision-making, and military brigades.[51] It was believed that this external leadership effectively vetoed a ceasefire agreement that Gaza-based leaders had reached with the PA in summer 1995.[52] Hamas's external leaders thereafter ordered some bombings without the knowledge of their Gaza colleagues, if not against their wishes.[53]

The PA was not a state able to impose policies on its population as fully constituted states can. As such, public opinion played an accentuated role in mediating the Palestinian government's decision-making in general, and its responses to Israel's attempted triadic coercion in particular. In facing off against each other, both the PA and Hamas were pushed, or restrained, by popular sentiment. In the context of the national struggle, political actors' main source of credibility remained the popular perception that they were advancing the cause of liberation. Arafat understood that he would face considerable backlash if, in fighting opposition groups, he appeared to be a lackey doing Israel's security work. "This is a real dilemma," one PA elite explained. "If we adhere strictly to the agreement and even just round up suspects, we are jeopardizing our legitimacy among our people."[54] This became especially the case as confidence in the peace process declined.

Though Hamas opposed the peace process, it was loathe to be seen as obstructionist whenever public support for negotiations ran high.[55] Hamas thus typically turned to violence when it anticipated that the public would reward it for such tactics. The Goldstein massacre appalled Palestinians; when Hamas responded with a suicide bombing, it did so in the expectation that such action would meet with broad popular backing, which it did.[56] Likewise, when Israel assassinated Ayyash, hundreds of thousands of Palestinians participated in mourning demonstrations. Emboldened by this reaction, together Hamas or Islamic Jihad launched four suicide attacks in Israeli cities between February 25 and March 4, 1996, leaving 59 dead and 214 injured.

These later attacks backfired for Hamas. Israel responded by imposing its most severe closure yet. In addition, faced with the possibility that the Likud would triumph in Israel's upcoming elections, the incumbent Labor government and the United States pressured Arafat to repress the opposition. Complying, Arafat ordered a sweeping campaign in March 1996. Though he resisted pressures to disarm Islamist organizations completely,[57] he arrested some 1,200 individuals and reportedly subjected scores to torture.[58] The PA also assailed the Islamists' institutional base, taking control of fifty-nine mosques and storming thirty Hamas civic institutions.[59]

Israeli triadic strategy against the PA, which involved policies that inflicted harm but fell short of military strikes, provided impetus for these actions against Hamas and Islamic Jihad. Nonetheless, Arafat would not have found it politically palatable to carry out a crackdown had Palestinian public opinion not supported it. Approximately 70 percent of Palestinians said that they did not support the Islamists' attacks, and 59 percent approved PA measures against them.[60] As indicated by opinion polls, support for Hamas dropped nearly in half from the February before the suicide bombings to the August after the bombings.[61] Aware that continued violence would provoke a costly intra-Palestinian showdown, Hamas reoriented its focus from military action to social activism and instructed its operatives not to resist PA security forces.[62] Israeli analyst Ori Slonim observed: "Hamas's military capability depends on its popular support and the degree of cooperation by supporters. The movement's difficulties to launch attacks since 1997 derive from changes in Palestinian society. As the PA continues to strengthen, Hamas's role as a channel of protest has diminished."[63] In this context, the PA also increased its security cooperation with Israel. As the head of Israel's Military Intelligence Evaluation Department remarked in 1997, "It's clear that the Palestinian Authority realizes today that terrorism and the peace process can't co-exist. Nowadays, I'm noticing more intensive effort on the part of the Palestinian Authority to prevent terrorism."[64]

Against this backdrop, violence against Israel dropped dramatically after 1996 (see figure 5.1). In this short window of time, therefore, triadic pressure was successful. The Palestinian Authority possessed enough security capacity to repress its opponents, given that Palestinian society generally supported suppressing them. Public opinion was thus a crucial variable; when it condemned opposition militancy, it compensated for the PA's weak cohesion and capacity and gave it the mandate it needed to do what would otherwise be too costly domestically. Nevertheless, public opinion proved an unstable substitute for regime strength. A critical mass of society could easily swing back in favor of militancy should it lose hope in the peace process or be provoked by Israeli violence. Israel's seeming triadic victory in 1996 was hence short-lived.

Netanyahu, the Tunnel Crisis, and Its Aftermath, 1996–1999

During the first years of the Oslo peace process, Israel's approach to triadic coercion against the PA was generally consistent with the Rabin Doctrine. Israel focused on positive inducements when it regarded Arafat as a partner. As Israeli decision-makers became convinced that he was enabling violence, however, they increasingly turned to more coercive tactics.[65]

Regardless, damage to the peace process had already become nearly irreparable. An Israeli extremist assassinated Rabin in November 1995, and in May 1996, Benjamin Netanyahu was elected on an anti-Oslo platform. Netanyahu insisted that he would authorize no further withdrawals until the PA demonstrated reciprocity with Israel's concessions and "full compliance" with its commitments.[66] In his campaign and then from the prime minister's office Netanyahu used savvy media and communication techniques to equate Arafat with terrorism.[67] This discourse promoted a set of beliefs and attitudes that encouraged the Israeli public to support heavy-handed triadic coercion as the appropriate strategy toward the PA.

In this context, the Netanyahu government refused to meet with Arafat, cancelled restrictions on settlement development, demolished Palestinian buildings in East Jerusalem, and froze the already-delayed withdrawal from Hebron.[68] Then, in September 1996, the Israeli government began excavating a tunnel alongside the Temple Mount/al-Aqsa mosque compound. This sparked Palestinian protests, which led to clashes with Israeli troops during which PA police used, for the first time, firearms against Israel. Five days of unrest saw some fifty-eight Palestinians and fifteen Israeli soldiers killed.[69] The violence ended only when U.S. president Bill Clinton called Arafat and Netanyahu to Washington for their first face-to-face meeting.

Israeli decision-makers generally believed that Arafat had purposely turned to violence to attain concessions from Netanyahu.[70] This assumption showed little attention to the role of PA regime strength in mediating these events. By contrast, Palestinian observers drew attention to precisely this factor. Analyst Mouin Rabbani explains that the protests were driven by grassroots frustration. PA security forces attempted to thwart the protests but failed. Israeli troops then fired upon Palestinian civilians, who, in turn, were outraged when their own police stood by. Rabbani argues that it was only after both civilians and Fatah activists "shamed" PA security officers that they returned fire. Their participation in armed confrontations was hence "imposed upon, rather than ordered by, Arafat," who then gave "tacit authorization" by not ordering otherwise.[71] A roundtable of Palestinian analysts concurred that the unrest was popular and spontaneous; once ignited, however, Arafat took the reins to channel and exploit it.[72]

These commentators also agreed that public opinion provided a conducive environment for anti-Oslo mobilization. Over the course of 1996, observers described Palestinians as expressing "a deep sense of frustration and discouragement, pessimism, and even alienation,"[73] if not being on the verge of explosion.[74] This sentiment changed when, in the clashes' aftermath, Netanyahu recommenced negotiations and later committed to withdraw from 80 percent of Hebron. Surveys revealed that 77 percent of Palestinian respondents believed that the tunnel confrontation had benefitted the Palestinian cause and 77.5 percent voiced support for the peace process.[75] Journalists noted an ascent in the popularity of Arafat and his security forces.[76]

The tunnel crisis was a game changer. Thereafter the Israeli military increasingly viewed the PA's predisposition as defiant. Escalatory trends in Israel's strategic culture intensified. In the realm of security decision-making, the tunnel events drove change in both the formal institutions and informal practices structuring Israel's military coercion. Within Israel's General Staff those who had gone to pains to convince their colleagues that peace was possible lost ground to skeptics who had never trusted Arafat.[77] Officers upholding the latter perspective were influential in the General Staff Intelligence Division's research unit, which, given the absence of any civilian intelligence system, dominated analysis of information on security matters for the government. The tunnel events hardened the Intelligence Division's conclusion that Arafat did not want peace and was bent on using violence to extort concessions from Israel. The division presented this assessment to the prime minister prior to the 2000 Camp David conference, and then again after the second Intifada began.[78]

Apart from reinforcing these security decision-making processes, the tunnel events also reinforced ideas that encouraged Israel's use of severe force. The IDF committee charged with investigating the crisis expressed concern that it had damaged the IDF's deterrent image in Palestinians' eyes.[79] On that basis, the army began making contingency plans detailing how to retake PA cities should Palestinians launch another uprising.[80] It pledged that Palestinians would never again extract political gain from violence. On the contrary, the army recommitted Israel to upholding what had long been a core plank of its security doctrine: in case of deterrence failure, "battlefield decision" must restore deterrence by forcing the adversary to pay a high price.[81]

These developments took on special weight in the context of the shift in the Israeli military, ongoing since the early 1990s, toward greater attention to low-intensity conflict, deterrence, and a "leveraging approach" that endorsed triadic coercion (see chapter 2). With the tunnel clashes, Israel increasingly came to believe that it should apply this approach to the PA, as it had applied it against Arab states. Many in Israel perceived that the PA was not a partner in peace, but rather a host regime that needed to be met with military pressure. Major General Gabi Ofir, top IDF commander in the West Bank at the time, expressed the prevalent opinion: "If the Palestinians conduct battles like that, we will have to respond much more harshly and painfully. The Palestinians will have to think very hard from the beginning if it makes sense for them to continue down this path."[82]

Not only did the Israel security establishment shift toward viewing the PA through the lens of triadic coercion, but it also did so with the four new emphases that we examine in chapter 2: a focus on the inherent rather than instrumental utility of actions in pursuit of deterrence, lack of nuance in the targeting of attacks, a preoccupation with enemy consciousness, and greater focus on military operations' appropriateness relative to their consequences. This moralistic turn was apparent in many military leaders' expression of personal outrage that the Palestinian security forces that they had trusted had turned their guns against Israel. "We felt betrayed," said IDF chief of staff Amnon Lipkin-Shahak, a top negotiator who had cultivated friendships with PA security commanders.[83] These sentiments marked an important moment in the evolution of Israel's strategic culture: more and more thereafter, Israel embraced triadic coercion because it regarded it as just and appropriate, not simply because of the concrete outcomes it was expected to yield.

In the years that followed the tunnel events, the IDF increasingly saw the PA's predisposition as defiant, not cooperative. It thus prepared itself for a potential future confrontation with Palestinian security forces. At the same time, Israel did not retire its will to circumvent the PA and target force directly at Palestinians it viewed as threats. It thus continued such policies as detention without trial, torture, house demolitions, and even a failed attempt to assassinate Hamas political leader Khaled Mishal in Jordan in 1997.[84]

Camp David and the Second Intifada, 2000–2004

The election of Labor's Ehud Barak as prime minister in May 1999 reinvigorated many people's hope for the peace process. Still, years of damage to Israeli-Palestinian trust could not easily be repaired. When violent conflict reignited in September 2000 it would reach unforeseeable levels, with long-lasting consequences for the Israeli-Palestinian conflict. Two factors at the core of our theory—the role of strategic culture in encouraging severe application of triadic coercion and the role of host regimes' weakness in undercutting the effectiveness of such policies—are indispensable for understanding this turn of events.

Indications of looming crisis came to the fore after May 15, 2000, when Palestinians commemorated the anniversary of the start of the 1948 War with demonstrations that escalated to clashes with Israeli troops at settlements and installations in the West Bank and Gaza Strip. The confrontations left six Palestinians dead and more than fifteen hundred injured as well as forty Israeli soldiers injured.[85] Despite the uneven toll of violence, the IDF was livid that Palestinians had again opened fire with weapons attained under the auspices of the peace process. Discussing the issue with American mediator Dennis Ross, Chief of Staff Shaul Mofaz expressed concerns that if Israel did not react even more forcefully to any future Palestinian threats, Palestinians would lose any remaining respect for the IDF. In Ross's words, "Mofaz told me that only an immediate, strong, and preemptory response would reestablish the Israeli deterrent."[86]

Israel's preoccupation with anything that might be perceived as a loss of deterrent posture gathered new urgency ten days later when the country officially ended its twenty-two-year occupation of southern Lebanon. While chapter 6 explores the significance of this withdrawal in the Lebanese context, it is crucial to note here its significance for Israeli-Palestinian relations. Several military commanders became gripped with worry that the withdrawal sent Israel's adversaries a dangerous message. Major General Moshe "Boogie" Ya'alon voiced this belief in April 2000:

> The withdrawal is perceived in the Arab world as an example of Arab force having succeeded in reclaiming land from Israel. The classic military questions such as who won, who inflicted greater losses and so forth have become irrelevant. . . . Israeli society . . . has proven unwilling to absorb losses in a campaign of attrition. . . . This lesson has not been lost on the extreme Islamic organizations opposed to the peace process. . . . At least some senior Palestinian Authority officials are willing, in light of the Lebanese outcome, to operate on the premise that force pays.[87]

This attitude both pulled on long-established beliefs about Arab hostility and pushed Israel's strategic culture toward preoccupation with enemy consciousness and Israel's deterrent posture. Increasingly, the IDF focused on symbolic issues quite distinct from objective military matters such as battlefield decision or balance of power.

It was against this backdrop that the United States convened Israeli and Palestinian negotiators in the July 2000 Camp David II Summit. This was a last effort to reach a final settlement by the September deadline set the previous year. Arafat agreed to attend only on President Clinton's assurance that he would not be blamed if it failed.[88] When the summit closed without an agreement, however, Clinton publicly praised Barak for his "courage and vision" and suggested that Arafat had not been forthcoming.[89]

Barak, intensely worried about competition from his critics on the right, went even further in putting all responsibility for the failure squarely on the Palestinians. Enlisting the head of the Foreign Ministry Information Department, Barak launched a campaign to "dictate . . . the media agenda" even while negotiations were ongoing.[90] No sooner had talks ended then Barak held a press conference with Israeli journalists at a Maryland hotel. He announced that he had "acted out of moral and personal commitment, and supreme national obligation to do everything possible to bring about an end to the conflict."[91] Invoking terms that would harden into stock phrases in Israeli popular discourse, Barak declared that he had left "no stone unturned" in the quest for peace but found "no partner" on the other side. The flight back to Israel became a "flying press conference" during which members of the negotiating team "rehashed the official version" of the summit praising Barak's "visionary" leadership.[92] Upon landing in Tel Aviv, Barak delivered a speech that entrenched those themes. He also communicated a threat to the PA: "Today the entire world knows that Israel desires peace. . . . To our neighbors, the Palestinians, I say today: We do not seek conflict. But if any of you should dare to put us to the test, we will stand together, strong and determined, convinced in the justness of our cause in the face of any challenge, and we shall triumph."[93]

In the months that followed, a media frenzy propagated a narrative that many in Israel and the United States came to regard as truth: Israel had offered the Palestinians everything, and Arafat showed his true face when he rejected it. Various Camp David participants later contested this interpretation, arguing that Israeli and American mistakes were to blame for the summit's failure at least as much as errors on the Palestinian side.[94] Revisionist accounts credit Barak for proposing staged withdrawals toward a Palestinian state in the Gaza Strip and some 92 percent of the West Bank, with a capital in East Jerusalem and shared control of Jerusalem holy sites. However, they also explain that Israel had not guaranteed Palestinian territorial contiguity in the West Bank, full sovereignty over East Jerusalem, or an acceptable compromise on refugees' right of return.[95] Barak's "generous offer" was thus not nearly as generous as he claimed.

Clayton Swisher, author of the most detailed history of Camp David, called the propagation of a false understanding of the summit "one of the greatest PR frauds in history."[96] Nonetheless, its effect on Israeli, and likewise American, public opinion cannot be overstated. The "myth" of Barak's generous offer reinforced a set of assumptions and attitudes that would encourage, if not compel, Israeli society to support triadic coercion against the PA should Palestinian actors forcibly protest the status quo. It also influenced Israel to prepare for such an eventuality. Hardly had Camp David ended before the IDF began carrying out large-scale exercises addressing various scenarios of confrontation with the PA, up to and including limited-scale war.[97]

Such was the tense environment when Ariel Sharon, Barak's leading Likud rival, made a controversial visit to the Temple Mount/al-Aqsa Mosque compound in September 2000. What Israelis viewed as a domestic political challenge, Palestinians saw as a provocative assertion of Israeli ownership of the holy site. The next afternoon, Palestinian protests sparked clashes that left 70 Israeli police officers injured, 220 Palestinians wounded, and 6 Palestinians dead. As demonstrations continued, the unrest came to be called a second Intifada, in a nod to the first mass uprising that had begun in the Occupied Territories in 1987. Palestinian protestors threw rocks and then Molotov cocktails at Israeli deployments across the West Bank and Gaza Strip. Israeli troops responded with extreme force. In the first days alone, the Israeli army reportedly fired a million shots—what a security official later dubbed "a bullet for every child."[98] Palestinian gunfire was confirmed on the fourth day, when PA policemen stationed at demonstrations entered the fray.[99]

In the weeks that followed, Palestinian activists shot at Israeli military installations, settlements, and roads in the Palestinian territories. Defining the uprising as an "armed conflict" short of war, the IDF deployed snipers and loosened its open-fire regulations.[100] It eventually used tanks, helicopter gunships, and warplanes to shell civilian areas from which gunmen were shooting.[101] Fatalities from the conflict totaled 53 after the first week, 112 after the second week, and 141 after the third week. More than 90 percent of these were Palestinian.[102] Claiming it necessary to clear away cover, Israel also bulldozed millions of dollars' worth of Palestinian houses, fields, and trees.[103] Israel blocked suspect movement by creating hundreds of new checkpoints, resulting in Palestinian economic losses of $8.45 million per day.[104] The IDF insisted that its response was defensive and restrained.[105] Palestinians and dozens of international and local investigations labeled it excessive, amounting to indiscriminate collective punishment and grave violations of human rights.[106]

Given the PA's status as a hybrid between a state-like government and a nonstate national movement, Israel's military response to the outset of the second Intifada was simultaneously direct and triadic. It sought direct coercion to the extent that it believed that Arafat was sponsoring violence and that the main perpetrators of attacks—Fatah members and PA security officers (many of whom were also Fatah members)—answered to his command. Yet Israel's mission also levied triadic coercion because it could not definitively know the degree to which the PA was involved in violence. Militants did not formally act as PA agents, and Arafat denied culpability. The Palestinian leadership insisted that violence was driven from below by grassroots frustration and activists' independent initiatives. Israel's leadership consistently dismissed these claims as an aversion of responsibility.[107] At the end of the Intifada's first week, Major General Ya'alon declared in a Paris conference that events in the West Bank and Gaza were "willed and initiated: a well-planned attack."[108] On these grounds, the Israeli government engaged in various forms of coercion against the PA to compel it to put an end to violence. It issued threats and, by the third week, targeted reprisals against PA military installations. Closure policies compounded pressure on the PA. Israel's refusal to transfer customs monies that it collected on the PA's behalf hastened an acute budget crisis, pressuring the PA even more.[109]

These measures aimed to punish the PA and hold it accountable for all violence emanating from its territory, even if it was not the PA that planned and executed it. As journalists Raviv Drucker and Ofer Shelah conclude in their authoritative study of Israel's strategy in the second Intifada, "In the first months, the IDF almost never targeted the terrorist organizations—Hamas and the Islamic Jihad. It deliberately attacked almost exclusively targets of the Palestinian Authority."[110] This strategy reflected what Gal Hirsch, head of IDF operations in the West Bank at the time, defined as the "leverages approach." As Hirsch explained, "The systemic idea of leverage was that through the use of various levels of pressure the Palestinian system would be convinced to act [against terrorists]—either because it is deterred or because it is in its own interests."[111]

This "leverages approach" was the closest the IDF came to speaking directly about triadic coercion. By "leverage" it meant that, instead of targeting nonstate perpetrators of violence directly, Israel would exert pressure on them indirectly by punishing both the state in which they resided and the civilian population in which they were based. Israel reasoned that the state and population would in turn pressure nonstate actors to cease their attacks. As Yoram Peri elaborates the logic, "By exerting heavy pressure on the Palestinian population, the Palestinians themselves—to ease the burden on their own lives—would rise up against their leadership and compel Arafat to change his policy and stop the armed struggle."[112]

A special General Staff task force established at the beginning of the Intifada and headed by Ya'alon focused on finding ways to use these "leverages" to pressure Arafat. This task force was solely focused on coercive leverage. Early in the discussion some members raised the idea of using "carrots," such as economic incentives and removal of checkpoints, in addition to "sticks." However, other task force members quickly dismissed this proposal, claiming that Arafat was not interested in peace—he was, in our terms, a "defiant host"—and therefore would not be influenced by positive incentives.[113]

Israel sustained this coercive approach as months became years. Israel tightened closure, established more checkpoints, and carried out heavy, mechanized attacks and incursions deep into PA areas. Especially after January 2002, the IDF used heavy artillery, Merkava tanks, F-15 and F-16 aircraft, and Cobra and Apache attack helicopters against PA targets.[114] One can conclude, as did Zeev Maoz, that "The basic post-Qiibya logic of hitting and hurting installations and political symbols of Arab regimes in order to compel them into curbing terrorism was applied to the PA."[115] Israel's strategy in confronting the second Intifada, in other words, was triadic coercion.

Strategic Culture: Decision-Making Processes

This embrace of triadic coercion was conditioned by Israel's strategic culture, in terms of both decision-making processes and ideas. Since statehood the defining characteristic of Israel's security decision-making had been the military's preeminence. Peri points out the most problematic aspects of Israel's permeable "political-military partnership," such as the military's monopoly on intelligence, insufficient institutionalization of civilian control, and the weak separation of the military from politics. He argues that, in fall 2000, all of these elements tipped even more "drastically" in favor of military power.[116] In particular, Peri chronicles the boldness of

Chief of Staff Mofaz, showing how he acted with such independence that he virtually became "acting defense minister." Continuing a public role that he had taken after the Lebanon withdrawal, Mofaz overstepped democratic constraints by leaking information and going directly to the press to criticize what he called the government's "excessive restraint" toward the PA. When Barak sought to maintain communication with the PA, Mofaz and other IDF leaders pushed for more forceful confrontation. Foreign Minister Shlomo Ben-Ami remarked, "If we had allowed the IDF to carry out all its plans, all of NATO would have been here already."[117] He added that, regardless, the government's opposition to this aggressive approach did not amount to much given its lack of effective and institutionalized control of the military. Of the chief of staff, Ben-Ami said he did "whatever he wanted."[118]

Apart from these skewed civil-military relations, the army's own organizational culture also encouraged its use of triadic coercion in the second Intifada. Taking advantage of the decentralized command, the top brass rallied lower-ranking officers with warnings about the existential threat that the Intifada posed. During the first month Deputy Chief of Staff Ya'alon met with hundreds of battalion commanders and told them that the "the battle taking place in the territories today is the most important struggle since the War of Independence," because Palestinians were engaged in a "clear, calculated, and deliberate war of independence."[119] Those commanders themselves reportedly responded that the government's policy of restraint "undermines defensive and offensive capabilities" and was being "perceived as weakness."[120]

Officers of varying ranks had considerable autonomy in acting on this impulse. In line with its "doer" valorization of improvisation and initiative in the field, the IDF leadership extended commanders' freedom of action as the Intifada progressed. Given this latitude, officers and soldiers were able to use their own judgment to delay, ignore, and undercut orders, to go beyond instructions, or to take action first and get political approval later. These tendencies typically enabled force more than they encouraged caution.[121] Dismayed with the resulting escalation, the deputy defense minister reportedly wrote to the prime minister, "From the chief of staff down to the last sergeant at the roadblock, no one is implementing your policy" because each is acting as "his own boss."[122]

Journalist Ben Caspit relays an anecdote that shows how these and other decision-making processes underlay and contributed to an Israeli strategic culture encouraging aggressive coercion. Upon assuming office, Barak had created a "Peace Administration" to coordinate civilian and military organs to advise the negotiations process. Acting on its traditional resistance to both abstract planning and civilian counterweights, the IDF undermined the Peace Administration by denying it maps and ignoring its meetings. When the second Intifada began, Barak ordered implementation of one of the Peace Administration's plans, the "gridding map," which detailed specific roads to close with the goal of containing conflict without escalating it. Caspit's description of the military's disrespect for this plan is worth quoting at length:

> The idea was to separate the territories from Israel while thinking of the political consequences. . . . It meant to isolate violent regions through a broad political vision, according to which the Palestinian population and the Israeli settlers should sustain minimal damage, while security is maximally guarded. The plan combined security-oriented concepts with political thinking and vision. . . .
>
> When the conflict started, Barak immediately ordered that the gridding plan be implemented at once, to minimize friction between Israelis and Palestinians, to isolate violent regions, and to avoid an escalation. Over the first four weeks of the fighting, Barak could not get his hands on true reports from the ground. . . . Later, after the dust has settled, it turned out that the IDF "grid" violently blocked hundreds of roads it was not supposed to, cut off dozens of villages, and turned entire regions into isolated enclaves. Every commander in the field felt free to build endless "escape routes" for the settlements and use the same bulldozers to block all the roads leading to and from Palestinian villages.
>
> Instead of taking pinpointed moves, moving gradually, collecting a price systematically, and letting the Palestinians understand that they would pay more every time violence escalates, the army slammed all across the sector and bet the jackpot. . . . The IDF bulldozers indiscriminately cut through roads, uprooted plantations, and left behind them scorched earth, a sense of despair, and a strong desire for revenge.[123]

As this and countless other examples illustrate, both formal and informal institutions of Israeli decision-making, and the structure of civil-military relations in particular, encouraged a rush to act even before (or at the expense of) careful consideration of the consequences. Reinforcing these dynamics was the pressure of public opinion. Mainstream Israeli society's esteem for the army and its own engrained belief in military force compounded the impulse pushing military and government leaders toward harsh application of triadic coercion. Indeed, an early October poll found that 56 percent of Israelis believed that the government was not activating security forces with the necessary firmness.[124] Right-leaning sectors of society expressed this view even more intensely. Columns in the *Jerusalem Post* decried the "self-imposed helplessness of the government,"[125] accused it of "castrat(ing) the IDF,"[126] and mocked its concern about "burning bridges" back to the negotiating table. Settlers launched a campaign to push the government toward a more hardline response, even gathering in a 1,500-person demonstration under the theme "Let the IDF Win."[127] They also delivered a petition threatening to take matters into their own hands if the army did not protect them.[128] One Shin Bet official likened settlers' mood to "lava seething under the surface which it is not known how, when, and where will erupt."[129]

Despite this mood, Barak sustained efforts to negotiate a resolution with the Palestinians. The January 2001 Taba conference between Israel and the PA made significant progress on core negotiation topics. Nevertheless, prospects for success were slim, given both political and public demand for belligerence. As Ben-Ami later remarked, "The pressure of Israeli public opinion against the talks could not be resisted."[130] Domestic political competition likewise pushed military escalation, especially after the Barak government lost its majority in the Knesset and an early election for prime minister was scheduled for that February. Sharon criticized Barak's weakness and campaigned on a promise to end peace talks and restore Israeli security. He was elected with 62 percent of the vote. By spring 2001, Israeli opinion polls found that "in the public mind, the chances of peace have never been lower, nor has the likelihood of war ever been higher." The ratio of those preferring a policy of sharp and immediate response to provocation over that of a policy of restraint was three to one.[131]

These trends marginalized the Israeli left and rendered the peace camp relatively silenced.[132] Consequently, those who called for greater force were less compelled to defend their position against alternative viewpoints. Public figures had incentives to ride the bandwagon in favor of strikes against the PA and disincentives for opening a debate about the risks of such strikes. This further pushed Israel's strategic culture toward triadic coercion, and away from alternative means of conflict resolution.

Strategic Culture: Ideas

Within this strategic culture, several ideas came to take on the weight of truth in Israel in fall 2000. Despite dubious empirical and analytical foundations, they became sustained through governmental, popular, and media discourse and institutionalized in political and military practices. Among them, four ideas emerged as particularly prominent in shaping the approach of the Israeli security elite, and the IDF command in particular, to their strategic environment. Though these ideas pertained to Israel's general strategic position, they had important applications for policies of triadic coercion against the PA in this and subsequent periods.

INHERENT RATHER THAN INSTRUMENTAL UTILITY OF ACTIONS IN PURSUIT OF DETERRENCE

The first idea was that actions taken in pursuit of deterrence were useful in their own right, independent of their actual effects in lessening violence. In this regard, Caspit was one of many who noted the military's claims that deterrence, once undermined, must be restored as a matter of pride as much as an outcome of rational calculations. "The Intifada found the IDF . . . in need of a swift victory, at all costs," he wrote. "It was aspiring to rehabilitate its lost deterrence powers, to find compensation for the Lebanon withdrawal, the Oslo Accords, the various interim accords, the humiliating contacts [with the Palestinians]."[133] Civilian leaders echoed this view, effectively shifting deterrence from a strategic tool vis-à-vis the Palestinians to an emotionally inflected principle vis-à-vis the entire Arab world. Knesset member Dan Meridor commented, "The biggest danger is the sense that there is a weakening of our deterrent might, and our image of strength. . . . When you hear Iraq's Saddam Hussein threatening Israel and you see how Syria allowed the kidnapping of our soldiers, you have to say to yourself that we have to restore the image of Israeli power and deterrence." Invoking the biblical names by which some Israelis refer to the West Bank, he added, "We can do it. The first front for this is in Judea and Samaria."[134]

The popular press echoed this view. "Israel will pay dearly if it acts as if the pursuit of peace can substitute for the restoration of deterrent power," the *Jerusalem Post* declared. "Israel's deterrent power—which means both the ability and willingness to use force—must be restored for peace to have a chance of success."[135] The logic of such claims remained woefully undeveloped. Advocates of a crackdown in the West Bank did not explain how it could change the calculations of the Iraqi or Syrian presidents or why it was requisite for the success of the peace process. Calls of this type came with little discussion of the potential costs of severe force in terms of blood, finances, and diplomatic relations. They did not evaluate whether the expected benefits really outweighed those costs. Far from it, they reflected a new strategic culture hardening around the conviction that military pressure must restore an image of toughness simply because an image of toughness must be restored. As Barak told the press in early October, "We are living in a very tough neighborhood where there is no mercy for the weak, no second opportunity for those who cannot defend themselves."[136] Former director of the Government Press Office Yossi Olmert agreed, writing, "When Israel is seen as weak and vulnerable, we can be sure that the Palestinians will try to take advantage. The lesson is clear: even when Israel takes a decision to concede politically to the Arabs, be they Lebanese or Palestinians, we can do it only from a position of military strength and superiority."[137]

These notions suggest that military action was becoming guided by strategic culture as much as by means-end thinking. Applied to triadic coercion, Israeli leaders justified targeting strikes against the PA due to a perceived lapse of deterrence in the past rather than a rational assessment of the circumstances that governed in the past and the best way to end violence in the present.

LACK OF NUANCE

In addition to pursuing a deterrent posture for its inherent as much as instrumental utility, Israeli strategic culture also became less and less nuanced in its approach to the punishment of host regimes. Adopting a "one-size-fits-all" policy, the Israeli government advocated use of military force against an undifferentiated enemy, without distinction among the discrete actors that might constitute such an enemy and without critical scrutiny of its actual, as opposed to assumed, motivations and capabilities. This lack of nuance came to the fore in the Israeli narrative that many Israelis came to regard as a truth: Israel's withdrawal from Lebanon "taught" Palestinians that Israel is weak and will surrender to violence. A November *Jerusalem Post* expressed this widespread view: "Now Israel is in the uncomfortable position of having to force the Palestinians to unlearn what for them was the graphic lesson of Lebanon: that Israel can be slowly bled into withdrawing from territory. Israel's current policy of restraint tends to confirm the relevance of the Lebanese model in the Palestinian mind."[138]

There were some examples of Palestinians voicing this "lesson of Lebanon."[139] Yet just as much evidence instead pointed to the contrary. A survey conducted one month after the Lebanon withdrawal asked Palestinians what strategy they would prefer should negotiators fail to reach a final agreement by the September 2000 deadline. More favored extending the date and continuing peace negotiations with Israel than endorsed other strategies, including confrontations and resistance.[140] Lebanon thus did not simply and uniformly push Palestinians toward violence. Rather, the main factor driving Palestinians' support for armed struggle in 2000 was consistent with what it had been before: decline in their confidence that peace negotiations could deliver an end to occupation. Palestinians' turn to military strategies remained linked to their assessment of the failure of political strategies more than to perceptions of Israel's deterrent strength or weakness.

Whether or not Palestinians had learned from Lebanon the lesson that "violence pays," many in Israel were convinced that they had.[141] Just one week after the Lebanon withdrawal, Mofaz invited PA Security Force leader Mohammed Dahlan to Tel Aviv to warn him that Palestinians should have no illusions that Israel had lost its "powers of dissuasion." Dahlan recalled retorting, "You're going to take revenge on us for the humiliation you suffered in Lebanon."[142] The upper echelons of the IDF adopted the conviction that military might was necessary to "teach the Palestinians" to unlearn the lessons of Lebanon. From there, Lipkin-Shahak reflected, "This perception trickled down, even when things were not said explicitly. The understanding was that if the Palestinians start something, we will prove to them that here is not Lebanon and the price they will pay will be high."[143]

This Israeli attitude pointed to inherited assumptions about Arab mentalities more than grounded scrutiny of what Palestinians themselves were saying and doing. It built on a culture advocating harsh punishment of adversaries across the board, not a tailored response to local and immediate circumstances. In this way, it ignored glaring differences between the Palestinians and Hezbollah. As Yezid Sayigh lamented, Palestinians' "chaotic" and "haphazard" armed activity was "a far cry" from the "precise political direction, disciplined implementation, organizational coherence" of the Lebanese group's military campaign.[144] Caspit added that the IDF's approach to the second Intifada, failing to differentiate among Palestinians themselves, even left the "classic Israeli code, according to which we must not view the entire Palestinian population as an enemy . . . smashed into pieces."[145]

The implicit assumption that "all Arabs are the same" resonated well with another generality underlying the lack of nuance in Israel's response to the second Intifada: the belief that Arafat was personally responsible for the violence. "He's violated every agreement," Barak said. "This wave of violence has been imposed upon us by the will of Arafat."[146] According to this narrative, the PA president deliberately pursued a policy of "talking and shooting" to escape the costs of overt sponsorship of armed groups while reaping whatever diplomatic rewards he might harvest from their violence.[147] Violence was thus a straightforward choice. "The Palestinians have once again decided to resort to violence for political gain," Israel's representative to the United Nations told the Secretary Council.[148]

This contention was dangerously oversimplified. It implied that armed strategies were a switch that Arafat turned on and off, not the outcome of a complex set of interactions between Israel and the Palestinians and amongst Palestinian groups themselves. It asserted that Arafat was an omnipotent decision-maker who could "control his people" if he wished, rather than a politician leading a regime severely lacking in cohesion and capacity. Though some Israeli planners recognized these constraints, they tended to conclude that all Palestinians would abide by Arafat's will if he were only coerced to impose it.[149] Ya'alon contended at the beginning of the Intifada that Arafat was to blame and that no hard intelligence was necessary to prove that obvious fact.[150] The few who contested this simplistic logic were marginalized.

Telling here is what would be called the "Amos vs. Amos" controversy.[151] In 2004, Major General Amos Malka, director of Military Intelligence at the outset of the Intifada, publicly accused Major General Amos Gilad, then head of Military Intelligence's research division, of distorting the assessments that he presented to political and defense leaders. Malka charged that Gilad persuaded decision-makers that Arafat had never abandoned the goal of eradicating Israel, deliberately ignoring significant intelligence to the contrary. Later intelligence indeed cast further doubt on Gilad's view: an interrogation of Fatah leaders arrested in 2002 revealed that, during the Intifada's initial stages, there was almost no centralized direction from Arafat or even from Marwan Barghouti.[152] The lack of nuance with which security leaders had come to view the Palestinian landscape, however, blinded them to such critical distinctions.

SHAPING ENEMY CONSCIOUSNESS

The lack of nuance characterizing Israel's understanding of the Intifada dovetailed with a third idea through which its strategic culture supported triadic coercion. Days after the Intifada's start, Ya'alon described the confrontation as a "war over narrative."[153] By this he meant that Israel needed not only to communicate its preferred interpretation of the Intifada to its own people and to the outside world but also to impose this narrative on the Palestinians themselves.

As discussed in chapter 2, the Operation Theory Research Institute (OTRI) developed ideas about targeting enemy populations' consciousness during the 1990s. In the second Intifada, Ya'alon became the main proponent of these ideas within the General Staff.[154] According to this view Israel was not merely striking the PA to alter its motivations or reduce it capacities but also to change how the "Palestinian street" understood the utility of violence against Israel. Becoming chief of staff in July 2002, Ya'alon actively promoted this view among the Israeli public.[155] That August a reporter quoted a leaked private conversation in which Ya'alon stated, "It is imperative that we win this conflict in such a way that the Palestinian side will burn into its consciousness that there is no chance of achieving goals by means of terror. If we don't do that, we will find ourselves on a slippery slope that will damage our deterrence."[156] Ya'alon then reiterated this position, directly connecting the issues of Palestinian consciousness and Israeli deterrence, in an interview with *Haaretz*.[157]

This new focus on enemy consciousness carried strategic problems. The effectiveness of coercion in changing foes' behavior can be easily verified by the subsequent rates of attacks. The effectiveness of coercion in influencing a change in foes' beliefs and attitudes, however, is very difficult to confirm. In making the latter the goal of military action, the IDF was adopting a policy impervious to evaluation; neither the government nor the public, nor indeed the army itself, could ever be certain that its objectives had been accomplished. The IDF's focus on enemy consciousness might not even have been a calculated objective as much as a rhetorical shield. Insofar as it did not specify the mechanisms by which its military punishments actually deterred nonstate actors' violence, Israeli leaders hid behind amorphous metaphors about "burning" lessons into enemy psyches. They therefore absolved themselves of the need to assess critically the assumptions that undergirded their choices and the actual consequences of those choices.

LOGIC OF APPROPRIATENESS

The final ideational component of Israel's strategic culture was the intensified role of a "logic of appropriateness," as opposed to a "logic of consequences," in justifying its actions. This sense of righteousness came to the fore in October 2000, when a Palestinian crowd took over a PA police station and beat to death two Israelis who had driven into Ramallah. According to Caspit, "Barak went wild," was "furious," and "declared 'an Armageddon war.'"[158] On the same day, Israeli helicopters bombed PA installations in Ramallah and Gaza. An unprecedented assault on the PA, the strikes unambiguously communicated that Israel held the Palestinian government responsible for Israeli deaths, even those perpetrated by enraged civilians.

Israeli leaders therefore advocated heavy-handed force against the PA because it was morally justified. This conclusion was the flipside of the conviction that Palestinians' actions were immoral. As Thomas Friedman argued in the *New York Times*, Arafat lacked the moral courage to make peace, and thus chose to "provoke the Israelis into brutalizing Palestinians again, and regain the moral high ground that way."[159] The head of the IDF Legal Division added that Arafat's reprehensible strategy was based on sacrificing his own people as well as innocent Israelis. "There is a definite interest on the Palestinian side to get large numbers of casualties, on both sides, so they can get more international involvement," he told a press conference.[160]

Just as Arafat's callous pursuit of bloodshed was morally repugnant, Israelis reasoned, Israel's use of force was legitimate, if not imperative. As Barak explained to NBC News, the correctness of Israel's military response was also in direct proportion to the generosity of its unprecedented concessions at Camp David:

> We voted to do whatever we can and to leave no stone unturned on the way to peace, but if we won't find partners, we will know what to do, and with the same determination, we will stand firm against whatever kind of challenge.... So we know that Arafat initiated this whole series of events, somehow using the willingness to sacrifice of [sic] his own people to draw the world attention back to his cause. We know that he can stop it. So if he doesn't, we cannot but draw the conclusion that if he doesn't want to make peace, it means that he deliberately decided to put an end to the peace process and to go into a conflict. Once he has done it, we don't have a choice but to respond.[161]

Barak's language invoked an expression dominant in Israel's security concept and discourse since statehood, that Israel had "no choice" (*ein brera*) but to fight wars that its adversaries consistently forced upon it.[162] This approach was resonant with inherited attitudes but departed from typical notions of rational calculus. To justify an action as the result of lack of choice, after all, was very different than asserting that it was the best choice selected from alternatives.

This rationale contributed to the crystallization in Israeli discourse of a circular logic that came to dominate conversations about security: exercise strength in order to avoid indicating weakness. This obtained the hallmark of a strategic culture, in Alastair Iain Johnston's sense of argumentation structures, languages, and analogies that establish preferences by formulating concepts about the efficacy of military force and "clothing these conceptions with such an aura of factuality that the strategic preferences seem uniquely realistic and efficacious."[163]

Role of Regime Weakness in Mediating Triadic Coercion Outcomes

Whereas Israel condemned the PA for masterminding an uprising, many Palestinians criticized it for failing to guide what they saw as a disorderly, if not "dysfunctional," revolt. Many bemoaned the "nonpresence" of the PA and begged it to take leadership.[164] That Arafat did not do so was predictable given his inability to escape the political binds in which Oslo had placed him. The peace process obligated the PA to suppress militancy while producing the disappointing outcomes that fueled it. Israel's triadic coercion at the outset of the Intifada did nothing to alleviate that contradiction. Thus Arafat, caught between a duty to uphold Oslo and the popular pressure to oppose it, did neither.[165] Even absent competing pressures, it is not clear what Arafat might have been able to do had he wished to act, given his regime's weak cohesion and capacity.

This choice was individually rational for Arafat, given the gap that Camp David had revealed between what Israel was willing to offer and what Palestinians were willing to accept. It was also rational given intra- and interfactional competition in the weak PA regime. The first to spearhead Intifada demonstrations and shootings were Fatah activists associated with Tanzim and Barghouti.[166] Many were deeply critical of the PA and eager to advance their own positions within Fatah. Their grassroots initiative presented a challenge to Arafat's leadership more than deference to it. If Arafat had forced a confrontation with the charismatic Barghouti, that cohort might have openly rebelled against Arafat.[167] At the same time, the crisis Fatah activists propelled could help Arafat escape from the Oslo stalemate.

These distinct and contradictory interests, compounded by interfactional competition and institutional incapacity, underlay the weakness of the PA regime. That weakness, in turn, was the defining context of the second Intifada. As Sayigh reflected, "All the flaws and weaknesses that had been built and reinforced and made a part of the [Palestinian] system over the previous six years became immediately apparent when faced under pressure."[168] Israel's policies of triadic coercion served as a main source of that pressure. They backfired, at least in the short term, because they aggravated PA regime weakness. They thereby enabled and encouraged violence by non-PA actors through several mechanisms.

Primarily, Israel's military repression—against the PA and Palestinians in general—contributed to radicalizing Palestinian society. Pounded by artillery and choked by closure, Palestinian confidence in the peace process plummeted, and calls for revenge surged, as they did in Israel. In Israel, however, this rightward shift in public opinion was channeled into elections and support for the one national army. Under the weak and fragmented PA, by contrast, it encouraged a range of groups other than the constituted government to take up arms. It also decreased the PA's capacity to resist such trends. Hamas did not become involved as an organization during the Intifada's first months, as it suspected that the uprising was a Fatah ploy to boost the peace process.[169] Its skepticism decreased as Palestinian casualties mounted, the PA weakened, popular calls for militancy intensified, and the Intifada became a new status quo. Judging that the damage to Oslo was irreversible, Hamas entered the Intifada on January 1, 2001, by carrying out its first suicide bombing inside Israel since 1998.[170]

Popular demonstrations receded as the Intifada became an armed free-for-all, with rival factions claiming responsibility for attacks. Hamas and Islamic Jihad routinized suicide bombings. The PFLP followed suit, lest it be left behind. Violence was encouraged by Palestinian public opinion; the percentage of Palestinians strongly or somewhat in support of suicide attacks rose from less than 26 percent in March 1999 to 73.7 percent in April 2001, and did not drop below 59.9 through June 2004.[171]

Israeli military force thus goaded Palestinian public opinion, which encouraged factions to carry out more and graver violence against Israel as a way of competing against each other. It also rendered the PA less capable of resisting such violence, physically and politically. Concerned about losing standing and cadres to other factions, Fatah activists announced their formation of a new militia force, the al-Aqsa Martyrs Brigade (AMB). AMB broke with Fatah's official condemnation of suicide attacks and carried out its first such bombing in early 2002. Over the next five years, AMB would claim more suicide attacks than would Hamas (see table 5.1).

For Israel, AMB vindicated charges that the PA was responsible for violence. Indeed, it would later capture documents based on which it would produce a 103-page report detailing, in the words of a cabinet member, "clear-cut, hard evidence that the Palestinian Authority under Yasser Arafat is a sponsoring and operating body in support of terror."[172] The alleged terror connection lay in the opaque overlaps between AMB, Fatah, and the

PA. An estimated 80 percent of AMB cadres were PA security force personnel.[173] Security force commanders typically served as patrons for AMB cells.

These linkages were predictable as long as the PA remained one expression of a multistranded nonstate struggle as much an authoritative government. Arafat had ultimate sway over AMB because he controlled Fatah's purse strings. According to the International Crisis Group, however, AMB "never formed a coherent, disciplined military organization led by a unified command implementing guidelines and decisions of a political leadership."[174] Human Rights Watch agreed that AMB fighters operated "under loose, personality-driven local command structures, with a degree of autonomy and improvisation."[175] Even within a single town, several cells sometimes functioned separately and competed for turf.[176]

AMB's fragmentation was a direct extension of the PA's regime weakness and incomplete institutionalization, especially manifest in lax regulation of multiple security branches, elite infighting, and use of public resources to create private fiefdoms. Arafat's patrimonial strategy of divide, conquer, and co-opt in a bloated security sector had bolstered his domination despite regime weakness. The precarious political system held as long as public opinion voiced confidence in the peace process. When negotiations collapsed, Fatah splintered, and parts bled into AMB. Israel's targeting of PA installations hastened this process, as the think tank Strategic Assessment Initiative explains:

> It was much easier to bomb a Palestinian police station than to locate a Hamas cell responsible for a suicide bombing. For organizations like Hamas which hoped to ultimately replace the PA, this proved fortuitous. By increasing attacks against Israel, they could effectively dismantle the apparatus of their chief rival while placing all the blame on Israel. . . . As Palestinian administrating institutions fragmented and the PA SF [security forces] were effectively wiped out, the only safe place to be was in the cell structure created by the militias.[177]

Israel's triadic coercion seemed tactically rational but was strategically counterproductive because it further undermined the Palestinian government's cohesion and capacity. This reduced the PA's ability to comply with the demand that it constrain nonstate rivals as well as cadres affiliated with its own ruling party. For Fatah and the police rank-and-file, joining an AMB cell under the sponsorship of some Fatah elite offered a guaranteed income at a time when unemployment was skyrocketing and the PA could not always pay employee wages.[178] For elites, sponsoring cells offered a way of vying with each other for who "controlled the street."

Fragmented from the start, what existed of AMB's command and control structure was further undermined by Israel's arrests of thousands of Intifada activists and fighters.[179] The IDF also embarked on a campaign of extrajudicial killings, assassinating 232 Palestinians at various levels of command between 2000 and 2008.[180] Those who filled the vacuum were typically young, inexperienced, and loyal to clans, cliques, or localities more than to any central leadership.[181] In rupturing AMB into smaller splinters, Israel eventually weakened its capacity to carry out attacks. Israel did not, however, establish deterrence in the sense of decreasing fighters' motivations to attack.

As the effects of triadic coercion accumulated, the PA gradually became a hollow shell unable to govern, provide services, or impose the rule of law. "The PA stopped being the arbiter of domestic political struggles and instead became a party to these struggles," an analyst in Gaza insisted. For him, the turning point arrived in 2001, when PA police attempted to arrest Hamas leaders, and residents of their Gaza neighborhoods came into the streets and forced the police away.[182] The most decisive blow to the PA's regime strength came after fifteen suicide attacks left seventy-eight Israelis dead in March 2002. Israel launched Operation Defensive Shield and reoccupied all West Bank cities except for Jericho. This move was no longer in the realm of either triadic coercion or deterrence but instead was an exercise of brute force. Giving up, at least temporarily, on the idea that the PA would clamp down on the Palestinian organizations perpetrating attacks, Israel decided to bypass the PA and directly target those organizations itself.[183]

Defensive Shield decreased the likelihood of triadic coercion success over the long-term. When Israel withdrew after forty-five days, it left a mammoth toll in Palestinian deaths, injuries, arrests, and property damage.[184] It also undid much of the state-building process undertaken in the 1990s. Journalist Amira Hass judged the army's raiding of governmental and nongovernmental offices, where computers were smashed and files burned, to be a systematic campaign to "destroy Palestinian civil institutions ... sending all of Palestinian society backward."[185] After the Operation's conclusion, Israeli troops confined Arafat to his Ramallah compound. Prime Minister Sharon and U.S. president George Bush declared him to be irrelevant. This gave the embittered PA president incentive to encourage violence against Israel as if to send the message, "Either deal with me or chaos." By June 2004, as many Palestinians said that they did not "feel the presence of the PA" as said that they did.[186] The decomposition of central institutions devolved political authority to the local level, where anyone with a weapon could assert his will.[187] Palestinians decried the "security lapse" and "chaos of weapons."[188]

The PA's weakening raised the relative clout and operational freedom of groups that rejected Israel. It also impeded the Palestinian leadership's efforts to end hostilities, even when leaders deemed it opportune. Over a dozen ceasefires collapsed or were foiled during the first three years of the Intifada alone. Many Israelis charged that Arafat wanted ceasefires to fail.[189] While we might never know the PA president's true intentions, we can trace how the political and institutional weakness of his regime reduced its ability to impose an end to the fighting. In the first five weeks of the uprising, Israeli and Palestinian representatives negotiated three ceasefires, one of which Arafat refused to sign and two of which did not take hold despite his official consent. Throughout that time, Tanzim and opposition factions denounced the leadership's willingness to collude with Israel while Palestinians buried their dead daily.[190]

The process of ending hostilities grew more complicated as the PA's nonstate rivals became emboldened. Then, even a unilateral Palestinian ceasefire came to require credible commitments from autonomous actors with divergent preferences.[191] On numerous occasions Israeli assassinations of Palestinian leaders led their factions to carry out revenge attacks and torpedo ceasefires.[192] At other junctures, factional leaders found that they could not guarantee enforcement of a ceasefire even among their own activists on the ground. As one Palestinian academic explained the failure of Palestinian factions to agree on a unilateral ceasefire in January 2003, "Most of the military operations [against Israel] are being carried out by gunmen who don't report to their political leaders. Even if the factions had reached an agreement, this wouldn't have meant a complete end to the violence."[193]

The rate of Palestinians' lethal attacks inside Israel declined dramatically after 2002 (see figure 5.1 and table 5.1). While many in the IDF credited Operation Defensive Shield for this success, one empirical study found that the crackdown had no effect on terrorist activity by Islamist militants and actually increased that by Fatah affiliates. Its results show that only defensive measures, namely the construction of a separation fence/wall in the West Bank beginning in 2002, had a statistically significant impact on reducing attacks.[194]

Triadic coercion appeared to play little role in this outcome. It did not "burn into Palestinians' consciousness" the lesson that violence does not pay but rather drove them to devise new ways of returning the infliction of pain. One such tactical innovation was homemade, unguided projectiles filled with explosives fired from the Gaza Strip into Israel. Not long after Hamas debuted its "Qassam rockets," Islamic Jihad and AMB began to launch them as well. The number of rockets consequently fired at Israel increased from 60 in 2001 to 861 in 2006.[195] The PA condemned rocket fire, its interior minister declaring in 2004 that "those who [launch rockets] are a certain group that does not represent the people and nation, doing it without thinking about the general interest."[196] Nonetheless, the PA lacked the cohesion and capacity to stop them. The weak PA was no longer able to do much, especially in Gaza, where Hamas was particularly strong. Taking the matter into its own hands, Israel carried out air strikes and raids that flattened homes and fields, destroyed utilities, left hundreds dead, and rendered whole communities without water. Still, it failed to stop the rocket fire.

Abbas and Regime Schism, 2005–2017

The second Intifada continued as a semi-war until Arafat's death in late 2004 invited a transition. Elected the PA's new president in January 2005, Mahmoud Abbas pledged to unify Palestinians under "one authority, one law, one gun." He knew that he needed to reconsolidate the PA if he were to use it as a tool to end the armed Intifada, which he had opposed since its inception.[197] With that end, Abbas convinced major Palestinian groups to accept a *tahdiyyah*, an open-ended calm toward Israel, that March. In exchange for Hamas's agreement to halt attacks against Israel, he promised it new parliamentary elections and entry into the PLO.

The regime that Abbas inherited, however, was acutely weak. A change in leadership alone would not resolve entrenched problems related to institutional capacities, elite fragmentation, and political legitimacy. Some high-ranking Fatah figures sought to create turmoil to prevent Abbas from implementing reforms that would undermine the power that they had acquired under Arafat. Fatah-affiliated fighters wanted to lash out at the system they accused of taking them for granted. Islamic Jihad ignored Abbas and carried out suicide bombings that claimed five Israeli lives in 2005. Various groups continued firing rockets from Gaza.

Facing domestic challenges, Abbas hoped concessions from Israel and aid from the United States would increase public support for a return to negotiations. These hopes were disappointed. Sharon evacuated some eight thousand settlers in Israel's unilateral disengagement from Gaza that summer but moved forward with plans to confiscate Palestinian land and expand other settlements in the West Bank.[198] Israel removed some checkpoints but put others in place.[199] It released a fraction of its Palestinian prisoners but detained far more new ones.[200] Ignoring Abbas, the IDF made some two thousand incursions into Palestinian areas and killed more than seven hundred Palestinians during the course of 2005.[201]

Caught between Israel and Palestinian militants, Abbas looked to the PA's January 2006 elections as a way of reining in parties that he was personally unable to control. Elections might have marked an advance toward strengthening the PA regime, as Hamas, Fatah, and other groups agreed to integrate into a single institution under a single set of rules. However, internal and external actors rejected the results: a victory for Hamas and affiliated independents with 78 of 132 seats. Israel refused both to deal with the PA and to transfer its custom revenues. The United States and the European Union announced that they would cut off aid to the PA until Hamas recognized Israel, denounced terrorism, and complied with all previous agreements. The new Hamas-led government refused to capitulate.

Fatah officially accepted the new government but unofficially sought to make it fail by ignoring Hamas ministers and stirring havoc in the streets. Under Arafat, political power had never been fully institutionalized, but at least had been concentrated in the person of the president. Now that power was split between two movements of comparable strength. The Saudi-brokered Mecca Agreement brought Fatah and Hamas together in a unity government. Yet Israel refused to recognize it, and the United States reportedly funded and armed Fatah to defeat the Islamists.[202] The long-boiling confrontation exploded in June 2007, when Hamas, accusing Fatah of plotting a coup, ousted Fatah-affiliated security forces and took control of the Gaza Strip in a few bloody days. The schism in the Palestinian body politic thus became geographic as well as political. Correspondingly, the PA was no longer a weak regime struggling to constrain a militant opposition. Rather, it became one of two factions struggling for power.

These changed circumstances rendered triadic coercion an inapt tool, even for Israeli decision-makers. The Fatah-led PA's claims to territorial control and political legitimacy were limited to the West Bank. Israel did not need to pressure Fatah to arrest, intimidate, and obstruct Hamas members in areas that Fatah controlled. The bitter internecine feud left Fatah predisposed to do so without any cajoling. Hamas was similarly ready to suppress Fatah supporters in Gaza.[203] Rather than triadic coercion, Israel, together with the United States, sought to help Abbas's PA consolidate power in the West Bank on the one hand, while isolating Hamas and sealing off Gaza on the other. Insistent on preventing Hamas from entering the ranks of legitimate political actors, Israeli governments also repeatedly intervened to disrupt Palestinian interfactional dialogue, reconciliation agreements, or unity governments.[204]

Israeli governments also undertook unilateral military action to stop rocket fire. Israel fought wars against the Gaza Strip in 2008–2009, 2012, and 2014. These left thousands of civilians dead and tens of thousands injured, and caused billions of dollars in material damage. Though each assault resulted in a momentary lull in rocket fire on Israel, none resolved the underlying issues propelling Palestinians' military activity. Approaching these confrontations, many in the Israeli defense establishment conceptually conflated the preventative notion of deterrence with the reactive notion of "destroying terrorist infrastructure." As of this writing, both the temporary and cumulative deterrent effectiveness of this new approach—increasingly labeled "mowing the grass"[205]—remain to be shown. Arguably, the assessment expressed by Malka in 2008 continues to hold: "What occurred and is still occurring in the Palestinian theater since the end of 2000 indicates the collapse of all the components of deterrence from both (the Israeli and Palestinian) directions."[206]

Nevertheless, the concept of triadic coercion has become so entrenched in Israel's strategic culture over the decades that it continues to reemerge in the state's security thinking. Thus, even as it refused to recognize Hamas, Israel paradoxically declared that it would hold Hamas accountable for any violence from the territory that it controlled. Accordingly, it targeted retaliation against Hamas for cross-border rocket fire from Gaza, even if it was launched by groups opposed to Hamas rule. Some of the most prominent groups of this sort identified with Salafism, a hardline kind of Islamism embracing a literal interpretation of the Quran.[207] For example, in May 2015 the IDF determined that the source of rocket fire toward the south of Israel was the Islamic Jihad. Regardless, it retaliated against Hamas, stating that "Hamas is the address and it is the one which should bear responsibility."[208] This showed how little Israel had learned from its checkered history of triadic coercion against the Palestinians and Arab states. Driven by an aggressive strategic culture and inattentive to the weakness of Palestinian governmental authority, Israel was poised to use triadic coercion under conditions in which it could not be effective.

Conclusion

Israel's triadic coercion against the PA was distinct from that against other countries because the PA was a self-governing apparatus rather than a state. In some respects, it was simply one of several groups competing for leadership of the Palestinian national movement. Yet it also sought to be the governing authority setting the rules of the political game for other actors in the territory that Israel transferred to it.

As a product of the Oslo Accords the PA promised to prevent Palestinian groups from using violence against Israel. Israel employed various strategies to hold the PA to that pledge. During the first years of the peace process Israel wielded both the promise of peace dividends and threats of delayed redeployments to encourage Arafat to fulfill his obligations. However, Palestinian groups opposed to both Arafat and Oslo did not abandon military means, and attacks took on the new form of suicide bombings inside Israel. Responding to terror, Israel increasingly turned to triadic coercion to pressure the PA to prevent violence. At the same time, Israel struck at Palestinian militants directly by carrying out arrests, raids, and extrajudicial killings. Israel's strategy was characterized by this dual use of triadic and direct coercion until 1996, when, in the course of confrontations between the IDF and Palestinian civilians, the Palestinian police opened fire on Israeli troops. This "tunnel crisis" was a turning point; in its wake, Israeli security planners came to regard the PA as a potential adversary more than as a partner.

The peace process continued, disappointing both Israeli and Palestinian expectations, until it hit the wall of the July 2000 Camp David II Summit.

Thereafter, a narrative took hold in Israel that it had offered generous concessions to the Palestinians, who, in rejecting them, proved that they did not want peace. That narrative dovetailed with shifts in Israeli security thinking that had been taking root since the mid-1990s with the increasing focus on low-intensity conflict, deterrence, and other related adaptations to the post–Cold War environment. This backdrop to Israel's strategic culture dramatically encouraged Israel's embrace of triadic coercion against the PA when protests spread across Palestinian communities that September.

The impact of strategic culture on Israel's use of triadic coercion against the second Intifada was evidenced in both its decision-making and ideational pillars. Various decision-making processes combined to encourage Israel to deploy punishing force against Palestinians in general and the PA in particular. Among the formal and informal institutional elements shaping Israel's strategic culture were the weakness of civilian checks on the military's towering role over security matters, the IDF's anti-intellectual preference for action over careful thinking, and the considerable autonomy of officers and soldiers in the field. In the realm of ideas, a set of assumptions and convictions crystalized that treated deterrence as a goal rather than a means; lacked nuanced differentiation among actors with different interests, structures, and capabilities; put exaggerated onus on enemy consciousness; and justified severe force on the basis of its moral appropriateness, not its expected outcomes. During the first months of the Intifada, this strategic culture led Israel to employ triadic coercion not only to compel the PA to stop all violence from areas under its control but also simply to prove that Israel was not weak.

Israeli decision-makers were rational in doubting Arafat's commitment to opposing violence. Yet they did not give adequate attention to the extent to which the PA's weakness as a regime conditioned Arafat's interests in allowing violence, to say nothing of his capacity to prevent it. The PA's deficient institutional capacity and territorial control sapped its ability to impose law, make arrests, and block attacks. Its lack of political cohesion constrained its ability to fight militants who were disaffected members of the ruling faction, and particularly those from rival factions. An important minority of Palestinians opposed Oslo and supported military activity as an alternative path for ending the occupation. This percentage contracted when the peace process appeared to be moving Palestinians closer to statehood and grew when the opposite held. That trend in public opinion gave a mandate to Hamas and other movements to use violence against Israel. Their own partisan interests did likewise. Inter- and intrafactional competition generated incentives for groups to attack Israeli targets as a way of bargaining or competing with each other. Had all Palestinian political actors deferred to the PA as a legitimate leader, they might have acceded to its negotiation strategies and ceasefires. In the absence of a truly authoritative political center, however, non-PA groups had significant autonomy to carry out violence for national, partisan, or private motives. Presiding over a political system lacking in cohesion and capacity, Arafat was continually apprehensive about his domestic standing. It was thus predictable that he did not take bolder stances in confronting, as opposed to accommodating, militant opposition.

Many Israeli military policies against the PA backfired because they aggravated, rather than alleviated, these sources of regime weakness. During the Oslo years, delaying and not implementing prior agreements reduced the legitimacy of the PA regime vis-à-vis its own society. Intensification of closure and expansion of Israeli settlements undermined the territorial bases of Palestinian autonomy and undercut public confidence in the peace process. In the second Intifada, Israel's attacking of PA security force installations encouraged officers to flee to the armed uprising. Those strikes, as well as withholding monies and other measures, directly weakened the PA's institutional capacity. They thereby diminished the PA's ability to be the governing arbiter of the Palestinian political system, rather than merely another faction competing for power. Israel's stance toward Arafat as a leader—first blaming him for rejecting a generous offer and then declaring him to be irrelevant—gave him no incentive to try to rein in violence, whether or not he could. Alongside Israel's targeting of the Palestinian leadership and government, its indiscriminate or collective punishments against Palestinian society as a whole destroyed what remained of Palestinians' initial embrace of Oslo. Palestinian public opinion was the main engine of the Intifada's escalation; as the population lost confidence in negotiations and became eager to avenge violence with violence, it voiced surging support for attacks against Israel.

The attitudes and assumptions guiding Israel's use of severe military force against the PA in the second Intifada represented the culmination of a strategic culture that, building on decision-making processes and ideas inherited from earlier eras, profoundly shaped triadic coercion. In turn, the second Intifada further entrenched Israel's strategic culture by shaping

Israelis' popular expectations about appropriate strategies for fighting terror, media discourse about what constituted national resolve, and political norms about what civilian and political decision-makers must do, lest they appear weak. One of the many damaging legacies of Israel's experience of the rise and fall of the Oslo peace process, therefore, was a renewed embrace of triadic coercion. By the mid-2000s, Israel was bringing a newly emotional and moralistic energy to its faith in military measures against governments that hosted militant nonstate actors, even under conditions when such measures were unlikely to accomplish Israel's goals.

CHAPTER 6

Lebanon Before and Since 2006

Strategic Culture at War

On July 12, 2006, Hezbollah carried out an ambush and kidnapping just inside the Israeli border. For Israel, this attack was a tactical surprise, not a strategic threat. Nevertheless, Israel responded with a thirty-four-day war that was devastating for Lebanon, and also very costly for Israel. One of Israel's key goals and justifications for the war was to reestablish its deterrent posture. By war's end, however, many elites and citizens expressed concern that the war had only degraded Israel's ability to deter its enemies. A decade later, many strategic analysts, noting general quiet in northern Israel since 2006, concluded that the deterrence effort was successful after all. They argued that the key to the war's effectiveness was its targeting of Lebanese infrastructure. They asserted that Israel must continue to pursue such policies of triadic coercion should nonstate actors attack again. Over the course of these oscillations, Israelis appeared to do little substantive thinking about what deterrence actually meant, who precisely was to be deterred, and how striking a weak host state could compel it to stop attacks by a strong nonstate actor.

We attribute the striking neglect of these issues, as well as the severe retaliations that they enabled, to developments in Israel's strategic culture and the ways that it encouraged and escalated triadic coercion. As in the past, Israel's defense establishment dominated security decision-making processes and used its formal and informal power to advocate direct threats and punishments against the Lebanese state. Those who opposed such a strategy did so primarily out of concern for diplomatic repercussions, not doubts about triadic coercion's effectiveness. At the same time, the push to inflict costs on Lebanon as a host state was not grounded in sound calculations about how and why that would terminate violence by nonstate actors. Rather, Israel's advocacy of triadic coercion reflected assumptions and attitudes that had become prominent in its security thinking during the prior decade through actions against the PA, as described in chapter 5. Among these were a focus on the inherent rather than instrumental utility of actions in pursuit of deterrence, lack of nuance in distinguishing among the heterogeneous actors and interests constituting what Israel homogeneously cast as "the enemy," emphasis on the appropriateness of retaliation regardless of its consequences, and a preoccupation with searing into the "consciousness" of adversaries a respect for Israel's strength and resolve.

Exploring these issues, we begin this chapter with a discussion of the institutional and political weakness of the Lebanese state and governmental system. In the next two sections we survey Israel's triadic relations with Lebanon from the start of Palestinian groups' attacks in the 1960s through the rise of Hezbollah after 1985. The fourth section analyzes Israel's 2000 withdrawal from Lebanon and its effect on strategic culture, arguing that this unilateral step produced a sense of humiliation that the IDF was eager to erase, as well as a sense that Israel was morally justified in responding to border violations with severe force. The fifth section turns to the 2006 War and demonstrates how Israel's strategic culture, in both its decision-making and ideational components, shaped the use of triadic coercion. The sixth section scrutinizes and criticizes the widespread view that developed in Israel after 2006, which further endorsed triadic coercion. The final section concludes with a recap of what we see as the flawed lessons that Israel derived from its long conflict with Lebanon and their potentially grave implications for the future.

State and Regime Weakness in Lebanon

Lebanon is typically regarded as having one of the weakest states in the Middle East. Whereas other Arab countries saw monarchs or "presidents for life" reign for decades of relative stability, Lebanon has been characterized by a fragmented arrangement of power sharing punctured by periods of internal upheaval. Lebanon is not dominated by a single family, political party, or individual, and thus is not typically regarded as having a "regime" as are other states in the region. However, as a state and political system, its weakness is apparent in its low levels of both cohesion and capacity, not unlike the weak regimes that we analyze in other chapters.

Lebanon's low level of internal political cohesion is a structural facet of its confessional political system. Since the nineteenth century, the most salient source of internal cleavage and conflict in Lebanon has been that between its eighteen different sectarian communities.[1] A system of confessional power sharing was instituted in the mid-nineteenth century and sustained under French colonial rule, which created Lebanon's current borders. Upon independence in 1943, leading Maronite Catholic and Sunni Muslim politicians forged the "National Pact." This unwritten agreement affirmed Lebanon to be a consociational democracy in which governmental and bureaucratic offices would be distributed among religious communities.[2]

While the consociational system helped forge a single state from disparate communities with different visions of the nation, it was, in Michael Hudson's words, "a remedy for the symptoms of sectarian strife rather than a cure."[3] Sectarian conflict undermined the legitimacy of state institutions, especially as communities' allotted political representation never accurately reflected their demographic weight, and did so even less over time.[4]

The dominant cleavage until the 1975 start of the civil war was that between Maronite Catholics, who held predominant political, economic, and social power, and Muslim communities and other oppositionists, which experienced various levels of disadvantage in the existent system. By the war's end in 1990, Sunni and Shiite movements were ascendant, and the Christian community stood militarily devastated, politically divided, and demographically weakened by emigration. Thereafter, politics became increasingly polarized between Sunni- and Shiite-dominated political blocs, each with different support bases, foreign policies, and patrons. Then, as now, competition within sects was often as acute as that between them. Regional identities, personal fiefdoms, interference by external parties, and sheer power politics added still other layers of crisscrossing complexity to this fragmented landscape. The result has been a plethora of groups that continually maneuver to protect and advance their power relative to each other, and political parties that form and break complex coalitions as they jockey for their share of public resources. The state is typically a tool or piece of turf in these battles, rather than an arbiter constraining factions for some greater collective good.[5]

Compounding the political system's poor cohesion is the state's deficient capacity. This deficiency is the result of both history and design insofar as it has been fundamental to the maintenance of the sectarian political order.[6] In coming together in the National Pact, confessional elites were fearful that an empowered state apparatus might interfere in confessions' private affairs or that their rivals might seize the state to act against them. At the same time, a weak state offered a context in which leaders could cooperate with each other in a shared interest in maintaining social peace. The corollary to the state's weakness was its economic noninterventionism: Lebanon was traditionally the foremost laissez-faire economy in the developing world.[7]

Since independence, Lebanon experienced recurrent crises and tumultuous transformations. Efforts were made to reform the system from above, such as under the state-strengthening efforts of President Fuad Chehab (1958–1964), or from below, such as the leftist movement whose call to end the sectarian system helped precipitate the civil war. Nevertheless, the rules of the political and economic game envisioned at the state's founding have largely persisted. The state functions as a pie to be divided among competing leaders as much as an independent actor. The sectarian system entails giving all political bosses a share in decision-making as well as participation in government ministries, control over licensing, and access to the contracts that are major sources of wealth. This practice not only leads to waste but also generates incentives for elites to create crises in an attempt to renegotiate the size of their share of government resources and decision-making.[8]

The reliance on elite consensus, rather than autonomous institutions and law, facilitates politicians' abuse of privilege and protects them from accountability, even when there is abundant evidence that they have committed crimes. The result is endemic corruption, vote buying, political interference in the judiciary, the emergence of monopolistic cliques in the private sector, and destruction with impunity of antiquities and the environment.[9] Some charge that a cabal of warlords and businessmen rule the country by means of a kind of institutionally legitimized money laundering.[10]

The result has been weak institutional capacity in several key realms of the state. In the economic sphere, Lebanon never created the empowered, centralized taxation system that is the hallmark indicator of a state's capacity and an essential component for the functioning of its other institutions.[11]

Rather, the bulk of state revenue comes from indirect taxes, which require much less institutional muscle to extract.[12] During the civil war, state taxation collapsed, and an illegal and thus inherently untaxable economy flourished.[13] Graft-ridden state spending and a lack of state definition and implementation of national development priorities further hampered the economy. Lebanon's public debt increased from US$2 billion in 1992 to US$42 billion at the end of 2007,[14] giving it the world's highest per capita public debt at that time.[15] Shackled state intervention in the economy has contributed to widespread economic inequality, a gap between wages and prices, and high unemployment. In consequence, the country is dependent on infusions of money from the estimated 10 to 25 percent of citizens who reside outside the country's borders.[16] Whereas many stronger states institute policies to channel migrant remittances to serve national development priorities, Lebanon's laissez-faire system leaves groups to vie over funds from the diaspora in their competition with each other.[17] Meanwhile, the state's inability to provide essential public goods and services leaves an array of nonstate actors to assume that role instead.[18]

Lebanon's lack of institutional capacity is also apparent in the marked weakness of its coercive and security apparatuses. The Lebanese army is weak due to lack of both resources and political consensus about its role.[19] Lebanon stands out among Middle Eastern states for the relatively small size of its military budget. Military expenditures amounted to less than $1.5 billion in 2004. This represented 4.5 percent of GDP (in contrast to Israel, where military expenditures were 8.1 percent of GDP) and 16.8 percent of central government expenditures (in contrast to Syria, where military expenditures were 28.3 percent of the government total).[20] In several incidents over the decades the Lebanese army attempted to confront armed threats but failed. On other occasions the army did not even make such attempts. In 1958, when President Camille Chamoun faced a Nasserite rebellion, the army positioned itself as neutral and refused to intervene.[21] Unable to command his own armed forces, the president resorted to requesting help from the United States, which dispatched Marines to Beirut. During the civil war, the government's order to attack opposition forces led some in the army to attempt a coup and others to desert en masse.[22] Later, facing interventions from the far superior Syrian and Israeli armies, the Lebanese army did not try to resist. In 2007, the army undertook what was lauded as a formidable demonstration of force when it assaulted the extremist group Ansar Al-Islam in northern Lebanon. That it took three months and the life of 168 soldiers to overcome the resistance of a small militia, however, was testimony to the ill preparation of Lebanon's national defense.[23]

This institutional and political weakness had direct implications for Lebanon's inability to exercise sovereignty over its own territory. The army failed in its attempts to wrestle authority over Palestinian refugee camps in the 1960s. After the start of the civil war, the PLO and its Lebanese allies controlled most of southern Lebanon, with the pro-Israel South Lebanon Army (SLA) militia controlling a thin strip directly north of the Israeli border. Only a few thousand strong at the outset of the war, the Lebanese army had no presence in either area.[24] From 1982 to 2000, Israel occupied southern Lebanon with the help of the SLA. Hezbollah, the largest militia not demobilized after the 1989 Taif Agreement terminated the civil war, became the effective military and political power in southern Lebanon from 2000 to 2006. It enjoys preponderant control in much of the South and the Bekaa Valley today.

Lebanon's complex relationship with Syria has further undermined its territorial control. In 1976, Syria sent troops into Lebanon in an attempt to quell the civil war. Throughout the next fifteen years of war it occupied parts of Lebanon or intervened on the part of this or that party, as served its interests. Syria thereby crucially influenced the balance of power among competing Lebanese factions and the fate of the overall struggle for Lebanon. After Taif, Syria supervised Lebanese foreign policy, controlled its security matters, manipulated elections, and generally regulated access to its high political posts, all the while extracting profits from its domination.[25]

Three other factors have further undermined the ability of the Lebanese state to penetrate and exercise authority over social forces. First, the real arbiters of power in society have traditionally not been government bodies but local strongman, notables, and political bosses. Citizens often access vital services and opportunities through such influential patrons rather than through the state; in turn it is they, not the state, who exercise meaningful authority over their clients.[26]

Second, the Lebanese state never tried to develop meaningful political authority over the approximately 10 percent of the population that are noncitizen Palestinian refugees.[27] Descendants of the some one hundred thousand refugees who crossed the northern border during the 1948 war, Palestinians in Lebanon have traditionally been legally disenfranchised, residentially segregated, economically deprived, and victims of social discrimination.[28] In this context PLO groups were able to create an effective state-within-a-state governing Palestinian camps and communities. In Lebanon's fragmented system, some elites perceived the PLO as a political threat, while others welcomed it as an ally.

Third, the state, as well as the dominant Christian and Sunni imaginings of the Lebanese nation, long marginalized Lebanese Shia.[29] In addition to having the least institutionalized power in terms of high government offices and parliamentary seats, the predominately Shiite South and the Bekaa Valley historically received a lesser share of government attention and funds, and thus ranked lower in development indicators.[30] State neglect, compounded by exploitation by a handful of Shiite aristocratic families and the monopolistic tobacco industry, left these regions the poorer "other Lebanon."[31] Landless Shiite sharecroppers carried that disadvantage with them when they migrated to the "misery belt" of the southern suburbs around the capital.[32]

In 1974, Musa al-Sadr mobilized the "Movement of the Deprived" to advance Shiite collective interests. The movement created Amal, a militia and then political party, from which some left to create Hezbollah in 1985. Denied fair representation in the state, Shia of various classes came to support these nonstate movements as the best protectors of their rights, dignity, and security.[33] Hezbollah gained broad popularity due to its reputation as an uncorrupt provider of the essential services that the state did not: a resistance force liberating Lebanese territory from occupation in a way that the state was not able and a political party ensuring Shia a seat at the governmental table that they otherwise would not have.[34] Had the state itself earned greater legitimacy among its Shiite population—now one of the two largest sects in Lebanon, if not the largest[35]—an armed nonstate powerhouse might not have come to possess such sweeping autonomy.

These multiple, self-reinforcing dimensions of state weakness greatly reduced the likelihood that Israel's triadic coercion could bring the Lebanese state to stop nonstate actors on its soil. The state's lack of territorial control gives nonstate actors considerable freedom to use state territory as a base for cross-border violence. The fact that real political power lies with elite bosses, rather than codified institutions, means that implementation of state policies is largely conditional on the consent and cooperation of individuals, not policies made at the political center. The alienation of the local population from the central government leaves an administrative and institutional void, which nonstate actors are ideally situated to fill. They might come to act as surrogate states, providing public goods or offering protection or representation that can help them garner support for their armed activity even from residents who do not necessarily support their military ambitions.[36] In such a context, the state might meet with few popular allies if it, under the pressure of triadic coercion, tries to coerce nonstate actors into submission.

Given the precarious bargaining that underlies the Lebanese political system, a political status quo is stable as long as there is consensus on preserving it. When there is no such consensus, the government easily plunges into crisis. This generates a built-in incentive for politicians to avoid difficult decisions that would antagonize other elites. Effective triadic coercion—upholding raison d'état in the face of opposition—depends precisely on a government's ability to undertake and sustain that kind of unpopular stance. The very nature of Lebanon's politics is thus an inherent obstacle to triadic coercion success.

Israel, Lebanon, and the PLO, 1949–1985

The Israeli-Lebanese border was largely quiet for the first fifteen years of Israeli statehood. No territorial disputes like the conflict with Syria over the Hula Valley caused militarized tensions. Palestinian refugee camps were not located near the border and were not militarized. This situation changed with the rise of Fatah and other guerrilla groups, after which Lebanon became an active arena for nonstate actors. Israel responded to Palestinian cross-border attacks with severe retaliation, including two massive invasions in 1978 and 1982. Nevertheless, it generally did not employ triadic coercion. Israel largely viewed the Lebanese regime as cooperatively predisposed against Palestinian nonstate actors. Following the Rabin Doctrine, it focused attacks directly on nonstate actors rather than on the state.

One notable exception to this pattern occurred in December 1968. Before 1967, Palestinian groups in Lebanon concentrated on attacking Israel across or inside its borders. Thereafter a new tactic emerged: international operations targeting Israeli civilians and interests outside the Middle East. According to Ariel Merari and Shlomo Elad, Palestinian groups executed 435 such attacks from 1968 to 1984.[37] For Israeli intelligence, identifying these groups' home bases became a top priority. In December 1968, the

PFLP attacked an El Al plane in Athens, killing one and injuring one. Determining that the perpetrators had come from Lebanon, the IDF staged a commando raid on the Beirut International Airport, during which it destroyed thirteen airliners owned predominantly by Lebanese and other Arab carriers.

Israel justified its attack in terms of triadic coercion. Defense Minister Moshe Dayan explained that it was "intended to bring the Arab states to reconsider whether their guerrilla warfare was worthwhile in the long run."[38] As Prime Minister Levy Eshkol elaborated, "It is the states that enable the sabotage organizations to prepare and commit terrorist acts that bear responsibility for the acts of aggression. They cannot disclaim this responsibility."[39] Addressing the Knesset, Eshkol added: "Lebanon cannot claim that it has no control over terrorist actions which are being organized in its territory. A state that does not want to control its citizens and residents, or is not capable of doing this, does not fulfill its basic political and humane obligations. Rules of international law stipulate clearly . . . that a state that shelters aggressors is an aggressor."[40]

That Israel was able to act inside Lebanon without interference precipitated a crisis in Lebanese politics. In April 1969, Palestinians and oppositionists defied a government ban on demonstrations and rallied thousands in a demonstration in support of the Palestinian guerrillas. Security forces cracked down, leaving eleven dead, eighty-three wounded, and two hundred arrested.[41] Lebanon's fragmentation and chronic weakness became further apparent in May, when the army clashed with Palestinian fighters but proved unable to stem either the fedayeen's rising numbers or their cross-border attacks on Israel. That August and September, Lebanese government forces attempted to impose a siege on Palestinian refugee camps but instead found themselves expelled by camp residents.[42]

Tension peaked in October, when another army attempt to lay siege to camps led to a general strike in solidarity with the fedayeen. Backlash forced state personnel to flee all refugee camps, and violent demonstrations resulted in casualties in several Lebanese cities. Militarily, the Lebanese state was no match for the PLO. Societally, large numbers of Lebanese civilians actively protested their state's policies. Diplomatically, several other Arab states criticized Lebanon, and Egypt intervened to push it to reconcile with the PLO. Unable to withstand domestic and regional pressure, the Lebanese government signed the Cairo Agreement that November. This turning-point accord allowed Palestinian military activity in the refugee camps and recognized the PLO as the sole authority there. Although the accord required Palestinian guerrillas to obtain state permission for any activity outside the camps, it served as an unambiguous testimony to the limits of the Lebanese state's authority over social forces in its own territory.[43]

Meanwhile, regional events further contributed to bolstering the influence of nonstate actors in Lebanon. After its 1970 expulsion from Jordan the Fatah-dominated PLO established its headquarters in Lebanon. Taking advantage of Lebanon's state weakness, guerrilla groups abrogated the terms of the Cairo Agreement by openly carrying weapons outside the camps, erecting roadblocks, and firing across the border without Lebanese army authorization.[44] Eventually the PLO became the major military power in southern Lebanon. Recognizing as much, Israel dubbed the area "Fatahland." The Lebanese army periodically attempted to assert control over the guerrillas, but the Lebanese were themselves conflicted about the PLO.[45] Unencumbered by state sovereignty, the PLO transformed Lebanon's South into a staging ground for attacks on Israel.[46]

Israel, meanwhile, generally abided by the Rabin Doctrine. It did not view Lebanon as a legitimate target of retaliation, as it had Syria or Egypt, but rather as a victim of violent nonstate actors.[47] Eschewing triadic coercion, Israel thus targeted most of its actions in Lebanon at nonstate actors themselves. Israel responded to the massacre of athletes in the Munich Olympics by launching another raid on Beirut in April 1973. Unlike the 1968 airport raid, however, it did not aim at Lebanese installations but sent its commandos to assassinate PLO officials directly. Prime Minister Golda Meier explained that IDF forces had been specifically ordered to avoid contact with Lebanese infrastructure, soldiers, and civilians.[48]

Israel sustained that policy as Lebanon slid into a civil war in 1975, the state collapsed, and the PLO expanded its control in the South. Then, in March 1978, a Lebanon-based PLO cell managed a major attack in Israel. In response Israel launched an unprecedented invasion and occupation of South Lebanon up to the Litani River.[49] As quoted in the *Washington Post*, the IDF spokesperson explained that Israel's goal was to destroy terrorists' capacities by striking directly at their bases, while taking care not "to harm the population, the Lebanese army or the [Syrian peacekeeping] force."[50] Defense Minister Ezer Weizman added that it was "not a reprisal operation in the usual sense."[51]

After four months, Israel withdrew and ceded control over the area to the United Nations Interim Force in Lebanon (UNIFIL) peacekeeping operation.⁵² Nevertheless, nonstate cross-border attacks continued. In June 1982, Israel launched Operation Peace for Galilee, a larger ground invasion that again sought to break the PLO, not pressure the Lebanese state. Israeli troops reached the outskirts of Beirut, and, after withstanding a nine-week siege, the PLO agreed to evacuate its forces from Lebanon. Israeli troops remained deployed deep in Lebanese territory until 1985, when they withdrew from all but a "security zone" in the South. It occupied that zone until 2000, using the SLA as a proxy militia to enforce its control.

Though Israel's operations responded to provocations by PLO groups, they did not constitute triadic coercion. Since the 1960s, Israel assessed the Lebanese government to be a cooperatively predisposed, hapless victim of nonstate actors. Adhering to the Rabin Doctrine, it thus targeted nonstate actors directly. In occupying Lebanon, Israel aimed at destroying, expelling, and preventing the regroup of Palestinian fighters; it sought to do what it perceived the Lebanese state was unable to do, not punish that state for its failures. The Lebanese would nevertheless pay a high price for Israel's intervention in terms of population displacement, economic deterioration, societal disruption, and the suffering of the population forced to live under Israeli control. Yet, in Israel's security and political thinking, it was not Israel's purpose to punish Lebanon as a state, government, or people. Even as it seized part of Lebanon, it continued to view Lebanon as not complicit in nonstate actors' crimes. This view would change as the occupation, paradoxically, gave rise to a new nonstate threat that fought not in the name of Palestine, but of liberating Lebanese territory.

Israel, Lebanon, and Hezbollah, 1985–2000

In 1985, Shiite Lebanese clerics and activists founded Hezbollah as an Islamic movement to carry out armed resistance against the Israeli occupation in South Lebanon. In the decades that followed, Hezbollah grew into a powerful, multifaceted political movement providing services, protection, social empowerment, and political representation to Shia in Lebanon.⁵³ Hezbollah was established with Iranian assistance and has remained dependent on Iranian funding and weaponry. It also relied on Syrian assistance as a political backer, conduit for Iranian weapons, and guarantor of training grounds in Lebanon's Bekaa Valley.⁵⁴ Nevertheless, Hezbollah was no mere proxy. It had its own leadership and support base and exercised genuine agency in determining its courses of military, political, and social action. It acted as a statelike authority in the area north of Israel's "security zone" and, beginning in 1992, participated in elections and won seats in parliament. It also became Israel's major nonstate adversary on its northern border, and the first non-Palestinian organization that it would fight using triadic coercion.

From 1985 to 2000, Hezbollah generally fought Israel by launching guerrilla-style strikes on troops in South Lebanon and firing mortars or rockets across the border. Israel typically responded by returning fire or carrying out ambushes and other operations aimed at Hezbollah forces. With time, Hezbollah became increasingly skilled in guerrilla strikes causing IDF casualties. Starting in 1992, it expanded its firing of Katyusha rockets at civilian targets inside Israel. Neither the IDF's superiority in firepower and technology, nor its capabilities in offensive conventional warfare, offered much advantage in low-intensity clashes with a nimble and motivated nonstate actor organically embedded in its own home turf. Defensive measures, such as hardened fortifications and IDF movement in convoys, likewise proved ineffective. Frustrated, the IDF command searched for other strategic options.[55] This search coincided with the crisis in Israeli strategic thinking discussed in chapter 2. Facing the changed environment of the 1990s, Israeli security elites evolved new ideas about how to transform conflicts with nonstate actors into the kind of interstate battles that Israel was skilled at fighting. These ideas endorsed triadic coercion as a strategy by which Israel would target states that hosted nonstate actors to "leverage" pressure to coerce them to restrain those nonstate actors.

Exercising leverages was no simple matter in the complex Lebanese political arena. During billionaire businessman Rafik Hariri's first term as prime minister (1992–1998), the government gained a degree of elite cohesion, and the country experienced economic recovery. Nevertheless, the main factor undergirding Lebanon's stability simultaneously demonstrated its weakness as a state. The Syrian army had sustained a presence in Lebanon since 1976, and the Taif Agreement effectively acknowledged its role as the power broker guaranteeing Lebanon's reconstitution as a nation-state. From 1989 to 2005, Lebanon (with the exception of the Israeli-occupied South) thus existed under what some called "Pax Syriana."[56] Using its large military and extensive intelligence services throughout Lebanon, as well as a network of Lebanese political allies, Syria maintained virtual control of Lebanese politics, especially as it pertained to security and foreign policy. This hegemony was institutionalized through the 1991 "Treaty of Brotherhood, Cooperation, and Coordination," followed by a Defense and Security Pact, which effectively subordinated Lebanese decision-making to Syrian approval.[57]

Against this backdrop, Israel judged that Lebanon's government was no longer positively predisposed toward cooperation with its demands. According to the Rabin Doctrine, Lebanon was now a legitimate target for Israeli triadic coercion. However, Lebanon remained a weak regime. The strong Syrian regime dominated it from behind the scenes, but the Lebanese government itself had few political or institutional resources with which to exercise authority over a powerful nonstate actor with fighters on the ground and representatives in the parliament.

Israel largely failed to distinguish among these different actors and interests operating on the Lebanese scene. It was in that context that Israel broke with the past and, in two massive operations in the 1990s, moved toward triadic coercion against Lebanon. Israel launched the first, Operation Accountability, in response to a series of Hezbollah attacks that killed seven IDF soldiers in July 1993. The IDF directed massive artillery shelling on areas of South Lebanon under Hezbollah control, and Hezbollah responded with Katyusha rockets to northern Israel. As the battle escalated, Israel declared that its aim was to destroy Hezbollah's infrastructure.[58] Israel did not target Lebanon directly as a host state. Nevertheless, its strategy resonated with the logic of triadic coercion insofar as it sought to create a crisis that would pressure both the Lebanese government and its Syrian patron to act against Hezbollah.[59] As Chief of Staff Barak told American diplomat Dennis Ross, Israel sought to exert leverage by triggering a massive wave of displaced villagers from the South into Beirut. Israel reasoned that it would thereby coerce Lebanon's government to plead with Damascus to rein in Hezbollah.[60]

This strategy proved ineffective. Neither the Lebanese government nor Syria took action against Hezbollah. Rather, Hezbollah recuperated from its material losses and continued attacks on IDF and SLA forces.[61] In March 1996, Israeli troops killed two Lebanese civilians in South Lebanon, and Hezbollah answered by firing Katyusha rockets on northern Israel. Israel responded with Operation Grapes of Wrath, a campaign of intensive bombing and shelling of both Hezbollah installations and civilian infrastructure in the South, the Bekaa Valley, and the southern suburbs of

Beirut.[62] In the course of these strikes, Israel forces unintentionally shelled a UN hospital in the village of Qana, killing 160 civilians. The United States then intervened to end hostilities. As in 1993, Israel's goal in the 1996 operation reflected logics of both a direct attack on a nonstate actor's capabilities and triadic coercion to alter state motivations. "The aim is Hezbollah," Israeli cabinet member Yossi Beilin explained. "The venue or the vehicle may be pressure on the government of Lebanon."[63]

The mechanism by which the identified "vehicle" would accomplish the stated goal, however, was unclear. Most accounts agree that Israel's primary objective was to generate leverage via a refugee crisis. According to the *Washington Post*, Israel declared that it aimed not to kill civilians but to scare them into fleeing north.[64] Israel thus distributed warnings, urging civilians to abandon their homes by a precise time before bombardment was to begin.[65] Beyond hoping to use population displacement to coerce the government, Israel also imposed triadic coercion more directly by blockading Lebanese seaports and bombing an electric power station. These targets, the *Washington Post* reported, "intended to wreak economic harm on Lebanon as additional pressure on its government to act to curb Hezbollah."[66]

Israel's thinking behind this strategy reveals a lack of clarity. On the one hand, some Israeli elites reasoned that military pressure would force Lebanon to act independently and authoritatively. As Barak, Israeli foreign minister at the time, declared on the operation's first day, "Lebanon must exert its sovereignty and bring about the disarmament of Hizbollah."[67] On the other hand, other officials appeared to reason that triadic coercion could be effective precisely because Lebanon was *not* independent and authoritative but rather reliant on Syria. As with Operation Accountability, some Israeli security elites apparently calculated that military pressure on the Lebanese government was desirable because it would put it in such a situation of crisis that Lebanon would beg Syria to intervene and crackdown on Hezbollah on its behalf.[68] Israel thus entertained triadic coercion as a means of indirectly coercing Syria on the grounds that Syria was both the major enabler of Hezbollah's violence and the real power broker in the Lebanese political system.

Whatever its rationale, Israel's triadic coercion against Lebanon in the 1990s proved unsuccessful. In Zeev Maoz's words, both Operation Accountability and Operation Grapes of Wrath applied "massive use of firepower in an effort to compel the civilian population to restrain Hezbollah" and "failed to yield such restraint."[69] Hezbollah attacks killed an average of twenty IDF soldiers per year in Lebanon from 1990 to 1996. In 1997, the year following Operation Grapes of Wrath, that toll rose to thirty. Hezbollah carried out an average of three hundred attacks per year in the "security zone" in the early 1990s. By 1998 that number was no less than one thousand.[70] Nor did triadic coercion yield new policies from the Lebanese government. Repeatedly, the Lebanese government declared that its own population would decry any action against Hezbollah as long as the Israeli occupation continued. Should it risk its own legitimacy and confront Hezbollah, it therefore risked provoking civil war.[71]

Regardless, as long as Syria dominated in Beirut and had an interest in Hezbollah activity against Israel, no Israeli pressure on the Lebanese state would bring that activity to a halt.[72] The indirect pressure that Israel was hoping to leverage against Syria was insufficient to force Assad to relinquish what he saw as his major asset in Lebanon. As Ross reflected on the 1993 operation, "The Israeli campaign was based on one flawed assumption. Assad did not care if the Lebanese were suffering; moreover, he was surely pleased by the situation that put the onus on Israel internationally. With 250,000 Lebanese streaming toward Beirut in a human caravan, Assad saw only gains, not losses."[73]

Under these circumstances, Israel's triadic coercion against Lebanon did not pressure Assad into opposition to Hezbollah. On the contrary, it elevated Syria's diplomatic status because Syria alone had the power to mediate an agreement with the organization. Indeed, as Operation Accountability unfolded, Damascus became the focal point of intense shuttle diplomacy. U.S. secretary of state Warren Christopher met with Assad in an effort to bring hostilities to an end. Israel, Lebanon, the United States, and France all sought Assad's approval on a ceasefire agreement. Once that was concluded, the situation on the border largely returned to what it had been previously. Triadic coercion thus failed, and both Assad and Hezbollah emerged from the operation emboldened.[74]

Israel's strategy against Lebanon in the 1990s did not demonstrate adequate attention to either the weakness of the Lebanese government or the complex relations between Lebanon, Syria, and Hezbollah. Rather, Israel seemed to hold that military pressure on the Lebanese state, whoever controlled it, would result in "leverage" that stopped nonstate actors. This approach manifested trends in Israel's strategic culture that would continue to grow thereafter.

Withdrawal from Southern Lebanon and Its Aftermath, 2000–2006

In May 2000, Israel unilaterally withdrew its troops from, and surrendered any authority over, South Lebanon. It is difficult to overstate the far-reaching effects of this historic event on Israeli strategic culture, especially in pushing it to embrace a moralistic logic of appropriateness in targeting enemy consciousness and to valorize the inherent utility of any operations that asserted a deterrent posture.

Prime Minister Barak pursued withdrawal from Lebanon for three main reasons. First, he believed that he would benefit politically as a result of extricating troops from what the public had come to see as a quagmire that killed an average of twenty Israeli soldiers annually. By the late 1990s, more than 40 percent of Israelis supported returning troops to the international border.[75] Specific events accelerated this sentiment, including a helicopter collision that killed seventy-three soldiers, a Hezbollah ambush that killed eleven, and an improvised explosive device that claimed the life of the highest-ranking IDF officer. Agitation by civil society groups such as "The Four Mothers," formed by the mothers of Israeli soldiers killed in Lebanon, had a similar effect. Campaigning in 1999, Barak promised to withdraw from Lebanon within a year. After Barak's victory, popular support for withdrawal climbed to 60 percent.[76] Second, Barak reasoned that international opinion would accept Israel's fighting Hezbollah from the Israeli side of the border more than from within occupied southern Lebanon.[77] Withdrawal would thus bolster the international legitimacy of Israel's confrontation with the nonstate actor. Third, Barak hoped withdrawal from Lebanon would aid his pursuit of a peace deal with Syria, which was his foreign policy priority. When talks with Syria broke down in January 2000, Barak embraced withdrawal as a fallback plan. Syria was using Hezbollah to exert pressure on Israel; withdrawal would deny Syria its claim that Hezbollah was legitimate resistance against an illegal occupation. It would likewise pressure Syria to withdraw its own forces from Lebanon, given that it justified that presence in part as resistance to the Israeli occupation.[78]

The IDF High Command was nearly unanimously opposed to Barak's withdrawal plan. In making that opposition public, the General Staff emphasized the harm to be done to Israel's deterrent posture.[79] It argued that, in the absence of Israeli forces in Lebanon, Hezbollah could position itself to fire rockets that could reach most of northern Israel. The General Staff also expressed fear that Hezbollah might gain command over the hills on the Lebanese side of the border, from where it could exercise tactical superiority over IDF bases and patrols in northern Israel. Military Intelligence Chief Amos Malka warned that this tactical advantage would dangerously raise the level of Israeli force needed to deter Hezbollah from striking Israel.[80]

In May 2000, the SLA began to disintegrate, and Hezbollah intensified its attacks on SLA and IDF positions. Barak decided to expedite his plan and, two months ahead of schedule, withdrew troops in one night. Israel's eighteen-year occupation of South Lebanon thus came to an abrupt end. Hezbollah fighters promptly took control of the abandoned territory and positioned themselves on the border.[81] Whether due to Syria's bidding or its own weakness or both, the Lebanese state did not move to impose state authority over the territory.

Israel's expedited withdrawal had an enduring effect on its strategic culture with regard to deterrence in general and triadic coercion in particular. Though no IDF soldiers were killed during the withdrawal from Lebanon, the Israeli public cringed to see images of them retreating hastily and under fire. IDF units left equipment behind, including weapons and armored vehicles. They left some posts intact, allowing Hezbollah to seize them wholesale. Israel also abandoned SLA militiamen who had been defending Israel's interests for more than two decades. Though some managed to flee with their families and find shelter in Israel, thousands were left to the mercy of their sworn enemy, Hezbollah.[82]

The Israeli military and public were dismayed by these developments, which they feared indicated Israel's weakness and unreliability. Deputy Minister of Defense Ephraim Sneh articulated the sentiments of much of the population when he said that, with the withdrawal, "deterrence was lost within forty minutes."[83] As distressing for Israelis was Hezbollah's quickness in declaring victory and championing itself as the first Arab force to liberate land from Israel militarily. The propaganda power of such claims was on full display when Hezbollah general secretary Hassan Nasrallah made an historic speech in the formerly occupied South:

> A few hundred Hizbollah fighters forced the most powerful state in the Middle East to wave a white flag. The era in which the Zionists

have intimidated the Lebanese and the Arabs is over. The Zionist entity lives in fear after the defeat of the occupation army at the hands of Islamic resistance fighters in Lebanon. This fear exists not only in northern Palestine but also in the heart of Tel-Aviv, in the depth of occupied Palestine. Israel, which has nuclear weapons and the strongest air force in the region—this Israel is weaker than a spider's web.[84]

Nasrallah's words, as in other declarations in which he asserted that Israeli society was fragile, cowardly, and unable to sustain sacrifices, had a profound impact on Israelis.[85] As Amir Rapaport observed, "Few are the Israelis who did not feel personally humiliated, as if the words were aiming directly at them, in their guts. One doubts that there was any speech that had so much effect, for years, as this speech."[86] Israelis were horrified that the image of military prowess that they had worked for decades to build was not only crumbling but also being mocked. David Makovsky notes that Deputy Chief of Staff Moshe Ya'alon would later "cite Nasrallah's 'spider web' speech as suggesting that Israel had lost its deterrent as Arabs no longer feared Israel's military might."[87]

In this view, Israeli leaders were regarding Nasrallah's speech as fact rather than the political rhetoric that it was. A more measured assessment would have noted that the withdrawal had not changed the balance of power in the region. If anything, it altered the "balance of interests" in Israel's favor, in the sense that Israel was motivated by the more vital imperative of defending its homeland. Hezbollah, no longer fighting a foreign occupation, had less pressing grievances with Israel and was thus less likely to challenge it militarily. Evidence of deterrence, or lack thereof, exists in practice, not performative speeches. And evidence, as detailed below, showed a significant decrease in Hezbollah's attacks following the withdrawal.

Nevertheless, the withdrawal fed intense Israeli fears that Israel had lost deterrence; should conditions so demand, it would need to reestablish deterrence by demonstrating its national and military might. Israeli leaders emphasized that this was not simply a strategic imperative but also a matter of moral and legal right. Barak had asserted this even before May 2000, when he argued that withdrawal would create "an invisible wall of lack of legitimacy" against Hezbollah's attacks.[88] After the withdrawal Israel spent tens of millions of shekels relocating to the south of the border the fences, patrol roads, and outposts that it had moved into Lebanese territory since 1982 in an effort to gain topographic advantage.[89] Israel devoted considerable effort to persuading the UN to confirm that Israel was thus in full compliance with UN Security Council Resolution 425, adopted in 1978 to demand Israel's withdrawal from Lebanon. It welcomed the UN secretary-general's June 2000 verification of the withdrawal as a kind of moral approbation.[90] In this context, many Israelis believed that they were accepting a new vulnerability in order to make a good-faith compliance with international law. Should adversaries exploit Israel's generosity, this thinking implied, Israel would be justified in punishing them with swift and exacting force. Visiting the Northern Command just before the withdrawal, Barak promised that, if Hezbollah dared to attack Israel with even a pistol, Israel's response would be unprecedented.[91] Chief of Staff Mofaz subsequently reiterated similar threats.[92]

Tough talk aside, from 2000 to 2006, a new set of implicit "rules of the game" developed between Israel and Hezbollah.[93] According to this unspoken, unformalized status quo, Hezbollah limited its provocations to the Mt. Dov/Sheba Farms area, which remained under Israeli control. Hezbollah regarded the area as Lebanese territory not yet liberated from Israeli occupation. Israel argued that it was a part of the Golan taken from Syria in 1967, and its final status was contingent on a peace deal with Syria.[94] Hezbollah mostly limited violence to this still-contested area. The IDF, not wanting to become re-entangled in Lebanon, usually returned fire in the same direction or shelled nearby Hezbollah positions. It dubbed this measured response "containment."[95]

Trends during this period ran counter to Israeli fears of lost deterrence. Hezbollah attacks against Israeli targets numbered 1,030 between 1992 and 1996, or roughly 250 attacks per year. Their total rose to 4,060 between 1996 and 2000, or about 1,000 per year. Between the May 2000 withdrawal and the July 2006 War, by contrast, Israel counted only twenty-six attacks, or four to five per year.[96] In those six years, seventeen Israeli soldiers and one Israeli civilian were killed in clashes with Hezbollah. Another five civilians and a soldier were killed by Palestinian militants who crossed the border with Hezbollah's assistance. The total number of casualties from cross-border attacks during all six years after the withdrawal is akin to the average annual casualty count from any single year before the withdrawal.[97]

The situation that evolved during these six years carries an important implication for our arguments about strategic culture, and in particular

Israel's gravitation toward an emphasis on the inherent rather than instrumental value of use of force in pursuit of deterrence. The numbers cited above suggest that Israeli deterrence was effective. Still, Israeli security elites concluded the opposite.[98] To the degree that they compared post-2000 border clashes to unrealistic expectations of total quiet rather than to pre-2000 levels of violence, they were necessarily disappointed. A complete cessation of hostilities was unlikely, as Hezbollah had strong incentive to sustain "resistance" in order to justify refusing disarmament, Syria wanted some level of violence to pressure Israel in future negotiations, and the Lebanese government was too weak to exert authority in the South.

In this context, Israeli leaders continued to think about triadic coercion as a potential strategy. Israel considered coercion against both Syria and Lebanon, with minimal attention to their strikingly different levels of regime strength or the complicated relationship between them. Triadic coercion against both featured prominently in Barak's first public address after announcing the withdrawal, when he repeatedly emphasized that, from then on, Israel would hold Lebanon and Syria accountable if Hezbollah continued to attack Israel.[99] Barak's words were meant not only for external ears. The Israeli security establishment expressed similar thinking in internal deliberations, as the Winograd Commission would later confirm:

> There developed within the IDF a notion that it was possible to exert influence on Hezbollah indirectly through the use of "leverages," which would be sufficient to restrain the organization. Among these "leverages" it included attacks of Syrian targets in Lebanon, attacks on Lebanese infrastructure sites, etc. The assumption was that, as a result of the functioning of such "leverages," Hezbollah would restrain its operations and limit its attacks against Israeli targets when needed.[100]

The military's contingency planning applied this triadic coercion logic. Immediately after the withdrawal, the IDF began to work on an operational plan in case of large-scale clashes with Hezbollah. Code-named Defense of the Land (*Magen Haaretz*) and officially adopted in 2004, the plan called for bombing and ground forces directed against Hezbollah but also emphasized targeting Syrian forces and installations in Lebanon. During IDF exercises the same year, Chief of Staff Ya'alon altered the plan to eliminate the ground invasion and intensify the bombing campaign. Aerial strikes would target Syria, which Ya'alon identified as "the center of gravity" that could best create leverage over Hezbollah, leading to a ceasefire on Israel's terms.[101] At the same time, bombardment would also strike Lebanese installations with the goal of inflicting hardship on the Lebanese state and people. This change put an even stronger emphasis on triadic coercion than had the original plan. Yet it did not go further in clarifying how the complex political relationship between Syria and the weak Lebanese state might mediate the effect of such coercion. These plans bore the heavy imprint of the "New Operational Concept," which became dominant among high-ranking officers in the 2000s and emphasized, among other elements, the need to alter enemies' perceptions and consciousness.[102]

Israel resorted to triadic coercion twice against Hezbollah between 2000 and 2006, both times aiming strikes at Syria.[103] The most important of the two strikes occurred in October 2000, when Hezbollah ambushed an Israeli patrol in the Sheba Farms area and kidnapped three soldiers. The IDF responded with limited strikes on Hezbollah positions in the vicinity, mostly seeking to block the kidnappers' escape routes. Israel also initiated strikes on a Syrian radar post in the Lebanese Bekaa Valley.[104] Barak explained the targeting of Syria's assets on NBC's "Meet the Press":

> I think that Hezbollah ran this operation, not the Syrians, but since Syria is the prominent power player in Lebanon, out of its own choice, I have no way but to see this reality, and identify the Syrians as the source of responsibility for any attack against Israel from the soil of Lebanon, whether they directly received an order like that last one, or indirectly. But, let me tell you more than that, if Syria would take all necessary acts or steps in order to put an end to the violence of Hezbollah, I would not hold them responsible. This is the same way that I don't hold responsible King Abdullah for what comes from Jordan, since I know that he takes all the measures to put an end to it. I don't hold Mubarak responsible for what comes from Egypt, since I know he takes all steps to avoid it. But, we cannot say this about Syria, they are the power player, they are responsible, and they might be addressed.[105]

Barak's comments echoed the logic of the Rabin Doctrine: states that were predisposed toward cooperation with Israel and opposition to violent nonstate actors would be spared Israeli strikes, but states that did not do all they could against nonstate actors should expect Israeli retribution. This assessment of Syria's role was valid for much of the 1990s, when the strong regime of Hafez al-Assad may indeed have been in a position to constrain Hezbollah's actions against Israel if it wished.[106]

This situation changed in the year 2000, which witnessed both the young, inexperienced Bashar al-Assad assume power in Damascus and a surge in Hezbollah's popularity after Israel left South Lebanon. As explained in chapter 4, these developments altered the relationship between Syria and Hezbollah from one of Syrian dominance to something closer to a symbiotic partnership. Hezbollah needed Syria as a military and political umbrella to deflect the demands of some Lebanese that it disarm as other militias did after Taif, especially when there was no longer an Israeli occupation to resist. Reciprocally, Syria wanted Hezbollah's political support to legitimize its presence in Lebanon and welcomed its continued military pressure on Israel as a tool for keeping the issue of the Golan alive.[107]

This political context rendered Syria even less likely to yield to Israel's triadic coercion than it might have been in the 1990s. The Lebanese government, given its ongoing weakness, was likewise unlikely to respond to triadic coercion as Israel wished. Returning to the premiership in 2000, Rafik Hariri was locked in polarized political competition with the pro-Syrian president, Emil Lahoud. As Hariri's Future Movement and other politicians mobilized stronger opposition to Syria's role in Lebanon, Hariri came into conflict with Syria's Lebanese nonstate allies, Hezbollah and Amal.[108] The rivalry intensified in 2004, when Lahoud sought to amend the constitution to retain the presidency for another three years. Hariri and other ministers protested what they saw as Syria's intervention in internal Lebanese politics to protect its own interests, including Hezbollah's freedom of maneuver against Israel.[109]

France and the United States took this matter to the UN Security Council, which adopted Resolution 1559, calling for withdrawal of any remaining foreign forces (meaning Syria) from Lebanon and the disarmament of any remaining militias (indicating Hezbollah). That October, Hariri resigned to lead the campaign to end Syrian hegemony. In February 2005 Hariri and twenty-two bystanders were killed by a car bomb in what most assumed to be an assassination in response to his anti-Syrian position. In what became known as the "Cedar Revolution," massive demonstrations rallied citizens of diverse backgrounds to demand accountability and an end to the Syrian occupation. Despite this show of grassroots solidarity, the sectarian-political fragmentation endemic to Lebanese politics eventually came to dominate events again. On March 8, Amal and Hezbollah mobilized hundreds of thousands to praise Syria and denounce UN and Western intervention. On March 14, an equally large counterdemonstration demanded Syria's complete withdrawal from Lebanon.[110]

Succumbing to pressure, Syria pulled its forces from Lebanon in April 2005. Thereafter, several bombings and assassinations killed a number of Lebanese public figures who vocally opposed Syria's continued interference. At the same time, Lebanese politics continued to polarize. Hariri's son Saad led the Sunni-dominant March 14 Alliance to win the May–June parliamentary elections. A new government, headed by Fouad Siniora, forged close relations with the United States, France, and Saudi Arabia. Hezbollah and Amal mobilized a pro-Iran, pro-Syrian opposition under the banner of the March 8 Alliance. It also attained seats in government, though the parties fell short of gaining blocking minority power.[111]

This end of direct Syrian hegemony elevated the autonomy of the Lebanese state in some respects. Nonetheless, the government was fragmented between rivals bitterly opposed on fundamental issues of foreign policy and Hezbollah's disarmament, and the state's structural incapacity remained as acute as ever.[112] Hezbollah's effective political and military domination in the South was evidence of the state's compromised territorial control.[113] Attempts to challenge this domination would have triggered a major political crisis; indeed, when March 14 ministers referred to the movement as a "militia" rather than a "resistance," March 8 shut down the government until the statement was retracted.[114] Labels aside, the Lebanese army would scarcely have been able to confront the better-equipped, better-trained nonstate actor even if ordered to do so. It is unclear whether it would have even tried, given that the army's composition reflected Lebanese society, which held no single position on Hezbollah.[115]

This evidence of regime weakness should have cautioned Israel against the notion that pressure on the Lebanese state could coerce it to stop Hezbollah. Yet IDF planners not only retained the triadic coercion at the base of the Defense of the Land plan but in fact shifted the target from Syria to the Lebanese government in the new operational plan Elevated Waters (*Mey Marom*).[116] The IDF Operation Branch later developed an alternative operational plan, called Ice Breaker (*Shoveret Kerach*), which was similar except in timing: Israel would begin with massive bombardment of both

Hezbollah and Lebanese state infrastructure, the latter with the aim of forcing the government to disarm the militant organization. Ground forces would be sent across the border a week later, if deemed necessary.[117]

On the eve of the 2006 War, therefore, the IDF's strategy centered on triadic coercion. The IDF's main operational plan for the contingency of renewed conflagration with Hezbollah was to target the weak Lebanese state rather than the relatively strong Syrian one.[118] Shai Feldman critiqued this approach, noting that, although Syria withdrew from Lebanon in 2005, "Israel seems to have failed to realize that its post-May 2000 compellence strategy—that was based on holding Syria accountable for any attack against Israel from Lebanese soil—needed to be revised."[119] Rather, as Amir Rapaport explained, "the perception that the government of Lebanon needed to bear the brunt of Hezbollah's actions became the dominant perception in the IDF."[120] Aimed at the institutionally cohesive and capable Syrian regime, triadic coercion might have been a rational strategy for attaining military and political leverage over the nonstate Hezbollah. Aimed at the weak Lebanese government, however, it could not succeed.

Israel's 2000 withdrawal from Lebanon was a critical event in its triadic coercion history. The withdrawal came after several years in which the security establishment was experimenting with new ideas that reinforced the centrality of deterrence in Israel's strategic culture. It also came after the Operations Accountability and Grapes of Wrath, which translated these ideas into action. These operations, though unsuccessful in achieving their strategic objectives, became the model for what the IDF would come to term "deterrence operations."[121] It would later enact that model in different arenas, such as in wars against the Gaza Strip in 2008–2009, 2012, and 2014. Israel's withdrawal from Lebanon also came after the 1996 West Bank tunnel clashes, which had further convinced the IDF of the need to respond to any enemy provocation with extreme force. In this context, Israeli military elites viewed the withdrawal from Lebanon as a humiliation and a failure, notwithstanding evidence that it actually led to a significant decrease in attacks and casualties. During the six years following the withdrawal, Israel responded to Hezbollah's limited provocations with small retaliation strikes targeted against both Lebanon and Syria. The fact that these retaliations did not completely stop Hezbollah from all border violations contributed to Israeli elites' conviction that Israel needed a massive operation of triadic coercion to restore its fading deterrence. These attitudes set the stage for war in 2006.

Triadic Coercion in the 2006 War

Hezbollah declared 2005 to be "the year of retrieving prisoners."[122] The movement repeatedly articulated the threat to kidnap Israeli soldiers as a bargaining chip for gaining the release of Lebanese prisoners held in Israel, and in November of that year attempted such a kidnapping.[123] Elected in February 2006, Prime Minister Ehud Olmert began receiving reliable intelligence that Hezbollah was likely to attempt a kidnapping.[124] The Israeli leadership was thus keenly aware that a kidnapping was merely a question of when, not if.[125] Despite this knowledge, Israel had no serious and organized discussion about how it would respond to such an event and with what strategic objective. It communicated no specific threats or clear "red lines" to Hezbollah, as the logic of deterrence theory requires.[126]

It was against this backdrop that, on July 12, 2006, Hezbollah carried out an ambush just inside Israel's border with Lebanon. It kidnapped two soldiers, killed three soldiers immediately, and then killed another five who followed in frantic pursuit of the perpetrators. The next thirty-four days saw what Israelis would call the "Second Lebanon War" and Lebanese the "July War." This war cost the lives of 165 Israelis (including 121 soldiers and 44 citizens) and almost 1,200 Lebanese (including several hundred Hezbollah fighters).[127] It injured approximately 1,500 Israelis and close to 4,500 Lebanese. It also forced 300,000 Israelis from their homes and displaced close to 1 million Lebanese (nearly a quarter of the population). It also caused billions of U.S. dollars in damage, overwhelmingly in Lebanon.[128]

Israel's massive use of military force reflected a doubling down on triadic coercion that cannot be fully understood without reference to its strategic culture. As in the past, this strategic culture was built on the two pillars of decision-making processes and ideas.

Strategic Culture: Decision-Making Processes

In the 2006 War, consistent with the institutionalized pattern in Israel, it was the IDF that proposed the goals of military operations to the civilian authority, not vice versa. These proposals, supported by nearly all of the top military echelon, called for triadic coercion targeting assets of the Lebanese state to force the government to act against Hezbollah.[129]

Chief of Staff Dan Halutz epitomized this consensus. Meeting with Minister of Defense Amir Peretz hours after the kidnapping, he forcefully advocated implementation of the Ice Breaker operational plan. "We need to hit Lebanese infrastructure, in the airport and other installations," Halutz declared. He added that it was also advisable to bomb Hezbollah targets.[130] The chief of staff provided a more detailed proposal when he met with Peretz again that afternoon. He recommended that Israel strike Lebanon's international airport, gas and transport infrastructure, as well as 20 to 25 percent of its electricity infrastructure.[131]

Military elites took the lead in determining this strategic vision, while the Israeli government largely complied with their recommendations. That evening, the IDF, Mossad, and Shin Bet chiefs presented Prime Minister Olmert with six proposed objectives for Israel's response. Of these, one was "to strengthen deterrence vis-à-vis Hezbollah and the entire region" and another was "to correct the prevailing system in Lebanon, based on an effective enforcement mechanism that is supported by international involvement." The latter objective was subsequently changed to "have the Lebanese government use the Lebanese army to impose its sovereignty over its entire territory."[132] While inclusion of the first objective demonstrated the centrality of deterrence in Israeli security thinking, the second objective, especially in the revised version, pointed directly to triadic coercion.

Some decision-makers—nearly exclusively civilian—articulated opposition to triadic coercion. However, they were concerned not about its efficacy, but rather international criticism. In a decisive meeting with Peretz and Halutz, Olmert explained that the Lebanese government had good relations with the West and the West would punish Israel if it went too far in assaulting Beirut.[133] There is some uncertainty about whether, in voicing this hesitation, Olmert was presenting his own viewpoint or was deferring to pressure from the U.S. secretary of state.[134] In either case, the prime minister did not consider whether the Lebanese state possessed the cohesion and capacity to act against Hezbollah, even if Israel could coerce it to try. His only concern appears to have been diplomatic backlash.

According to existing sources, the only high-ranking Israeli leader who openly questioned the strategic efficacy of triadic coercion was Peretz—tellingly, the member of the security leadership with the least military experience. In an early meeting, Peretz reportedly asked the director of Military Intelligence how he would react if he were a Christian in Beirut who found himself with no electricity due to Israeli bombardment. The director replied that he would be angry with Hezbollah. Peretz retorted, "Do you know what I'd say? I'd say that Hezbollah was right—those Jews are crazy."[135] Against the recommendation of the generals, Peretz argued that the IDF should concentrate on Hezbollah, not Lebanese assets.

Peretz's view was backed by Olmert, and eventually the government, later that day. That night, the Israeli Air Force destroyed between one-third and one-half of Hezbollah's stockpiles of Iranian-made midrange Fajr missiles as well as fifty-nine stationary rocket launchers. This targeted operation took only half an hour and cost the life of an estimated twenty Lebanese civilians, even though rockets were hidden in homes.[136] In retrospect this mission was considered the IDF's most important and successful move in the war.[137] The General Staff had originally opposed it, however, because it was overwhelmingly focused on triadic coercion. The IDF top brass judged that striking the Lebanese government on the supposition that it would punish Hezbollah would yield greater benefit than using Israel's own military and technological superiority to punish Hezbollah directly.

Although Israel had destroyed Hezbollah's Fajr missiles, Hezbollah retained thousands of short-range Katyusha rockets. For the next month it launched those relentlessly at Israel.[138] During that time the IDF never got the authorization it sought for a sweeping triadic coercion operation, mostly due to U.S. opposition.[139] Nevertheless, the strategy crept into Israeli operations. Beginning in the first assault, the army added some public infrastructure to the target list, arguing that this was necessary to carry out operations or to impede Hezbollah's movement and weapons transportation. Thus, even though the government formally rejected the IDF's operational plan to focus the war on the Lebanese state and government, a significant part of military operations aimed at precisely that.[140] Israel neutralized Lebanon's airports and seaports and damaged the Beirut-Damascus Highway. It bombed forty-six gas stations, several fuel depots, ninety-two bridges, eighty-two communication lines, fourteen radar stations, fifty-two road tunnels, and numerous roads and interchanges throughout the country.[141] It also demolished much of Dahiya, the predominantly Shiite southern suburb of Beirut that offered a base of popular support for Hezbollah. Though bombardment of this civilian neighborhood might have intended to pressure Hezbollah directly, it also carried an element of triadic coercion. Israeli strategists believed that destruction of a residential area of the capital sent the government a uniquely strong message about Israel's capabilities and willingness to wield them. It communicated to all Lebanese, and indeed all Arab countries, that Israel would hold its state adversaries responsible for guarding their frontiers with Israel.[142]

The use of triadic coercion by the IDF, despite the government's official rejection of that strategy, reveals the imprint of Israel's particular strategic culture of decision-making. That the government did adopt targeting of the Lebanese state demonstrates the imbalance between civil and military authority in both strategic planning and operational details, as well as the force-escalating aspects of the army's own structure and organizational approach.[143] It also shows how Israel's action often preceded thinking, with war starting even before war aims were determined.[144] This indicates the Israeli military's persistent anti-intellectualism, a tradition even more apparent in the ideational dimensions of Israel's strategic culture.

Strategic Culture: Ideas

The role of strategic culture in shaping triadic coercion emerged in assumptions and contentions that, having taken root in prior years, heavily impacted events in 2006. Four ideational trends proved especially dominant in Israel's strategy against Lebanon, just as they had against the PA during the second Intifada.

INHERENT UTILITY OF ACTIONS IN PURSUIT OF DETERRENCE

In advocating triadic coercion, military elites appeared to be acting on an inherited faith in military force more than a reasoned assessment of how the costs of such actions compared with their likely benefits. Dag Henrikson explains: "Israel's decision to go to war was not based on a thorough in-depth analysis of the specific situation at hand, but rather rooted in its strategic outlook cultivated in the decades preceding the war. This thinking has largely focused on the concept of deterrence, and should deterrence fail, to restore deterrence."[145]

This circular thinking was front and center in the IDF command's first meeting with the minister of defense after the abduction. Halutz argued that Hezbollah's attack was a breach of Israeli sovereignty, which was made all the more intolerable by Hamas's kidnapping of a corporal near Gaza three weeks earlier. "We have to restore our deterrence, which got hit by the abduction of Gilad Shalit, and now received another blow," Halutz said.[146] This perspective informed the IDF's design of goals for the operation in Lebanon. Among the most paramount was "to strengthen deterrence against Hezbollah and the entire region."[147]

It does not appear that high-ranking officers stopped to spell out the logic by which their military strikes would generate deterrence. In this sense they seemed to focus on the pursuit of a deterrent posture as a goal in and of itself, rather than regarding such activity as a tool whose value lay in its ability to produce greater security. According to available records, the closest that decision-makers came to probing the instrumental, rather than inherent, utility of deterrence strikes came in an exchange between Halutz and then deputy prime minister Shimon Peres. Halutz reportedly declared, "Israel's deterrence will not be maintained just because they [Arabs] think we have this or that stuff. Even if we have them, it does not prove itself on the ground. The fact is that things [like the abduction] occur."[148] Peres asked the assembled leaders to think a few steps into the future and to consider what might be Arab responses to Israeli actions, Israel's counterresponses, and so on. Both the chief of staff and the prime minister reportedly brushed his comments aside.[149]

Just as the defense establishment appears to have made no serious effort to evaluate the expected benefits of operations to "restore deterrence," they seemed to make little attempt to assess their potential costs. In leading books of investigative reporting by Israeli journalists one is hard pressed to identify evidence of someone in the Israeli government or military command undertaking any serious reckoning of this type during or even after the war.[150] Neither does the meticulously detailed Winograd report offer such an account.[151]

As such, we were unable to find any sort of retrospective, counterfactual analysis that compares Israel's material and human losses in 2006 to a forecasting of what losses might have been had Israel not gone to war and instead sustained the prewar status quo. Bracketing Lebanese losses, which are worthy of study in their own right, this kind of an analysis is useful for gauging the effectiveness of Israel's strategy for protecting its own citizens. In the six years between Israel's withdrawal from Lebanon in 2000 and the 2006 War, four Israelis lost their lives on average each year to Hezbollah's attacks, most of them soldiers. Assuming continuation of the same pattern, it would have taken almost forty years for Israel to suffer the same number of fatalities that it suffered in the war (165).[152] Of course, there is no assurance that the nonoccurrence of the 2006 War would have yielded continuation of the same casualty rates. Nevertheless, they offer a sound starting point for a rational calculation about the expected costs and benefits of war. To our knowledge, no such calculation was made. In choosing war, Israeli leaders did not ask whether existing trends in border clashes were tolerable or intolerable. Rather, they interpreted Hezbollah's abduction raid to represent a lapse of deterrence and judged that to be the one loss that Israel could not tolerate.

LACK OF NUANCE

Israel's drive for deterrence painted the threat to its north with a very broad brush. Decision-makers made insufficient distinctions among the different actors constituting the Lebanese landscape, not to mention their varied interests and resources. As Ofer Shelah and Yoav Limor observed, "Few [in Israel's leadership] were concerned with nuances, such as the differentiation between 'good' and 'bad' Lebanese—not only as targets of shelling but as future levers to achieve the goal of strengthening internal pressure on Hezbollah."[153] They cite a telling example. As the war began, the speaker of the Lebanese Parliament, Nabih Berri, reportedly sent a secret message to Israel promising to remain neutral in the war as long as Israel did not attack his Amal movement, a Shiite rival to Hezbollah. Ignoring this offer, Israel attacked the movement on July 14.[154]

Just as damaging was a lack of serious thinking about the weakness of the Lebanese state and government, and how this would mediate triadic coercion. All indicators suggest that the IDF did not act on the basis of convincing analysis indicating that Lebanese authorities had the capacity to coerce Hezbollah into submission or that Israeli pressure could even compel them to try. Such analysis would have required attention to the Lebanese government's institutional competencies, relationship to social forces, structure of political incentives, and domestic constraints. It would likewise have demanded an estimation of how, precisely, strikes on infrastructure would increase the likelihood that this government would assume the sovereign responsibility that Israel had never observed it assuming in the past. Halutz and the rest of the General Staff showed no interest in careful forecasting of this type. "Halutz," Harel and Issacharoff commented, "was keen to strike immediately. He didn't mull over a detailed analysis of power centers in Lebanon."[155]

The lack of nuanced thinking came to the fore on August 9, when the cabinet discussed going beyond the bombing campaign to launch a massive ground invasion. Referring to the Lebanese government, Halutz reportedly said: "We tell them pay attention: The electricity supply will start to decrease by small portions, the fuel will stop flowing in portions.... We will present steps: ten percent, twenty-five, thirty, seventy, a hundred. I don't know a stronger signal for taking responsibility."[156] One minister asked Halutz if the government in Beirut had the capacity to stop Hezbollah even if it wanted to. "That," Halutz reputedly responded, "is not my business."[157] The chief of staff thus relieved himself from the need to account for how exactly his plan would leverage pressure on the state to influence the nonstate actor. He simply assumed it would.

This and other anecdotes from the war suggest that IDF leaders approached the problem of restoring deterrence with a simple, one-size-fits-all solution. The IDF's almost automatic transfer of the target of triadic coercion from Syria in the Defense of the Land operational plan to Lebanon in the Elevated Waters and Ice Breaker plans points to the same unnuanced way of thinking. Military leadership did not devote careful attention to precisely whom the IDF should try to coerce and how this would increase Israeli security rather than yield new security problems. Instead, the defense establishment, as well as the civilian leaders who trusted its judgment, adopted the assumption that the harder the blow to Lebanon, the more Israel's deterrence would be restored.

LOGIC OF APPROPRIATENESS

The discussion thus far has critiqued the strategic soundness of Israeli leaders' choice of triadic coercion in the 2006 War. However, decision-makers often justified triadic coercion on grounds that had nothing to do with strategic soundness, instead asserting *moral* appropriateness. This conviction stemmed from the widespread view among Israelis that, in withdrawing from Lebanon in 2000, Israel had prioritized international principles and obligations, even at jeopardy to its own national security.

This understanding carried two implications. First, in Israeli eyes, taking the risk of pulling back to its own side of the border subsequently legitimated nearly whatever Israel believed it was necessary to do to defend that border. In demanding an end to border hostilities, the state was not advancing expansionist or otherwise questionable ambitions. Rather, it was protecting its land and innocent civilians. Fulfilling that mission was the government's and the army's obligation to its people. Second, if Israel was demonstrating its respect for Lebanon's territorial and national sovereignty, then it was Lebanon's obligation to do the same for Israel. Israelis believed that they had made great sacrifices and endured great expense to show the world that it was committed to complying with UN resolutions. The Lebanese now had to do likewise. This was particularly the case after Syria's withdrawal from Lebanon. Israel concluded that there was no longer any denying that the Lebanese state was the rightful custodian of its frontiers and thus the correct address to which to direct any complaint about violations.

Prime Minister Olmert evoked this reasoning when, during a press conference with the visiting Japanese prime minister, he made his first public remarks after the abduction:

> The events of this morning cannot be considered a terrorist strike; they are the acts of a sovereign state that has attacked Israel without cause and without provocation. The Lebanese government, which Hezbollah is part of, is trying to upset regional stability. Lebanon will bear the consequences of its action. The IDF is operating in Lebanon, and the government will be meeting this evening in order to approve more operations. I am confident that these reactions will reverberate in the right places and with the appropriate force.[158]

What is striking about this statement is that it contradicted what Olmert, given the high quality of military intelligence that he possessed, knew to be the facts. The prime minister was well aware that Hezbollah conducted the attack and that the Lebanese government had no say in the administration or control of its southern region. Still, his remarks suggest the opposite. Olmert's public statement might be seen as simply a political show to gain international support for Israel's offensive, if the IDF leadership had not been expressing a similar logic in closed-door discussions. In the first meeting of the General Staff after the kidnapping, Halutz proclaimed: "I suggest making the Lebanese jump so that Lebanon takes responsibility once and for all."[159] Most of the General Staff echoed this opinion. Head of the IDF Planning Division, Yitzhak Harel, reportedly said, "We should attack Beirut. For a year now we have been saying that the responsibility should lay upon the Lebanese government. Now we need to implement it at long last."[160] Gadi Eisenkott, head of the IDF Operations Branch, articulated a similar stance.[161]

The rationale underpinning such arguments was moralistic, not strategic. Israel asserted what the Lebanese government *ought* to do, not what it could do or was likely to do. It ignored the weakness of the Lebanese political order in terms of institutional capacities, authority over social forces, territorial sovereignty, and internal cohesion. Lebanon's entrenched structural problems suggested that it was not able to act autonomously. Nonetheless, as Harel and Issacharoff wrote, "Israel's official spokespersons constructed a theory according to which Lebanon was a sovereign state." They added that "it is one thing to tout this publicly; to believe in it and act accordingly is another."[162] In the 2006 War, Israeli decision-makers did both. They thereby acted on a logic of appropriateness more than a logic of consequences.

Israel was convinced that it was right and justified in carrying out disproportionate strikes. Whether or not they could actually have any effect on Lebanese state decision-making was a lesser concern.

ENEMY CONSCIOUSNESS

As in its repression of the second Intifada, Israel embraced overpowering retaliation against Lebanon with the objective of proving that Israel was not weak and making sure its adversaries never again thought otherwise. This obsession with the consciousness and attitudes of its enemies continued in the 2006 War, albeit with a new twist: in striking at what it saw as enemies' perceptions, it was in part seeking to rectify its own perception of itself.

This impulse was rooted in Israel's 2000 withdrawal and Nasrallah's subsequent "spider web speech." It is unclear to what extent either the act of leaving South Lebanon or Hezbollah's rhetorical framing of that act actually convinced the Arab world that Israeli society was cowardly and breakable. There is little doubt, however, that these events convinced *Israelis* that its Arab adversaries had come to view them in this way. Politicians, military elites, and civilians alike interpreted Nasrallah's derisive words as a reflection of his (and other Arabs') real perception of Israel, not as rhetoric.

As Gil Murciano wrote, "The images of Israel's hasty retreat coupled with humiliating messages relayed by Nasrallah were ingrained in the consciousness of the Israeli public and leadership in what could be defined as a 'formative humiliation.'"[163]

These feelings were especially formative in the IDF. Israeli generals would often cite Nasrallah's spider web speech as evidence that Israel had lost its deterrent power, because its adversaries no longer feared Israel.[164] Gadi Eizenkot, head of the Northern Command at the time of the speech, reportedly kept a copy of the spider web speech in his desk drawer.[165] One day after the 2006 abduction, a senior Military Intelligence officer told members of the Knesset Foreign Affairs and Defense Committee that Hezbollah's policy was based on the assumption that Israeli society is fragile. He likewise mentioned the spider web speech as evidence.[166]

For Israel, there was an urgent need to change these supposed beliefs. Israel's war strategy thus made the consciousness of the Lebanese people, and not merely the capacity of Hezbollah to carry out attacks, a deliberate target. This became particularly salient in two operations during the war. The first was not triadic coercion but direct retaliation aimed at Bint Jbail, the town in in South Lebanon that Nasrallah had chosen as the venue for his spider web speech. In the last week of July 2006, the IDF ordered ground forces to seize the town. The impetus driving this move was emotional more than strategic. As Deputy Chief of Staff Moshe Kaplinski admitted, "There is no military-tactical significance for taking over Bint Jbail. There is a different meaning here . . . a symbolic meaning."[167] The IDF planned to hold a victory parade in Bint Jbail after conquering it. The objective of this show of might—complete with tanks and a speech already written for the occasion by the "Consciousness Center" of the Northern Command's Ninety-first Brigade—was to promote the IDF's image of fortitude and invincibility.[168]

The fact that the IDF even had a Consciousness Center is indicative of the importance that the Israeli military assigned to its mission to reshape Arab attitudes. Likewise pointing in this direction is Israeli officers' diversion of scarce assets to strike symbolic (yet militarily unimportant) targets. As Shelah and Limor conclude: "It was clear throughout the operation . . . that the consciousness question, which so preoccupied the military command, was floating in the background."[169] As further evidence, the authors note that the IDF command referred to the assault on Bint Jbail as

Operation Webs of Steel, a metaphorical indication of Israel's desire to crush Nasrallah's spider web and impose a coercive web of its own.

Israel's second operation targeting enemy consciousness was the bombing of Dahiya, the southern suburbs of Beirut, on July 14 and 15. Israel gave residents advance warning to evacuate, and thus the area was largely empty of both civilians and Hezbollah fighters by the time it was bombed. Nevertheless, the Israeli Air Force's bombing destroyed a huge portion of the neighborhood.[170] Israeli decision-makers did not appear to be seeking to destroy Hezbollah's vital military capabilities, given that Hezbollah had removed them from Dahyia by then. Rather, it main aim appeared to be sending a larger "message" to the movement, its supporters, Lebanon, and the larger Arab world: Israel is strong and resolute.[171] Israel would not hesitate to destroy civilian infrastructure as a means to apply pressure on Hezbollah and the state that hosted it.[172]

Triadic Coercion since 2006: Israel's Lessons Learned

What lessons did Israel learn from the war? In the immediate wake of the ceasefire, conventional wisdom in Israel regarded the war as a failure. An August 2006 survey found that 68.3 percent of the Jewish Israeli population thought that the country's deterrence posture had eroded or significantly eroded as a result of the war.[173] Publications issued in or after the summer of 2006 reiterated this opinion, among them books with titles such as Rapaport's *Friendly Fire: How We Failed Ourselves in the Second Lebanon War* and articles with headlines such as Avi Kover's "The Israel Defense Forces in the Second Lebanon War: Why the Poor Performance?" Much of the criticism by these analysts focused on deterrence. Writing in 2007, Yair Evron noted that Israeli media commentary and public debate at this time continuously repeated the idea that the war had left Israel's deterrence "considerably damaged."[174]

The most politically weighty criticism came from the Winograd Commission, which the government formed to investigate Israel's conduct in the war. In January 2008 it issued its six-hundred-page report detailing Israel's civilian and military decision-making processes and military and diplomatic performance during the war. Among its many criticisms, the report leveled a scathing censure of the leadership's lack of serious deliberation about either the war's objectives or the relationship between those objectives and the means used to achieve them.[175] The report concluded that these oversights had detrimental implications for Israeli deterrence and the overall balance of power in the region.[176] Deferring to this censure, Chief of Staff Halutz resigned in January 2007.

As time passed, the security establishment's assessment became more mixed. In fall 2006, director of military intelligence, Major General Amos Yadlin, lamented that Israeli deterrence suffered as a result of the IDF's poor performance in the war. In September 2007, he declared that Israeli deterrence was "very strong."[177] Other security elites echoed this new view. As former deputy minister of defense Ephraim Sneh said in 2010, "The war reinforced Israel's deterrence by making every Arab ruler realize that he doesn't want his country to look like the Dahiya quarter of Beirut."[178] Analyst Gabriel Siboni agreed, adding, "What the public thinks is irrelevant. . . . If we have managed to create eight to ten years of quiet, we did well."[179]

Israeli military observers who evaluated these medium-term effects positively seem to derive two lessons from the war. The first is that, should deterrence fail, Israel should restore it by using unrestrained firepower to destroy not only the source of fire or enemy headquarters but also their greater surroundings. Major General Gadi Eisenkott described this model: "What happened in the Dahiya quarter of Beirut in 2006 will happen in every village from which Israel is fired on. . . . We will apply disproportionate force on it and cause great damage and destruction there. From our standpoint, these are not civilian villages, they are military bases."[180] Like most other elements of Israeli strategic thought, what came to be known as the "Dahiya Doctrine" is not an official policy as much as an operational concept.[181] It has won increasing support among military and civilian strategists. For example, both Siboni and former head of the Israel National Security Council Giora Eiland published articles conceptualizing the need for massive retaliation to any provocation as a strategy for promoting deterrence.[182]

The second lesson that Israel seems to have learned from the 2006 War is that triadic coercion is the key to fighting nonstate actors based in neighboring states. In a 2015 op-ed Yadlin argued that, while generally successful, Israel's campaign in Lebanon would have ended the war more quickly, and with a more enduring impact for Israeli deterrence, had Lebanese infrastructure been the main target.[183] Other military leaders called even more forcefully for this targeting of the Lebanese state. In a 2008 article tellingly titled "The Third Lebanon War: Target Lebanon," Eiland was unequivocal: "The state of Israel failed in the Second Lebanon War (and may also fail in a subsequent encounter) because it targeted the wrong enemy. Israel fought against Hezbollah instead of fighting against the Republic of Lebanon."[184] Another former high-ranking military intelligence officer agreed:

> We should stop dealing with Hezbollah and we should start confronting Lebanon. This is a process. Its foundation started in 2006. When a violent incident occurs with Lebanon, our leaders refer to Hezbollah only. We should stop using the word "Hezbollah" and say instead "Lebanon": "Lebanon got more weapons." . . . There is a failure in marketing and branding the Lebanese arena as one that is the responsibility of the Lebanese government, rather than the responsibility of Hezbollah.[185]

Siboni added that the imperative to hold Lebanon accountable for the actions of Hezbollah would become stronger should Hezbollah come to play a larger role in the Lebanese government. Under those conditions, Israel need not differentiate between the movement and the state. Instead, it could treat both as a single enemy entity.

Discussions of these lessons rarely attended to the mechanisms by which either factor, massive retaliation or the targeting of such retaliation, would actually bring about deterrence. They presumably rested on the assumption (more implied than elaborated) that Israel's application of punishing force would cause the target population or state so much suffering that they would demand nonstate actors stop their anti-Israeli activity. Israeli advocates of this logic did not typically give evidence or explain how populations or governments were expected to exert influence over nonstate actors. Nor did they entertain the possibility that Israel's strikes might instead make it more difficult for populations or governments to take any position that could be seen as succumbing to or collaborating with foreign aggression. They considered even less how the relative strength of host regimes would mediate these processes. Rather than engaging such strategic questions, advocates of triadic coercion justified their policy on the grounds of righteousness or appropriateness. As Yadlin argued, "Attacking infrastructures, while insisting on the principle of 'the state's responsibility,' is at the basis of Israel's security perception." Israel, he insisted, "must go back to the principle it set in the 1950s and 1960s: casting state responsibility on the country from which the enemy operates against Israel."[186]

As years passed, triadic coercion became the official policy of Israel toward Lebanon. Prime Minister Benjamin Netanyahu communicated that policy publicly and privately.[187] In 2012, Chief of Staff Benni Gantz was asked about the possibility of another war between Israel and Hezbollah. He said that, in such a case, he would "not advise any Lebanese to be in Lebanon."[188] In a 2016 interview Ehud Barak said that Israel made a fundamental strategic error in the 2006 War when, in bowing to U.S. demands, it attacked only Hezbollah and avoided targeting high-value Lebanese assets. Barak explained:

> Israel undercut its own well-known stated deterrence policy vis-à-vis Lebanon and Hezbollah. . . . [Had Israel targeted Lebanon's main infrastructure assets in 2006] . . . not only would Hezbollah have been forced to choose between its various competing identities and loyalties, but the Lebanese government itself would have been compelled to, and would have found itself effective in acting quickly to put an end to the conflict in order to cut losses and damage and rescue its value assets. Under such circumstances, Hezbollah would have found it complicated to resist the demand to stop the fighting and rocket launching.[189]

To assess the validity of these conclusions, we explore two questions. First, as of this writing, has the 2006 War increased Israel's deterrence vis-à-vis Hezbollah? Richard Ned Lebow and Janice Gross Stein explain that deterrence can be deemed effective when an actor deliberately refrains from carrying out an attack due to expectations of punishment (as opposed to not carrying out an attack because it has no wish to attack).[190] In the case of Hezbollah, it is not clear which was the case in the decade following the 2006 War. From the summer of 2006 through the end of 2015, there were only ten incidents involving exchanges of fire across the border. These resulted in three Israeli dead and several wounded.[191] Several of these incidents, including one in which an Israeli colonel was killed, involved the Lebanese army or Palestinian factions, not Hezbollah. Hezbollah itself aimed its few attacks on the Sheba Farms area, though Israel also attributes to Hezbollah a 2012 attack on Israeli tourists in Bulgaria that killed five.[192] Hezbollah's relative restraint has been apparent in word as well as deed.

Nasrallah publicly admitted that, had he known that abducting Israeli soldiers would lead to a war of the magnitude it did, he would "absolutely not" have endorsed the kidnapping.[193] Hezbollah's restraint held despite significant Israeli provocations, including attacks on Syria since 2011 such as the February 2014 bombing of a weapons shipment en route to Hezbollah bases in Lebanon.[194] It also held in spite of assassinations of senior Hezbollah commanders, among them Imad Mughniyah, killed in Damascus in February 2008.[195] Though Israel did not take responsibility for the assassination, it did not deny it.

This record seems to point to Israel's successful deterrence of Hezbollah.[196] Alternatively, Hezbollah might have refrained from attacks because it had other priorities. The years after 2006 witnessed intensification of Hezbollah's domestic political struggles with the rival March 14 Alliance, even escalating to armed clashes. After 2011 the movement became increasingly deeply involved in the Syrian war, resulting in significant costs for the movement in terms of casualties and expense.[197] Under such conditions, opening a second front against Israel would be so disadvantageous that some judged that it was Hezbollah that sought to deter conflict with Israel rather than the reverse. As one strategic analysis concluded in 2016: "At the moment, Hezbollah is stretched too thin in Syria to pick a fight with Israel. . . . The prospect of coming under attack from Israel while the group is distracted in Syria is a constant concern for Hezbollah leaders. Consequently, the group has tried to deter Israeli aggression through limited operations in response to Israeli strikes."[198]

Whether or not one attributed the relative quiet on the Lebanon-Israel border to Israeli deterrence, a second question was in order: Could any effective deterrence be attributed to Israel's use of triadic coercion, specifically? Though Israeli strategists claimed that it could, evidence was scant. Fifteen days into the war, Lebanese prime minister Fouad Siniora proposed a ceasefire plan entailing the Lebanese government's imposition of authority on the border and disarmament of all forces other than the Lebanese army, as stipulated by the Taif Agreement.

Siniora did not need Israel to push him to make these demands. He had already sought to strip Hezbollah of its weapons in the wake of Hariri's assassination, but that initiative failed because he did not command a government with the cohesion needed to override opposition or the capacity required to assert a state monopoly on the legitimate use of violence.[199] In those regards, Israel's use of triadic coercion may have undermined rather than increased Lebanese authorities' abilities to impose their will on the country's powerful nonstate actor. William Harris judged that many Lebanese were "furious" with Hezbollah's dragging the country to war without consultation. Nonetheless, "Israel's assault on the international airport roads and bridges everywhere, together with the mounting civilian deaths in the Shiite areas, brought a general 'street' coalescence with Hezbollah."[200] The Lebanese government undertook challenges to Hezbollah after the war, but these continued to be motivated by domestic political considerations, not Israeli pressure. Then, too, assertions of state power failed due to the government's weakness and the nonstate actor's relative strength. For example, when Siniora attempted to dismantle Hezbollah's private communication network in 2008 and subordinate it to state authority, Nasrallah responded that this was a declaration of war on the organization. Hezbollah troops clashed with Sunni militias in Beirut and Tripoli, and with Druze forces in the Chouf mountains. Hezbollah easily prevailed. Within a week, Siniora's government was forced to retract its decision.[201]

If triadic coercion had been effective, evidence would show the Lebanese state's acting upon Hezbollah, militarily or politically, to cease strikes on Israel. That did not occur. As Anthony Cordsman observed, "Israel had no success during the conflict in forcing Lebanon to become and act as an accountable state or in ending the status of Hezbollah as a state within a state."[202] Far from it, Hezbollah forced Lebanese governments to collapse in late 2006 and again in 2010. As of this writing, Hezbollah is the most powerful political party in the country. It also remains in control of South Lebanon. Should it decide to attack Israel, neither the Lebanese army nor UN border forces could stop it. The movement's arsenal of rockets and missiles appeared larger and more sophisticated a decade after the war than before it.[203] Disarmament of Hezbollah is simply not on the Lebanese political agenda.

Israel's use of triadic coercion against the Lebanese state in the 2006 War thus arguably appeared to have no effect in deterring Hezbollah. It might even have been counterproductive to the degree that it was part of the processes strengthening Hezbollah's standing vis-à-vis a politically autonomous Lebanese government. Under these circumstances, any lull in Hezbollah cross-border activity that is attributable to Israeli actions—rather than the Syrian war or other factors—appears to be direct deterrence of the movement stemming from the direct costs it suffered in 2006. It cannot be attributed to triadic coercion operating via the Lebanese state.[204]

Conclusion

During the first two decades after the 1949 armistice agreement between Lebanon and Israel, their shared border was largely quiet. This changed when the PLO shifted its bases from Jordan to Lebanon in 1970–1971. Nevertheless, with few exceptions, Israel did not employ triadic coercion against Lebanon until the 1990s. Rather, following the Rabin Doctrine, it judged that Lebanon was cooperatively predisposed toward Israel's demands. As Lebanon was not supporting nonstate actors' attacks, Israel turned its fire on nonstate actors directly.

Israel's approach changed in the 1990s, by which time its main nonstate adversary in Lebanon was no longer the PLO but the Lebanese movement Hezbollah. In 1993 and 1996, Israel responded to Hezbollah's attacks with massive bombardment operations that aimed to produce a wave of refugees from South Lebanon and thereby pressure authorities in Beirut to terminate the nonstate actor's strikes. Imposed upon a state and government with markedly deficient cohesion and capacity, both triadic coercion campaigns failed. Though Hezbollah's rates of attacks were higher in the second half of the decade than in the first, Israeli strategists continued to endorse such large-scale triadic coercion. It believed that such offensives, later dubbed "deterrence operations," would demonstrate Israel's superior capacity and thereby convince adversaries not to challenge it.

Israel redoubled its endorsement of severe retaliation and triadic coercion after its withdrawal from South Lebanon in 2000. Many military elites saw the hasty and unilateral retreat as a humiliating display of weakness that showed the Arab world that Israel surrenders to violence. Even Israelis who did not view the withdrawal as dishonorable believed that their state had taken the moral high ground in respecting the international border and would thus be morally justified in using force should Lebanese forces violate it. These two sensibilities, a compulsion to show resolute strength and a conviction that past concessions legitimated strong retaliation against any provocation, helped root new preferences for triadic coercion in Israel's strategic culture. Further compounded by the sense of outrage set aflame by the second Intifada, these ideas crystalized into a narrative emphasizing the need to assert a "deterrent posture" at all costs and the conviction that Israel's show of force would automatically result in strengthened deterrence.

The 2006 War dramatically demonstrated this strategic culture. When Hezbollah kidnapped two Israeli soldiers and killed three, Israel retaliated with a severe bombing campaign and ultimately a ground invasion. Hezbollah responded with rocket fire, and the result was a thirty-four-day war claiming the lives of 165 Israelis and almost 1,200 Lebanese, and devastating Lebanon with billions of dollars in material damage. Israel's war strategy entailed both direct strikes against Hezbollah and triadic coercion that aimed at state and civilian targets in order to force the Lebanese government to "take responsibility" and restrain Hezbollah.

Israel's turn to triadic coercion revealed the culmination of patterns in its strategic culture that were decades in the making. In terms of decision-making processes, it demonstrated the dominant influence of the military's personnel, intelligence, and assessments in shaping Israeli foreign and security policy. From the first hours, military elites pushed for massive destruction of Lebanese infrastructure. To the degree that the Israeli civilian leadership limited implementation of such proposals, it was not out of critique of their presumed efficacy as much as concern for the potential diplomatic fallout. With regard to strategic ideas, Israel's use of both massive force and triadic coercion was encouraged by regard for the inherent, as opposed to instrumental, utility of actions in pursuit of deterrence; a lack of nuance in distinguishing among different actors, glossed over as a monolithic adversary; an emphasis on the logic of appropriateness, rather than strategic outcomes, as a criterion for adopting military strategy; and an emotion-laden calling for severe punishment to burn into enemies' "consciousness" a fear of Israel's might and resolve. These tendencies elevated moralistic convictions and dubious assumptions at the expense of measured calculations about the costs and benefits of military force. They gave precious little consideration to how the strength of a targeted host state mediates the effectiveness of triadic coercion. In calling to pound Lebanon, the defense establishment did not specify how this famously weak state and perilously divided government would manage to control a nonstate actor that was not only one of the most politically powerful forces in the country but also stronger than the national army.

Initial Israeli lamentations about the failure of the 2006 War gave way, with the passage of years, to a general belief that overpowering bombardment had restored Israel's deterrence and ought to be used with even more intensity against any future violations of the northern border. This increased support for triadic coercion ignored the very mixed record of triadic coercion going back to the early years of Israeli statehood. In particular, it neglected to note how the strength or weakness of a targeted host regime affects its ability to exert meaningful authority over nonstate actors on its soil. In light of these considerations, we conclude that the 2006 War was not a success story for triadic coercion. Perceiving the war as such is a distorted lesson with potentially grave consequences for the future.

CHAPTER 7

Triadic Coercion Beyond the Arab-Israeli Conflict

In the previous chapters we presented arguments about the sources and outcomes of Israeli triadic coercion policy and demonstrated them through detailed case studies from the Arab-Israeli conflict. Are these relationships unique to Israel and its neighbors, or does their logic apply beyond it?

Evaluating the generalizability of these arguments is no straightforward affair. Our claims about the sources of Israel's use of triadic coercion center on the role of strategic culture. As strategic culture differs from one country to another, we expect the frequency and magnitude with which other countries engage in triadic coercion to vary. We also expect the way decision-makers approach triadic coercion to diverge. By contrast, we expect the consequences of triadic coercion to reveal similar patterns across cases, despite their many other differences. Regardless of how contexts vary, triadic coercion is most likely to be effective when aimed against strong regimes. Triadic coercion is likely to fail or backfire when used against weak regimes.

To explore the larger validity of these claims beyond the Arab-Israeli conflict, this chapter briefly examines the plausibility of our arguments for explaining patterns in two other countries: India and Turkey. We chose to analyze these two cases because they provide rich data and long histories of triadic conflicts. Like Israel, both have faced protracted violence from nonstate actors operating from neighboring states or with the aid of those states. Both India and Turkey have accused host states of aiding or abetting these groups' attacks against their countries and demanded that they cease such support. Have they used triadic coercion to that end? If yes, under what circumstances and with what effects? If not, why?

India

India and Pakistan have been locked in an enduring rivalry since partition of the subcontinent in 1947. Their bilateral confrontation has encompassed nearly every type of conflict studied in international relations, including a nuclear standoff, arms race, conventional wars, and intrastate conflict between different ethno-religious communities. The conflict between the two countries has also entailed an intense territorial dispute over the region of Kashmir. This dispute stems from the 1947 partition of the subcontinent, when the Hindu prince (Maharaja) of Kashmir chose for Kashmir to remain within India, contrary to the wishes of the state's majority Muslim population. When war began between India and Pakistan, Kashmiri tribesmen supporting accession to Pakistan rebelled against the Maharaja. The ceasefire ending the war divided Kashmir, leaving roughly two-thirds under Indian control as the state of Jammu and Kashmir, and the remaining one-third under Pakistani control. While India was generally satisfied with that territorial status quo, Pakistan did not accept it.[1]

In the decades that followed, nonstate actors struggling for Kashmir's independence or accession to Pakistan carried out attacks against India. These group were often based in Pakistan or received aid from the Pakistani military and intelligence services.[2] The ongoing conflict between India, Pakistan, and Kashmiri nonstate actors was thus triadic in nature. Since independence India's leadership has dealt with nonstate actors through both defensive measures and belligerent acts such as collective punishments repressing the civilian Kashmiri population. Over the years India also attempted fleeting or partial instances of triadic coercion, with very limited success. For the most part, however, it avoided striking the state of Pakistan as a strategy for deterring, retaliating against, or otherwise compelling an end to violence by nonstate actors. Since the start of the twenty-first century, India has begun to restructure its military doctrine in ways that have allowed for greater aggressiveness in triadic situations. Nevertheless, it remains unlikely that triadic coercion will ever reach the level in

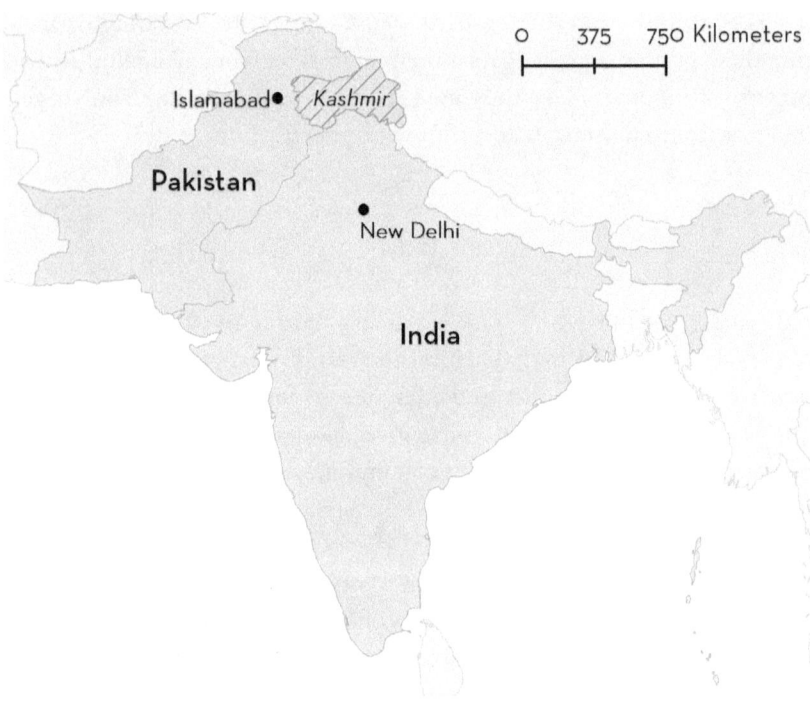

India that it has in Israel. We attribute this to India's strategic culture. Whereas Israel's offense-oriented strategic culture has consistently encouraged aggressive measures, including triadic coercion, India's defense-oriented strategic culture long discouraged it. We believe that it will continue to do so.

As in the case of Israel, India's strategic culture is a product of both ideas and decision-making processes. Former defense minister George Fernandes described India's doctrine as "a non-aggressive, non-provocative defense policy based on the philosophy of defensive defense."[3] Stephen Cohen and Sunil Dasgupta attribute this policy to India's relative poverty at independence, its political leaders' preference for nonalignment during the Cold War, and its society's belief that military power evoked legacies of colonialism and thus should be avoided. This ideological preference for defensive, rather than offensive, approaches has been consolidated and institutionalized in decision-making processes since the early decades of statehood.[4] Civilian authorities have typically dominated the state's handling of security matters, while military officers have played a subordinate role.

In addition, security decision-making processes are highly bureaucratic in nature and include multiple veto points. Some criticize this cumbersome organizational structure for being inefficient in times of crisis. However, it has reinforced a tendency toward caution in use of military force. In thwarting rash escalatory decisions, it has created space and time for diplomacy to attempt to resolve problems politically.[5]

This defensive doctrine and nonmilitaristic norms helped shape India's decision not to engage in triadic coercion during the first three of its four major wars with Pakistan, even though all involved triadic conflict with Pakistan and Kashmiri groups in some way. The 1947–1948 war, which immediately followed the partition of the Indian subcontinent, started after armed groups from Pakistan's frontier invaded Kashmir in October 1947. Kashmir's besieged ruler requested armed assistance from India and in exchange pledged to join India as one of its provinces. Despite the triadic element of this conflict, India restricted its operations to the territory of Kashmir and did not attempt to punish Pakistan beyond this territory. Its goal was not to deter Pakistan's assistance to nonstate actors but rather to secure the territory as part of India.

The war ended in January 1949 with the establishment of a ceasefire line partitioning Kashmir. In 1965 the countries again went to war after Pakistan covertly encouraged and organized the infiltration of Kashmiri guerrillas into Indian-administered Jammu and Kashmir. Indian troops responded by crossing the international border near Lahore. Three weeks of fighting ended with a UN-sponsored ceasefire.[6] Again, India and Pakistan engaged in a war over territory, but India did not employ triadic coercion.

The third war began in 1971, as Pakistan descended into civil conflict after East Pakistan demanded autonomy and later independence. Millions of civilians fled to India, which invaded East Pakistan in support of its secession and there fought directly against the Pakistani army. The war neither centered on triadic conflict nor entailed elements of triadic coercion. The war ended in the creation of Bangladesh and the signing of the Simla Accord in 1972. The accord called for a final settlement of the Kashmir dispute and included provisions to transform the unofficial Kashmir ceasefire line into a "Line of Control" that both parties promised to respect until a more permanent settlement was achieved.[7]

After more than two decades of relative quiet, the Kashmiri conflict erupted again in 1987, when the incumbent coalition of the National

Conference and Congress parties reportedly rigged state elections in Jammu and Kashmir. The Jammu and Kashmir Liberation Front (JKLF) gained increased popularity against that backdrop, which many Kashmiris saw not only as a violation of democratic principles but also as a surrender of Kashmiri autonomy to dictates from Delhi. The JKLF began insurgent attacks against Indian authorities in Kashmir and mobilized mass demonstrations demanding independence. Pakistan actively assisted the JKLF with weapons, military training, and bases in Pakistani Kashmir beyond the Line of Control, in violation of the Simla Accord.[8] India responded harshly, clamping down on dissent by imposing a curfew, conducting mass arrests, shooting at protesters, and torturing detainees, among other methods.[9] This repression contributed to escalating tension to a full-blown conflict in the Kashmir Valley by summer 1988. Nevertheless, and despite Pakistani assistance to Kashmiri separatists, India did not undertake triadic coercion.

The years that followed witnessed other shifts in the triadic conflict between India, Pakistan, and Pakistani-aided nonstate actors. Ideological tensions grew between the largely secular, pro-independence JKLF and the Pakistani regime, which favored groups that embraced Islamism and the goal of Kashmiri accession to Pakistan.[10] In this context, Hizb-ul-Mujahideen—an organization that supported unification of Kashmir with Pakistan and was closely affiliated with the Pakistani Islamist group Jamaat-i Islami—became the most important Pakistan-backed nonstate actor fighting Indian authorities in Kashmir in the 1990s. Rather than using triadic coercion, India directly targeted counterinsurgency against this and other nonstate Kashmiri actors, successfully weakening them.[11]

As the decade progressed, the Pakistani army and Inter-Services Intelligence (ISI), the state's premier agency collecting and assessing information on security affairs, increasingly invested resources in Lashkar-e-Taiba (LeT). LeT was a Pakistani nonstate actor founded by militants who had fought against the USSR in Afghanistan. In the mid-1990s LeT began attacking both the Indian military and Hindu civilians in Kashmir. Based on interviews and secondary sources, Stephen Tankel enumerated the multiple ways in which Pakistan's security apparatus was assisting the group through "funding, assistance with organizing, combat training; campaign guidance; provision of weapons and kit, including sophisticated communications equipment; hides, launching pads and fire support for cadres crossing into Indian-administered Kashmir; assistance infiltrating into or exfiltrating out of India and other countries; intelligence on targets and threats; diplomatic support; and, of course, safe haven and protection in Pakistan."[12] Other nonstate actors also continued to operate in Kashmir. In the year 2000, for example, the al-Qaeda-linked Kashmiri jihadist organization, Jaish-e Mohammed (JeM), emerged and began engaging in insurgency and terrorism against India. ISI was believed to be involved in its creation as well.

The structure of India's conflict with these Pakistan-supported insurgents was definitively triadic in nature. Nevertheless, India's response centered on targeting nonstate actors directly, with a focus on often-brutal counterinsurgency tactics such as arrests, killing of cadres, and intimidation of potential supporters. By the turn of the century India also undertook civilian initiatives such as local elections aimed to increase the legitimacy of Indian rule in Jammu and Kashmir.[13] Throughout, India did not undertake measures targeting Pakistan as a complicit or actively implicated host state.

Between 1981 and 2004 India adopted what it called the "Sundarji Doctrine," which added more offensive options to its operational menu of choices. Still, the Indian state and army remained relatively oriented toward defense. The doctrine called for seven defensive "holding corps" to be deployed near the border regions with Pakistan. Their primary role was to check an enemy advance in the event of a war. The Sundarji Doctrine also called for the establishment of three Strike Corps, but based these contingents in central India, a significant distance from the international border. This location deliberately slowed any potential military reaction to tension with Pakistan: Should political leaders call for mass mobilization, it would take nearly three weeks for the Strike Corps to reach the border. This enabled time for diplomacy to take effect before any engagement of troops commenced.[14]

The fourth war between India and Pakistan was the Kargil War of 1999. It began when Pakistani soldiers and Pakistani-supported nonstate insurgents infiltrated Indian-controlled Kashmir and launched a surprise attack on remote Indian military positions. After about two months of fighting, coupled with international pressure on Pakistan, India recaptured most of the positions on the Indian side of the Line of Control, and Pakistani forces withdrew from the remaining positions.[15] In the war's aftermath Indian decision-making circles deepened their attention to triadic coercion as a strategy and escalation control as an operational priority. Officials became increasingly concerned that Pakistan's nuclear arsenal might nullify India's conventional superiority and embolden attacks by Pakistani-supported nonstate actors. These concerns were aggravated by severe attacks in and around Kashmir by Pakistani-supported organizations, including LeT and JeM. JeM, for example, was responsible for an October 2001 attack that killed thirty-eight near the state parliament of Jammu and Kashmir.[16]

In December 2001, six individuals believed to be a part of LeT attacked the Parliament House in New Delhi. The ensuing gun battle left dead all six attackers and eight security force members. Responding to the attack, the Indian government broke with past practices and targeted its military threats not at the nonstate actors themselves but at Pakistan. It issued five demands, respectively requiring Pakistan to ban the LeT and JeM organizations, extradite twenty individuals whom India accused of having carried out terrorist attacks on its soil, end the Pakistani army's assistance to insurgents' infiltrations into Kashmir, stop arming terrorists, and cease hosting terrorist training camps.[17] Clearly communicating a threat of force if these demands were not met, India launched Operation Parakram, through which it deployed eight hundred thousand troops on the border with Pakistan.[18]

This combination of military ultimatums and mass mobilization constituted an act of triadic coercion. Faced with attacks by nonstate actors, India directed coercion at the state implicated in hosting and aiding those actors. It had some impact: Pakistan seized JeM's and LeT's funds and arrested over two thousand members, including their leaders. Pakistani president Pervez Musharraf declared that he was banning LeT and JeM and would not permit terrorism on any territory that Pakistan controlled.[19] Nevertheless, triadic coercion did not resolve the crisis. In May 2002, escalation renewed when LeT attacked military housing for Indian soldiers and their families in Indian-Kashmir, leaving fifty dead or wounded. Amidst widespread outrage, India doubled down on triadic coercion. Demanding that Musharraf take responsibility, India threatened imminent military action and called for the Pakistani high commissioner to leave New Delhi. Then, in mid-October, India formally declared victory on the grounds that the international community had recognized Pakistan's role in supporting terrorism.[20] It ended Operation Parakram and withdrew its troops from the border.

Despite India's triumphant claims, most analysts agree that Operation Parakram had limited effects. The ISI continued working with nonstate actors covertly and thereby minimized the actual impact of their having been officially banned. It warned groups such as the LeT and JeM in advance about impending raids by Pakistani police and guided them to change their names and financial allocations in ways that would allow them to operate despite the prohibition against them. Gradually, Pakistani authorities released militants whom they had arrested earlier while under Indian (and American) pressure.[21]

Just as India's triadic coercion did not force sustained or meaningful change in Pakistan's behavior, it also did not result in tangible change in the conditions of insurgency on the ground in Kashmir. Militias that were believed to be acting with Pakistani support killed 445 Indian civilians and 250 security personnel in 2001. In 2002, even after Operation Parakram, they killed 465 civilians and 195 security personnel. Hussein Haqqani and Ashley Tellis concluded that "India did not secure the one thing its military mobilization was intended to achieve: conclusive termination of Pakistan's involvement in terrorism directed against India."[22] Patrick Bratton agreed, finding no evidence that the Pakistani government took seriously India's threat to invade if Pakistan continued supporting LeT, JeM, and other similar groups.[23] India's political leaders and military leadership likewise recognized that triadic coercion failed to stop the violence of nonstate actors. The military, in particular, understood that Operation Parakram was a massive but blunt tool. If India wanted to avoid an all-out war with its nuclear-armed neighbor, it needed the means to enact sharp and pinpointed retaliation. Moreover, during Operation Parakram it took the Indian Strike Corps more than three weeks to prepare for attack on the western border, by which time the Pakistani army was fully mobilized and international pressure to avoid confrontation was mounting.[24]

Based on the limited success of triadic coercion, the Indian military undertook a shift in strategy and in 2004 announced a new doctrine that became known as Cold Start.[25] In Walter Ladwig's words, Cold Start "marked a break from the fundamentally defensive orientation that the Indian military . . . employed since independence in 1947."[26] Drawing on Israeli and Soviet security concepts, Cold Start outlined an offensive doctrine of blitzkrieg.[27] It sought to build India's capacity to carry out conventional retaliatory strikes against the Pakistani army that would inflict significant harm before any international actors could intervene. These middle-ranging attacks were intended to pursue objectives that were sufficiently narrow to discourage Pakistan from responding by escalating to conventional or nuclear war. Cold Start also directed the Indian army to make structural changes to its fighting forces. It called for transformation of its force structure from three large Strike Corps to eight forward-deployed "Integrated Battle Groups." Those groups emphasized speed and combined infantry and air force operations to achieve limited objectives.[28]

Experts debate the extent to which the Cold Start was fully implemented with regard to military procurement, restructuring, training, and readiness.[29] The limits of the doctrine's application came to the fore in November 2008, when LeT carried out a series of simultaneous shootings and bombings in Mumbai that killed 164 and wounded at least 308. India again demanded that Pakistan halt assistance to the organization and arrest its leaders and fighters. Those demands were fairly similar to those made after the 2001 attack on Parliament. The method by which the Indian army sought to compel compliance, however, was very different.[30] In response to the 2001 attack, India targeted Pakistan with military mobilization that was public, yet slow. In 2008, by contrast, India made a quiet threat of severe action. In a message sent to the Pakistani leadership via U.S. senator John McCain, Indian prime minister Manmohan Singh threatened to begin air attacks on Pakistan if the latter did not arrest those involved in the Mumbai attack.[31] Reports circulated that the Indian military was ready to take action whenever an order arrived.

The Pakistani army put its forces on alert in response. A situation of tense standoff persisted for about a month, after which the Indian government began to deescalate the crisis by using more moderate rhetoric and military demobilization. The leaders of both armies spoke on the direct telephone red line established to avert nuclear confrontation. Though India's coercive tactics in 2008 differed from those in 2001, the strategic impact was similarly marginal. Pakistan neither enacted a serious crackdown on nonstate actors nor curbed its own security forces' assistance to those actors.[32] In the long term, there was no significant change in nonstate actors' behavior.

Beyond these two high-profile crises, India and Pakistan also engaged in many smaller skirmishes along the Kashmiri border in the twenty-first century. These incidents sometimes pushed India to use triadic coercion, namely threats or retaliations, against what it viewed as Pakistan's support for insurgents challenging Indian rule in Kashmir. For example, in September 2016, militants carried out a raid on an Indian barrack in Kashmir that killed eighteen soldiers. India accused JeM of executing it, with assistance from Pakistan. Indian media, as well as government ministers, called for retaliation against Pakistan.[33] Less than two weeks after the attack,

India claimed to have launched a "surgical strike" by helicopters and ground troops against terrorist "launch pads" across the Line of Control. A senior Indian army official said that "significant casualties have been caused to the terrorists and those who are trying to support them." Pakistani officials reported that two Pakistani soldiers were also killed.[34] Those casualties suggest that India was not strictly targeting the nonstate actor but also engaged in triadic coercion aimed at Pakistan as a host state.

Nevertheless, as in the past, there was little indication that triadic coercion was effective or that it would be effective in the future. David Carter identified the weakness of the Pakistani regime as the main reason for the failure of India's attempts to compel Pakistan to act against violent nonstate actors.[35] Given our assessment of the conditions for triadic coercion success, we concur. In Pakistan the state is indeed strong in terms of military capacity. The state commands a sizable military, which in 2014 included 925,800 troops.[36] Apart from possessing nuclear weapons, Pakistan's conventional forces are well equipped. In 2015 Pakistan spent 3.4 percent of its GDP on its military, amounting to more than $9 billion.[37]

These figures suggest that the Pakistani government possesses the capability to stop nonstate actors' cross-border activity should it wish. Nevertheless, its weak regime cohesion greatly impedes such action. Since independence, Pakistan has faced a plethora of challenges to its unity and stability as a state. Several powerful social groups with different worldviews compete to advance their vision of the state and its identity, among them middle-class professionals, the state bureaucracy, the military, rural elites, clergy, and business elites. Their conflicting interests impede the creation of coherent governments with single, unified agendas.[38] Beyond this fragmentation, the high rate of turnover in government, much of it attributable to the military's dominant role in politics, has been another key factor undermining regime cohesion. From independence to 2006, Pakistan had four military heads of state and twenty-seven civilian prime ministers, some of whom served under an overarching military authority. Only one elected government completed its five-year term in office.[39] Several governments fell due to direct military coups or military-backed maneuvering by the opposition. Thus, as T. V. Paul argues, the national army—an instrument created and empowered to protect the state from external enemies—"made Pakistan less secure and unified as a coherent political unit."[40]

Another factor weakening the Pakistani regime was a high level of internal violence. Pakistan's decision to ally with the U.S. War on Terror changed its position on Afghanistan and al-Qaeda. Jihadi groups such as the Pakistani Taliban, which once enjoyed support from the Pakistani state, targeted violence against their former backers.[41] Between 1996 and 2005, terrorist attacks in Pakistan killed an average of 77 people per year. Between 2006 and 2015, this average climbed to 1,046. In 2013, terrorist attacks resulted in a peak of 2,159 fatalities.[42] These new stresses acted upon a state already beleaguered by economic woes and political instability. In consequence, Pakistan's ranking in the Fund for Peace's "Fragile States Index" worsened from thirty-fourth in 2005 to fourteenth in 2016.[43]

This regime weakness directly undermined the success of India's triadic coercion. For example, after the 2001 attack on Parliament, Pakistan officially succumbed to Indian demands to repress militant insurgents, yet surreptitiously continued to facilitate them. In taking this course, Pakistan's government might have been circumvented by its own intelligence service—testimony to the state's incomplete power over its subsidiary agencies. Alternatively, the government might have been complicit in allowing nonstate actors to continue their operations out of fear that these actors would otherwise turn their attacks against the regime itself or that repressing them would dangerously provoke opposition among the Pakistani population.[44] In either scenario, the regime's lack of legitimacy, stability, and capacity was on display.

Similar evidence of the role of regime weakness, and in particular weak cohesion, in impairing Pakistan's ability to control nonstate actors emerged in the wake of India's use of triadic coercion in response to the 2008 Mumbai attack. As a RAND study concluded about the attack, "Indian and American officials by and large believe that Pakistan's civilian government does not control the military's (or the ISI's) policies toward militant groups operating in and from Pakistan."[45] In these and other cases, Pakistan's wavering in implementing its own commitments to crack down on violent nonstate actors revealed the limits of its regime strength. While Pakistan was a nuclear power and boasted a sizeable military, its regime lacked autonomy from and authority over political and social forces within its own borders. It thus calculated that the immediate domestic costs of fully repressing nonstate actors outweighed the risks of potential war with India. Raison d'état clearly demanded avoiding interstate war, but the weak Pakistani regime was unable to prioritize those demands.

India has been aware of this political weakness, and that awareness has served as an additional brake on its use of triadic coercion. Discussing the

Mumbai attack, Carter concludes that "Indian concerns about the internal stability of Pakistan and the standing of the fragile civilian government relative to the LeT and their supporters made compellent punishment much too costly and likely counterproductive."[46] India's attention to its rival's cohesion and capacity, and deliberate consideration of such factors in deciding whether or not to use military threats to demand that Pakistan take action against nonstate actors, stand in sharp contrast to Israel's repeated disregard of the same matters. The contrast of these two cases suggests how different strategic cultures can lead coercer states to very different approaches in similarly structured triadic conflicts. India's primarily defensive strategic culture has promoted caution in its retaliation against Pakistan in scenarios in which Israel's strategic culture would have pushed it toward an aggressive approach.

Since the start of the twenty-first century, India has moved closer to adopting triadic coercion as a strategy than it had in the past. In Operation Parakram and the subsequent partial adaptation of Cold Start, India carried out threats and limited action against Pakistani state assets. This trend shows worrisome signs of adoption of something akin to Israel's logic of triadic coercion. Nevertheless, India's military actions and threats aimed to compel Pakistan to act against nonstate actors have proven largely ineffective due to the weakness of the Pakistani regime. Given India's own cautious strategic culture, it should be easier for India to learn from its mistakes. It is thus unlikely to get caught in the pattern, typified in the Israeli experience, of adhering to a policy of triadic coercion even under conditions when it is unlikely to be effective.

Turkey

Like Israel and India, Turkey has also engaged in protracted conflict with nonstate actors supported or abetted by neighboring states. The most significant actor has been the Kurdistan Workers' Party (PKK), a militant leftist organization committed to using armed struggle to attain the goal of an independent Kurdish state. Since its founding, the Turkish Republic has sought to assimilate ethnic Kurds, who currently represent approximately 15 to 20 percent of the population.[47] The state has tended to view Kurds' political ambitions, including any mobilization around the demand for cultural and linguistic rights, as a dangerous separatist challenge to its

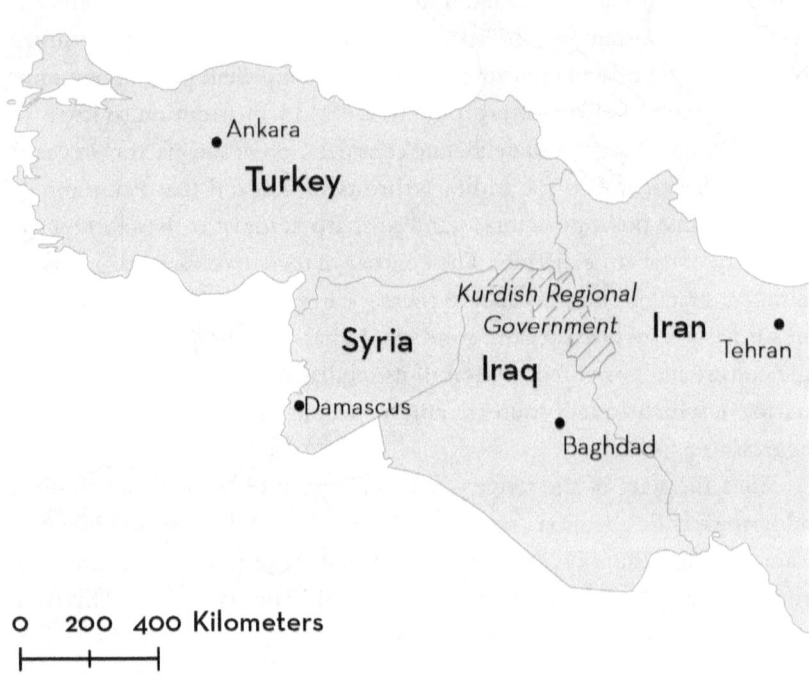

territorial integrity and national cohesion. The state has variously banned publicly speaking, broadcasting, or publishing in Kurdish and, until now, has not allowed education in Kurdish.[48]

The PKK was formed in 1984. At its peak the organization enjoyed a strength of some fifteen thousand fighters and fifty thousand sympathizers. The PKK employed guerrilla and hit-and-run tactics, including shootings, armed assaults, bombings, and detonation of landmines and other explosive substances. It also engaged in terrorism, including suicide bombings in urban areas and tourist sites.[49] Turkey consistently viewed the PKK as one of the gravest threats to its national security. In the late 1980s, Turkish officials tended to say that the country did not have a Kurdish problem, only a "terrorist" problem.[50] By the mid-1990s, Turkey was devoting almost a third of its security personnel to fighting the PKK. According to unofficial estimates as of 2012, the conflict had cost approximate thirty-five thousand lives and displaced nearly three million people.[51]

This conflict was not merely a fierce intrastate struggle. It was also a triadic conflict insofar as the states of Iraq, Syria, and Iran supported the

PKK to various extents at various times. Turkey viewed this foreign support as crucial for the movement's survival and capacity to use violence. In Galia Lindenstrauss's assessment, Turkey perceived the Kurdish threat "to be mastered and encouraged by hostile outside forces . . . trying to meddle in its politics" if not "tear the country apart."[52] As one Turkish government minister said, "The only people prepared to call themselves Kurds are militants, tools of foreign ideologies."[53] The conflict dynamics that can encourage triadic coercion thus existed in Turkey for decades. Nevertheless, Turkey, like India, adopted responses that differed significantly from those of Israel. It rarely aimed military threats and strikes at states aiding the PKK; when it did, it seemed to take into consideration the strength of the targeted regime. These responses were grounded in both the decision-making and ideational elements of Turkey's strategic culture.

In terms of security decision-making, the military was perhaps the most powerful institution in the late Ottoman state.[54] The founding fathers of the Turkish Republic were successful generals. The military acted as guarantor of a single-party regime until 1946 and a central political actor in the multiparty parliamentary system that subsequently took shape. Claiming the need to defend order and the republic's key principles, officers took over the government in 1960 and 1971, unsuccessfully attempted coups in 1962 and 1963, and seized the state and ruled by decree from 1980 to 1983. In 1997, the military launched what some called a "postmodern" coup-by-memorandum, causing the collapse of the sitting government. It continued to intervene in politics until the Justice and Development Party (AKP) won elections in 2002 and thereafter gradually chipped away at military power and brought the military under civilian control.[55]

Turkish armed forces wielded particular influence, and indeed enjoyed extraordinary powers, to repress domestic groups perceived as challenging Mustafa Kemal's vision of a secular and culturally homogenous nation-state.[56] This intensified the state's militaristic stance toward Kurdish mobilization. In 1987, just three years after the PPK's formation, the government declared a state of emergency in the largely Kurdish southeastern provinces.[57] Parliament renewed this state of emergency every four months until 2002.[58] Over the years, various army-linked forces carried out violent measures, including burning villages and forcibly migrating civilians.[59]

While these aspects of security decision-making processes encouraged Turkey's use of force against the PKK, the ideas at the heart of the country's strategic culture impeded this force from taking the form of triadic coercion. Turkey's foreign policy orientation has traditionally been characterized by caution, moderation, and avoidance of conflict with other states. This orientation has roots in the late Ottoman Empire, which, by the eighteenth century, manifested acute awareness of European countries' comparative strength. Fear of loss of territory encouraged the Ottomans to adopt a defensive realpolitik emphasizing balance-of-power diplomacy.[60] This legacy continued to dominate the Turkish Republic. During the Cold War, Turkish foreign policymaking won praise for "its high degree of rationality, sense of responsibility, long term perspective, and realism."[61] There have been exceptions to Turkey's emphasis on nonaggression and noninterference, such as the 1974 invasion of northern Cyprus. Still, the country's strategic culture during the Cold War largely manifested "guarded neutrality" and "extreme caution" to avoid antagonizing world powers or regional neighbors.[62]

From the 1990s to mid-2010s, the Turkish government undertook a more assertive stance that some described as a "new activism." Yet even this fresh ambition appeared to balance "daring and caution" and did not abandon valorization of moderation.[63] In the words of Nimet Beriker-Atiyas, "Post-Cold War Turkish foreign policy is static, defensive, and reactive, and avoids taking risks."[64] After 2002, AKP governments led by prime minister, and then president, Recep Tayyip Erdoğan became increasingly bold in asserting Turkey as a central player in the Middle East and as a global and trade power bridging East and West.[65] At the same time, this more activist vision explicitly sought to avoid conflict. This was embodied in Foreign Minister Ahmet Davutoglu's 2009 declaration of a "zero problems with neighbors" policy, aiming for "limitless cooperation" with states in the region.[66] The 2011 Arab uprisings, and especially Turkey's vocal support for the rebellion against Bashar al-Assad in Syria, rattled this stance. Turkey's own increasing domestic instability did likewise. By 2013, some observers suggested that Turkey had gone from "zero problems with neighbors" to "zero friends,"[67] a trend that seems to have only increased since then.

For decades, therefore, triadic conflict remained one of Turkey's enduring problems. Turkish officials believed that neighboring countries were supporting the PKK, and that belief was one of the key determinants of its relations with each of them.[68] Nevertheless, Turkey largely eschewed strikes and threats against those states. Rather, it typically sought to combat PKK forces outside its borders by targeting military strikes directly at the movement's bases, assets, and personnel. In adopting this approach, Turkey showed awareness that neighboring countries that have assisted the PKK have not done so out of sympathy for Kurdish autonomy but as a tool to advance their own political goals vis-à-vis Turkey. Indeed, these same states share concerns about Kurdish irredentism within their own borders. Turkey largely acted in ways that tried to take advantage of these common interests, not opt for harsh militarized action that would undermine them. In this spirit, it traditionally sought diplomatic resolutions to triadic conflicts. It also made use of its strong trade relations with states assisting the PKK and sometimes employed economic pressure, such as threatening or imposing sanctions, as a form of influence.[69]

These patterns are apparent in Turkey's relations with each of the states perceived to host or assist the PKK. Vis-à-vis Syria before 2011, Turkey preferred nonmilitary efforts at persuasion. Until 1998, Syria was considered to have been the PKK's most important state backer.[70] In aiding the group, it appeared that Hafez al-Assad was using the Kurds as a "card" with which to pressure Turkey to make concessions on other matters, such as access to water from the Tigris and Euphrates Rivers.[71] Though Assad denied it, both Turkey and NATO countries were convinced that PKK fighters were training in Syria and Syrian-controlled Lebanon. PKK leader Abdullah Ocalan maintained an office in Damascus and was believed to possess a Syrian resident permit.[72]

To convince Syria to terminate this support, Turkey turned first to diplomacy. It thus signed security protocols with Syria in 1987, 1992, and 1993. Still, such accords failed to end Syrian support for the PKK. In 1998, Turkey finally escalated to triadic coercion. It mobilized tens of thousands of troops on the Syrian border and threatened military action unless Syria expelled Ocalan and ceased its sheltering of PKK bases and fighters.[73] Facing the prospect of war, Assad conceded to Turkey's demands by withdrawing his support of the PKK and deporting Ocalan, whom Turkey captured the following year. Turkey and Syria went on to sign the Adana Agreement, which established security cooperation between the two countries.[74]

The 1998 confrontation confirms two findings from our analysis of the Israeli case. First, the very rareness of militarized brinkmanship and tension demonstrates the role of Turkey's strategic culture in limiting escalation in triadic coercion. That this example of military threats against a host state stands out as the single triadic coercion exception in Turkey's battle with the PKK is testimony to the traditional prudence of Turkish military and political decision-makers in this regard.[75] Second, the consequences of this incident affirm our finding that triadic coercion is only effective when exercised against strong regimes. The regime of Hafez al-Assad in the late 1990s, as detailed in chapter 4, had sufficient cohesion to recognize that a military conflict with Turkey did not serve its national security interests, and sufficient capacity to do what was needed to avoid such escalation. Under these circumstances, as we would predict, Turkey's threats of triadic coercion proved effective.

Turkey's triadic conflict with Iran offers further evidence of Turkey's aversion to triadic coercion. In the first decades after the Islamic Revolution, Iran and Turkey were at odds in terms of their international relations and visions of the role of religion in the public sphere. Nonetheless, the two countries engaged in extensive trade and economic cooperation. This included Iran's use of Turkish ports for war imports during the Iran-Iraq War and Turkey's sale of goods and technical assistance to Iran in return for oil and gas. Still, triadic conflict created tension between the two countries.[76] Iran gave overt or covert support to the PKK and other Kurdish groups in an apparent bid to challenge Turkey's growing stature in the Middle East, the Caucuses, and Central Asia.[77] During the peak of PKK attacks between 1992 and 1995, PKK militants freely crossed Iranian borders. Nonetheless, Turkey did not resort to triadic coercion against Iran but instead pursued PKK fighters directly. This drove Turkey to make some incursions into Iranian territory, which the Iranian government condemned. Throughout these actions, however, Turkey was careful not to target Iran as a state.

Using diplomacy to deescalate the crisis, Turkey held eight diplomatic and national security meetings with Iran between 1992 and 1994. In November 1993, the two states signed a joint security protocol stipulating that neither would permit any terrorist organization on its territory. In June 1994, they reached an agreement in which Iran promised to satisfy three main Turkish goals: prevent passage of PKK members from northern Iraq to Iran, prevent the PKK's passage to Armenia, and grant Turkey's request to bomb roads in Iran used by the PKK.[78] In exchange for

Iranian cooperation on these matters, the Turkish government pledged that it would move against Iranian opposition groups based in Turkey.

Rather than using triadic coercion, therefore, Turkey sought to combat nonstate actors by cultivating reciprocal collaboration and common ground. This investment in cooperation intensified after Turkey's 1999 arrest of Ocalan sparked demonstrations and unrest by Kurds throughout the Middle East, including in Iran. Newly wary of the threat of Kurdish separatism (as well as other potential regional transformations in the wake of September 11), Iran suspended relations with the PKK. Turkey seized upon those favorable circumstances to pursue further resolution of its triadic conflict with Iran through diplomatic collaboration. Against this backdrop, the Turkey-Iran Commission on Security Cooperation held its eighth joint security meeting in October 2001. In these talks Iran promised to prevent the PKK from launching attacks into Turkey. Again offering reciprocity on nonstate actors of concern to Iran, Turkey pledged to end support for an Azerbaijani liberation movement, as Iran demanded.[79]

In the years that followed, Turkey and Iran continued to work together against both the PKK and other Kurdish groups operating from northern Iraq.[80] By 2011, Erdoğan even signaled that Turkey would launch a joint operation with Iran against Kurdish militants' main base in northern Iraq.[81] Though competing interests in regional power continued to impede full realization of this and other forms of Turkish-Iranian cooperation, it was noteworthy that Turkey did not pursue any kind of direct military coercion to compel Iran to cease support for nonstate actors attacking Turkey. This was judicious, given Turkey's awareness of Iran's political and military power and Turkey's own reliance on Iranian oil.[82] In this context, Turkish decision-makers calculated that severing relations with Iran due to its alleged support of terrorism, or even threatening Iran militarily, would present Turkey with more costs than benefits.

Turkey's nonuse of triadic coercion was apparent not only in its relations with Syria and Iran but also with Iraq. Before the 1990s, Turkey and Iraq cooperated against Kurdish insurgents. Then Turkey joined the U.S.-led coalition in the 1990–1991 Gulf War.[83] In the wake of the Gulf War, Turkey accused Saddam Hussein of giving assistance to the PKK, though Baghdad officially denied that.[84] An even graver threat for Turkey in the 1990s was the creation in northern Iraq of the Kurdistan Regional Government (KRG). Turkey not only viewed this de facto Kurdish autonomy as a dangerous regional precedent but also accused Iraqi Kurdish groups of allowing PKK training camps in KRG territory.

In the context of the 1990s, the PKK repeatedly used territory loosely controlled by the KRG as a base for attacks across the border into Turkey. The Turkish army made repeated incursions into northern Iraq. Lasting several weeks, these assaults often entailed aerial bombardment of targets suspected to be PKK bases as well as infantry searches for militants.[85] While violations of Iraqi territory, such military actions were not triadic coercion because they aimed at the nonstate PKK directly. At the same time, after 1992, Turkey established an informal alliance with the two major Iraqi Kurdish parties, the Kurdish Democratic Party (KDP) and the Patriotic Union of Kurdistan (PUK), against the PKK. In March 1995, Turkey launched a particularly large operation in northern Iraq, deploying fighter planes, tanks, and thirty-five thousand troops.[86] This massive operation again aimed specifically at fighting nonstate actors in the semi-autonomous regions of Iraq, not the Iraqi state.

Gradually, the rivalry between the Iraqi Kurdish parties escalated to civil war. As the PKK allied with the PUK, Turkey in turn allied with the KDP. In May 1997, Turkey launched another major assault, dubbed Operation Hammer, during which it coordinated with KDP forces to attack the PUK and attempt to expel the PKK from Iraq.[87] Another cross-border operation in September 1997 sought a similar aim. These maneuvers clearly centered on military force. Yet again, they aimed at nonstate actors directly and did not constitute triadic coercion.

Turkey's triadic conflict with Iraq underwent another turn after the 2003 U.S. invasion toppled Saddam Hussein. This historic event transformed the Iraqi state and its place in the Middle East. Still, it did not immediately alter Turkey's aversion to triadic coercion. Turkey largely did not target triadic pressure at the Iraqi central government until 2006, when it threatened to limit economic and trade relations if Iraq did not take all necessary actions to uproot the PKK from the border area. After PKK attacks killed more than forty Turks in one month in 2007, the Turkish National Security Council announced its endorsement of a food and energy embargo against Iraq.[88] According to those plans, Turkey would cut electricity to the region, close the border crossing between Turkey and Iraq, end Turkish firms' commercial activities in the region, and control activities of firms trading with the family of KRG president Masoud Barzani.[89] These plans marked an unambiguous escalation in pressure tactics, yet they continued to fall short of military coercion. Turkey avoided holding the Iraqi central state in Baghdad responsible for Kurdish strategies.

Turkey continued with this nonmilitary approach to triadic conflict when it hosted the "Extended Neighbors of Iraq" conference in November 2007. Turkish representatives' intense lobbying bore fruit as conference delegates approved a statement that upheld Turkey's opposition to the PKK.[90] By 2008, President Erdoğan had shifted from hints that he was considering an embargo of Iraq to a public pledge of increased economic ties with Iraq. The Iraqi central government responded to these inducements. As Stephen Flanagan and Samuel Brannen noted, "Baghdad recognizes that the Kurdish issue is the potential spoiler of the relationship and is therefore working to balance its interests and cooperation with Turkey carefully."[91]

Even as it sought to cultivate cooperation with the Iraqi government, Turkey continued its assaults on nonstate threats. In 2008 it launched a large-scale land, air, and artillery operation against PKK forces in northern Iraq. During the operation, the Turkish government and army emphasized repeatedly that their only target was the PKK and that they were making all efforts to avert civilian casualties.[92] In addition, that year Turkey, Iraq, and the United States signed an agreement in which they pledged "to continue close cooperation in strengthening and maintaining military and security institutions and democratic political institutions in Iraq, including, as may be mutually agreed, cooperation in training, equipping, and arming the Iraqi Security Forces, in order to combat domestic and international terrorism and outlaw groups."[93] This agreement marked another step away from interstate military action and toward diplomatic cooperation, including with Iraq, as a strategy against nonstate threats.

Since the withdrawal of U.S. troops from Iraq in 2011, Turkey's policy toward the KRG has likewise shifted from antagonism to cooperation. Opening a Turkish consulate in Erbil and participating in various development projects, Turkey appeared to embrace Kurdish autonomy in Iraq at least in part in the hope of curbing the demands of its own Kurdish population and of eliciting KRG collaboration against the PKK.[94] At the same time, Turkey worked to strengthen and bolster the central government in Baghdad in an effort to stabilize the country and contain the scope of Iraqi Kurdish independence.[95] Turkey understood that military coercion against the Iraqi regime would be ineffective precisely because that regime was weak. It thus not only avoided taking military action against that regime but instead actively supported building its cohesion and capacity.

In 2013, peace talks between the Turkish government and the PKK led to a ceasefire. The truce lasted until 2015, when the AKP lost its majority in the June elections. Upon maneuvering to hold new snap elections that November, Erdoğan also moved to extract political advantage from the state's conflict with the PKK. He appeared to calculate that renewed assaults on PKK militants could serve him by discrediting the Kurdish-linked HDP opposition party and rallying both Turkish nationalist voters and conservative Kurdish voters to the AKP.[96] Against this backdrop, he ordered the bombing of PKK bases in Turkey and in northern Iraq, resulting in hundreds of casualties and widespread destruction. The PKK retaliated, precipitating a resurge of violence. The AKP regained its majority that November. By July 2016, enflamed hostilities had left 1,700 people dead and more than 350,000 displaced.[97]

As of this writing, Turkey's once-stable democracy has been unsettled not only by bloody conflict with the PKK but also by a coup attempt in 2016, a rash of terrorist attacks carried out by ISIS or other extremist groups, serious economic decline, unprecedented violations of human rights and crackdowns on freedom of speech and opposition, and the increasing authoritarianism of the political system. This tumult in Turkish domestic politics is intertwined with the multidimensional war next door in Syria, where Turkey has perceived a national security threat from both ISIS and Kurdish groups asserting autonomy in the North. Turkey forcefully intervened in fighting against Syria's most powerful Kurdish faction, the Party of Democratic Union (PYD), which had close ties to the PKK. In Operation Euphrates Shield in 2016–2017, Turkey carried out a major military intervention into northern Syria seeking to create a security buffer that would both force ISIS from the border and contain the PYD east of the Euphrates. Ryan Gingeras judged that the latter goal was Turkey's top priority, as it was a "natural extension" of its war with the PKK.[98] In this context, in early 2018, Turkey led Syrian forces that it backed in invading the northwest Syrian district of Afrin and violently taking it over from the Kurdish groups that had held it for years. Meanwhile, the AKP government also attempted to counter the PYD in Syria and the PKK in Turkey by intensifying cooperation with the KRG. In the process, it sidelined the

Iraqi government in ways that stoked tension with the central Iraqi government and Iran.[99]

Increasingly isolated, the Erdoğan government found itself beleaguered by millions of Syrian refugees, worsening relations with both Iran and Israel, new tensions with its NATO allies, and extraordinary levels of political polarization within its own population. It became entangled with jihadist groups on the one hand and victims of their attacks on the other. Its fraught relationship with Russia vacillated between diplomatic conflict and cooperation, all against a backdrop made complex by energy dependence and different positions toward the Assad regime.[100] Navigating these perilous and explosive contradictions, Erdoğan showed himself willing to commit unbridled abuses against the rights of his own citizens and use severe force against Kurdish groups, sometimes for cynical domestic or regional motives. Yet even as the Turkish government courted escalatory conflict on many fronts, it remained markedly prudent in averting escalation in specifically triadic conflicts. Consistent with a long, though now evolving, tradition of realism and restraint in foreign policy, Turkey largely eschewed triadic coercion. It thereby avoided allowing nonstate actors to drive new conflagrations with host states.

Lessons from India and Turkey

This brief examination of the Indian and Turkish cases affirms the arguments that we have demonstrated across Israeli history. First and foremost, whether or not a coercer state adopts policies of triadic coercion is very much affected by its own strategic culture. Both Turkey and India faced ample threats from nonstate actors hosted or assisted by neighboring states. Nonetheless, neither responded by directing military threats and strikes at those states as consistently or aggressively as did Israel. On the contrary, both states focused on fighting nonstate actors directly and frequently employed nonmilitary strategies such as diplomacy or economic sanctions. This aversion to triadic coercion was predictable, given India's traditional emphasis on defensive doctrines and Turkey's long-standing caution in foreign affairs. India and Turkey did carry out triadic coercion in a few instances that served as exceptions to these rules. In recent times, both countries have become more assertive, and Turkey has become embroiled in regional conflict. Nevertheless, the effect of each country's strategic culture on its approach to triadic conflict offered a stark contrast to Israel, which used aggressive triadic coercion disproportionately, nearly instinctively, and as an assertion of moral principle as much as a result of strategic calculation.

On those rare occasions in which India and Turkey resorted to triadic coercion, outcomes similarly confirmed the conditions for success that we demonstrate in the Israeli case. India's one major move toward triadic coercion against Pakistan, the 2001 Operation Parakram, proved largely futile due to the weak cohesion of the Pakistani regime. The Pakistani government pledged to abide by India's demands to ban nonstate actors but did not follow through. In this, Pakistan might have been circumvented by its own intelligence service, which feared the domestic backlash of repressing Kashmiri separatist groups and worried that a crackdown would bring insurgents to turn their violence from India to Pakistan itself. Regardless of the precise mechanism through which regime weaknesses impacted state behavior, the consequence was the same: the Pakistani regime was unable to uphold the national security imperative to reduce the chances of war, even as Indian armed forces mobilized on its border.

Inversely, Turkey's sole clear application of triadic coercion, its 1998 deployment of forces on the Syrian border and threats of "repercussions" if Syria did not expel Ocalan, was effective because of the capable and highly cohesive regime in Damascus. Hafez al-Assad commanded remarkably centralized authority over state policy-making. When he judged that something was in the political interests of his regime or the national security interests of his state, he took and implemented that decision. Rationally calculating that the risk of war with Turkey far outweighed the benefits of abetting the PKK, the Syrian president promptly complied with Turkey's demands. Turkey's use of triadic coercion proved effective in this instance, and the state did not again use it under conditions when such effectiveness was unlikely to recur.

Though a more comprehensive investigation of the Indian and Turkish cases is needed to verify these findings in full detail, the comparative analysis offered in this chapter testifies to the greater generalizability of this book's central claims. Our study of the Indian and Turkish experiences with triadic conflict, juxtaposed with the prior chapters' in-depth scrutiny of the Israeli experience, demonstrates how differing strategic cultures affect different approaches to applying triadic coercion. It also confirms that host state strength mediates the likelihood that triadic coercion will succeed in realizing coercers' aims. Demonstration of these patterns strengthens our conclusion that policy-makers should exercise caution when aiming strikes at host states as a strategy for combatting nonstate actors. They should employ such strategies only under the particular conditions that enable their effectiveness, and they should be vigilant in considering how their own inherited assumptions and norms might move them to do otherwise.

Conclusion

Richard Ned Lebow and Janice Stein once wrote that models of rational deterrence are "theories about nonexistent decision makers operating in nonexistent environments."[1] The same could be said about the broader arena of theories of coercion, which includes both deterrence and compellence. Taking a grounded empirical approach, this book has scrutinized real decision-makers in their actual environments. Specifically, it has endeavored to understand a particular kind of coercion—what we call triadic coercion—in which a state directs military threats or strikes at another state to force it to take action against a nonstate actor to which it offers shelter or assistance. Our aim has been to use in-depth historical analysis and process tracing to uncover and evaluate causal relationships regarding both why states undertake triadic coercion and the conditions under which that strategy yields the desired results. This conclusion reviews the main takeaways of each chapter; highlights the key lessons, contributions, and extensions of the book as a whole; and derives recommendations for policy-makers.

Chapter Synopses

The seven previous chapters of this book craft a new framework for understanding triadic conflict, present hypotheses about the causes and effects of triadic coercion, and evaluate those propositions through qualitative empirical analysis. Chapter 1 begins by making the case for examining triadic coercion as a particular kind of strategic interaction demanding analysis in its own right. It then moves to present a rational "decision-making tree" that lays out three questions that a coercer state decision-maker should ask in determining the appropriateness of employing triadic coercion: (1) Does a favorable interstate balance of power allow the coercer to threaten the host credibly? (2) Does the host state's predisposition render it inclined to defy or cooperate with demands to stop the nonstate actors' violence? (3) Is the host state's regime strong?

Employing this schema, the chapter puts forth two major arguments that guide the remainder of the book. First, considering the *outcomes* of triadic coercion, we argue that—regardless of a host state's defiant or cooperative predisposition—triadic coercion is only likely to succeed when targeted against a host state that possesses a regime that is strong. The stronger a regime, in terms of both cohesion and capacity, the more it can prioritize national interests over nonstate actor ambitions, design actions as triadic coercion demands, and carry them out despite potential opposition. Conversely, when regimes are internally fragmented and institutionally weak, they will be unable to respond coherently to coercers' credible threats. Therefore, triadic coercion aimed at host states with weak regimes is likely to be ineffective or even counterproductive.

Second, we ask if triadic coercion is likely to succeed only against strong regimes, why do many states nevertheless employ it against weak ones? Here, turning to the *sources* of triadic coercion, we argue that the use or nonuse of this strategy is not strictly the result of rational, cost-benefit analysis. Rather, we propose that it is also profoundly shaped by a coercer state's own strategic culture, in the sense of its historically shaped and socially reinforced ideas, attitudes, traditions, preferences, and habits related to security matters. We examine strategic culture as the product of the institutional arrangements that structure decision-making processes and the ideas and assumptions that influence the content of those decisions. In determining whether to strike at states that host nonstate actors, a coercer state's unique strategic culture may lead decision-makers to emphasize only certain levels of the decision tree and disregard others, such as regime strength. When a strategic culture encourages it, a coercer state can come to regard triadic coercion as appropriate on moral, rather than instrumental, grounds. It can also view forceful action in pursuit of deterrence as necessary and beneficial, regardless of its actual effect in establishing deterrence.

Israel's long and varied history of conflict with its neighbors has offered an ideal laboratory for this analytical undertaking. Chapter 2 outlines how Israel's application of triadic coercion has evolved since statehood. The initial crystallization of the policy in the 1950s was heavily affected by interaction with Egypt and, even more importantly, with Jordan. Confronting border violations from individuals and groups, Israel first targeted reprisals against civilian communities that it believed to support or harbor infiltrators. As that strategy garnered international criticism, Israel instead began to strike state installations in the countries from which infiltrations originated. From 1956 until the mid-1990s, Israel adapted this application of triadic coercion in accord with its perception of host states' predispositions. When it believed that a host state was defiant and supported nonstate actors' violence—for example, Egypt between 1952 and 1956 and Syria between 1963 and 1970—it attacked that state. When it regarded the host state as cooperative and not an accomplice to attacks—for example, Jordan in the 1960s or Lebanon before the 1990s—it instead aimed coercion directly at nonstate actors themselves. This approach, which we follow Menachem Klein in calling the "Rabin Doctrine," showed a level of nuance beyond a focus on mere interstate balance of power, as blunt deterrence theory might predict. Nevertheless, it failed to take into account another crucial variable: the strength of the host state's regime.

The 1990s saw a crisis in Israel's security concept, as its main security concern shifted from conventional interstate war to asymmetric threats, and this prompted a reworking of its traditional national security concept. The ensuing developments in strategic culture hardened four tendencies in Israel's practice of triadic coercion. First, it brought Israel to advocate forceful action in pursuit of asserting a deterrent posture as a goal in and of itself rather than as a means to the greater goal of actually reducing violence. Second, despite high levels of intelligence to the contrary, Israel's strategic culture encouraged decision-makers to view its varied adversaries as one and the same, neglecting their different identities, interests, and capacities. Third, strategic culture reinforced the idea that coercive force should aim not simply at enemies' capabilities but also at their consciousness, in order to change their beliefs about Israel. In particular, Israel's aim became convincing its enemies of Israel's will and overwhelming capacity to punish any who dared to oppose it. Fourth, Israel's strategic culture increasingly emphasized a "logic of appropriateness" that justified actions on the basis of moral righteousness rather than rational calculations about the expected impact on the targeted actor.

Chapter 3 analyzes Israel's triadic coercion against Egypt, with an emphasis on how variation in the strength of the regime in Cairo mediated the effectiveness of Israel's efforts to force it to act against nonstate actors on its soil. In the early 1950s, Israel faced the problem of what it called infiltrations from the Egyptian-controlled Gaza Strip. Israel's efforts to respond with military force against this host state repeatedly failed. Before 1954, the Egyptian government attempted to restrict infiltrations but was unable due to the regime's institutional weakness and domestic crises. Lack of cohesion and capacity likewise drove President Gamal Abdel Nasser to support infiltrations in 1955 and 1956, even though doing so goaded his more powerful adversary. The 1956 Suez War transformed this situation because it helped Nasser centralize authority and consolidate political capacity. He used this enhanced regime strength to curb nonstate actors. Only under those conditions did Israel's efforts at triadic coercion become effective. This situation remained on the border until Israel's 1967 occupation of Gaza and the Sinai Peninsula, and subsequently the 1979 Israel-Egypt peace treaty, rendered moot the question of triadic coercion. The triadic equilibrium held through 2011, when a popular uprising forced the resignation of President Hosni Mubarak and Egypt entered into a new phase of regime instability and uncertainty. As government authority weakened in the Sinai Peninsula, extremist organizations, sometimes together with local Bedouin communities, took up arms. While their insurgency aimed predominantly against Cairo, they also directed some lethal attacks across the border at Israel. This generated a new arena of triadic conflict. Nevertheless, Israel largely refrained from applying triadic coercion. Influenced by years of peace with Egypt and the belief that the Egyptian regime under Abdel Fattah el-Sisi was positively predisposed against nonstate actors, Israel instead chose to cooperate with Cairo in confronting what both states regarded as a threat.

Chapter 4 uncovers similar patterns in Israel's use of triadic coercion against Syria, again pointing to the importance of host regime cohesion and capacity in mediating triadic coercion outcomes. Nonstate actors' attacks from Syria to Israel did not reach significant levels until after 1963, a period when the establishment of a new Ba'ath Party regime coincided with the rise of the Palestinian guerrilla movement. The government in

Damascus was committed to the Palestinian struggle. Perhaps more than ideology, however, it was the regime's extreme internal factionalism and weak institutions that created the context within which Syria became a champion of guerrilla strikes against Israel. Consistent with the Rabin Doctrine, Israel targeted reprisals against the Syrian state in the belief that it was predisposed to defiance. It did not consider how the Ba'ath regime's lack of cohesion and capacity was crucial in enabling nonstate violent activity or how Israel's coercive measures actually aggravated those dimensions of regime weakness. Under these conditions, triadic coercion repeatedly failed. This pattern changed dramatically as Hafez al-Assad consolidated a cohesive, centralized, and capable regime after 1970. Though Assad encouraged nonstate attacks from other territories, he prohibited them from Syria in a pragmatic commitment to safeguard his state from Israeli triadic coercion. Thereafter, any continued Israeli coercion targeting the Syrian state became more effective. This was due not to a change in Syria's predisposition but to a change in the strength of its regime. This status quo persisted until 2011, when the regime brutally repressed a popular uprising, spurring its descent into a multidimensional war. Since then, territorial fragmentation and state withdrawal has ceded new autonomy to nonstate actors on Syrian soil, though its consequences for conflict with Israel remain to be seen.

Chapter 5 illustrates the flexibility of our arguments about triadic coercion by extending their application to an atypical quasi-state actor: the Palestinian Authority (PA). Though the PA is not an independent state, Israel has often treated it as such by employing triadic coercion in the demand that it stop violence by militant groups in the West Bank or Gaza Strip. In the immediate wake of the 1993 Oslo Accords, Israel regarded the PA as something of a security partner; it thus generally sought to support the PA in fighting Palestinian opposition groups, while also reserving its own discretion to suppress those groups directly, as it saw necessary. After 1996, Israel came to view the PA as a potential enemy warranting both direct and triadic coercion. This shift was precipitated by the Jerusalem tunnel clashes and hastened by the new evolution in Israeli security thinking in the 1990s. These trends fed Israel's intense preoccupation with any perceived weakening in its deterrence and the need to restore it, at all costs. These and other trends in Israel's strategic culture came to fruition, and hardened, during the second Intifada. Given the PA's weak cohesion and capacity, it was highly questionable if it had the political or institutional ability to fulfill Israel's demands to end attacks by rival movements such as Hamas or even disaffected members of the ruling Fatah faction. Nevertheless, Israel both escalated its coercion and increasingly justified it with rationales that were less grounded in fact-based calculations about how to reduce violence than they were in morally infused assumptions and convictions. Among these were the need to sear into "enemy consciousness" the lesson that Israel does not surrender to force, the legitimacy of reprisals due to their appropriateness as much as their expected utility, a general dearth of nuance in identifying the targets of coercion, and advocacy of military force to assert a deterrent posture on the basis of its inherent rather than merely instrumental value. These notions had long roots in Israeli decision-making and ideas but reached new heights in the early 2000s and thereafter compounded a markedly aggressive streak in strategic culture. These new trends would prove critical in shaping Israel's subsequent approach to triadic coercion.

Chapter 6 traces the impact of this strategic culture on Israel's use of triadic coercion against Lebanon. From the late 1960s until 1982, Israel's main nonstate adversaries from Lebanese territory were Palestinian fedayeen. Israel recognized that the Lebanese government was cooperatively predisposed against these groups and thus followed the Rabin Doctrine and largely aimed its force at nonstate actors directly. By the 1990s, Israel's main nonstate foe in Lebanon was Hezbollah. In sync with changes in its strategic culture in that era, Israel turned to triadic coercion when it responded to Hezbollah provocations with large-scale bombing operations in 1993 and 1996, whose targeting went far beyond Hezbollah specifically. These campaigns embraced what Israeli security planners called a "leverages" approach, meaning pressuring a host state as a kind of lever or weight against nonstate actors. However, they revealed a lack of nuance and clarity as to whether Israel intended to coerce the Lebanese government, the Syrian regime that militarily controlled Lebanon, Lebanese civilians, or all of the above. Neither did military leaders devote clear attention to how, precisely, use of force would bring any of these actors to change their behavior. Moreover, these actions showed Israel's inattention to how its triadic coercion could be rendered ineffective by Lebanon's acutely low levels of institutional capacity and high levels of political fragmentation.

These complications aside, the Israeli security establishment's enthusiasm for triadic coercion, without regard to host regime weakness, continued to harden after its 2000 withdrawal from southern Lebanon. It reached dramatic new heights in the 2006 War. Though the government rejected the IDF's most extreme plans due to American pressure, Israel caused unprecedented destruction through direct strikes against Hezbollah and triadic coercion aimed to force the Lebanese government to "take responsibility" and restrain Hezbollah. Israel's massive show of force demonstrated both the military's dominance in foreign and security policy and the elevation of a moralistic, emotion-laden call for the appropriateness of actions that asserted a deterrent posture. Israel did not consider how Lebanon's weak state and divided government could actually control a nonstate actor that was more powerful than Lebanon's own army. In the aftermath of the war Israel did not question this dubious emphasis on triadic coercion but rather doubled down in support of it. Security elites increasingly reiterated a promise that, in any future conflict with Hezbollah, they would regard Lebanon itself as the primary enemy. The Israeli security establishment thus elevated triadic coercion to an axiom of national strategy, without ever subjecting that strategy to a systematic, penetrating analysis about its proven success or failure.

Chapter 7 looks beyond the Israeli experience to probe the validity and generalizability of our arguments about the causes and effects of triadic coercion. We briefly examine two other cases of triadic conflict: India's conflict with Pakistan due to the latter's backing of Kashmiri separatist groups and Turkey's conflict with Syria, Iran, and Iraq over their support for the PKK. The Indian and Turkish experiences validate the contentions of this book both due to the ways that they are distinct from Israel and the ways in which they were similar. With regard to differences, as we predict, these states' different strategic cultures guided them to undertake very different approaches to triadic coercion. India's strategic culture is grounded in a security policy that emphasizes defense and strict civilian control over the military. Though India's military doctrine moved in a somewhat more offensive direction in the early 2000s, the continued dominance of a defensive approach was vital in shaping India's general avoidance of triadic coercion against Pakistan. Similarly, Turkey's strategic culture has traditionally emphasized caution, moderation, and realism. The state's doctrine of noninterference eroded in the context of the post-2011 Syrian war. Still, it long played a role in discouraging Turkey from undertaking triadic coercion against neighboring states and instead encouraging it to combat PKK forces directly. In this way, the Indian and Turkish cases illustrate how triadic coercion is not an automatic, rational outcome of all triadic situations but rather a choice deeply shaped by a coercer state's security ideas and decision-making processes.

With regard to similarities, in the rare instances that India and Turkey did employ policies resembling triadic coercion, the effectiveness of those policies was mediated by the targeted host regime, as history had shown to be the case with Israel. In the 2001–2002 Operation Parakram, India mobilized troops on the Pakistani border in a clear signal of its readiness to engage militarily if Pakistan did not comply with its demands to crack down on militant groups fighting for Kashmir's independence. Though Pakistan made some efforts against militants, India's use of triadic coercion ultimately did not yield significant achievements due to the Pakistani regime's lack of cohesion. The government did not fully control the military or intelligence services, which appeared to circumvent civilian dictates and continue to abet insurgents. In addition, the regime's fear of domestic backlash discouraged it from taking an unequivocal stance against nonstate actors. Whereas host regime weakness thus undermined the success of India's experiment with triadic coercion, host regime strength enabled success when Turkey turned to the same strategy. After several security accords failed to terminate Syria's support for the PKK, Turkey mobilized troops on the border in 1998 and threatened military action. The Assad regime had the cohesion to recognize the dangers of conflict with Turkey and the capacity to take the actions necessary to avert such escalation. It thus quickly complied with Turkey's demands to dismantle PKK bases and expel its leadership.

Comparative analysis of India and Turkey, juxtaposed with analysis of seventy years of Israeli practice of triadic coercion, thus offers insight on various dimensions and dynamics constituting three-player conflicts involving states and nonstate actors. The sum of this research gives us confidence that our arguments about the sources and outcomes of triadic coercion can plausibly be extended to explain still other cases of triadic conflict as well.

Contributions and Extensions

This book's theoretical framework, causal arguments, and empirical analysis make contributions to different strands of scholarship on international relations, intrastate conflict, security studies, and Middle East politics. We highlight three in particular. First, this study combines ideas taken from research on coercion and on counterinsurgency in order to create a novel understanding of a particular type of strategic situation. Research on deterrence, and similarly on compellence, has long sought to establish the conditions under which different strategies are more or less likely to succeed. Most models, emphasizing elements such as balance of power, resolve, and clear communication, implicitly or explicitly assume conventional conflicts between two states.

In the post–Cold War era, a new research agenda termed "complex deterrence," or the "fourth wave of deterrence," has shed light on more multifaceted situations, including those that involve asymmetrical conflict with nonstate actors. Works on complex deterrence point out that, in such situations, states might be unable to achieve deterrence even if they are more powerful and more determined than their adversaries and communicate their strength and will clearly. This literature helpfully shows how sheer balance of power is not sufficient to achieve deterrence and compellence in complex situations, which instead demand strategies that are nuanced and tailored to the challenges at hand. Yet existing scholarship has not adequately addressed the unique qualities of triadic conflicts. As a result, it has not considered how characteristics of the states that host nonstate actors—such as the strength of their regimes in terms of political cohesion and institutional capacity—mediate the effectiveness of other states' efforts to pressure them to take action against nonstate violence.

Scholarship on insurgency, on the other hand, does consider how states' internal strength influences their relations to nonstate actors based in their territory. While strong states are likely to restrict the autonomy and violent activities of nonstate actors within their borders, weak states are often unable to limit the action of such groups. A state's counterinsurgency against militant groups is also unlikely to succeed if it lacks the institutional capacity to offer the services and security that win the population over from fighters. This literature amply shows why, for these reasons, weak states are more likely than strong ones to host insurgent groups. However, such studies tend to focus on these kinds of dynamics inside state boundaries and by and large do not address how state strength or weakness also affects conflict with other states, much less one state's ability to deter violence from another state's territory.

Our book has combined ideas from these two distinct bodies of literature in order to cover blind spots left by both. In creating an analytical framework with which to examine triadic conflicts, we took on a particular kind of conflict yet to be theorized sufficiently in work on either deterrence or counterinsurgency. Our research reveals that triadic conflicts have dynamics and conditions for success that differ significantly from conflicts that are strictly either interstate or intrastate. Our approach sustains the significance of some traditional deterrence variables, such as a coercer state's ability to make and effectively communicate credible threats. At the same time, we show how those variables do not fully explain varied outcomes in triadic conflicts.

Second, we contribute to scholarship on strategic culture by extending its applicability to a new domain. Existing research relating strategic culture to coercion predominantly probes how national security ideas and norms create "sticky" habits of thinking about the use of nuclear weapons.[2] We show how strategic cultures can similarly harden approaches to conventional warfare and even asymmetrical threats, and with grave consequences. Our conceptualization of strategic culture as a product of two elements, decision-making processes and ideas, offers a parsimonious yet powerful way of encapsulating an array of elements determining the system of beliefs, values, traditions, and practices that shape security policies and military behavior. In addition, we show how strategic culture explains otherwise puzzling patterns in coercive policies. For example, over the decades Israeli decision-makers have viewed their use of triadic coercion as the straightforward strategic choice of an optimal method for combatting nonstate actors. We take up the notion of strategic culture to contest this view. In the process, we illustrate how socially conditioned attitudes can become engrained and appear self-evidently rational even when they are not. We thus offer new evidence and analysis demonstrating the utility of strategic culture as an analytical tool.

Third, our study contributes to scholarship on Israel and the Arab-Israeli conflict. Research of these subjects is vast, and we have used and cited hundreds of sources that have examined it from a plethora of angles over the course of decades. Still, our concentration on triadic coercion is novel and fresh. It has provided a new focal point on which to bring together knowledge about an array of different aspects of Middle East politics and history and a new research agenda with which to use this knowledge in identifying and explaining heretofore understudied puzzles. Many works on Israeli security issues consider particular eras (such as Israel's border conflicts in the 1950s and 1960s), particular events (such as the 2006 Lebanon War), or particular topics (such as deterrence or counterterrorism). These works often mention moments akin to what we call triadic conflict but do not theorize them as distinct strategic situations worthy of theorization or empirical scrutiny in their own right. In highlighting and investigating the breadth of Israel's triadic conflicts over the full length of its history we have put existing sources in a new dialogue that reveals neglected instances of both variation and continuity over time. Our work brings to the fore patterns, such as triadic coercion's different outcomes against strong and weak host regimes, as well as puzzles, such as Israel's persistent use of triadic coercion even under conditions in which its own past suggests it to be ineffective. The multicase and *longue durée* design of our research thus shines a spotlight on questions that had yet to be asked. We hope that our answers to those questions will advance an overdue debate on triadic coercion.

Recommendations

What can decision-makers learn from this study? The most important lessons follow our main questions and arguments. Consistent with our findings about the conditions for triadic coercion success, decision-makers who consider using this strategy should give the utmost attention to the weakness of any regimes that they might target and avoid any military action that risks further weakening them.

Consistent with our findings about the drivers of triadic coercion adoption, decision-makers ought to be aware of the potentially perverse effects of strategic culture on their security choices. Politicians, military elites, and publics at large might be convinced that a particular response to an insurgent challenger is the necessary, the intrinsically appropriate, or even the only course of action. Yet what seems like a self-evidently rational strategy might also be conditioned by uncalculated factors, such as socially engrained assumptions, inherited dispositions, and institutionally reinforced attitudes. Decision-makers should subject the instinct to use military force to critical scrutiny and a comprehensive weighing of all available policy options in light of their expected costs and benefits. Our survey of Israel's history suggests that triadic coercion may not always be a misguided strategic choice. But it often is. Those who advocate this approach must be vigilant in establishing that it passes the test of the logic of consequences, and not that it simply seems to them to be appropriate. In particular, security elites must be wary of using military strikes for the sake of asserting a deterrent posture as a goal in and of itself.

In the Israeli case, this lesson has never been more urgent. The states and governments on Israel's borders are engulfed in unprecedented crisis. Egypt's economy is in free fall, its military dictatorship depends on repression to forestall opposition, and the state cannot stop extremist groups in the Sinai Peninsula. Syria is being torn apart by a brutal war in which foreign powers are shredding its national sovereignty, hundreds of different rebel battalions are vying for control of territory, and the internationally recognized regime slaughters civilians in a bid to hold power. Palestinian national institutions are corrupt, hollowed-out shadows of their once unifying selves, and the West Bank and Gaza Strip are split between two rival governments, neither of which command much legitimacy with the people over whom they purport to rule. Lebanon remains the weak state that it has always been and now also finds its two main political blocs divided on opposite sides of the Syrian war and its infrastructure buckling under the weight of some one million Syrian refugees. Triadic coercion cannot be effective against these acutely weak regimes; rather, it could be perilously counterproductive. Should nonstate actors based in any of these areas attack Israel, our study suggests that it would be highly unwise for Israel to respond by "holding responsible" the nominal government.

As we write these words, the dangers of triadic coercion in the Middle East are staggeringly grave. This is not only because the probable utility of triadic coercion as a strategy for ending violence is rapidly diminishing but also because Israel's enthusiasm for the strategy continues to rise. The "IDF Strategy" document of 2015, Israel's first written military doctrine, wholeheartedly endorses such coercive strategies. Israeli political and military discourse about Hezbollah suggests that, should Israel find itself in confrontation with the nonstate actor in the future, Israel is likely to adopt an even more aggressive approach targeting the Lebanese state. Facing the Gaza Strip, Israel increasingly threatens triadic coercion to force the Hamas government to rein in rival groups just as it once threatened triadic coercion against Arafat to force it to rein in Hamas. In August 2016, for example, the IDF bombed several Hamas targets in response to a rocket launched by a Salafi organization ideologically affiliated with ISIS. Israeli military intelligence ascertained that the group had launched the rocket at least in part to challenge Hamas's authority. Nevertheless, it was quick to declare,

"Hamas is the sovereign in the Gaza Strip, and it will bear responsibility for any terrorist incident emanating from it."[3]

The history of Israel's triadic coercion need not repeat itself. India shows how a different kind of strategic culture can push a state toward caution rather than aggression in triadic relations. Turkey demonstrates how triadic coercion can be applied only where it's likely to succeed: against a strong regime. These cases also illustrate how our arguments about triadic coercion and about strategic culture are generalizable beyond the Arab-Israeli conflict. More academic and policy attention is necessary to continue to trace their dynamics in a range of settings across time and space.

Ultimately, the Arab-Israeli conflict is much larger than triadic coercion. The key to sustainable and just peace in the region does not lie simply in enforcing quiet along borders that have been determined by war and dispossession. Nor can genuine peace be built on thwarting violence by nonstate actors while ignoring the much larger popular and historical grievances that animate their struggles. Peace requires political agreements that address all peoples' aspirations for freedom, security, dignity, and national self-determination. Effective triadic coercion is not a substitute for political solutions that safeguard individual and collective rights. Misapplied triadic coercion, however, can cause tremendous and unnecessary destruction and bloodshed, and everything should be done to avoid such needless violence.

To that end, we propose that states should institutionalize alternative centers of decision-making authority and empower them with the ability to weigh in on important strategic decisions as well as the means to promote meaningful consideration of different avenues of security thought and action. Where armies tend toward severe and disproportionate force, greater civilian scrutiny of military decision-making is needed to check that tendency. Even given these institutional reforms and paradigm shifts, resolving triadic conflicts will not be easy. Yet the lessons of Israeli history, like those of India and Turkey, show how strictly military solutions are seldom sufficient against complex problems involving national conflicts over sovereignty and territory. Genuine peace requires negotiation and significant sacrifice. As difficult as they might be, sacrifices for peace are dwarfed by those extracted by perpetual war.

Notes

Unless otherwise noted, all translations are the authors'.

1. Understanding Triadic Coercion

1. "Text of Bush's Address," CNN, September 11, 2001, accessed October 26, 2015, http://edition.cnn.com/2001/US/09/11/bush.speech.text/.
2. Other scholars have addressed similar dynamics. What we call "triadic coercion" is similar to what Keren Fraiman calls "transitive compellence" and David Carter dubs "the compellence dilemma." See Keren E. Fraiman, "Understanding Weak States and State Sponsors: The Case for Base State Coercion," in *Coercion: The Power to Hurt in International Politics*, ed. Kelly M. Greenhill and Peter Krause (New York: Oxford University Press, 2018), 117–37; David B. Carter, "The Compellence Dilemma: International Disputes with Violent Groups," *International Studies Quarterly* 59 (2015): 461–76.
3. Idean Salehyan, "Transnational Rebels: Neighboring States as Sanctuary for Rebel Groups," *World Politics* 59, no. 2 (2007): 217–42.
4. However, the United States has been reluctant to use coercion in Pakistan. Paul D. Miller, "How to Exercise U.S. Leverage Over Pakistan," *Washington Quarterly* 35, no. 4 (2012): 37–52; Stephen D. Krasner, "Talking Tough to Pakistan: How to End Islamabad's Defiance," *Foreign Affairs* 91, no. 1 (February 2012): 87–96.
5. Christopher Phillips, "Turkey and Syria," in *Turkey's Global Strategy* (London: London School of Economics Reports, 2011), 36; Hasan Turunc, "Turkey and Iraq," in *Turkey's Global Strategy* (London: London School of Economics Reports,

2011), 40–42; Elliot Hentov, "Turkey and Iran," in *Turkey's Global Strategy* (London: London School of Economics Reports, 2011), 29.
6. Sumit Ganguly and Michael R. Kraig, "The 2001–2002 Indo-Pakistani Crisis: Exposing the Limits of Coercive Diplomacy," *Security Studies* 14, no. 2 (2005): 290–324.
7. Idean Salehyan, *Rebels Without Borders: Transnational Insurgencies in World Politics* (Ithaca, N.Y.: Cornell University Press, 2009), 174.
8. Ibid., 126–44.
9. Boaz Atzili and Wendy Pearlman, "Triadic Deterrence: Coercing Strength, Beaten by Weakness," *Security Studies* 21 (2012): 301–35.
10. Rudra Sil and Peter J. Katzenstein, *Beyond Paradigms: Analytic Eclecticism in the Study of World Politics* (Basingstoke: Palgrave Macmillan, 2010); for a similar approach, see Charles Kupchan, *How Enemies Become Friends: The Sources of Stable Peace* (Princeton, N.J.: Princeton University Press, 2010).
11. Thomas Schelling, *Arms and Influence* (New Haven, Conn.: Yale University Press, 1966), 2–3.
12. See, e.g., Jeffrey W. Knopf, "The Fourth Wave in Deterrence Research," *Contemporary Security Policy* 31, no. 1 (2010): 1–33; Paul K. Davis and Brian M. Jenkins, *Deterrence & Influence in Counterterrorism: A Component in the War on Al Qaeda* (Santa Monica, Calif.: RAND, 2002), xii, http://www.dtic.mil/dtic/tr/fulltext/u2/a409007.pdf; Alex Wilner, "Deterring the Undeterrable: Coercion, Denial, and Delegitimization in Counterterrorism," *Journal of Strategic Studies* 34, no. 1 (2011): 3–37.
13. See Robert A. Pape, "The Strategic Logic of Suicide Terrorism," *American Political Science Review* 97, no. 3 (2003): 343–61; David A. Lake, "Rational Extremism: Understanding Terrorism in the Twenty-First Century," *Dialogue IO* 1, no. 1 (2002): 15–29; Max Abrahms, "What Terrorists Really Want: Terrorist Motives and Counterterrorism Strategy," *International Security* 32, no. 4 (2008): 78–105.
14. Martha Crenshaw, "Coercive Diplomacy and the Response to Terrorism," in *The United States and Coercive Diplomacy*, ed. Robert Art and Patrick Cronin (Washington, D.C.: U.S. Institute of Peace Press, 2003), 310–13; Richard K. Betts, "The Soft Underbelly of American Primacy: Tactical Advantages of Terror," *Political Science Quarterly* 117, no. 1 (2002): 31; Emanuel Adler, "Complex Deterrence in the Asymmetric-Warfare Era," in *Complex Deterrence: Strategy in the Global Age*, ed. James J. Wirtz, Patrick M. Morgan, and T. V. Paul (Chicago: University of Chicago Press, 2009), 85–108; Janice Gross Stein, "Rational Deterrence Against 'Irrational' Adversaries? No Common Knowledge," in *Complex Deterrence: Strategy in the Global Age*, ed. T. V. Paul, Patrick M. Morgan, and James J. Wirtz (Chicago: University of Chicago Press, 2009), 58–82; Davis and Jenkins, "Deterrence & Influence in Counterterrorism," 4.
15. Crenshaw, "Coercive Diplomacy and the Response to Terrorism," 311–12; Betts, "Soft Underbelly of American Primacy," 31; Knopf, "Fourth Wave in Deterrence Research," 21.
16. Crenshaw, "Coercive Diplomacy and the Response to Terrorism," 311–12.
17. Ibid.

18. Knopf, "Fourth Wave in Deterrence Research," 23.
19. Ibid., 11; see also Robert F. Trager and Dessislava P. Zagorcheva, "Deterring Terrorism: It Can Be Done," *International Security* 30, no. 3 (2005): 87–123; Boaz Ganor, *The Counter-Terrorism Puzzle: A Guide for Decision Makers* (New Brunswick, N.J.: Transaction Publishers, 2005), 81–82; Neil J. Smelser and Faith Mitchell, eds., *Discouraging Terrorism: Some Implications of 9/11* (Washington, D.C.: National Academies Press, 2002); Betts, "Soft Underbelly of American Primacy."
20. Daniel Byman, *Deadly Connections: States That Sponsor Terrorism* (Cambridge: Cambridge University Press, 2005), 12.
21. On the distinction between deterrence and compellence, see Thomas C. Schelling, *The Strategy of Conflict* (Cambridge, Mass.: Harvard University Press, 1960), chap. 2. For a discussion of the term "coercion" as encompassing both deterrence and compellence, see Robert J. Art and Kelly M. Greenhill, "Coercion: An Analytical Overview," in *Coercion: The Power to Hurt in International Politics*, ed. Kelly M. Greenhill and Peter Krause (New York: Oxford University Press, 2018), 4–5.
22. Alexander George, "The Need for Influence Theory and Actor-Specific Behavioral Models of Adversaries," *Comparative Strategy* 22, no. 5 (2003): 463–87; Davis and Jenkins, "Deterrence & Influence in Counterterrorism."
23. Fraiman, "Understanding Weak States and State Sponsors," 137.
24. Byman, *Deadly Connections*, 6.
25. Jonathan Shimshoni, *Israel and Conventional Deterrence: Border Warfare from 1953 to 1970* (Ithaca, N.Y.: Cornell University Press, 1988), 226.
26. Paul R. Pillar, *Terrorism and U.S. Foreign Policy* (Washington, D.C.: Brookings Institution Press, 2001), 178–79.
27. Byman, *Deadly Connections*, 11–15.
28. David Brown, *The State and Ethnic Politics in Southeast Asia* (New York: Routledge, 1994), 3.
29. Though we define such aspects of political control in terms of regime capacity, some scholars include them in their definition of state capacity. See, e.g., Cullen S. Hendrix, "Measuring State Capacity: Theoretical and Empirical Implications for the Study of Civil Conflict," *Journal of Peace Research* 47, no. 3 (2010): 273–85; Kalevi Holsti, *The State, War and the State of War* (Cambridge: Cambridge University Press, 1996), 82–98.
30. This builds on Wendy Pearlman, *Violence, Nonviolence, and the Palestinian National Movement* (Cambridge: Cambridge University Press, 2011), 9.
31. Gary W. Cox and Kenneth A. Shepsle, "Majority Cycling and Agenda Manipulation: Richard McKelvey's Contributions and Legacy," in *Positive Changes in Political Science: The Legacy of Richard McKelvey's Most Influential Writings*, ed. John H. Aldrich, James E. Alt, and Arthur Lupia (Ann Arbor: University of Michigan Press, 2007), 35.
32. Holsti, *State, War and the State of War*.
33. Steven R. David, "Explaining Third World Alignment," *World Politics* 43, no. 2 (1991): 233–56.
34. Ibid., 236.

35. Doug McAdam, Sidney G. Tarrow, and Charles Tilly, *Dynamics of Contention* (Cambridge: Cambridge University Press, 2001), 78.
36. Michael Mann, *The Sources of Social Power*, vol. 2, *The Rise of Classes and Nation-States, 1760–1914*, 2nd ed. (Cambridge: Cambridge University Press, 2012); see also Hillel Soifer and Matthias vom Hau, "Unpacking the Strength of the State: The Utility of State Infrastructural Power," *Studies in Comparative International Development* 43, no. 3–4 (2008): 219–30.
37. Theda Skocpol, *States and Social Revolutions: A Comparative Analysis of France, Russia, and China* (Cambridge: Cambridge University Press, 1979); Jeffrey Ira Herbst, *States and Power in Africa: Comparative Lessons in Authority and Control* (Princeton, N.J.: Princeton University Press, 2000); Hendrix, "Measuring State Capacity"; Cameron G. Thies, "War, Rivalry, and State Building in Latin America," *American Journal of Political Science* 49, no. 3 (2005): 451–65.
38. Max Weber, "Politics as a Vocation," in *From Max Weber: Essays in Sociology*, ed. Hans Heinrich Gerth and C. Wright Mills (New York: Oxford University Press, 1958), 78.
39. Holsti, *State, War and the State of War*, 84–86.
40. Carter, "Compellence Dilemma."
41. Byman, *Deadly Connections*, 13.
42. David, "Explaining Third World Alignment."
43. Carter, "Compellence Dilemma."
44. Salehyan, *Rebels Without Borders*, 114–16.
45. Dylan Craig, "Developing a Comparative Perspective on the Use of Nonstates in War," *African Security* 4, no. 3 (2011): 171–94; William Minter, *Apartheid's Contras: An Inquiry into the Roots of War in Angola and Mozambique* (Johannesburg: Witwatersrand University Press, 1994).
46. Gérard Prunier, *Africa's World War: Congo, the Rwandan Genocide, and the Making of a Continental Catastrophe* (New York: Oxford University Press, 2009); Boaz Atzili, *Good Fences Bad Neighbors: Border Fixity and International Conflict* (Chicago: University of Chicago Press, 2012), 183–87; William Reno, *Warlord Politics and African States* (Boulder, Colo.: Lynne Rienner, 1998), 147–87.
47. John A. Nagl, *Counterinsurgency Lessons from Malaya and Vietnam: Learning to Eat Soup with a Knife* (Westport, Conn.: Praeger, 2002).
48. Glenn Herald Snyder, *Deterrence and Defense: Toward a Theory of National Security* (Princeton, N.J.: Princeton University Press, 1961); for studies that challenge this formula, see Paul Huth and Bruce Russett, "What Makes Deterrence Work? Cases from 1900 to 1980," *World Politics* 36, no. 4 (1984): 496–526; Richard Ned Lebow and Janice Gross Stein, "Rational Deterrence Theory: I Think, Therefore I Deter," *World Politics* 41, no. 2 (1989): 208–24.
49. Douglas M. Gibler, "Outside-In: The Effects of External Threat on State Centralization," *Journal of Conflict Resolution* 54, no. 4 (2010): 519–42.
50. Lewis A. Coser, *The Functions of Social Conflict* (Glencoe, Ill.: Free Press, 1956), 92.
51. Atzili, *Good Fences Bad Neighbors*; Gibler, "Outside-In."
52. Atzili, *Good Fences Bad Neighbors*, 33–56; Gibler, "Outside-In," 521–22.

53. Colin S. Gray, *Modern Strategy* (Oxford: Oxford University Press, 1999), 51; see also Kerry Longhurst, "The Concept of Strategic Culture," in *Military Sociology: The Richness of a Discipline*, ed. Gerhard Kümmel, Andreas Prüfert, and Astrid Albrecht-Heide (Baden-Baden: Nomos, 2000), 200; Lawrence Sondhaus, *Strategic Culture and Ways of War* (London: Routledge, 2006), 123–30.
54. Alastair Iain Johnston, "Cultural Realism and Strategy in Maoist China," in *The Culture of National Security: Norms and Identity in World Politics*, ed. Peter J. Katzenstein (New York: Columbia University Press, 1996), 216–68.
55. Thomas Berger, "Norms, Identity, and National Security in Germany and Japan," in *The Culture of National Security: Norms and Identity in World Politics*, ed. Peter J. Katzenstein (New York: Columbia University Press, 1996), 326.
56. Colin S. Gray, "National Style in Strategy: The American Example," *International Security* 6, no. 2 (1981): 21–47; Colin S. Gray, "Out of the Wilderness: Prime Time for Strategic Culture," *Comparative Strategy* 26, no. 1 (2007): 1–20.
57. Matthew Evangelista, *Innovation and the Arms Race: How the United States and the Soviet Union Develop New Military Technologies* (Ithaca, N.Y.: Cornell University Press, 1988).
58. Dima Adamsky, *The Culture of Military Innovation: The Impact of Cultural Factors on the Revolution in Military Affairs in Russia, the US, and Israel* (Stanford, Calif.: Stanford University Press, 2010).
59. Elizabeth Kier, *Imagining War: French and British Military Doctrine Between the Wars* (Princeton, N.J.: Princeton University Press, 1997).
60. Thomas G. Mahnken, *Technology and the American Way of War* (New York: Columbia University Press, 2008).
61. See chapters in Peter J. Katzenstein, ed., *The Culture of National Security: Norms and Identity in World Politics* (New York: Columbia University Press, 1996); Jack L. Snyder, *The Soviet Strategic Culture: Implications for Limited Nuclear Operations*, (Santa Monica, Calif.: RAND Corporation, September 1977), http://www.dtic.mil/dtic/tr/fulltext/u2/a046124.pdf; Shu Guang Zhang, *Deterrence and Strategic Culture: Chinese-American Confrontations, 1949–1958* (Ithaca, N.Y.: Cornell University Press, 1992).
62. Amir Lupovici, *The Power of Deterrence: Emotions, Identity, and American and Israeli Wars of Resolve* (New York: Cambridge University Press, 2016).
63. James G. March and Johan P. Olsen, *Rediscovering Institutions: The Organizational Basis of Politics* (New York: Free Press, 1989).
64. Jon Elster, *Alchemies of the Mind: Rationality and the Emotions* (New York: Cambridge University Press, 1999), 285.
65. Alastair Iain Johnston, "Thinking about Strategic Culture," *International Security* 19, no. 4 (1995): 32–64.
66. Bernard Brodie, "Implications for Military Policy," in *The Absolute Weapon: Atomic Power and World Order*, ed. Bernard Brodie (New York: Harcourt, Brace and Company, 1946); Schelling, *Strategy of Conflict*; Snyder, *Deterrence and Defense*.
67. Huth and Russett, "What Makes Deterrence Work?"; Alexander L. George and Richard Smoke, *Deterrence in American Foreign Policy: Theory and Practice* (New York: Columbia University Press, 1974); Robert Jervis, *Perception and Misperception*

in *International Politics* (Princeton, N.J.: Princeton University Press, 1976); Robert Jervis, Richard Ned Lebow, and Janice Gross Stein, *Psychology and Deterrence* (Baltimore, Md.: Johns Hopkins University Press, 1985).

68. Amir Lupovici, "The Emerging Fourth Wave of Deterrence Theory—Toward a New Research Agenda," *International Studies Quarterly* 54, no. 3 (2010): 705–32; Knopf, "Fourth Wave in Deterrence Research"; T. V. Paul, "Complex Deterrence: An Introduction," in *Complex Deterrence: Strategy in the Global Age*, ed. T. V. Paul, Patrick M. Morgan, and James J. Wirtz (Chicago: University of Chicago Press, 2009), 1–27; also see Patrick M. Morgan, *Deterrence Now* (Cambridge: Cambridge University Press, 2003); Stephen M. Saideman and Marie-Joëlle Zahar, "Causing Security, Reducing Fear: Deterring Intra-State Violence and Assuring Government Restraint," in *Intra-State Conflict, Governments And Security: Dilemmas Of Deterrence And Assurance*, ed. Stephen M. Saideman and Marie-Joelle Zahar (London: Routledge, 2008); Andreas Wenger and Alex Wilner, eds., *Deterring Terrorism: Theory and Practice* (Stanford, Calif.: Stanford University Press, 2012).

69. James D. Fearon and David D. Laitin, "Ethnicity, Insurgency, and Civil War," *American Political Science Review* 97, no. 1 (2003): 75–90; Sarah Kenyon Lischer, *Dangerous Sanctuaries: Refugee Camps, Civil War, and the Dilemmas of Humanitarian Aid* (Ithaca, N.Y.: Cornell University Press, 2005); James A. Piazza, "Incubators of Terror: Do Failed and Failing States Promote Transnational Terrorism?," *International Studies Quarterly* 52, no. 3 (2008): 469–88; Salehyan, *Rebels Without Borders*; Boaz Atzili, "State Weakness and 'Vacuum of Power' in Lebanon," *Studies in Conflict & Terrorism* 33, no. 8 (2010): 757–82.

70. David Kilcullen, *Counterinsurgency* (New York: Oxford University Press, 2010), 146–61; Daniel Byman, "Friends Like These: Counterinsurgency and the War on Terrorism," *International Security* 31, no. 2 (2006): 95–99.

71. Salehyan, *Rebels Without Borders*; Kenneth A. Schultz, "The Enforcement Problem in Coercive Bargaining: Interstate Conflict over Rebel Support in Civil Wars," *International Organization* 64, no. 2 (2010): 281–312.

72. Michael Mastanduno, David A. Lake, and G. John Ikenberry, "Toward a Realist Theory of State Action," *International Studies Quarterly* 33, no. 4 (1989): 457–74; Holsti, *State, War and the State of War*, 82–98, 150–82.

73. David, "Explaining Third World Alignment."

2. Israel's Use of Triadic Coercion: Sources and Historical Evolution

1. Yehuda Ben Meir, *Civil-Military Relations in Israel* (New York: Columbia University Press, 1995), 178; Charles D. Freilich, *Zion's Dilemmas: How Israel Makes National Security Policy* (Ithaca, N.Y.: Cornell University Press, 2012), 65.

2. Yoram Peri, *Between Battles and Ballots: Israeli Military in Politics* (New York: Cambridge University Press, 1985); Yoram Peri, *Generals in the Cabinet Room: How the*

Military Shapes Israeli Policy (Washington, D.C.: United States Institute of Peace, 2006), 17–32.
3. Ben Meir, *Civil-Military Relations in Israel*, 126–27.
4. Peri, *Between Battles and Ballots*, 175–91; Freilich, *Zion's Dilemmas*, 67–68.
5. Freilich, *Zion's Dilemmas*, 68–71.
6. See Peri, *Generals in the Cabinet Room*.
7. Ben Meir, *Civil-Military Relations in Israel*, 145.
8. Freilich, *Zion's Dilemmas*, 238–43.
9. Martin Van Creveld, *The Sword and the Olive: A Critical History of the Israeli Defense Force* (New York: Public Affairs, 1998), 109.
10. Avi Kober, "What Happened to Israeli Military Thought?," *Journal of Strategic Studies* 34, no. 5 (2011): 707–32; Dima Adamsky, *The Culture of Military Innovation: The Impact of Cultural Factors on the Revolution in Military Affairs in Russia, the US, and Israel* (Stanford, Calif.: Stanford University Press, 2010); Gil-li Vardi, "'Pounding Their Feet:' Israeli Military Culture as Reflected in Early IDF Combat History," *Journal of Strategic Studies* 31, no. 2 (2008): 295–324.
11. Van Creveld, *Sword and the Olive*, 126; Eliot A. Cohen, Michael Eisenstadt, and Andrew J. Bacevich, *Knives, Tanks, and Missiles: Israel's Security Revolution* (Washington, D.C.: Washington Institute for Near East Policy, 1988), 71–75; Adamsky, *Culture of Military Innovation*, 110–11.
12. See Shimon Naveh, "The Cult of the Offensive Preemption and Future Challenges for Israeli Operational Thought," *Israel Affairs* 2, no. 1 (1995): 169; Eliyahu Winograd, "Final Report: The Inquiry Commission to Examine the Events of the Military Campaign in Lebanon 2006" [in Hebrew] (State of Israel, Tel Aviv, January 30, 2008), 397–98.
13. Adamsky, *Culture of Military Innovation*, 117–19.
14. Freilich, *Zion's Dilemmas*, 27–36, 45–59.
15. Peri, *Between Battles and Ballots*.
16. Vardi, "'Pounding Their Feet,'" 296.
17. Benjamin Miller, "The Concept of Security: Should It Be Redefined?," in *Israel's National Security Towards the 21st Century*, ed. Uri Bar-Joseph (London: Routledge, 2001), 1–12; Yoav Ben-Horin and Barry Posen, *Israel's Strategic Doctrine* (Santa Monica, Calif.: RAND Corporation, 1981), http://www.rand.org/pubs/reports/R2845.html.
18. Quoted in Avner Yaniv, *Deterrence Without the Bomb: The Politics of Israeli Strategy* (Lexington, Mass.: Lexington Books, 1987), 13; See also Zeev Maoz, *Defending the Holy Land: A Critical Analysis of Israel's Security & Foreign Policy* (Ann Arbor: University of Michigan Press, 2006), 7–8; Ben-Horin and Posen, *Israel's Strategic Doctrine*, 4–5.
19. United Nations DESA/Population Division, "World Population Prospects 2017," accessed April 14, 2018, https://esa.un.org/unpd/wpp/Download/Standard/Population/.
20. Bernard Wasserstein, *Israelis and Palestinians: Why Do They Fight? Can They Stop?* 2nd ed. (New Haven, Conn.: Yale University Press, 2004), 24.

21. Ariel Levite, *Offense and Defense in Israeli Military Doctrine* (Boulder, Colo.: Westview Press, 1989), 33–35.
22. Efraim Inbar, "The 'No Choice War' Debate in Israel," *Journal of Strategic Studies* 12, no. 1 (1989): 22–37; Martin Van Creveld, *The Land of Blood and Honey: The Rise of Modern Israel* (New York: Thomas Dunne Books, 2010), 125.
23. See Levite, *Offense and Defense in Israeli Military Doctrine*, 31.
24. Adamsky, *Culture of Military Innovation*, 12.
25. Uri Bar-Joseph, "Introduction," in *Israel's National Security Towards the 21st Century*, ed. Uri Bar-Joseph (London: Frank Cass, 2001), 2; Adamsky, *Culture of Military Innovation*, 112.
26. For "immediate deterrence," see Patrick M. Morgan, *Deterrence Now* (Cambridge: Cambridge University Press, 2003). For its implementation in Israeli strategy, see Uri Bar-Joseph, "Variations on a Theme: The Conceptualization of Deterrence in Israeli Strategic Thinking," *Security Studies* 7, no. 3 (2007): 145–81; Yaniv, *Deterrence Without the Bomb*.
27. Maoz, *Defending the Holy Land*, 15–16; Bar-Joseph, "Variations on a Theme"; Amos Malka, "Israel and Asymmetrical Deterrence," *Comparative Strategy* 27, no. 1 (2008): 1–19.
28. Bar-Joseph, "Variations on a Theme"; Doron Almog, "Cumulative Deterrence and the War on Terrorism," *Parameters* 34, no. 4 (2004): 4–19; Maoz, *Defending the Holy Land*, 15–16.
29. Naveh, "Cult of the Offensive Preemption" Adamsky, *Culture of Military Innovation*, 112–13. The "cult of offensive" is a term first used by Stephen Van Evera to describe the offensive bias of all major powers' militaries on the eve of World War I. See Stephen Van Evera, "The Cult of the Offensive and the Origins of the First World War," *International Security* 9, no. 1 (1984): 58–107. In this original formulation, the "cult of offensive" stems from organizational pathologies. Yet the term may in fact be more amenable to a cultural context than an organizational one, as the word "cult" suggests an ideational core. The use of this term is thus appropriate the context of Israeli strategic culture.
30. Dov Tamari, "Offense or Defense: Do We Have a Choice?" [in Hebrew], *Maarachot* 289–290 (October 1983): 5–11.
31. Israel Defense Forces, "IDF Strategy" Document: *Deterring Terror, How Israel Confronts the Next Generation of Threats*, trans. Susan Rosenberg, Belfer Center Special Report (Cambridge, Mass.: Belfer Center, August 2016), chap. 3, sec. 20, clause B, http://www.belfercenter.org/sites/default/files/legacy/files/IDF%20doctrine%20translation%20-%20web%20final2.pdf.
32. Dima Adamsky, "From Israel with Deterrence: Strategic Culture, Intra-War Coercion and Brute Force," *Security Studies* 26, no. 1 (2017): 157–84.
33. Ami Pedahzur, *The Israeli Secret Services and the Struggle Against Terrorism* (New York: Columbia University Press, 2009).
34. Yael Zerubavel, *Recovered Roots: Collective Memory and the Making of Israeli National Tradition* (Chicago: University of Chicago Press, 1997); Edna Lomsky-Feder and Eyal Ben-Ari, *The Military and Militarism in Israeli Society* (Albany: State University of New York Press, 1999).

35. Naveh, "Cult of the Offensive Preemption."
36. Interview with a senior Israeli decision-maker by author Boaz Atzili, June 2010, not for attribution.
37. Adamsky, *Culture of Military Innovation*, 113. For a similar argument about the realm of counterterrorism, see Pedahzur, *Israeli Secret Services*.
38. Vardi, "'Pounding Their Feet,'" 296.
39. Benny Morris, *The Birth of the Palestinian Refugee Problem, 1947–1949* (Cambridge: Cambridge University Press, 1989).
40. Benny Morris, *Israel's Border Wars, 1949–1956: Arab Infiltration, Israeli Retaliation, and the Countdown to the Suez War* (Oxford: Clarendon Press, 1993), 18–19. The data are from the IDF and Israeli police. Note that the actual numbers may have been in fact much higher, as many infiltrations went unnoticed.
41. Ibid., 49.
42. Ibid., chap. 2.
43. Ibid., 51; Barry M. Blechman, "The Consequences of the Israeli Reprisals: An Assessment" (PhD diss., Georgetown University, 1971); Zeev Maoz, "Arab Non-state Aggression and Israeli Limited Uses of Force Dataset," *The Quantitative History of the Arab-Israeli Conflict*, 2008, http://vanity.dss.ucdavis.edu/~maoz/quanthist.htm.
44. Maoz, "Arab Nonstate Aggression Dataset." The data are taken from a variety of sources, including archival records, newspapers, and books. Maoz defines Israeli raids as "any use of force that exceeds the immediate purpose of self-defense and was also defined (either in official reports or by historians) as an act of retaliation to a non-state act of violence or as a preemptive initiative in order to prevent a non-state attack."
45. Mixed Armistice Commissions were separate UN-led committees composed of military officers from Israel and Egypt, Jordan, Syria, and Lebanon under the authority of the UN Truce Supervision Organization (UNTSO). Their role was to supervise the implementation and maintenance of the 1949 armistice agreements. In case of complaints about breaches, the committees would investigate, file a report with UNTSO and the UN Secretary General, and, if justified, issue a condemnation. See Michael B. Oren, "Escalation to Suez: The Egypt-Israel Border War, 1949–56," *Journal of Contemporary History* 24, no. 2 (1989): 347–73; E. L. M. Burns, *Between Arab and Israeli* (London: G. G. Harrap, 1962).
46. Nathan Albert Pelcovits, *The Long Armistice: UN Peacekeeping and the Arab-Israeli Conflict, 1948–1960* (Westview Press, 1993), 38–80. See, for example, the case of a 1954 attack that killed eleven riders on an Israeli bus in Maale Akrabim in the Negev, when Israel petitioned the UN Security Council against Jordan (58–64).
47. Originally called Hayl Hasfar (Border Corps).
48. Morris, *Israel's Border Wars*, 119–21; Hanon Alon, *Countering Palestinian Terrorism in Israel: Toward a Policy Analysis of Countermeasures*, International Security and Arms Control (Santa Monica, Calif.: RAND Corporation, 1980), 15–16.
49. Avi Shlaim, *Israel and Palestine: Reappraisals, Revisions, Refutations* (Brooklyn, N.Y.: Verso, 2010), 86; Morris, *Israel's Border Wars*, 135.
50. Morris, *Israel's Border Wars*, 100–108.

51. "Meeting of the Senior Staff of the Ministry of Foreign Affairs (Tel Aviv, 2 February 1953)," in *Documents on the Foreign Policy of Israel*, ed. Yemima Rosenthal (Jerusalem: Israel State Archives, 1995), 223–24.
52. Maoz, *Defending the Holy Land*, 66–70; Mordechai Bar-On, *The Gates of Gaza: Israel's Road to Suez and Back, 1955–1957* (New York: St. Martin's Press, 1995), 39–40.
53. Quoted in Mordechai Bar-On, *Moshe Dayan: Israel's Controversial Hero* (New Haven, Conn.: Yale University Press, 2012), 49.
54. Maoz, "Arab Nonstate Aggression Dataset."
55. Morris, *Israel's Border Wars*, 183.
56. Ibid., 183–84.
57. "Meeting of the Senior Staff," 57.
58. Zeev Schiff, *A History of the Israeli Army, 1874 to the Present* (New York: Macmillan, 1985), 72. Note that these numbers include raids in 1953 by Unit 101. If these were excluded, the failure rate of the raids would be even higher.
59. "British Embassy in Tel Aviv, 28th February 1953, 1033/73/53," in *Records of Jordan 1919–1965*, ed. Jane Priestland (Cambridge: Cambridge Archive Editions, 1996), 8:27.
60. Jonathan Shimshoni, *Israel and Conventional Deterrence: Border Warfare from 1953 to 1970* (Ithaca, N.Y.: Cornell University Press, 1988), 44; Edward Luttwak and Dan Horowitz, *The Israeli Army* (London: Harper & Row, 1975), 107.
61. Luttwak and Horowitz, *Israeli Army*, 71–74; Avraham Avi-Hai, *Ben Gurion, State Builder: Principles and Pragmatism, 1948–1963* (Jerusalem: Israel Universities Press, 1974), 115–19.
62. Luttwak and Horowitz, *Israeli Army*, 106–7.
63. Ibid., 108.
64. Ibid., 108–10.
65. Ibid., 109–10; Morris, *Israel's Border Wars*, 236–44.
66. Morris, *Israel's Border Wars*, 184.
67. Ibid., 236–44; Luttwak and Horowitz, *Israeli Army*, 111.
68. Quoted in Morris, *Israel's Border Wars*, 177.
69. Ibid., 244–62.
70. Pelcovits, *Long Armistice*, 57; Avi Shlaim, *The Iron Wall: Israel and the Arab World* (New York: Norton, 2001), 90–94.
71. Pelcovits, *Long Armistice*, 57.
72. Morris, *Israel's Border Wars*, 259.
73. Maoz, *Defending the Holy Land*, 236–37; Van Creveld, *Sword and the Olive*, 133; Morris, *Israel's Border Wars*, 262.
74. Morris, *Israel's Border Wars*, 185.
75. Moshe Dayan, "Military Operations in Peacetime," [in Hebrew], *Maarachot* 118–19 (1959): 57.
76. Burns, *Between Arab and Israeli*, 1962, 58.
77. Luttwak and Horowitz, *Israeli Army*, 113.
78. Morris, *Israel's Border Wars*, 382–402; Bar-On, *Gates of Gaza*, 201–18.
79. Morris, *Israel's Border Wars*, 421.

80. Quoted in ibid., 399.
81. Moshe Dayan, *Diary of the Sinai Campaign* (New York: Harper & Row, 1966), 56.
82. Ranan D. Kuperman, "The Impact of Internal Politics on Israel's Reprisal Policy During the 1950s," *Journal of Strategic Studies* 24, no. 1 (2001): 1–28; Avi Shlaim, "Conflicting Approaches to Israel's Relations with the Arabs: Ben Gurion and Sharett, 1953–1956," *Middle East Journal* 37, no. 2 (1983): 180–201.
83. This is consistent with Blechman, "Consequences of the Israeli Reprisals" and Shimshoni, *Israel and Conventional Deterrence*.
84. In the Pearson linear test, "1" means a perfect correlation and "0" indicates no correlation at all. As it is exceedingly rare for tests to produce a perfect "0," outcomes of less than 0.1, either positive or negative, are regarded as effectively indicating no relationship.
85. Daniel Byman, *A High Price: The Triumphs and Failures of Israeli Counterterrorism* (New York: Oxford University Press, 2011), 21. This conclusion also echoes Shimshoni, *Israel and Conventional Deterrence*, 51–53, 92–96.
86. Almog, "Cumulative Deterrence and the War on Terrorism," 9.
87. Dayan, "Military Operations in Peacetime," 57.
88. Maoz, *Defending the Holy Land*, 60–61.
89. Shmuel Bar, "Deterring Terrorists: What Israel Has Learned," *Policy Review* 149 (2008): 42.
90. Menachem Klein, "The 'Tranquil Decade' Re-Examined: Arab-Israeli Relations During the Years 1957–67," in *Israel: The First Hundred Years*, vol. 2, *From War to Peace?*, ed. Efraim Karsh (London: Routledge, 2000), 71–72. Klein associates this doctrine with the period 1965–1967, but we argue that its basic idea could be expanded to encompass Israel's retaliation policy in general between 1956 and the early 1990s.
91. Quoted in Michael Oren, *Six Days of War: June 1967 and the Making of the Modern Middle East* (New York: Oxford University Press, 2002), 52. See also Moshe Shemesh, "The IDF Raid on Samu': The Turning-Point in Jordan's Relations with Israel and the West Bank Palestinians," *Israel Studies* 7, no. 1 (2002): 139–67.
92. Klein, "'Tranquil Decade' Re-Examined," 71–72.
93. Anne Mariel Peters and Pete W. Moore, "Beyond Boom and Bust: External Rents, Durable Authoritarianism, and Institutional Adaptation in the Hashemite Kingdom of Jordan," *Studies in Comparative International Development* 44, no. 3 (2009): 264–65.
94. Ibid., 267.
95. Sean Yom, *From Resilience to Revolution: How Foreign Interventions Destabilize the Middle East* (New York: Columbia University Press, 2016), 159–60.
96. Kamal Salibi, *The Modern History of Jordan* (London: I. B. Tauris, 1993), 166.
97. Joseph Nevo, *King Abdallah and Palestine: A Territorial Ambition* (London: Macmillan, 1996), 198–99.
98. Yom, *From Resilience to Revolution*, 164.
99. Arthur R. Day, *East Bank/West Bank: Jordan and the Prospects for Peace* (New York: Council on Foreign Relations), 28–29.

100. William L. Cleveland, *A History of the Middle East* (Boulder, Colo.: Westview Press, 1994), 331.
101. Day, *East Bank/West Bank*, 29–31; Uriel Dann, *King Hussein and the Challenge of Arab Radicalism: Jordan, 1955–1967* (New York: Oxford University Press, 1989), 39–67.
102. Clinton Bailey, *Jordan's Palestinian Challenge, 1948–1983: A Political History* (Boulder, Colo.: Westview Press, 1984), 11.
103. Peters and Moore, "Beyond Boom and Bust," 268.
104. See Yom, *From Resilience to Revolution*, 165–79.
105. Bailey, *Jordan's Palestinian Challenge*, 5.
106. Yezid Sayigh, *Armed Struggle and the Search for State: The Palestinian National Movement, 1949–1993* (Oxford: Oxford University Press, 1997), 138–39; Shemesh, "IDF Raid on Samu'," 140–45; Maoz, *Defending the Holy Land*, 241.
107. Maoz, *Defending the Holy Land*, 247.
108. "Israel Force Crosses Border with Jordan," Jerusalem Israel Domestic Service, November 13, 1966, in Foreign Broadcast Information Service (FBIS) Daily Reports; Moshe Shemesh, *Arab Politics, Palestinian Nationalism and the Six Day War: The Crystallization of Arab Strategy and Nasir's Descent to War, 1957–1967* (Brighton: Sussex Academic Press, 2008), 151.
109. Avi Shlaim, "Jordan: Walking the Tight Rope," in *The 1967 Arab-Israeli War: Origins and Consequences*, ed. Avi Shlaim and William Roger Louis (New York: Cambridge University Press, 2012), 100.
110. Shemesh, "IDF Raid on Samu'," 151.
111. Ibid.
112. Shlaim, "Jordan: Walking the Tight Rope," 101.
113. Shemesh, "IDF Raid on Samu'," 153–55.
114. Ibid., 161.
115. Shlaim, *Iron Wall*, 234.
116. Shlaim, "Jordan: Walking the Tight Rope," 100.
117. Quoted in Shlaim, *Iron Wall*, 234.
118. Shlaim, "Jordan: Walking the Tight Rope," 101–2.
119. Quoted in ibid., 101.
120. Based on United Nations Relief and Works Agency for Palestinian Refugees (UNRWA) registration. See Luisa Gandolfo, *Palestinians in Jordan: The Politics of Identity* (New York: I. B. Tauris, 2012), 9.
121. Sayigh, *Armed Struggle and the Search for State*, 177–78.
122. Maoz, *Defending the Holy Land*, 244–46.
123. Yezid Sayigh, "Turning Defeat into Opportunity: The Palestinian Guerrillas after the June 1967 War," *Middle East Journal* 46, no. 2 (1992): 244–65.
124. Sayigh, *Armed Struggle and the Search for State*, 144.
125. John W. Amos, *Palestinian Resistance: Organization of a Nationalist Movement* (New York: Pergamon Press, 1980), 35; Ehud Yaari, *Strike Terror: The Story of Fateh*, trans. Esther Yaari (New York: Sabra Books, 1970), 199; Helena Cobban, *The Palestinian Liberation Organisation: People, Power, and Politics* (Cambridge: Cambridge University Press, 1984), 49.

126. Yehoshafat Harakabi, *Fedayeen Action and Arab Strategy*, Adelphi Papers, no. 53 (London: Institute for Strategic Studies, December 1968), 29.
127. Avi Shlaim, *Lion of Jordan: The Life of King Hussein in War and Peace* (New York: Knopf, 2009), 315–26.
128. Nigel J. Ashton, "Pulling the Strings: King Hussein's Role During the Crisis of 1970 in Jordan," *International History Review* 28, no. 1 (2006): 100.
129. Shlaim, *Lion of Jordan*, 141–42; Ashton, "Pulling the Strings," 100; Iris Fruchter-Ronen, "Black September: The 1970–71 Events and Their Impact on the Formation of Jordanian National Identity," *Civil Wars* 10, no. 3 (2008): 245.
130. Chris Sibilla, "Jordan's Black September, 1970," *Moments in U.S. Diplomatic History*, July 8, 2015, Association for Diplomatic Studies and Training, http://adst.org/2015/07/jordans-black-september-1970/. See also Fruchter-Ronen, "Black September."
131. Shlaim, *Lion of Jordan*, 307. See also Ashton, "Pulling the Strings."
132. Ashton, "Pulling the Strings;" Sayigh, *Armed Struggle and the Search for State*, 243–61.
133. For a detailed description of the battles and the politics of the war, see Sayigh, *Armed Struggle and the Search for State*, 262–81.
134. Cited in Levite, *Offense and Defense in Israeli Military Doctrine*, 25.
135. Stuart A. Cohen, *Israel and Its Army: From Cohesion to Confusion* (London: Routledge, 2008), 45–48.
136. Avi Kober, "The Intellectual and Modern Focus in Israeli Military Thinking as Reflected in Ma'arachot Articles, 1948–2000," *Armed Forces & Society* 30, no. 1 (2003): 154.
137. Adamsky, "From Israel with Deterrence"; Avi Kober, "A Paradigm in Crisis? Israel's Doctrine of Military Decision," *Israel Affairs* 2, no. 1 (1995): 207.
138. Niccolò Petrelli, "Deterring Insurgents: Culture, Adaptation and the Evolution of Israeli Counterinsurgency, 1987–2005," *Journal of Strategic Studies* 36, no. 5 (2013): 667–68.
139. See Dov Tamari and Meir Califi, "The IDF's Operational Concept" [in Hebrew], *Maarachot* 423 (2009): 32.
140. Naveh, "Cult of the Offensive Preemption," 169.
141. Kober, "A Paradigm in Crisis?"; Uri Bar-Joseph, ed., *Israel's National Security Towards the 21st Century* (London: Frank Cass, 2001).
142. Peri, *Generals in the Cabinet Room*, 123–24.
143. Petrelli, "Deterring Insurgents," 671; Cohen, *Israel and Its Army*, 48–49.
144. Adamsky, *Culture of Military Innovation*, 102–3; Tamari and Califi, "The IDF's Operational Concept"; Akiva Bigman, "Bogie Yaalon's Post-Modern IDF," *MIDA*, October 12, 2014, http://mida.org.il/2014/10/12/bogie-yaalons-post-modern-idf/.
145. Petrelli, "Deterring Insurgents." OTRI is best known for the "New Operational Concept," which was officially adopted but not implemented, and then discarded after the 2006 Lebanon war. See Adamsky, "From Israel with Deterrence"; Tamari and Califi, "IDF's Operational Concept."
146. Adamsky, "From Israel with Deterrence."

147. Israeli Defense Forces Chief of Staff Office, "IDF Strategy" [in Hebrew], chap. A, section 5, August 2015, https://go.ynet.co.il/pic/news/16919.pdf.
148. Adamsky, "From Israel with Deterrence," 169–70. These concepts are used in IDF parlance and included in the "IDF Strategy" document in the original Hebrew.
149. David E. Sanger and Mark Mazzetti, "Israel Struck Syrian Nuclear Project, Analysts Say," *New York Times*, October 14, 2017, http://www.nytimes.com/2007/10/14/washington/14weapons.html; Ian Black, "'Israeli Attack' on Sudanese Arms Factory Offers Glimpse of Secret War," *Guardian*, October 25, 2012, https://www.theguardian.com/world/2012/oct/25/israeli-sudanese-factory-secret-war; Jack Khoury, "Israeli Jets Attack Near Damascus, Syria Confirms; 'Hezbollah Arms Targeted,'" *Haaretz*, November 30, 2016, http://www.haaretz.com/israel-news/1.756132.
150. Adamsky, "From Israel with Deterrence," 164.
151. Gal Hirsch, "From 'Cast Lead' to 'Other Way': The Development of the Campaign in the Central Command, 2000–2003" [in Hebrew], *Maarachot* 393 (February 2004): 28. Also see Peri, *Generals in the Cabinet Room*, 116–29.
152. Gal Hirsch, *War Story, Love Story* [in Hebrew] (Tel Aviv: Miskal, 2009), 170.
153. Amir Lupovici, *The Power of Deterrence: Emotions, Identity, and American and Israeli Wars of Resolve* (New York: Cambridge University Press, 2016), 53–58.
154. U.S. Department of Defense, *Strategic Deterrence Joint Operating Concept, Version 1.0* (Offutt Air Force Base, Nebraska: U.S. Strategic Command, February 2004). See also Jeffrey S. Lantis, "Strategic Culture and Tailored Deterrence: Bridging the Gap Between Theory and Practice," *Contemporary Security Policy* 30, no. 3 (2009): 467–85.
155. Israel Defense Forces, "IDF Strategy," chap. 3, section 27.
156. Efraim Inbar and Eitan Shamir, "'Mowing the Grass': Israel's Strategy for Protracted Intractable Conflict," *Journal of Strategic Studies* 37, no. 1 (2014): 65–90.
157. Ibid., 68. Brigadier General (Ret.) Gabriel Siboni uses the term similarly in an interview with author Boaz Atzili, July 2013.
158. See, e.g., U.S. Army, "Insurgencies and Countering Insurgencies" (Washington, D.C.: Department of the Army, May 2014), https://fas.org/irp/doddir/army/fm3-24.pdf; David Kilcullen, *Counterinsurgency* (New York: Oxford University Press, 2010), 37.
159. Partially this is a reflection of what Ami Pedahzur calls "the war model" of counterterrorism. See Pedahzur, *Israeli Secret Services*, 1–13.
160. Cited in Peri, *Generals in the Cabinet Room*, 124.
161. The Belfer Center's English translation refers to this as "public perception," but we maintain that "consciousness" better captures the original intent in Hebrew.
162. "Public Perceptions actions" in the Belfer Center translation. See Israel Defense Forces, "IDF Strategy," chap. C, clause 28, i, b.
163. Quoted in Nadir Tzur, "The Test of Consciousness: The Crisis of Meanings in the IDF and Israeli Society and Their Exposure in the Second Lebanon War" [in Hebrew], *Military and Strategy* 2, no. 2 (2010): 15, http://heb.inss.org.il/upload images/Import/(FILE)1286797368.pdf.
164. Adamsky, "From Israel with Deterrence."

165. Almog, "Cumulative Deterrence and the War on Terrorism."
166. Bigman, "Bogie Yaalon's Post-Modern IDF."
167. Israel Defense Forces, "IDF Strategy," chap. 2, sections 22, 35, 36.
168. See, e.g., Adamsky, *Culture of Military Innovation*, 115–16.
169. James G. March and Johan P. Olsen, *Democratic Governance* (New York: Free Press, 1995).

3. Egypt Since 1949: Triadic Coercion from Raids to Peace

1. Angela Seay and Patricia Toye, eds., *Israel: Boundary Disputes with Arab Neighbours, 1946–1964* (Cambridge: Cambridge Archive Editions, 1995), 3:299.
2. Avner Yaniv, *Deterrence Without the Bomb: The Politics of Israeli Strategy* (Lexington, Mass.: Lexington Books, 1987), 75.
3. Zeev Maoz, *Defending the Holy Land: A Critical Analysis of Israel's Security & Foreign Policy* (Ann Arbor: University of Michigan Press, 2006), 77.
4. Jonathan Shimshoni, *Israel and Conventional Deterrence: Border Warfare from 1953 to 1970* (Ithaca, N.Y.: Cornell University Press, 1988), 120.
5. Lawrence Freedman, *Deterrence* (Cambridge: Polity Press, 2004), 29–32.
6. Elli Lieberman, *Reconceptualizing Deterrence: Nudging Toward Rationality in Middle East Rivalries* (London: Routledge, 2013), 70–71.
7. Ibid., 56.
8. Benny Morris, *Israel's Border Wars, 1949–1956: Arab Infiltration, Israeli Retaliation, and the Countdown to the Suez War* (Oxford: Clarendon Press, 1993).
9. Baruch Kimmerling and Joel S. Migdal, *The Palestinian People: History* (Cambridge, Mass.: Harvard University Press, 2003), 229.
10. Michael B. Oren, *Origins of the Second Arab-Israel War: Egypt, Israel and the Great Powers 1952–56* (London: Frank Cass, 1992), 12–13.
11. Elmo H. Hutchison, *Violent Truce: A Military Observer Looks at the Arab-Israeli Conflict 1951–1955* (New York: Devin-Adair, 1956), 117.
12. United Nations Department of Public Information, *Yearbook of the United Nations, 1955* (New York: UN Department of Public Information, 1956), Part 1, Section 1, Chapter 4: "The Palestine Question," 32.
13. Cited in Barry M. Blechman, "The Consequences of the Israeli Reprisals: An Assessment" (PhD diss., Georgetown University, 1971), 65.
14. Morris, *Israel's Border Wars*, 31–32; Oren, *Origins of the Second Arab-Israel War*, 11.
15. Oren, *Origins of the Second Arab-Israel War*, 13.
16. Blechman, "Consequences of the Israeli Reprisals," 73–74.
17. Morris, *Israel's Border Wars*, 84.
18. Quoted in E. L. M. Burns, *Between Arab and Israeli* (London: G. G. Harrap, 1962), 58.
19. Ibid.
20. Oren, *Origins of the Second Arab-Israel War*, 11.
21. Shimshoni, *Israel and Conventional Deterrence*, 93; Oren, *Origins of the Second Arab-Israel War*, 12; Morris, *Israel's Border Wars*, 95; Jean-Pierre Filiu and John King,

Gaza: A History, Comparative Politics and International Studies (New York: Oxford University Press, 2014), 80; Ilana Feldman, Governing Gaza: Bureaucracy, Authority, and the Work of Rule, 1917–1967 (Durham, N.C.: Duke University Press, 2008); Ilana Feldman, Police Encounters: Security and Surveillance in Gaza under Egyptian Rule (Stanford, Calif.: Stanford University Press, 2015).

22. Ehud Yaari, Egypt and the Fedayeen, 1953–1956 [in Hebrew] (Givat Haviva: Center for Arabic and Afro-Asian Studies, 1975), 12.
23. Ibid., 22.
24. See Feldman, Police Encounters, 26–34; also see Feldman, Governing Gaza, 128.
25. Feldman, Police Encounters, 26–27, 29–30.
26. Jason Brownlee, Authoritarianism in an Age of Democratization (New York: Cambridge University Press, 2007), 49.
27. Michael B. Oren, "Escalation to Suez: The Egypt-Israel Border War, 1949–56," Journal of Contemporary History 24, no. 2 (1989): 351–52.
28. Oren, Origins of the Second Arab-Israel War, 13.
29. Oren, "Escalation to Suez," 351.
30. Yezid Sayigh, Armed Struggle and the Search for State: The Palestinian National Movement, 1949–1993 (Oxford: Oxford University Press, 1997), 61.
31. Shimshoni, Israel and Conventional Deterrence, 74.
32. Feldman, Police Encounters, 6, 33.
33. Quoted in Seay and Toye, Israel, 2:604.
34. P. J. Vatikiotis, The History of Modern Egypt: From Muhammad Ali to Mubarak, 4th ed. (Baltimore, Md.: Johns Hopkins University Press, 1991), 371–72; Kirk J. Beattie, Egypt During the Nasser Years: Ideology, Politics, and Civil Society (Boulder, Colo.: Westview Press, 1994), 55.
35. A. I. Dawisha, Egypt in the Arab World: The Elements of Foreign Policy (New York: John Wiley, 1976), 13; P. J. Vatikiotis, Nasser and His Generation (New York: St. Martin's Press, 1978), 128.
36. P. J. Vatikiotis, The Egyptian Army in Politics: Pattern for New Nations? (Bloomington: Indiana University Press, 1961), 133.
37. See Alan Richards and John Waterbury, A Political Economy of the Middle East, 2nd ed. (Boulder, Colo.: Westview Press, 1996), 155.
38. Peter Mansfield, Nasser's Egypt (Baltimore, Md.: Penguin Books, 1965), 45.
39. Keith Wheelock, Nasser's New Egypt: A Critical Analysis (New York: Praeger, 1960), 38–39.
40. Vatikiotis, History of Modern Egypt, 383–84.
41. Ibid., 394.
42. John Waterbury, The Egypt of Nasser and Sadat: The Political Economy of Two Regimes (Princeton, N.J.: Princeton University Press, 1983), 57.
43. Ibid., 60–62; Edward Owen and Şevket Pamuk, A History of Middle East Economies in the Twentieth Century (Cambridge, Mass.: Harvard University Press, 1999), 128–29.
44. Patrick Karl O'Brien, The Revolution in Egypt's Economic System: From Private Enterprise to Socialism, 1952–1965 (New York: Oxford University Press, 1966), 336.
45. Vatikiotis, Nasser and His Generation, 136.

46. Brownlee, *Authoritarianism in an Age of Democratization*, 53.
47. Vatikiotis, *Nasser and His Generation*, 143, 149; R. Hrair Dekmejian, *Egypt under Nasir: A Study in Political Dynamics* (Albany: State University of New York Press, 1971), 30.
48. Shimshoni, *Israel and Conventional Deterrence*, 102–3.
49. Wheelock, *Nasser's New Egypt*, 209, 222.
50. Dekmejian, *Egypt under Nasir*, 44.
51. Blechman, "Consequences of the Israeli Reprisals," 70.
52. Sayigh, *Armed Struggle and the Search for State*, 61.
53. Ibid., 351–57; Morris, *Israel's Border Wars*, 312–16; Blechman, "Consequences of the Israeli Reprisals," 64–80; Filiu and King, *Gaza*, 86.
54. Blechman, "Consequences of the Israeli Reprisals," 76.
55. Oren, "Escalation to Suez," 355.
56. Morris, *Israel's Border Wars*, 85.
57. Oren, "Escalation to Suez," 355.
58. Blechman, "Consequences of the Israeli Reprisals," 68.
59. Shimshoni, *Israel and Conventional Deterrence*, 93; Filiu and King, *Gaza*, 84–85.
60. Filiu and King, *Gaza*, 85.
61. Mansfield, *Nasser's Egypt*, 56.
62. Filiu and King, *Gaza*, 85.
63. Morris, *Israel's Border Wars*, 84–91; Oren, "Escalation to Suez," 370.
64. Morris, *Israel's Border Wars*, 89–90.
65. Yaari, *Egypt and the Fedayeen*, 42.
66. Sayigh, *Armed Struggle and the Search for State*, 61–62.
67. Yaari, *Egypt and the Fedayeen*, 43.
68. Ibid., 12.
69. Ibid., 43.
70. Benny Morris, *Israel's Border Wars, 1949–1956: Arab Infiltration, Israeli Retaliation, and the Countdown to the Suez War* (Oxford: Clarendon Press, 1993), 92.
71. Burns, *Between Arab and Israeli*, 89.
72. Cited in Morris, *Israel's Border Wars, 1949–1956*, 85.
73. Wheelock, *Nasser's New Egypt*, 42. See also Vatikiotis, *Nasser and His Generation*, 142.
74. Beattie, *Egypt During the Nasser Years*, 99; Vatikiotis, *History of Modern Egypt*, 386.
75. Brownlee, *Authoritarianism in an Age of Democratization*, 55.
76. Yaari, *Egypt and the Fedayeen*, 17.
77. Anouar Abdel-Malek, *Egypt: Military Society: The Army Regime, the Left, and Social Change under Nasser* (New York: Random House, 1968).
78. O'Brien, *Revolution in Egypt's Economic System*, 336.
79. Abdel-Malek, *Egypt: Military Society*, 88.
80. Joel S. Migdal, *Strong Societies and Weak States: State-Society Relations and State Capabilities in the Third World* (Princeton, N.J.: Princeton University Press, 1988), 181–205.
81. Dekmejian, *Egypt under Nasir*, 35–36.
82. Wheelock, *Nasser's New Egypt*, chap. 8.

83. Mansfield, *Nasser's Egypt*, 56.
84. Wheelock, *Nasser's New Egypt*, 209.
85. Ernest Stock, *Israel on the Road to Sinai, 1949–1956: With a Sequel on the Six-Day War, 1967* (Ithaca, N.Y.: Cornell University Press, 1967), 119.
86. Yaari, *Egypt and the Fedayeen*, 12.
87. Filiu and King, *Gaza*, 85–86.
88. Sayigh, *Armed Struggle and the Search for State*, 62.
89. Dekmejian, *Egypt under Nasir*, 38–39.
90. Shimshoni, *Israel and Conventional Deterrence*, 93.
91. Wheelock, *Nasser's New Egypt*, 226; Shimshoni, *Israel and Conventional Deterrence*, 94.
92. Wheelock, *Nasser's New Egypt*, 210.
93. Stock, *Israel on the Road to Sinai*, 71.
94. Filiu and King, *Gaza*, 87.
95. Wheelock, *Nasser's New Egypt*, 223; Stock, *Israel on the Road to Sinai*, 126.
96. See also Wheelock, *Nasser's New Egypt*, 222; Jonathan B. Isacoff, *Writing the Arab-Israeli Conflict: Pragmatism and Historical Inquiry* (Lanham, Md.: Lexington Books, 2006), 50; Filiu and King, *Gaza*, 87.
97. "Report to the Security Council Concerning 28 February, 1955; Incident near Gaza; Egypt—Israel Mixed Armistice Commission Report; Text on Egypt-Israel Mixed Armistice Commission's Resolution on Nahal Oz Incident," in *Israel: Boundary Disputes with Arab Neighbours, 1946–1964*, ed. Angela Seay and Patricia Toye (Cambridge: Cambridge Archive Editions, 1995), 7:447.
98. Ariel Sharon and David Chanoff, *Warrior: An Autobiography*, 2nd ed. (New York: Simon & Schuster, 2001), 109.
99. Shimshoni, *Israel and Conventional Deterrence*, 114.
100. Moți Golani, *Israel in Search of a War: The Sinai Campaign, 1955–1956* (Brighton: Sussex Academic Press, 1998); Jonathan B. Isacoff, "Between Militarism and Moderation in Israel: Constructing Security in Historical Perspective," in *Redefining Security in the Middle East*, ed. Tami Amanda Jacoby and Brent E. Sasley (Manchester: Manchester University Press, 2002), 50–51.
101. Kennett Love, *Suez: The Twice-Fought War: A History* (New York: McGraw-Hill, 1969), 83, 81; Filiu and King, *Gaza*, 87.
102. Morris, *Israel's Border Wars*, 427.
103. Stock, *Israel on the Road to Sinai*, 115.
104. Shimshoni, *Israel and Conventional Deterrence*, 111–12.
105. Yaari, *Egypt and the Fedayeen*, 42–43.
106. Love, *Suez*, 83; Filiu and King, *Gaza*, 85.
107. Filiu and King, *Gaza*, 88.
108. Salah Khalaf (Abu Iyad) with Eric Rouleau, *My Home, My Land: A Narrative of the Palestinian Struggle*, trans. Linda Butler Koseoglu (New York: Times Books, 1981), 22.
109. Ibid.
110. Filiu and King, *Gaza*, 88.
111. Love, *Suez*, 85.

112. Shimshoni, *Israel and Conventional Deterrence*, 95, 102.
113. Mansfield, *Nasser's Egypt*, 56; Wheelock, *Nasser's New Egypt*, 51.
114. Avraham Sela, *The Decline of the Arab-Israeli Conflict: Middle East Politics and the Quest for Regional Order* (Albany: State University of New York Press, 1998), 43; David Tal, "The 1956 Sinai War: A Watershed in the History of the Arab-Israeli Conflict," in *Reassessing Suez 1956: New Perspectives on the Crisis and Its Aftermath*, ed. Simon C. Smith (Aldershot: Ashgate, 2008), 142–43.
115. Abdel-Malek, *Egypt: Military Society*, 103; Vatikiotis, *Egyptian Army in Politics*, 159.
116. Dekmejian, *Egypt under Nasir*, 113.
117. Ali Al'Amin Mazrui and Christophe Wondji, eds., *Africa since 1935* (Berkeley: University of California Press, 1993), 840.
118. Ali E. Hillal Dessouki and Adel al-Labban, "Arms Race, Defense Expenditures and Development: The Egyptian Case 1952–1973," in *The Conflict with Israel in Arab Politics and Society*, ed. Ian Lustick (New York: Garland, 1994), 119.
119. Love, *Suez*, 83.
120. Ibid., 86.
121. Morris, *Israel's Border Wars*, 91; Sayigh, *Armed Struggle and the Search for State*, 63–65; Shimshoni, *Israel and Conventional Deterrence*, 81–82; Love, *Suez*, 85; Stock, *Israel on the Road to Sinai*, 73–74.
122. Wheelock, *Nasser's New Egypt*, 226.
123. Blechman, "Consequences of the Israeli Reprisals," 88. See also Dawisha, *Egypt in the Arab World*, 13; Burns, *Between Arab and Israeli*, 97.
124. Cited in Shimshoni, *Israel and Conventional Deterrence*, 81.
125. Alan Dowty, *Israel/Palestine*, 3rd ed. (Cambridge: Polity, 2012), 110.
126. Shimshoni, *Israel and Conventional Deterrence*, 82.
127. Maoz, *Defending the Holy Land*, 55; and Shimshoni, *Israel and Conventional Deterrence*, 43.
128. Moshe Dayan, *Diary of the Sinai Campaign* (New York: Harper & Row, 1966), 9.
129. Mansfield, *Nasser's Egypt*, 56.
130. Mordechai Bar-On, *The Gates of Gaza: Israel's Road to Suez and Back, 1955–1957* (New York: St. Martin's Press, 1995), 1–24.
131. Ibid., 16–17.
132. Burns, *Between Arab and Israeli*, 99.
133. Bar-On, *Gates of Gaza*, 18.
134. Wheelock, *Nasser's New Egypt*, 51; Dekmejian, *Egypt under Nasir*, 44.
135. Vatikiotis, *Egyptian Army in Politics*, 71.
136. Dawisha, *Egypt in the Arab World*, 11–15.
137. Bar-On, *Gates of Gaza*, 37–55.
138. Fred J. Khouri, "The Policy of Retaliation in Arab-Israeli Relations," *Middle East Journal* 20, no. 4 (1966): 453; Zeev Maoz and Ben D. Mor, *Bound by Struggle: The Strategic Evolution of Enduring International Rivalries* (Ann Arbor: University of Michigan Press, 2002), 145.
139. Michael N. Barnett, *Confronting the Costs of War: Military Power, State, and Society in Egypt and Israel* (Princeton, N.J.: Princeton University Press, 1992), 93–94.

140. Walter Laqueur, *The Road to Jerusalem: The Origins of the Arab-Israeli Conflict, 1967* (New York: Macmillan, 1968), 36.
141. P. J. Vatikiotis, *The History of Egypt*, 2nd ed. (Baltimore, Md.: Johns Hopkins University Press, 1980), 385.
142. Roger Owen, *State, Power and Politics in the Making of the Modern Middle East*, 3rd ed. (London: Routledge, 2004), 28.
143. Vatikiotis, *Nasser and His Generation*, 175.
144. Ibid., 154, 172.
145. Dekmejian, *Egypt under Nasir*, 226–27.
146. Ibid.
147. Wheelock, *Nasser's New Egypt*, chaps. 4 and 6.
148. Vatikiotis, *History of Egypt*, 393–94.
149. Robert Mabro, *The Egyptian Economy, 1952–1972* (Oxford: Clarendon Press, 1974), 168; O'Brien, *Revolution in Egypt's Economic System*, 336; and Waterbury, *Egypt of Nasser and Sadat*, 201.
150. Vatikiotis, *History of Egypt*, 393.
151. Owen, *State, Power and Politics*, 24–25.
152. Mansfield, *Nasser's Egypt*, 111; Tom Little, *Modern Egypt* (London: Ernest Benn, 1967), 245.
153. Dawisha, *Egypt in the Arab World*, 87.
154. For the increase in Egyptian military personnel between 1955 and 1966, see Owen, *State, Power and Politics*, 24–25. For Nasser's popularity, see Dawisha, *Egypt in the Arab World*, 13–14.
155. Shimshoni, *Israel and Conventional Deterrence*, 120.
156. Yezid Sayigh, "Escalation or Containment? Egypt and the Palestine Liberation Army, 1964–67," *International Journal of Middle East Studies* 30, no. 1 (1998): 98.
157. Feldman, *Governing Gaza*, 8–9.
158. Feldman, *Police Encounters*, 7.
159. Kimmerling and Migdal, *The Palestinian People*, 238.
160. Wendy Pearlman, "The Palestinian National Movement," in *The 1967 Arab-Israeli War: Origins and Consequences*, ed. Avi Shlaim and William Roger Louis (New York: Cambridge University Press, 2012), 126–48.
161. Sayigh, *Armed Struggle and the Search for State*, 98–106.
162. Ibid., 106–7.
163. Moshe Shemesh, *Arab Politics, Palestinian Nationalism and the Six Day War: The Crystallization of Arab Strategy and Nasir's Descent to War, 1957–1967* (Brighton: Sussex Academic Press, 2008), 12; Sayigh, *Armed Struggle and the Search for State*, 67–70, 98–106.
164. Sayigh, *Armed Struggle and the Search for State*, 98.
165. Pearlman, *Violence, Nonviolence*, 65.
166. Shemesh, *Arab Politics, Palestinian Nationalism*, 96.
167. Moshe Shemesh, "The Fida'iyyun Organization's Contribution to the Descent to the Six-Day War," *Israel Studies* 11, no. 1 (2006): 10; Shemesh, *Arab Politics, Palestinian Nationalism*, 99–101.
168. Pearlman, "Palestinian National Movement."

169. Dekmejian, *Egypt under Nasir*, 244, 253.
170. "Egypt's Lawless Peninsula," *Al Jazeera*, August 14, 2013, http://www.aljazeera.com/programmes/insidestory/2013/08/20138146027683120.html.
171. "Special Briefing: Attacks Against Security Forces Continue in Egypt's North Sinai," Tahrir Institute for Middle East Policy, September 11, 2017, https://timep.org/special-reports/special-briefing-attacks-against-security-forces-continue-in-egypts-north-sinai/.
172. Avi Issacharoff, "The Egyptian Revolution Has Created a Vacuum in Sinai," *Haaretz*, August 19, 2011, http://www.haaretz.com/blogs/2.244/the-egyptian-revolution-has-created-a-vacuum-in-sinai-1.379438.
173. More attempted attacks were thwarted by Israeli or Egyptian forces.
174. Allyn Fisher-Ilan, "Israel Shoots down Rocket Targeting Resort City Eilat," *Reuters*, August 12, 2013; Ruth Eglash, "As ISIS Roils Neighboring Sinai, Israel Keeps This Border Highway Empty," *Washington Post*, November 14, 2016; "ISIS Claims Rocket Attack on Israel," *Jerusalem Post*, April 10, 2017; Peter Beaumont, "Rockets Fired into Southern Israel from Egypt's Sinai," *Guardian*, February 20, 2017.
175. See, e.g., James D. Fearon and David D. Laitin, "Ethnicity, Insurgency, and Civil War," *American Political Science Review* 97, no. 1 (2003): 75–90.
176. Amr Yossef, "Securing the Sinai," *Foreign Affairs*, September 28, 2011, https://www.foreignaffairs.com/articles/middle-east/2011-09-28/securing-sinai.
177. Ibid.
178. Amy Austin Holmes, "There Are Weeks When Decades Happen: Structure and Strategy in the Egyptian Revolution," *Mobilization* 17, no. 4 (2012): 405.
179. Ehud Yaari and Normand St. Pierre, "Sinai: The New Frontier of Conflict?," Washington Institute, November 20, 2011, http://www.washingtoninstitute.org/policy-analysis/view/sinai-the-new-frontier-of-conflict.
180. Yossef, "Securing the Sinai"; Zack Gold, "Security in the Sinai: Present and Future" (ICCT Research Paper, The Hague, International Centre for Counter-Terrorism, March 2014), http://www.icct.nl/download/file/ICCT-Gold-Security-In-The-Sinai-March-2014.pdf.
181. Yaari and St. Pierre, "Sinai."
182. Robert F. Worth, "Lawless Sinai Shows Risks Rising in Fractured Egypt," *New York Times*, August 10, 2013, http://www.nytimes.com/2013/08/11/world/middleeast/lawless-sinai-shows-risks-rising-in-fractured-egypt.html; Nikola Kovac and Trista Guertin, "Armed Groups in the Sinai Peninsula," Civil-Military Fusion Centre, February 2013, http://www.operationspaix.net/DATA/DOCUMENT/7805~v~Armed_Groups_in_the_Sinai_Peninsula.pdf.
183. See Gold, "Security in the Sinai"; "Factbox: Key Violent Incidents in Sinai since 2004," *Egypt Independent*, May 21, 2013, http://www.egyptindependent.com/news/factbox-key-violent-incidents-sinai-2004; Vivian Salama, "What's Behind the Wave of Terror in the Sinai," *Atlantic*, November 22, 2013, http://www.theatlantic.com/international/archive/2013/11/whats-behind-the-wave-of-terror-in-the-sinai/281751/; Holly Cramer et al., "Special Feature: Terrorism in Sinai," Middle East Institute, n.d., http://www.mei.edu/sinai-terrorism.

184. Ashgan Harb, "Gas Pipeline in Sinai Bombed for 15th Time since Revolution Started," *Egypt Independent*, October 4, 2015, http://www.egyptindependent.com/news/gas-pipeline-sinai-bombed-15th-time-revolution-started.
185. Amr Nasr El-Din, "And Then There Was Sinai," Carnegie Endowment for International Peace, July 11, 2013, http://carnegieendowment.org/sada/52366.
186. Lisa Watanabe, "Sinai Peninsula—from Buffer Zone to Battlefield," (CSS Analysis in Security Policy, Center for Security Studies, February 2015), http://www.css.ethz.ch/publications/pdfs/CSSAnalyse168-EN.pdf.
187. Kovac and Guertin, "Armed Groups in the Sinai Peninsula."
188. El-Din, "And Then There Was Sinai."
189. Augustus Richard Norton, "The Return of Egypt's Deep State," *Current History* 112, no. 758 (2013): 338–44.
190. "Egypt: Roadmap to Repression: No End in Sight to Human Rights Violations," Amnesty International, January 23, 2014, https://www.amnesty.org/en/documents/MDE12/005/2014/en/.
191. Gold, "Security in the Sinai," 3.
192. "Egypt's Security: Threat and Response," Tahrir Institute for Middle East Policy, October 27, 2014, http://timep.org/commentary/egypts-security-threat-response/.
193. Worth, "Lawless Sinai Shows Risks."
194. Steven A. Cook, *Ruling but Not Governing: The Military and Political Development in Egypt, Algeria, and Turkey* (Baltimore, Md.: Johns Hopkins University Press, 2007); Yezid Sayigh, "Above the State: The Officers' Republic in Egypt," (Carnegie Papers, Carnegie Endowment for International Peace, Washington, D.C., August 2012), http://carnegieendowment.org/files/officers_republic1.pdf.
195. Ursula Lindsey, "The Cult of Sisi," *New York Times*, September 12, 2013, http://latitude.blogs.nytimes.com/2013/09/12/the-cult-of-sisi/.
196. "Egypt Declares State of Emergency in Sinai," *Al Jazeera*, October 25, 2014, http://www.aljazeera.com/news/middleeast/2014/10/egypt-declares-state-emergency-sinai-2014102422836500878.html; "Special Report: How Cairo Is Taking the Fight to Sinai Militants," *Reuters*, February 5, 2015, http://www.reuters.com/article/2015/02/05/us-egypt-sinai-militants-specialreport-idUSKBN0L80XM20150205.
197. David D. Kirkpatrick, "Militant Group in Egypt Vows Loyalty to ISIS," *New York Times*, November 10, 2014, http://www.nytimes.com/2014/11/11/world/middleeast/egyptian-militant-group-pledges-loyalty-to-isis.html?_r=0; Watanabe, "Sinai Peninsula"; Allison McManus, "The Battle for Egypt's Sinai," Tahrir Institute for Middle East Policy, December 5, 2014, http://timep.org/commentary/battle-egypts-sinai/.
198. "Special Report."
199. Yoram Schweitzer, "Egypt's War in the Sinai Peninsula: A Struggle That Goes Beyond Egypt," *INSS Insight*, Institute for National Security Studies, February 3, 2015, http://www.inss.org.il/publication/egypts-war-in-the-sinai-peninsula-a-struggle-that-goes-beyond-egypt/; Ahmed Mohamed Hassan and Yusri

Mohamed, "At Least 23 Egyptian Soldiers Killed in Deadliest Sinai Attack in Years," *Reuters*, July 7, 2017, https://www.reuters.com/article/us-philippines-quake-idUSKBN1AR0EJ.

200. Anshel Pfeffer, "Coordinated Attacks in South Kill 8," *Haaretz*, August 19, 2011, http://www.haaretz.com/coordinated-attacks-in-south-israel-kill-8-1.379428; El-Din, "And Then There Was Sinai"; "Egyptians Tear Down Israeli Flag as Hundreds Storm Cairo Embassy," *Haaretz*, September 9, 2011, http://www.haaretz.com/israel-news/egyptians-tear-down-israeli-flag-as-hundreds-storm-cairo-embassy-1.383568.

201. Zack Gold, "Sinai Security: Opportunities for Unlikely Cooperation Among Egypt, Israel, and Hamas" (Saban Center Analysis Paper, no. 30, Brookings Institution, Washington, D.C., 2013), 13. Though part of the reason for the construction of the barrier was, in addition to the security threat, to obstruct the movement of refugees from Africa to Israel via Egypt and to prevent cross-border smuggling. See Daniel Byman and Khaled Elgindy, "The Deepening Chaos in Sinai," *National Interest* 127 (October 2013): 47.

202. Gabi Siboni and Ram Ben-Barak, "The Sinai Peninsula Threat Development and Response Concept" (Saban Center Analysis Paper, no. 31, Brookings Institution, Washington, D.C., 2014), 11.

203. Byman and Elgindy, "Deepening Chaos in Sinai," 46–47.

204. Gold, "Sinai Security," 12.

205. Gili Cohen and Reuters, "Defense Minister: Sinai Militants Will Strike Again, but Iron Dome Will Keep South Israel Safe," *Haaretz*, August 13, 2013, http://www.haaretz.com/israel-news/.premium-1.541259.

206. Watanabe, "Sinai Peninsula," 4; Gold, "Sinai Security," 17–18.

207. Samira Shackle, "Unprecedented Security Cooperation Between Egypt and Israel in the Sinai," *Middle East Monitor*, January 27, 2014, https://www.middleeastmonitor.com/20140127-unprecedented-security-cooperation-between-egypt-and-israel-in-the-sinai/; Jack Khory and Gilli Cohen, "Egyptian Officials: Israeli Drone Strikes Sinai Rocket-Launching Site, Kills Five," *Haaretz*, August 11, 2013, http://www.haaretz.com/israel-news/.premium-1.540699; Beaumont, "Rockets Fired"; Yoram Schweitzer and Ofir Winter, "Egypt's War on Terrorism in the Sinai Peninsula: Alliance with Tribes, Partnership with Israel?," *INSS Insight*, Institute for National Security Studies, June 15, 2017, http://www.inss.org.il/publication/egypts-war-terrorism-sinai-peninsula-alliance-tribes-partnership-israel/.

208. Ehud Yaari, Aaron Zelin, and Matthew Levitt, "Israel's Evolving Terrorist Threats from Sinai to Syria" (2014 Weinberg Founders Conference, Washington Institute for Near East Policy, 2014), http://www.washingtoninstitute.org/policy-analysis/view/israels-evolving-terrorist-threats-from-sinai-to-syria; Gold, "Sinai Security," 19–20.

209. Amos Harel and Avi Issacharoff, "Israel-Sinai Border Attack Thwarted, but Ominous Signs Loom Ahead," *Haaretz*, August 6, 2012, http://www.haaretz.com/blogs/east-side-story/israel-sinai-border-attack-thwarted-but-ominous-signs-loom-ahead-1.456350.

210. Zachary Laub, "Security in Egypt's Sinai Peninsula," Council of Foreign Relations, December 11, 2013, https://www.cfr.org/backgrounder/security-egypts-sinai-peninsula.
211. Gold, "Sinai Security," 12.
212. Anna Ahronheim, "Liberman: Ties Between Israel, Arab States, 'More Crucial for Them Than Us,'" *Jerusalem Post*, April 28, 2017, http://www.jpost.com/Magazine/Liberman-Its-not-about-us-and-Gaza-489139.
213. "Israel-Egypt Cooperation Surpasses Expectation," *Middle East Monitor*, January 28, 2015, https://www.middleeastmonitor.com/news/middle-east/16624-israeli-tv-israeli-egyptian-cooperation-surpasses-expectation; Ben Caspit, "Israel-Egypt Anti-Terrorism Cooperation at Zenith—Al-Monitor: The Pulse of the Middle East," *Al-Monitor*, May 23, 2014, http://www.al-monitor.com/pulse/originals/2014/05/israel-egypt-security-cooperation-netanyahu-livni-nuclear.html.
214. Moran Stern, "The Reality of Israel-Egypt Relations," *MenaSource* (blog), Atlantic Council, October 28, 2016, http://www.atlanticcouncil.org/blogs/menasource/the-reality-of-israel-egypt-relations.
215. Dov Lieber, "Egypt Foreign Minister Makes a Rare Visit for Netanyahu Meet," *Times of Israel*, July 10, 2016, http://www.timesofisrael.com/egyptian-foreign-minister-to-visit-tel-aviv-for-netanyahu-meeting/.
216. Ronit Zilberstein, "Sinai Is Becoming a Terrorist Launching Pad, Netanyahu Says," *Israel Hayom*, April 5, 2012, http://www.israelhayom.com/site/newsletter_article.php?id=3832.
217. Yossef, "Securing the Sinai."
218. El-Din, "And Then There Was Sinai."
219. "Sinai Residents Complain of Violations by Egypt Army," *Al-Monitor*, May 7, 2014, http://www.al-monitor.com/pulse/originals/2014/05/egypt-sinai-war-on-terror-civilians.html; Mohannad Sabry, "By Military or Militants, Society Is the Casualty in Sinai," Tahrir Institute for Middle East Policy, July 24, 2014, http://timep.org/esw/articles-analysis/military-militants-society-casualty-sinai/.
220. Watanabe, "Sinai Peninsula"; Helena Burgrová, "The Security Question in the Post-Mubarak Egypt: The Security Void in Sinai," *Obrana a Strategie*, no. 1 (2014): 65–76, http://www.obranaastrategie.cz/cs/aktualni-cislo-1-2014/clanky/the-security-question-in-the-post-mubarak-egypt.html#.WtTv4NPwaqA.

4. Syria Since 1949: Triadic Coercion from Coups to Revolution

1. Unlike in Egypt's case, systematic data on infiltration from Syria are not available. The main databases, such as that by Maoz, do not count the country of origin but the region of Israel in which attacks occur. Attacks in northern Israel could have their origins in Syria, Lebanon, or Jordan.
2. Barry M. Blechman, "The Consequences of the Israeli Reprisals: An Assessment" (PhD diss., Georgetown University, 1971)," 96; Elmo H. Hutchison, *Violent Truce:*

A Military Observer Looks at the Arab-Israeli Conflict 1951–1955 (New York: Devin-Adair, 1956), 107.
3. This section draws heavily on Fred J. Khouri, "Friction and Conflict on the Israeli-Syrian Front," *Middle East Journal* 17, no. 1/2 (1963): 16.
4. Ibid., 19–20.
5. Ibid., 21.
6. Moshe Maoz, *Syria and Israel: From War to Peacemaking* (Oxford: Oxford University Press, 1995), 49–50.
7. Khouri, "Friction and Conflict," 24, 27.
8. E. L. M. Burns, *Between Arab and Israeli* (London: G. G. Harrap, 1962), 111.
9. Khouri, "Friction and Conflict," 31–32.
10. Quoted in Maoz, *Syria and Israel*, 50.
11. Ibid., 44.
12. Andrew Rathmell, *Secret War in the Middle East: The Covert Struggle for Syria, 1949–1961* (London: I. B. Tauris, 1995), 130.
13. Ibid., 125.
14. Raymond A. Hinnebusch, *Authoritarian Power and State Formation in Ba'thist Syria: Army, Party, and Peasant* (Boulder, Colo.: Westview Press, 1990), chaps. 2–3.
15. Ibid., 17.
16. Patrick Seale, *The Struggle for Syria: A Study of Post-War Arab Politics 1945–1958* (New Haven, Conn.: Yale University Press, 1987), 319.
17. Ibid., 307.
18. "W. Eytan (Tel Aviv) to the Israel Missions Abroad. 9 April 1951," in *Documents on the Foreign Policy of Israel*, ed. Yemima Rosenthal (Jerusalem: Israel State Archives, 1995), 101.
19. Maoz, *Syria and Israel*, 53.
20. Blechman, "Consequences of the Israeli Reprisals," 101–2.
21. Maoz, *Syria and Israel*, 44.
22. Hinnebusch, *Authoritarian Power*, 103; Raymond A. Hinnebusch, *Syria: Revolution from Above* (London: Routledge, 2002), 34.
23. Daniel Byman, *Deadly Connections: States That Sponsor Terrorism* (Cambridge: Cambridge University Press, 2005), 120.
24. Seale, *Struggle for Syria*, 307.
25. Hinnebusch, *Authoritarian Power*, 113.
26. Hanna Batatu, *Syria's Peasantry, the Descendants of Its Lesser Rural Notables, and Their Politics* (Princeton, N.J.: Princeton University Press, 1999), 144–45.
27. Patrick Seale and Maureen McConville, *Assad of Syria: The Struggle for the Middle East* (London: I. B. Tauris, 1988), 85.
28. Cited in ibid., 124.
29. Salah Khalaf (Abu Iyad) and Eric Rouleau, *My Home, My Land: A Narrative of the Palestinian Struggle*, trans. Linda Butler Koseoglu (New York: Times Books, 1981), 42.
30. Maoz, *Syria and Israel*, 82.
31. Moshe Shemesh, *Arab Politics, Palestinian Nationalism and the Six Day War: The Crystallization of Arab Strategy and Nasir's Descent to War, 1957–1967* (Brighton:

Sussex Academic Press, 2008), 103–4; Moshe Shemesh, "The Fida'iyyun Organization's Contribution to the Descent to the Six-Day War," *Israel Studies* 11, no. 1 (2006): 7.

32. Maoz, *Syria and Israel*, 84; Malcolm H. Kerr, "Hafiz Asad and the Changing Patterns of Syrian Politics," *International Journal* 28, no. 4 (1973): 697.
33. David Lesch, "Syria: Playing with Fire," in *The 1967 Arab-Israeli War: Origins and Consequences*, ed. Avi Shlaim and William Roger Louis (New York: Cambridge University Press, 2012), 86.
34. Batatu, *Syria's Peasantry*, 171.
35. Steven Heydemann, *Authoritarianism in Syria: Institutions and Social Conflict, 1946–1970* (Ithaca, N.Y.: Cornell University Press, 1999), 181.
36. Itamar Rabinovich, *Syria under the Ba'th, 1963–66: The Army-Party Symbiosis* (Jerusalem: Israel Universities Press, 1972), 113–14.
37. Hinnebusch, *Authoritarian Power*, 254–56.
38. Mark A. Tessler, *A History of the Israeli-Palestinian Conflict* (Bloomington: Indiana University Press, 1994), 366; Byman, *Deadly Connections*, 121.
39. Seale and McConville, *Assad of Syria*, 125.
40. Moshe Maoz and Avner Yaniv, eds., *Syria under Assad: Domestic Constraints and Regional Risks* (New York: St. Martin's Press, 1986), 192.
41. Tessler, *History of the Israeli-Palestinian Conflict*, 377; Maoz and Yaniv, *Syria under Assad*, 193; Maoz, *Syria and Israel*, 82.
42. Cited in Yezid Sayigh, *Armed Struggle and the Search for State: The Palestinian National Movement, 1949–1993* (Oxford: Oxford University Press, 1997), 104.
43. See Rabinovich, *Syria under the Ba'th*, 130–31.
44. Abraham Ben-Tzur, ed., "The Syrian Ba'ath Party and Israel: Documents from the Internal Party Publications," in *Explicit Proof of Artificial Creation of Tension along the Israeli Border by Syrian Authorities and the Inter-Arab Command for Purely Inner Syrian Purposes* (Givat Haviva: Center for Arabic and Afro-Asian Studies, 1968), 11–12.
45. Rabinovich, *Syria under the Ba'th*, 127.
46. Batatu, *Syria's Peasantry*, 171.
47. Fred Haley Lawson, *Why Syria Goes to War: Thirty Years of Confrontation* (Ithaca, N.Y.: Cornell University Press, 1996), 43.
48. Hinnebusch, *Authoritarian Power*, 133. For more on the dynamics of fragmentation and institution building, see Wendy Pearlman, *Violence, Nonviolence, and the Palestinian National Movement* (Cambridge: Cambridge University Press, 2011).
49. Quoted in Nikolaos van Dam, *The Struggle for Power in Syria: Politics and Society under Asad and the Ba'th Party*, 4th ed. (London: I. B. Tauris, 2011), 34–35. Emphasis in the original.
50. Maoz and Yaniv, *Syria under Assad*, 193.
51. Maoz, *Syria and Israel*, 84.
52. Volker Perthes, *The Political Economy of Syria under Asad* (London: I. B. Tauris, 1995), 188.
53. Yaacov Bar-Siman-Tov, *Linkage Politics in the Middle East: Syria Between Domestic and External Conflict, 1961–1970* (Boulder, Colo.: Westview Press, 1983), 152.

54. Menachem Klein, "The 'Tranquil Decade' Re-Examined: Arab-Israeli Relations During the Years 1957–67," in *Israel: The First Hundred Years*, vol. 2, *From War to Peace?*, ed. Efraim Karsh (London: Routledge, 2000), 71.
55. Avi Shlaim, *The Iron Wall: Israel and the Arab World* (New York: W.W. Norton, 2001), 229.
56. Ibid.
57. Lesch, "Syria: Playing with Fire," 86.
58. Tom Segev, *1967: Israel, the War, and the Year That Transformed the Middle East*, trans. Jessica Cohen (New York: Metropolitan Books, 2007), 194.
59. Quoted in Klein, " 'Tranquil Decade' Re-Examined," 72.
60. Sayigh, *Armed Struggle and the Search for State*, 104–29.
61. Shemesh, "Fida'iyyun Organization's Contribution," 2.
62. Bar-Siman-Tov, *Linkage Politics in the Middle East*, 148.
63. John F. Devlin, "The Baath Party: Rise and Metamorphosis," *American Historical Review* 96, no. 5 (1991): 1403; van Dam, *Struggle for Power in Syria*, 62.
64. Martin Seymour, "The Dynamics of Power in Syria since the Break with Egypt," *Middle Eastern Studies* 6, no. 1 (1970): 44.
65. Hinnebusch, *Authoritarian Power*, 132.
66. Seale and McConville, *Assad of Syria*, 104.
67. Maoz, *Syria and Israel*, 89.
68. Shemesh, "Fida'iyyun Organization's Contribution," 2.
69. Bar-Siman-Tov, *Linkage Politics in the Middle East*, 152–53.
70. Sayigh, *Armed Struggle and the Search for State*, 139.
71. Pearlman, *Violence, Nonviolence*, chap. 3.
72. Shlaim, *Iron Wall*; Zeev Maoz, *Defending the Holy Land: A Critical Analysis of Israel's Security & Foreign Policy* (Ann Arbor: University of Michigan Press, 2006), 106–8.
73. Lesch, "Syria: Playing with Fire," 86.
74. Seale and McConville, *Assad of Syria*, 25.
75. Avi Shlaim and William Roger Louis, eds., *The 1967 Arab-Israeli War: Origins and Consequences* (New York: Cambridge University Press, 2012).
76. See Lawson, *Why Syria Goes to War*, 21; Shlaim, *Iron Wall*, 235; and Maoz, *Syria and Israel*, 89.
77. Joseph Mann, "The Syrian Neo-Ba'th Regime and the Kingdom of Saudi Arabia, 1966–70," *Middle Eastern Studies* 42, no. 5 (2006): 768; Hinnebusch, *Authoritarian Power*, 22.
78. Devlin, "Baath Party," 1403; Maoz, *Syria and Israel*, 117–18; Mann, "Syrian Neo-Ba'th Regime," 768; Moshe Maoz, *Asad: The Sphinx of Damascus: A Political Biography* (New York: Weidenfeld & Nicholson, 1988), 36; Kerr, "Hafiz Asad," 699.
79. Kerr, "Hafiz Asad," 698.
80. Hinnebusch, *Authoritarian Power*, 22; Maoz, *Asad: The Sphinx of Damascus*, 36.
81. Batatu, *Syria's Peasantry*, 173.
82. Sayigh, *Armed Struggle and the Search for State*, 187.
83. Daniel Dishon, ed., *Middle East Record*, vol. 5, 1969–1970 (Jerusalem: Israel Universities Press, 1977), 1149.

84. Ibid.
85. John W. Amos, *Palestinian Resistance: Organization of a Nationalist Movement* (New York: Pergamon Press, 1980), 101–2.
86. Daniel Dishon, ed., *Middle East Record*, vol. 4, 1968 (Jerusalem: Israel Universities Press, 1973), 322–24; Dishon, *Middle East Record*, 5:203.
87. Dishon, *Middle East Record*, 5:118; Kerr, "Hafiz Asad," 698.
88. Maoz, *Syria and Israel*, 118.
89. Raymond A. Hinnebusch, "Revisionist Dreams, Realist Strategies: The Foreign Policy of Syria," in *The Foreign Policies of Arab States*, ed. Ali E. Hillal Dessouki and Bahgat Korany (Boulder, Colo.: Westview Press, 1991), 392.
90. Bar-Siman-Tov, *Linkage Politics in the Middle East*, 164–65.
91. Sayigh, *Armed Struggle and the Search for State*, 265.
92. Ibid., 264.
93. Dishon, *Middle East Record*, 5:1150.
94. Helena Cobban, *The Palestinian Liberation Organisation: People, Power, and Politics* (Cambridge: Cambridge University Press, 1984), 52.
95. Cited in Kerr, "Hafiz Asad," 699–700.
96. Maoz, *Asad: The Sphinx of Damascus*, 36; Batatu, *Syria's Peasantry*, 173–74.
97. Hinnebusch, *Authoritarian Power*, 139–40.
98. Ibid., 145–47.
99. Hinnebusch, *Syria: Revolution from Above*, 72.
100. Ibid., 73.
101. Bassam Haddad, *Business Networks in Syria: The Political Economy of Authoritarianism* (Stanford, Calif.: Stanford University Press, 2012).
102. Hinnebusch, *Syria: Revolution from Above*, 67.
103. Perthes, *Political Economy of Syria*, 109–13.
104. Batatu, *Syria's Peasantry*, 177–78.
105. See Radwan Ziadeh, *Power and Policy in Syria: Intelligence Services, Foreign Relations and Democracy in the Modern Middle East* (London: I. B. Tauris, 2011), 23–24.
106. Middle East Watch, *Syria Unmasked: The Suppression of Human Rights by the Asad Regime* (New Haven, Conn.: Yale University Press, 1991), 41.
107. Eyal Zisser, *Asad's Legacy: Syria in Transition* (New York: New York University Press, 2001), 29. See also James T. Quinlivan, "Coup-Proofing: Its Practice and Consequences in the Middle East," *International Security* 24, no. 2 (1999): 131–54.
108. Batatu, *Syria's Peasantry*, 277.
109. Alasdair Drysdale and Raymond A. Hinnebusch, *Syria and the Middle East Peace Process* (New York: Council of Foreign Relations, 1991), 44.
110. Ibid.
111. Maoz and Yaniv, *Syria under Assad*, 44–45.
112. Hinnebusch, *Authoritarian Power*, 191.
113. Maoz and Yaniv, *Syria under Assad*, 72.
114. Maoz, *Asad: The Sphinx of Damascus*, 58–59.
115. Ibid., 179.
116. Batatu, *Syria's Peasantry*, 279.

117. Raymond A. Hinnebusch, "The Foreign Policy of Syria," in *The Foreign Policies of Middle East States: Between Agency and Structure*, ed. Anoushiravan Ehteshami and Raymond A. Hinnebusch (Boulder, Colo.: Lynne Rienner, 2002), 148, 151.
118. Hinnebusch, *Syria: Revolution from Above*, 68.
119. Raymond A. Hinnebusch, *The International Politics of the Middle East* (New York: Palgrave, 2003), 133.
120. Byman, *Deadly Connections*, 125.
121. Sayigh, *Armed Struggle and the Search for State*, 288–89.
122. Batatu, *Syria's Peasantry*, 291.
123. Sayigh, *Armed Struggle and the Search for State*, 288.
124. See also Amos, *Palestinian Resistance*, 187–89; Sara Bar-Haim, "The Palestine Liberation Army: Stooge or Actor?," in *The Palestinians and the Middle East Conflict: Studies in Their History, Sociology and Politics*, ed. Gabriel Ben-Dor (Ramat Gan: Turtledove Publishing, 1978), 173–92.
125. Sayigh, *Armed Struggle and the Search for State*, 288–89; Amos, *Palestinian Resistance*, 102.
126. Batatu, *Syria's Peasantry*, 306.
127. Maoz, *Defending the Holy Land*, 331.
128. Terrence Smith, "Scores of Israeli Planes Strike 10 Guerrilla Bases in a Reprisal for Munich," *New York Times*, September 9, 1972.
129. Sayigh, *Armed Struggle and the Search for State*, 312.
130. Maoz, *Syria and Israel*, 124.
131. Juan de Oniss, "Syria Said to Tell Guerrillas to Quit Villages Near Heights," *New York Times*, January 24, 1973.
132. Bard O'Neill, *Armed Struggle in Palestine: A Political-Military Analysis* (Boulder, Colo.: Westview Press, 1978), 178.
133. Kerr, "Hafiz Asad," 705.
134. Seale and McConville, *Assad of Syria*, 282.
135. Lisa Wedeen, *Ambiguities of Domination: Politics, Rhetoric, and Symbols in Contemporary Syria* (Chicago: University of Chicago Press, 1999), 54; Batatu, *Syria's Peasantry*, 202.
136. "Israeli Chief of Staff on Terrorism, Security," Jerusalem Domestic Service, August 2, 1985, Foreign Broadcast Information Service Daily Reports.
137. Boaz Atzili, *Good Fences Bad Neighbors: Border Fixity and International Conflict* (Chicago: University of Chicago Press, 2012), 176–79; Naomi Joy Weinberger, *Syrian Intervention in Lebanon: The 1975–76 Civil War* (New York: Oxford University Press, 1986); Karen Rasler, "Internationalized Civil War: A Dynamic Analysis of the Syrian Intervention in Lebanon," *Journal of Conflict Resolution* 27, no. 3 (1983): 421–56.
138. Bar-Haim, "Palestine Liberation Army," 174.
139. Sayigh, *Armed Struggle and the Search for State*, chaps. 15–16.
140. Maoz, *Asad: The Sphinx of Damascus*, 122.
141. Augustus Richard Norton and Jillian Schwedler, "(In)security Zones in South Lebanon," *Journal of Palestine Studies* 23, no. 1 (1993): 65.

142. Tabitha Petran, *The Struggle over Lebanon* (New York: Monthly Review Press, 1987), 299.
143. Norton and Schwedler, "(In)security Zones in South Lebanon," 67.
144. Sayigh, *Armed Struggle and the Search for State*, 507.
145. Maoz and Mor, *Bound by Struggle*, 193.
146. Batatu, *Syria's Peasantry*, 202.
147. Cited in ibid., 302.
148. Maoz, *Defending the Holy Land*, 194–226.
149. Sayigh, *Armed Struggle and the Search for State*, 560–61.
150. Maoz and Yaniv, *Syria under Assad*, 191; Sayigh, *Armed Struggle and the Search for State*, 561; Batatu, *Syria's Peasantry*, 304–5.
151. Sayigh, *Armed Struggle and the Search for State*, 582.
152. Maoz, *Asad: The Sphinx of Damascus*, 175.
153. Cited in Byman, *Deadly Connections*, 136.
154. Ibid., 129.
155. Maoz, *Asad: The Sphinx of Damascus*, 175.
156. Byman, *Deadly Connections*, 119.
157. Hinnebusch, "Revisionist Dreams, Realist Strategies," 381.
158. Avner Yaniv, *Deterrence Without the Bomb: The Politics of Israeli Strategy* (Lexington, Mass.: Lexington Books, 1987), 167; Maoz, *Syria and Israel*, 162; Itamar Rabinovich, *The View from Damascus: State, Political Community and Foreign Relations in Modern and Contemporary Syria* (London: Vallentine Mitchell, 2008), 180.
159. U.S. Department of State, "Chapter 3: State Sponsors of Terrorism," *Country Reports on Terrorism, 2008*, April 30, 2009, http://www.state.gov/j/ct/rls/crt/2008/122436.htm.
160. Byman, *Deadly Connections*, 129–30, 135.
161. Augustus Richard Norton, *Hezbollah: A Short History* (Princeton, N.J.: Princeton University Press, 2007), 26–45; Fred Haley Lawson, *Global Security Watch—Syria* (Santa Barbara, Calif.: Praeger, 2013), 113.
162. Sune Haugbolle, *The Alliance Between Iran, Syria and Hizbollah and Its Implications for the Political Development in Lebanon and the Middle East* (Copenhagen: Danish Institute for International Studies, 2006), 9.
163. "Syria under Bashar (I): Foreign Policy Challenges," Middle East Report, no. 24, (Brussels: International Crisis Group, February 11, 2004), 14.
164. Volker Perthes, *Syria under Bashar Al-Asad: Modernisation and the Limits of Change* (Oxford: Oxford University Press, 2004), 62.
165. Eyal Zisser, *Commanding Syria: Bashar Al-Asad and the First Years in Power* (London: I. B. Tauris, 2007), 150.
166. Quoted in ibid., 160; Lawson, *Global Security Watch—Syria*, 117.
167. Perthes, *Syria under Bashar Al-Asad*, 55.
168. Zisser, *Commanding Syria*, 150.
169. Ibid., 159–62.
170. Ibid.
171. "Syria under Bashar (I)," 9.

172. "Israel Hits Palestinian 'Camp' in Syria," *BBC News*, October 5, 2003, http://news.bbc.co.uk/2/hi/middle_east/3165394.stm; "Syria under Bashar (I)," 13.
173. "Syria under Bashar (I)," 10, 14.
174. U.S. Department of State, "Chapter 3."
175. "Syria under Bashar (I)," 9.
176. Abbas William Samii, "A Stable Structure on Shifting Sands: Assessing the Hizbullah-Iran-Syria Relationship," *Middle East Journal* 62, no. 1 (2008): 45.
177. Amos Harel and Avi Issacharoff, *34 Days: Israel, Hezbollah, and the War in Lebanon* (New York: Palgrave Macmillan, 2008), 162–63.
178. Seale, *Struggle for Syria*, xv.
179. Anthony Shadid, "Syrian Elite to Fight Protests to 'the End,'" *New York Times*, May 10, 2011, http://www.nytimes.com/2011/05/11/world/middleeast/11makhlouf.html.
180. Wendy Pearlman, "Palestinians and the Arab Spring," in *Civil Resistance and the Arab Spring*, ed. Adam Roberts, Timothy Garton Ash, and Michael Willis (Oxford: Oxford University Press, 2016), 248–69.
181. See Jonathan Steele, "How Yarmouk Refugee Camp Became the Worst Place in Syria," *Guardian*, March 5, 2015, http://www.theguardian.com/news/2015/mar/05/how-yarmouk-refugee-camp-became-worst-place-syria.
182. Harriet Sherwood, "Thirteen Killed as Israeli Troops Open Fire on Nakba Day Border Protests," *Guardian*, May 15, 2011, http://www.theguardian.com/world/2011/may/15/israeli-troops-kill-eight-nakba-protests.
183. Rabinovich, *View from Damascus*, 377.
184. For example, see Herb Keinon and Yaakov Lappin, "2 Israelis Injured by Cross-Border Fire from Syria," *Jerusalem Post*, August 27, 2014, http://www.jpost.com/Middle-East/Syrian-mortar-falls-in-northern-Golan-Heights-lightly-injuring-one-372526.
185. Barak Ravid, "Netanyahu Says Israel to Determine If Syrian Mortar Fire Was Intentional," *Haaretz*, November 12, 2012, http://www.haaretz.com/israel-news/netanyahu-says-israel-to-determine-if-syrian-mortar-fire-was-intentional.premium-1.477228; Adam Withnall, "Israel Launches Attack on Syria with Air Strikes in Response to Death," *Independent*, June 23, 2014, http://www.independent.co.uk/news/world/middle-east/israel-launches-attack-on-syria-with-air-strikes-in-response-to-death-of-golan-heights-teenager-9556153.html.
186. Withnall, "Israel Launches Attack on Syria."
187. Dan Williams, "Israel Didn't Target Iranian General in Strike: Source," Reuters, January 20, 2015, http://www.reuters.com/article/2015/01/20/us-mideast-crisis-israel-syria-idUSKBN0KT1HQ20150120.
188. Itamar Rabinovich, "A New Israeli Policy on Syria: Should Israel Threaten Intervention?," *Order from Chaos* (blog), Brookings Institution, February 13, 2015, http://www.brookings.edu/blogs/order-from-chaos/posts/2015/02/13-new-israeli-policy-on-syria-rabinovich.
189. Phillip Smyth, "Israel Is the New Front in the Syrian War," *Foreign Policy*, January 28, 2015, https://foreignpolicy.com/2015/01/28/israel-is-the-new-front-in-the-syrian-war/.

190. Syrian Centre for Policy Research, "Alienation and Violence: Impact of the Syria Crisis Report 2014," March 15, 2015, http://www.unrwa.org/resources/reports/alienation-and-violence-impact-syria-crisis-2014.
191. Simon Tisdall, "Syrian President Admits Military Setbacks, in First Public Speech for a Year," *Guardian*, July 26, 2015, http://www.theguardian.com/world/2015/jul/26/syrian-president-public-speech-bashar-al-assad.
192. Marisa Sullivan, "Hezbollah in Syria," Middle East Security Report 19, Institute for the Study of War, April 2014, http://www.understandingwar.org/report/hezbollah-syria; Michael Herzog, "The Next Battle in the Israel-Hezbollah War Is Unfolding in Southern Syria," *Business Insider*, March 5, 2015, http://www.businessinsider.com/the-next-battle-in-the-israel-hezbollah-war-is-unfolding-in-southern-syria-2015-3.
193. Byman, *Deadly Connections*, 125.

5. Israel and the Palestinian Authority Since 1993: Strategic Culture in Asymmetric Conflict

1. See Zeev Maoz, *Defending the Holy Land: A Critical Analysis of Israel's Security & Foreign Policy* (Ann Arbor: University of Michigan Press, 2006); Keren Sharvit et al., "The Effects of Israeli Use of Coercive and Conciliatory Tactics on Palestinian's Use of Terrorist Tactics: 2000–2006," *Dynamics of Asymmetric Conflict* 6, no. 1–3 (2013): 22–44.
2. Sergio Catignani, "The Strategic Impasse in Low-Intensity Conflicts: The Gap Between Israeli Counter-Insurgency Strategy and Tactics During the Al-Aqsa Intifada," *Journal of Strategic Studies* 28, no. 1 (2005): 57–75; Daniel Byman, "Curious Victory: Explaining Israel's Suppression of the Second Intifada," *Terrorism and Political Violence* 24, no. 5 (2012): 825–52.
3. Laura Dugan and Erica Chenoweth, "Moving Beyond Deterrence: The Effectiveness of Raising the Expected Utility of Abstaining from Terrorism in Israel," *American Sociological Review* 77, no. 4 (2012): 597–624.
4. See the discussion of our concept of "strategic culture" in chapter 1.
5. Sara M. Roy, "Palestinian Society and Economy: The Continued Denial of Possibility," *Journal of Palestine Studies* 30, no. 4 (2001): 10.
6. See, among others, Edward Said, *Peace and Its Discontents: Gaza-Jericho, 1993–1995* (New York: Vintage, 1995); Mona Naim and Joe Stork, "Interview with Mahmoud Darwish, 'My Opposition to the Terms of the Accord Is a Measure of My Attachment to Real Peace,'" *Middle East Report* 194/195 (August 1995): 18–19.
7. Palestinian fatalities were 364 in the six-year period after the Oslo Agreement and 1,162 in the six-year period before it. See Na'ama Carmi, "Oslo: Before and after: The Status of Human Rights in the Occupied Territories," Information Sheet (Jerusalem: B'Tselem, May 1999), 7.
8. Raphael Ahren, "Rabin Formally Opposed a Palestinian State More than a Year after White House Handshake, Letter from 1994 Shows," *Times of Israel*,

December 31, 2012, http://www.timesofisrael.com/rabin-formally-opposed-a-palestinian-state-more-than-a-year-after-white-house-handshake-letter-from-1994-shows/.
9. See Wendy Pearlman, *Violence, Nonviolence, and the Palestinian National Movement* (Cambridge: Cambridge University Press, 2011).
10. Max Weber, "Politics as a Vocation," in *From Max Weber: Essays in Sociology*, ed. Hans Heinrich Gerth and C. Wright Mills (New York: Oxford University Press, 1958), 78.
11. See Jamil Hilal, *The Palestinian Political Order after Oslo: A Critical Analytical Study* [in Arabic] (Ramallah, West Bank: Muwatin, 1998); Nigel Craig Parsons, *The Politics of the Palestinian Authority: From Oslo to Al-Aqsa* (New York: Routledge, 2005).
12. See "Index of CPRS Polls," Palestinian Center for Policy and Survey Research, August 2, 2013, http://www.pcpsr.org/en/node/151.
13. See Efraim Karsh, "Arafat's Grand Strategy," *Middle East Quarterly* 11, no. 2 (Spring 2004): 1–9.
14. Mark A. Tessler, *A History of the Israeli-Palestinian Conflict* (Bloomington: Indiana University Press, 1994), 776–78; Itamar Rabinovich, *Waging Peace: Israel and the Arabs, 1948–2003* (Princeton, N.J.: Princeton University Press, 2004), 67.
15. Shmuel Bar, "Deterrence of Palestinian Terrorism," in *Deterring Terrorism: Theory and Practice*, ed. Andreas Wenger and Alex Wilner (Stanford, Calif.: Stanford University Press, 2012), 213.
16. Jeff Jacoby, "Would Rabin Have Pulled the Plug on a 'Peace Process' That Failed?," *Boston Globe*, October 22, 2015, https://www.bostonglobe.com/opinion/2015/10/22/would-rabin-have-pulled-plug-peace-process-that-failed/fgHF1Y8bkh7leSbtgHfleL/story.html.
17. Daniel Byman, *A High Price: The Triumphs and Failures of Israeli Counterterrorism* (Oxford: Oxford University Press, 2011), 82.
18. Boaz Ganor, "Israel, Hamas, and Fatah," in *Democracy and Counterterrorism: Lessons From the Past*, ed. Robert J. Art and Louise Richardson (Washington, D.C.: U.S. Institute of Peace Press, 2007), 271.
19. Sara M. Roy, "Why Peace Failed: An Oslo Autopsy," in *Failing Peace: Gaza and the Palestinian-Israeli Conflict* (London: Pluto, 2007), 245.
20. Yuval Ginbar, "Routine Torture: Interrogation Methods of the General Security Service" (Jerusalem: B'Tselem, February 1998), http://www.btselem.org/publications/summaries/199802_routine_torture.
21. Amira Hass, "Israel's Closure Policy: An Ineffective Strategy of Containment and Repression," *Journal of Palestine Studies* 31, no. 3 (2002): 5–20.
22. Roy, "Why Peace Failed," 242.
23. "Chronology: 16 May–15 August 1994," *Journal of Palestine Studies* 24, no. 1 (1994): 173.
24. Ami Pedahzur, *The Israeli Secret Services and the Struggle Against Terrorism* (New York: Columbia University Press, 2009), 98.
25. Roy, "Why Peace Failed," 13, 24.
26. Ganor, "Israel, Hamas, and Fatah," 271–72.

27. Quoted in Byman, *High Price*, 105.
28. Ibid., 83–84.
29. Tessler, *History of the Israeli-Palestinian Conflict*, 778.
30. Byman, *High Price*, 84; Pedahzur, *Israeli Secret Services*, 99.
31. Ganor, "Israel, Hamas, and Fatah," 272.
32. Tessler, *History of the Israeli-Palestinian Conflict*, 778.
33. "Chronology: 16 May–15 August 1994," 164.
34. Yezid Sayigh, *Armed Struggle and the Search for State: The Palestinian National Movement, 1949–1993* (Oxford: Oxford University Press, 1997), 654–55, 690–91.
35. Hilal, *Palestinian Political Order after Oslo*.
36. See Amira Hass, "Gaza Workers and the Palestinian Authority," *Middle East Report* 194 (August 1995): 25–28; Ishac Diwan and Radwan A. Shaban, eds., *Development under Adversity: The Palestinian Economy in Transition* (Washington, D.C.: The World Bank and Palestine Economic Policy Research Institute, 1999), 4–5, 68–69.
37. Roy, "Why Peace Failed," 242.
38. Salem Aljuni, "The Palestinian Economy and the Second Intifada," *Journal of Palestine Studies* 32, no. 3 (2003): 64–73.
39. Laetitia Bucaille, *Gaza: La Violence de La Paix* (Paris: Presses de Science Po, 1998); Parsons, *Politics of the Palestinian Authority*.
40. Rex Brynen, "The Neopatrimonial Dimension of Palestinian Politics," *Journal of Palestine Studies* 25, no. 1 (1995): 23–36; Sayigh, *Armed Struggle and the Search for State*, 454–60.
41. See Amnesty International, *Amnesty International Report 1996* (London: Amnesty International, January 1996); *Amnesty International Report 1997* (London: Amnesty International, June 1997); *Amnesty International Report 1998* (London: Amnesty International, January 1998); *Amnesty International Report 1999* (London: Amnesty International, June 1999); *Amnesty International Report 2000* (London: Amnesty International, June 2000); *Amnesty International Report 2001* (London: Amnesty International, June 2001). Note that each annual report covers events of the preceding year, January through December.
42. See David Samuels, "In a Ruined Country," *Atlantic Monthly*, September 2005.
43. See Jeroen Gunning, *Hamas in Politics: Democracy, Religion, Violence* (New York: Columbia University Press, 2008), chap. 2.
44. See Shaul Mishal and Avraham Sela, *The Palestinian Hamas: Vision, Violence, and Coexistence* (New York: Columbia University Press, 2006).
45. Graham Usher, *Palestine in Crisis: The Struggle For Peace and Political Independence after Oslo*, Transnational Institute Series (London: Pluto Press, 1995), 74–75; Khalil Shikaki, "Palestinians Divided," *Foreign Affairs* 81, no. 1 (2002): 89–105.
46. Graham Usher, "Fatah's Tanzim: Origins and Politics," *Middle East Report* 217 (Winter 2000): 6–7; Parsons, *Politics of the Palestinian Authority*, 137–38.
47. Jeroen Gunning, "Peace with Hamas? The Transforming Potential of Political Participation," *International Affairs* 80, no. 2 (2004): 243.
48. Graham Usher, "Hamas Seeks a Place at the Table," *Middle East International*, no. 476 (May 13, 1994): 17–18.

49. See Wendy Pearlman, "Spoiling Inside and Out: Internal Political Contestation and the Middle East Peace Process," *International Security* 33, no. 3 (Winter 2008): 101; Khaled Hroub, "The Hamas Movement Between the Palestinian Authority and Israel: From the Triangle of Forces to the Hammer and Anvil" [in Arabic], *Majallat Al-Dirasat Al-Filastiniyah* 18 (Spring 1994): 28–29; Mishal and Sela, *Palestinian Hamas*, 73.
50. Bar, "Deterrence of Palestinian Terrorism," 221.
51. See Mishal and Sela, *Palestinian Hamas*, 56, 58–59.
52. Ibid., 73–74.
53. Graham Usher, *Dispatches From Palestine: The Rise and Fall of the Oslo Peace Process* (London: Pluto Press, 1999), 86; Ghazi A. Hamad, "The Relationship Between Hamas and the Palestinian National Authority (PNA): The Conflictual Past and the Unknown Future," in *Palestinian Perspectives*, ed. Wolfgang Freund (Frankfurt am Main: Peter Lang, 1999), 182.
54. Cited in Lamis Andoni, "Palestinian Islamist Group Signals Shift in Strategy," *Christian Science Monitor*, September 13, 1994.
55. See Barry M. Rubin, "The Future of Palestinian Politics: Factions, Frictions and Functions," *Middle East Review of International Affairs* 4, no. 3 (September 2000), http://www.rubincenter.org/2000/09/rubin-2000-09-07/; Khaled Hroub, *Hamas: Political Thought and Practice* (Washington, D.C.: Institute for Palestine Studies, 2000), 100, 119–20; Mishal and Sela, *Palestinian Hamas*, 71–72; Charmaine Seitz, "Coming of Age: HAMAS's Rise to Prominence in the Post-Oslo Era," in *The Struggle for Sovereignty: Palestine and Israel, 1993–2005*, ed. Joel Beinin and Rebecca L. Stein (Stanford, Calif.: Stanford University Press, 2006), 113–17.
56. Hroub, "The Hamas Movement," 28–29.
57. Yoram Meital, *Peace in Tatters: Israel, Palestine, and the Middle East* (Boulder, Colo.: Lynne Rienner, 2006), 45.
58. Amira Hass, *Drinking the Sea at Gaza: Days and Nights in a Land under Siege*, trans. Elana Wesley and Maxine Kaufman-Lacusta (New York: Henry Holt, 1999), 91–93; see also Charles Enderlin, *Shattered Dreams: The Failure of the Peace Process in the Middle East, 1995–2002* (New York: Other Press, 2003), 32–33.
59. Graham Usher, "Closures, Cantons and the Palestinian Covenant," *Middle East Report* 199 (Summer 1996): 33–37.
60. Center for Palestine Research and Studies, "Public Opinion Poll No. 22," March 29, 1996, http://www.pcpsr.org/sites/default/files/cprs%20poll%2022.pdf.
61. Jerusalem Media and Communication Centre (JMCC), "Public Opinion Poll," February 1996,August 1996, http://www.jmcc.org/polls.aspx. The JMCC is a polling organization that issues periodic reports of surveys of Palestinian public opinion. The numbers cited here were collected and tallied from these reports by the author. All reports are available on the cited JMCC website.
62. Sara M. Roy, "The Transformation of Islamist NGOs in Palestine," *Middle East Report* 214 (Spring 2000): 24–26; Byman, *High Price*, 109.
63. Ori Slonim, "The Hamas and Terror: An Alternative Explanation for the Use of Violence," *Strategic Assessment* 2, no. 3 (December 1999), http://www.inss.org.il

/publication/the-hamas-and-terror-an-alternative-explanation-for-the-use-of-violence/.
64. Quoted in Enderlin, *Shattered Dreams*, 69–70.
65. Bar, "Deterrence of Palestinian Terrorism," 213.
66. Rabinovich, *Waging Peace*, 95–96, 107–8; Meital, *Peace in Tatters*, 46; Tessler, *History of the Israeli-Palestinian Conflict*, 786.
67. Enderlin, *Shattered Dreams*, 69.
68. Palestinian Academic Society for the Study of International Affairs, *Annual Report 1996* (Jerusalem: PASSIA, 1997).
69. "Playing with Fire on the Temple Mount: Use of Lethal and Excessive Force by the Israel Police Force," Case Study No. 7 (Jerusalem: B'Tselem, December 1996), http://www.btselem.org/publications/summaries/199612_playing_with_fire.
70. Andrea Levin, "The Media's Tunnel Vision," *Middle East Quarterly* 3, no. 4 (1996): 3–9; Efraim Karsh, *Arafat's War: The Man and His Battle for Israeli Conquest* (New York: Grove Press, 2007), 147–51.
71. Mouin Rabbani, "Palestinian Authority, Israeli Rule: From Transitional to Permanent Arrangement," *Middle East Report* 201 (1996): 2–6, 22; see also Enderlin, *Shattered Dreams*, 55–56; Graham Usher, "Picture of War," *Middle East International* 535 (October 4, 1996), 3–5.
72. "IPS Forum: The Tunnel Crisis," *Journal of Palestine Studies* 26, no. 2 (Winter 1997): 95–101.
73. Mustafa Barghouti, "Posteuphoria in Palestine," *Journal of Palestine Studies* 25, no. 4 (1996): 87.
74. See, for example, Ilene R. Prusher, "Palestinians Talk of a New Intifadah," *Christian Science Monitor*, August 19, 1996.
75. Jerusalem Media and Communication Centre, "Public Opinion Poll No. 17," November 1996, www.jmcc.org. .
76. See Ghassan Khatib, "A Bloody Peace Process?," *Palestine Report*, October 4, 1996; Stephanie Nolen, "Arafat Moves to Consolidate Renewed Support," *Palestine Report*, October 4, 1996; Graham Usher, "Resistance and Negotiations," *News from Within* 12, no. 10 (November 1996): 7–9.
77. Yoram Peri, *The Israeli Military and Israel's Palestinian Policy: From Oslo to the Al Aqsa Intifada*, Peaceworks, no. 47 (Washington, D.C.: United States Institute of Peace, 2002), 30.
78. Ibid., 31.
79. Amos Harel and Avi Issacharoff, *The Seventh War* [in Hebrew] (Tel Aviv: Miskal, 2004), 56.
80. Enderlin, *Shattered Dreams*, 60–61; Ben Caspit, "Israel Is Not a Country with an Army, but an Army with an Attached Country," *Maariv*, September 6, 2002.
81. Efraim Inbar and Shmuel Sandler, "Israel's Deterrence Strategy Revisited," *Security Studies* 3, no. 2 (Winter 1993/1994): 332.
82. Quoted in Yoav Limor, "If the Palestinians Will Conduct Battles—We Will Respond in a Harsh Manner," *Maariv*, July 18, 1997; Jeremy Pressman, "The Second Intifada: An Early Look at the Background and Causes of Israeli-Palestinian Conflict," *Journal of Conflict Resolution* 22, no. 2 (2003): 114–41.

83. Quoted in Byman, *High Price*, 90; see also Peri, *Israeli Military and Israel's Palestinian Policy*, 28–29.
84. Human Rights Watch, *World Report 1997* (New York: HRW, 1998), *World Report 1998* (New York: HRW, 1999), *World Report 1999* (New York: HRW, 2000).
85. Clayton E. Swisher, *The Truth about Camp David: The Untold Story about the Collapse of the Middle East Peace Process* (New York: Nation Books, 2004), 216.
86. Dennis Ross, *The Missing Peace: The Inside Story of the Fight for Middle East Peace* (New York: Farrar, Straus and Giroux, 2004), 731.
87. Quoted in Amos Harel, "Not Mutual Trust, Just Interests," *Haaretz*, April 28, 2000.
88. Swisher, *Truth about Camp David*, 242; Robert Malley and Hussein Agha, "Camp David: The Tragedy of Errors," *New York Review of Books*, August 9, 2001, http://www.nybooks.com/articles/2001/08/09/camp-david-the-tragedy-of-errors/.
89. Swisher, *Truth about Camp David*, 336–37.
90. Aluf Benn, "The Selling of the Summit," *Haaretz*, July 27, 2001.
91. Swisher, *Truth about Camp David*, 337–38.
92. Benn, "Selling of the Summit."
93. Swisher, *Truth about Camp David*, 340.
94. Malley and Agha, "Camp David"; Swisher, *Truth about Camp David*; Deborah Sontag, "And Yet So Far: A Special Report. Quest for Mideast Peace: How and Why It Failed," *New York Times*, July 26, 2001.
95. Jeremy Pressman, "Visions in Collision: What Happened at Camp David and Taba?," *International Security* 28, no. 2 (2003): 5–43.
96. Swisher, *Truth about Camp David*, 386.
97. Suzanne Goldenberg, "Barak Rushes to Blame Unyielding Arafat," *Guardian*, July 26, 2000; Nina Gilbert, "Mofaz Warns of Conflict Following Summit Failure," *Jerusalem Post*, July 26, 2000.
98. Caspit, "Israel Is Not a Country with an Army"; Reuven Pedatzur, "More Than a Million Bullets," *Haaretz*, June 29, 2004.
99. "Chronology," *Journal of Palestine Studies* 30, no. 2 (Winter 2001): 198.
100. Amira Hass, "Don't Shoot till You Can See They're over the Age of 12," *Haaretz*, November 20, 2000; "Press Briefing by Colonel Daniel Reisner—Head of the International Law Branch of the IDF Legal Division," Israel Ministry of Foreign Affairs, November 15, 2000, http://mfa.gov.il/MFA/PressRoom/2000/Pages/Press%20Briefing%20by%20Colonel%20Daniel%20Reisner-%20Head%20of.aspx.
101. See "Excessive Force: Human Rights Violations during IDF Actions in Area A" (Jerusalem: B'Tselem, December 2001), https://www.btselem.org/download/200112_excessive_force_eng.pdf; PHRMG, "Overkill: Israeli Bombardment and Destruction of Palestinian Civilian Homes and Infrastructure," *The Monitor* 5, no. 1 (February 2001).
102. See "Excessive Force."
103. See "Question of the Violation of Human Rights in the Occupied Arab Territories, Including Palestine: Report of the Human Rights Inquiry Commission Established Pursuant to Commission Resolution S 5/1 of 19 October 2000"

(United Nations Economic and Social Council Commission on Human Rights [UN-ECOSOC], March 16, 2001), 23; "The Intifada In Figures: Statistics on Israel's Violations of Human Rights in the Occupied Palestinian Territories, September 28, 2000–September 28, 2003" (Gaza: Al-Mezan Center for Human Rights, 2003); "Israel and the Occupied Territories: Under the Rubble: House Demolition and Destruction of Land and Property" (Amnesty International, May 18, 2004); "Policy of Destruction: House Demolitions and Destruction of Agricultural Land in the Gaza Strip" (Jerusalem: B'Tselem, February 2002); *Razing Rafah: Mass Demolitions in the Gaza Strip* (New York: Human Rights Watch, October 2004); World Bank, *Fifteen Months—Intifada, Closures, and Palestinian Economic Crisis: An Assessment* (Washington, D.C.: World Bank Group, March 2002), http://documents.worldbank.org/curated/en/394371468049795957/Fifteen-months-Intifada-closures-and-Palestinian-economic-crisis-an-assessment.

104. See Leila Farsakh, "Under Siege: Closure, Separation and the Palestinian Economy," *Middle East Report* 217 (Winter 2000): 22–25; World Bank, *West Bank and Gaza Update: One Year of Intifada, Closures and Palestinian Economic Crisis* (West Bank and Gaza Strip: World Bank Group, November 2001); Hass, "Israel's Closure Policy."

105. See "Statement by Israel Ambassador Lancry to 10th Emergency Session of the UN General Assembly," October 18, 2000, http://mfa.gov.il/MFA/InternatlOrgs/Speeches/Pages/Statement%20by%20Israel%20Ambassador%20Lancry%20to%2010th%20Emer.aspx; "Press Briefing by Colonel Daniel Reisner."

106. Apart from reports and press releases by Palestinian human rights organizations, see Amnesty International, *Broken Lives—One Year of Intifada: Israel/Occupied Territories/Palestinian Authority* (London: Amnesty International UK, 2001); "Illusions of Restraint: Human Rights Violations During the Events in the Occupied Territories 29 September—2 December 2000" (Jerusalem: B'Tselem, December 2000); "Question of the Violation of Human Rights," 15; "Excessive Force"; *Center of the Storm: A Case Study of Human Rights Abuses in Hebron District* (New York: Human Rights Watch, April 1, 2001); "Trigger Happy: Unjustified Shooting and Violation of the Open-Fire Regulations During the Al-Aqsa Intifada" (Jerusalem: B'Tselem, March 2002); "Implementation of the Fourth Geneva Convention in the Occupied Palestinian Territories: History of a Multilateral Process (1997–2001)," *International Review of the Red Cross*, no. 847 (September 30, 2002): 661–98.

107. Peri, *Israeli Military and Israel's Palestinian Policy*, 6.

108. Raviv Drucker and Ofer Shelah, *Boomerang: The Failure of Leadership in the Second Intifada* [in Hebrew] (Jerusalem: Keter, 2005), 81.

109. Harel and Issacharoff, *The Seventh War*, 86.

110. Drucker and Shelah, *Boomerang*, 54.

111. Gal Hirsch, *War Story, Love Story* [in Hebrew] (Tel Aviv: Miskal, 2009), 170.

112. Peri, *Generals in the Cabinet Room*, 116.

113. Drucker and Shelah, *Boomerang*, 95; see also Peri, *Generals in the Cabinet Room*, 116–29.

114. Catignani, "Strategic Impasse in Low-Intensity Conflicts," 108–9; Hirsch, *War Story, Love Story*, 168–70.
115. Maoz, *Defending the Holy Land*, 264.
116. Peri, *Israeli Military and Israel's Palestinian Policy*.
117. Quoted in "Israel's Mufaz—Cabinet Rejected 'Dozens' of IDF Plans Against Palestinians," *Hatzofe*, November 24, 2000.
118. Quoted in Peri, *Israeli Military and Israel's Palestinian Policy*, 35.
119. "Israeli Army Officers Criticize IDF's 'Policy of Restraint,' 'Weakness,'" *Maariv*, November 27, 2000, 5.
120. Yoav Limor, "IDF Battalion Commanders Are Sharply Criticizing the Policy of Restraint," *Maariv*, November 27, 2000.
121. Drucker and Shelah, *Boomerang*, 41–58; Peri, *Israeli Military and Israel's Palestinian Policy*, 34–35, 39.
122. Caspit, "Israel Is Not a Country with an Army."
123. Ben Caspit, "The Army Will Decide and Approve," *Maariv*, September 13, 2002.
124. "Great Majority: Apply More Power; Rise to Netanyahu," *Hatzofe*, October 13, 2000.
125. "Blind Restraint," *Jerusalem Post*, November 15, 2000.
126. Uri Dan, "Know Thine Enemy," *Jerusalem Post*, November 9, 2000.
127. Etgar Lefkovits and Margot Dudkevitch, "1,500 Protest in Capital against 'Restraint,'" *Jerusalem Post*, November 15, 2000; "Clinton Telephones His 'bridging Proposals' to Barak and Arafat," *Mideast Mirror*, November 15, 2000.
128. "Israeli Settlers Decide to Drop Restraint, Stage Anti-Palestinian Protests," *BBC News*, November 6, 2000.
129. Yossi Levi, "Shin Bet Fears Emergence of New Jewish Underground in Territories," *Maariv*, November 15, 2000.
130. Quoted in Sontag, "And Yet So Far."
131. Asher Arian, "Israeli Public Opinion on National Security 2001," Memorandum no. 60 (Jaffee Center for Strategic Studies, Tel Aviv University, August 2001), 21, 29.
132. Tamar Hermann, *The Israeli Peace Movement: A Shattered Dream* (New York: Cambridge University Press, 2009), chap. 4.
133. Caspit, "Army Will Decide and Approve."
134. Quoted in Arieh O'Sullivan, "How Far Can Our War for Peace Go?," *Jerusalem Post*, October 10, 2000.
135. "A Time to Deter," *Jerusalem Post*, November 10, 2000.
136. "Interview with Israel PM Barak on NBC News Meet the Press," Israel Ministry of Foreign Affairs, October 8, 2000, http://mfa.gov.il/MFA/PressRoom/2000/Pages/Interview%20with%20Israel%20PM%20Barak%20on%20NBC%20News%20Meet%20th.aspx.
137. Yossi Olmert, "Arabs Read Prudence As Weakness," *Jerusalem Post*, October 17, 2000.
138. "Blind Restraint."
139. See Harel and Issacharoff, *The Seventh War*, 62–65.

140. See "Public Opinion Poll No. 37," June 2000, http://www.jmcc.org/documentsandmaps.aspx?id=463.
141. Mark A. Heller, "Implications of the Withdrawal from Lebanon for Israeli-Palestinian Relations," *Strategic Assessment* 3, no. 1 (June 2000), http://www.inss.org.il/publication/implications-of-the-withdrawal-from-lebanon-for-israeli-palestinian-relations/; Shlomo Brom, "The Withdrawal from Southern Lebanon: One Year Later," *Strategic Assessment* 4, no. 2 (August 2001), http://www.inss.org.il/publication/the-withdrawal-from-southern-lebanon-one-year-later/; Ronen Sebag, "Lebanon: The Intifada's False Premise," *Middle East Quarterly* 9, no. 2 (Spring 2002): 13–21. For more analysis, see Caspit, "The Army Will Decide and Approve"; Peri, *Israeli Military and Israel's Palestinian Policy*, 33.
142. Quoted in Enderlin, *Shattered Dreams*, 153.
143. Quoted in Harel and Issacharoff, *The Seventh War*, 64.
144. Yezid Sayigh, "Arafat and the Anatomy of a Revolt," *Survival* 43, no. 3 (September 2001): 52–53.
145. Caspit, "Army Will Decide and Approve."
146. "Interview with Israel PM Barak on NBC News Meet the Press."
147. Charles Krauthammer, "Arafat's Strategy," *Washington Post*, October 20, 2000; Ely Karmon, "Arafat's Strategy—Lebanonization and Entanglement" (Herzliya, Israel: International Institute for Counter-Terrorism, November 16, 2000), https://www.ict.org.il/Article.aspx?ID=794; Karsh, *Arafat's War*; Michael Herzog, "The Palestinian Intifada (Part I): Palestinian Lessons and Prospects," *Policywatch* (Washington, DC: Washington Institute for Near East Policy, September 29, 2004).
148. Mark Devenport, "Feelings Run High at the UN," BBC News, October 4, 2000, http://news.bbc.co.uk/2/hi/middle_east/955223.stm.
149. "Press Conference with Acting Foreign Minister Ben-Ami," Israel Ministry of Foreign Affairs, October 1, 2000, http://mfa.gov.il/MFA/ForeignPolicy/MFADocuments/Yearbook13/Pages/171%20%20Press%20conference%20with%20Acting%20Foreign%20Minister.aspx.
150. Drucker and Shelah, *Boomerang*, 80.
151. Akiva Eldar, "Military Intelligence Presented Erroneous Assumption on Palestinians," *Haaretz*, June 10, 2004; Gideon Alon and Akiva Eldar, "Opposition Demands Probe of Gilad's 'Erroneous' Evaluations," *Haaretz*, June 11, 2004; Harel and Issacharoff, *The Seventh War*, 86.
152. Harel and Issacharoff, *The Seventh War*, 87–88.
153. Drucker and Shelah, *Boomerang*, 14.
154. Harel and Issacharoff, *The Seventh War*, 59. See chapter 2 in this book for more discussion.
155. Peri, *Generals in the Cabinet Room*, 141.
156. Quoted in Ewen MacAskill, "We Must Destroy Palestinian Threat, Army Chief Says," *Guardian*, August 26, 2002, https://www.theguardian.com/world/2002/aug/27/israel.
157. Peri, *Generals in the Cabinet Room*, 141.
158. Caspit, "Israel Is Not a Country with an Army."

159. Thomas L. Friedman, "Foreign Affairs; Arafat's War," *New York Times*, October 13, 2000.
160. "Press Briefing by Colonel Daniel Reisner."
161. "Interview with Israel PM Barak on NBC News Meet the Press."
162. Efraim Inbar, "The 'No Choice War' Debate in Israel," *Journal of Strategic Studies* 12, no. 1 (1989): 22–37.
163. Alistair Iain Johnston, "Thinking about Strategic Culture," *International Security* 19, no. 4 (1995): 32–64.
164. Roy, "Palestinian Society and Economy," 9; Edward Said, "The Tragedy Deepens," *Al-Ahram Weekly*, December 7, 2000; Ashraf al-Agrami, "National Unity: The Need to Reconsider," *Al-Ayyam*, January 13, 2003.
165. Sayigh, "Arafat and the Anatomy of a Revolt," 48–49.
166. Eitan Y. Alimi, "Contextualizing Political Terrorism: A Collective Action Perspective for Understanding the Tanzim," *Studies in Conflict & Terrorism* 29, no. 3 (2006): 263–83.
167. Sayigh, "Arafat and the Anatomy of a Revolt"; Ali Jarbawi, "Critical Reflections on One Year of the Intifada," *Between the Lines* 1, no. 12 (October 2001): 9–14.
168. Yezid Sayigh, "Palestine—Where To?" (presentation, PASSIA Roundtable Meeting and Discussion, Jerusalem, July 9, 2002), http://passia.org/meetings/54?year=2002; see also "For the Record: Interview with Yezid Sayigh," *Palestine Report*, March 7, 2001.
169. Ghazi Hamad, "The Islamist Catch-22," *Palestine Report*, December 13, 2000.
170. *Erased in a Moment: Suicide Bombing Attacks Against Israeli Civilians* (New York: Human Rights Watch, October 2002), 1.
171. Jerusalem Media and Communication Centre, "Public Opinion Polls," *Poll Finder*, n.d., http://www.jmcc.org/polls.aspx.
172. Lee Hockstader, "Israel Sets Out Charges Arafat Supported Terror," *Washington Post*, May 6, 2002.
173. "Who Governs the West Bank? Palestinian Administration under Israeli Occupation," Middle East Report, no. 32 (Amman/Brussels: International Crisis Group, September 28, 2004), 24–25.
174. Ibid., 26; see also Parsons, *Politics of the Palestinian Authority*, 267–68.
175. *Erased in a Moment*, 62–63.
176. See Toufic Haddad, "Overcoming the Culture of Petitions: Critiquing the Role and Influence of Palestinian 'Secular, National, Democratic' Forces," *Between the Lines* 11, no. 14 (March 2002): 30–36.
177. Strategic Assessment Initiative, *Planning Considerations for International Involvement in the Palestinian Security Sector* (Washington, D.C.: Strategic Assessment Initiative, July 2005), 13, http://www.strategicassessments.org/ontherecord/saipublications/SAI-Planning_Considerations_for_International_Involvement_July_2005.pdf, accessed August 19, 2007.
178. "Fateh Can Be Rescued from Itself," *Mideast Mirror*, October 25, 2004; "Al-Aqsa Commander: No One Can Unilaterally End De-Escalation," *Financial Times*, April 28, 2005.

179. "Statistics on Palestinians in the Custody of the Israeli Security Forces," (Jerusalem: B'Tselem, August 9, 2017), http://www.btselem.org/statistics/detainees_and_prisoners.
180. "Fatalities Before Operation 'Cast Lead,'" B'Tselem, n.d., http://www.btselem.org/statistics/fatalities/before-cast-lead/by-date-of-event.
181. James Bennet, "A People Adrift: In Chaos, Palestinians Struggle for a Way Out," *New York Times*, July 15, 2004; Graham Usher, "Facing Defeat: The Intifada Two Years On," *Journal of Palestine Studies* 32, no. 2 (2003): 34.
182. Author Wendy Pearlman interview with analyst, Gaza City, July 2005.
183. Hirsch, *War Story, Love Story*, 170–75; Peri, *Generals in the Cabinet Room*, 129–33.
184. "Report of the Secretary-General Prepared Pursuant to General Assembly Resolution ES-10/10" (United Nations, July 30, 2002), https://unispal.un.org/DPA/DPR/unispal.nsf/0/FD7BDE7666E04F5C85256C08004E63ED; Amira Hass, "Operation Destroy the Data," *Haaretz*, April 24, 2002.
185. Hass, "Operation Destroy the Data."
186. Jerusalem Media and Communication Centre, "Public Opinion Poll No. 51," June 2004.
187. "Who Governs the West Bank?" See also Azmi Bishara, "Beyond Belief," *Al-Ahram Weekly*, July 25–31, 2002, http://www.fikrwanaqd.net/site/topics/article.asp?cu_no=1&item_no=331&version=1&template_id=273&parent_id=29; "Fateh Can Be Rescued from Itself"; and Bennet, "A People Adrift."
188. "Misuse of Weapons on the Part of Palestinian Security Force Personnel, 2001" [in Arabic] (Ramallah, West Bank: PICCR, 2002); PHRMG, "The 'Intra'fada: The Chaos of Weapons—an Analysis of Internal Palestinian Violence," *The Monitor* 7, no. 1 (April 2004); PHRMG, "Gaza in Turmoil: The Power Struggle within the Palestinian Authority," *The Monitor* 8, no. 1 (May 2005); on the Palestinian Legislative Council (PLC) inquiry into this internal situation, see Arnon Regular, "Palestinian Inquiry Blames Yasser Arafat for Anarchy," *Haaretz*, August 10, 2004.
189. See Yossi Olmert, "Arafat's Little Game of Cease-Fires," *Jerusalem Post*, June 10, 2001; Yoel Marcus, "Dr. Cease-Fire and Mr. Terror," *Haaretz*, June 12, 2001.
190. "Fateh Al-Tanzim Leader in West Bank Marwan Al-Barghuthi Interviewed on Intifadah," *Al-Majallah*, October 29, 2000; "'Peaceful Intifada' Will Go on," *Mideast Mirror*, November 2, 2000; Mouin Rabbani, "Negotiating Over the Clinton Plan," Press Information Note, no. 43, *Middle East Report*, January 6, 2001, http://www.merip.org/mero/mero010601.
191. Pearlman, *Violence, Nonviolence*, 174–79.
192. Usher, "Facing Defeat."
193. Cited in Khaled Abu Toameh, "Talking at Cross Purposes," *Jerusalem Post*, January 31, 2003.
194. Sharvit et al., "Effects of Israeli Use," 39.
195. "The Nature and Extent of Palestinian Terrorism, 2006," Israeli Ministry of Foreign Affairs, March 1, 2007, http://www.mfa.gov.il/mfa/foreignpolicy/terrorism/palestinian/pages/palestinian%20terrorism%202006.aspx.
196. Cited in Regular, "Palestinian Inquiry."

197. Ali Jarbawi and Wendy Pearlman, "Struggle in a Post-Charisma Transition: Rethinking Palestinian Politics after Arafat," *Journal of Palestine Studies* 36, no. 4 (2007): 6–21.
198. "Under the Guise of Security: Routing the Separation Barrier to Enable Israeli Settlement Expansion in the West Bank" (Jerusalem: B'Tselem, December 2005).
199. "West Bank Closure Count and Analysis" (Jerusalem: United Nations Office for the Coordination of Humanitarian Affairs, January 2006), https://www.ochaopt.org/content/west-bank-closure-count-and-analysis-january-2006.
200. Amnesty International, *Amnesty International Report 2005* (London: Amnesty International, January 2006).
201. Human Rights Watch, *World Report 2005* (New York: HRW, 2006).
202. International Institute for Strategic Studies, "Hamas Coup in Gaza: Fundamental Shift in Palestinian Politics," *Strategic Comments* 13, no. 5 (June 2007); David Rose, "The Gaza Bombshell," *Vanity Fair*, April 2008.
203. Nathan J. Brown, "The Hamas-Fatah Conflict: Shallow but Wide," *Fletcher Forum of World Affairs* 34, no. 2 (Summer 2010): 35–49.
204. Yazan al-Saadi, "Palestinian Reconciliation: A History of Documents," *Al-Akhbar*, April 28, 2014, http://english.al-akhbar.com/node/19580.
205. Efraim Inbar and Eitan Shamir, "'Mowing the Grass:' Israel's Strategy for Protracted Intractable Conflict," *Journal of Strategic Studies* 37, no. 1 (2014): 65–90.
206. Amos Malka, "Israel and Asymmetrical Deterrence," *Comparative Strategy* 27, no. 1 (2008): 13.
207. Colin P. Clarke, "How Salafism's Rise Threatens Gaza: What It Means for Hamas and Israel," *Foreign Affairs*, October 11, 2017, https://www.foreignaffairs.com/articles/israel/2017-10-11/how-salafisms-rise-threatens-gaza.
208. Yaakov Lappin, Khaled Abu Toameh, and Lahav Harkov, "Gaza Will Pay a 'Heavy Price' for Rocket Fire, Says Ya'alon," *Jerusalem Post*, May 28, 2015; William Booth and Hazem Balousha, "Amnesty International: Hamas Guilty of Torture, Summary Executions," *Washington Post*, May 27, 2015.

6. Lebanon Before and Since 2006: Strategic Culture at War

1. See Ussama Samir Makdisi, *The Culture of Sectarianism: Community, History, and Violence in Nineteenth-Century Ottoman Lebanon* (Berkeley: University of California Press, 2000); Samir Khalaf, *Civil and Uncivil Violence in Lebanon: A History of the Internationalization of Communal Conflict* (New York: Columbia University Press, 2002).
2. See Michael C. Hudson, *The Precarious Republic: Political Modernization in Lebanon* (Boulder, Colo.: Westview Press, 1985).
3. Ibid., 44.
4. See Rania Maktabi, "The Lebanese Census of 1932 Revisited: Who Are the Lebanese?," *British Journal of Middle Eastern Studies* 26, no. 2 (1999): 219–41; Muhammad A. Faour, "Religion, Demography, and Politics in Lebanon," *Middle Eastern Studies* 43, no. 6 (2007): 909–21.

5. William Harris, "Lebanon's Roller Coaster Ride," in *Lebanon: Liberation, Conflict, and Crisis*, ed. Barry M. Rubin (New York: Palgrave Macmillan, 2009), 63–82.
6. Leonard Binder, ed., *Politics in Lebanon* (New York: Wiley, 1966); Hudson, *Precarious Republic*; Elizabeth Picard, *Lebanon: A Shattered Country: Myths and Realities of the Wars in Lebanon* (New York: Holmes & Meier, 1996); Fawwaz Traboulsi, *A History of Modern Lebanon*, 2nd ed. (London: Pluto Press, 2012).
7. Toufic K. Gaspard, *A Political Economy of Lebanon, 1948–2002: The Limits of Laissez-Faire* (Leiden: Brill, 2004), xix; Carolyn Gates, *The Merchant Republic of Lebanon: Rise of an Open Economy* (London: I. B. Tauris, 1998).
8. Charles Adwan, "Corruption in Reconstruction: The Cost of National Consensus in Post-War Lebanon" (Washington, D.C.: Center for International Private Enterprise, December 1, 2004).
9. See Mohammad F. Mattar, "On Corruption," in *Options for Lebanon*, ed. Nawaf Salam (London: I. B. Tauris, 2004), 173–208; Khalil Gebara, "Reconstruction Survey: The Political Economy of Corruption in Post-War Lebanon" (Beirut: Lebanese Transparency Association, 2007); Adwan, "Corruption in Reconstruction."
10. Kamal Dib, *Warlords and Merchants: The Lebanese Business and Political Establishment* (Reading, UK: Ithaca Press, 2004).
11. Joyce R. Starr, "Lebanon's Economy: The Costs of Protracted Violence," in *The Emergence of a New Lebanon: Fantasy or Reality?*, ed. Edward E. Azar (New York: Praeger, 1984), 69–78.
12. Jonathan Haughton, "An Assessment of the Tax System in Lebanon" (Suffolk University, Boston, 2004).
13. Starr, "Lebanon's Economy."
14. Michael Bluhm, "Finance Ministry Puts Public Debt at $42 Billion," *Daily Star*, January 31, 2008.
15. Augustus Richard Norton, *Hezbollah: A Short History* (Princeton, N.J.: Princeton University Press, 2007), 122.
16. See Charbel Nahas, "Émigration," *Le Commerce Du Levant*, October 2007, 32–38; Charbel Nahas, "Émigration (2)," *Le Commerce Du Levant*, November 2007, 42–44.
17. Wendy Pearlman, "Competing for Lebanon's Diaspora: Transnationalism and Domestic Struggles in a Weak State," *International Migration Review* 48, no. 1 (Spring 2014): 34–75.
18. Melani Claire Cammett, *Compassionate Communalism: Welfare and Sectarianism in Lebanon* (Ithaca, N.Y.: Cornell University Press, 2014); Megan Stewart, "Civil War as State-Making: Strategic Governance in Civil War," *International Organization* 72, no. 1 (Winter 2018): 205–26.
19. See Oren Barak, *The Lebanese Army: A National Institution in a Divided Society* (Albany: State University of New York Press, 2009); R. D. McLaurin, "Lebanon and Its Army: Past, Present, and Future," in *The Emergence of a New Lebanon: Fantasy or Reality*, ed. Edward E. Azar (New York: Praeger, 1984), 79–114; Farid El-Khazen, *The Breakdown of the State in Lebanon, 1967–1976* (Cambridge, Mass.: Harvard University Press, 2000).

20. Stockholm International Peace Research Institute (SIPRI), "SIPRI Military Expenditure Database," *SIPRI Databases*, 2016, https://www.sipri.org/databases/milex.
21. Barak, *Lebanese Army*, 51–62.
22. Ibid., 93–110.
23. See ibid., 1.
24. Walid Khalidi, *Conflict and Violence in Lebanon: Confrontation in the Middle East* (Cambridge, Mass.: Harvard University Press, 1983), 108.
25. Volker Perthes, *Syria under Bashar Al-Asad: Modernisation and the Limits of Change* (Oxford: Oxford University Press, 2004), 53.
26. Samir Khalaf, *Lebanon's Predicament* (New York: Columbia University Press, 1987); Maroun Kisirwani and William M. Parle, "Assessing the Impact of the Post Civil War Period on the Lebanese Bureaucracy: A View from Inside," *Journal of Asian and African Studies* 22, no. 1 (1987): 17–32; El-Khazen, *Breakdown of the State*, 29–86.
27. See "Lebanon," United Nations Relief and Works Agency, July 1, 2014, http://www.unrwa.org/where-we-work/lebanon.
28. See Fawaz Turki, *The Disinherited: Journal of a Palestinian Exile* (New York: Monthly Review Press, 1972); Rosemary Sayigh, *The Palestinians: From Peasants to Revolutionaries* (New York: Zed Books, 2007).
29. Lara Deeb, *An Enchanted Modern: Gender and Public Piety in Shi'i Lebanon* (Princeton, N.J.: Princeton University Press, 2006), chap. 2; Roschanack Shaery-Eisenlohr, *Shi'ite Lebanon: Transnational Religion and the Making of National Identities* (New York: Columbia University Press, 2008), 2.
30. Boutros Labaki, "The Balance of Power Between Sects and the Making of Internal Conflict in Lebanon" [in Arabic], *Al-Waqia* 5–6 (1983): 215–45.
31. Picard, *Lebanon*, 39–41.
32. Salim Nasr, "Roots of the Shi'i Movement," *MERIP Reports* 133 (May/June 1985): 10–16.
33. See Graham E. Fuller and Rend Rahim Francke, *The Arab Shi'a: The Forgotten Muslims* (Basingstoke: St. Martin's Press, 1999), chap. 9; Simon Haddad, "The Origins of Popular Support for Lebanon's Hezbollah," *Studies in Conflict & Terrorism* 29, no. 1 (2006): 25–26; Norton, *Hezbollah*, 46.
34. Mona Harb and Reinoud Leenders, "Know Thy Enemy: Hizbullah, 'Terrorism' and the Politics of Perception," *Third World Quarterly* 26, no. 1 (2005): 187.
35. Faour, "Religion, Demography, and Politics in Lebanon," 919.
36. Alexus G. Grynkewich, "Welfare as Warfare: How Violent Non-State Groups Use Social Services to Attack the State," *Studies in Conflict & Terrorism* 31, no. 4 (2008): 350–70; Boaz Atzili, "State Weakness and 'Vacuum of Power' in Lebanon," *Studies in Conflict & Terrorism* 33, no. 8 (2010): 757–82.
37. Ariel Merari and Shlomo Elad, *The International Dimension of Palestinian Terrorism* (Jerusalem: Jerusalem Post Press, 1986), 5–6, 120.
38. "Dayan Comment," Jerusalem Domestic Service, December 30, 1968, in Reports regarding raid on Beirut Airport, Israel, H5, Foreign Broadcast Information Service (FBIS) Daily Reports.

39. "Eshkol Statement," Jerusalem Domestic Service, December 29, 1968, in Reports regarding raid on Beirut Airport, Israel, H3, Foreign Broadcast Information Service (FBIS) Daily Reports. See also "Reasons for Action," Jerusalem Domestic Service, December 28, 1968, in Reports regarding raid on Beirut Airport, Israel, H2, FBIS Daily Reports.
40. "Eshkol Addresses Knesset in Beirut Operation," Jerusalem Domestic Service, December 31, 1968.
41. El-Khazen, *Breakdown of the State*, 140–45.
42. Sayigh, *Armed Struggle and the Search for State*, 190–91.
43. El-Khazen, *Breakdown of the State*, 140–68; Khalidi, *Conflict and Violence in Lebanon*, 185–87.
44. El-Khazen, *Breakdown of the State*, 161–68.
45. Augustus Richard Norton and Jillian Schwedler, "(In)security Zones in South Lebanon," *Journal of Palestine Studies* 23, no. 1 (1993): 62.
46. El-Khazen, *Breakdown of the State*, 179–92.
47. Menachem Klein, "The 'Tranquil Decade' Re-Examined: Arab-Israeli Relations During the Years 1957–67," in *Israel: The First Hundred Years*. Vol. 2, *From War to Peace?*, ed. Efraim Karsh (London: Routledge, 2000), 68–82.
48. "Golda Meir's Knesset Remarks," Jerusalem Domestic Service, April 10, 1973, in Reportage on Beirut Attack Continues, Israel, H1, FBIS Daily Reports; Terence Smith, "Explanation in Tel Aviv; Brennan Urges Minimum Wage Rise," *New York Times*, April 11, 1973, 1.
49. Norton and Schwedler, "(In)security Zones in South Lebanon," 65.
50. Richard L. Homan, "Israelis Launch Attack into Lebanon," *Washington Post*, March 15, 1978, A16.
51. H.D.S. Greenway, "Israel's Aim: A Buffer Zone Free of Palestinians," *Washington Post*, March 16, 1978, A1.
52. Zeev Maoz, *Defending the Holy Land: A Critical Analysis of Israel's Security & Foreign Policy* (Ann Arbor: University of Michigan Press, 2006), 176.
53. Norton, *Hezbollah*, 27–46.
54. Daniel Byman, *Deadly Connections: States That Sponsor Terrorism* (Cambridge: Cambridge University Press, 2005), 79–115; Norton, *Hezbollah*, 34–35; Hussain Sirriyeh, "The Emergence of Hizbollah and the Beginning of Resistance, 1982–85," in *Israel and Hizbollah: An Asymmetric Conflict in Historical and Comparative Perspective*, ed. Clive Jones and Sergio Catignani (New York: Routledge, 2010), 41–42.
55. Sergio Catignani, "Israeli Counter-Insurgency Strategy and the Quest for Security in the Israeli-Lebanese Conflict Arena," in *Israel and Hizbollah: An Asymmetric Conflict in Historical and Comparative Perspective*, ed. Clive Jones and Sergio Catignani (New York: Routledge, 2010), 76–88.
56. Rola El-Husseini, *Pax Syriana: Elite Politics in Postwar Lebanon* (Syracuse, N.Y.: Syracuse University Press, 2012).
57. Ohannes Geukjian, "Political Instability and Conflict after the Syrian Withdrawal from Lebanon," *Middle East Journal* 68, no. 4 (2014): 524.

58. Jerrold Kessel, "Israel Takes Its Revenge On Hizbullah," *Guardian*, July 27, 1993, 9.
59. Zeev Schiff, quoted in ibid.; Julian Ozanne and Mark Nicholson, "Israel Steps up Attacks on South Lebanon," *Financial Times*, July 28, 1993; Jerrold Kessel, "250,000 Flee from Israel's Onslaught; Scores of Lebanese Civilians Dead and Hundreds Injured in Three-Day Attack," *Guardian*, July 29, 1993.
60. Dennis Ross, *The Missing Peace: The Inside Story of the Fight for the Middle East Peace* (New York: Farrar, Straus and Giroux, 2004), 109–10.
61. Elli Lieberman, *Reconceptualizing Deterrence: Nudging Toward Rationality in Middle East Rivalries* (London: Routledge, 2013), 180; Judith Palmer Harik, *Hezbollah: The Changing Face of Terrorism* (New York: I. B. Tauris, 2004), 116–17.
62. Lieberman, *Reconceptualizing Deterrence*, 180–81; Daniel Sobelman, "Hizbollah: From Terror to Resistance," in *Israel and Hizbollah: An Asymmetric Conflict in Historical and Comparative Perspective*, ed. Clive Jones and Sergio Catignani (Routledge, 2010), 58–59.
63. Barton Gellman, "Raids Draw Wide Praise In Israel; Lebanon Operation Boosts Peres' Image," *Washington Post*, April 14, 1996.
64. Ibid.
65. *Civilian Pawns: Laws of War Violations and the Use of Weapons on the Israeli-Lebanese Border* (New York: Human Rights Watch, May 1996).
66. Barton Gellman, "If It's Lights Out for Israeli Synagogue, Beirut Must Go Dark Too," *Washington Post*, April 15, 1996. See also Ross, *Missing Peace*, 250.
67. Quoted in Sobelman, "Hizbollah," 58.
68. Ibid.
69. Maoz, *Defending the Holy Land*, 225.
70. Lieberman, *Reconceptualizing Deterrence*, 180–81.
71. Hala Jaber, *Hezbollah: Born with a Vengeance* (New York: Columbia University Press, 1997), 195.
72. Emile El-Hokayem, "Hizballah and Syria: Outgrowing the Proxy Relationships," *Washington Quarterly* 30, no. 2 (2007): 35–52.
73. Ross, *Missing Peace*, 110.
74. Ibid., 251–55; Maoz, *Defending the Holy Land*, 255; Lieberman, *Reconceptualizing Deterrence*, 180–81.
75. Maoz, *Defending the Holy Land*, 226–29.
76. Ibid.
77. Author Boaz Atzili interview with retired senior IDF general, Tel-Aviv, July 29, 2010.
78. Amos Harel and Avi Issacharoff, *Spider Webs* [in Hebrew] (Tel Aviv: Miskal, 2008), 15–29.
79. Ibid.
80. Daniel Sobelman, *New Rules of the Game: Israel and Hizbollah after the Withdrawal from Lebanon* (Tel Aviv: Jaffee Center for Strategic Studies, 2004), 32–33.
81. Ibid., 27–39.
82. Amir Rapaport, *Friendly Fire* [in Hebrew] (Tel Aviv: Maariv, 2007), 64–70.

83. Ephraim Sneh (former Israeli deputy-minister of defense), interview with author Boaz Atzili, Netanya, Israel, July 19, 2010.
84. Eyal Zisser, "Hizbollah: The Battle over Lebanon," *Military and Strategic Affairs* 1, no. 2 (October 2009): 47–59, as cited in Lieberman, *Reconceptualizing Deterrence*, 204.
85. Meir Elran, "The Civilian Front in the Second Lebanon War," in *The Second Lebanon War: Strategic Perspectives*, ed. Meir Elran and Shlomo Brom (Tel Aviv: Institute for National Security Studies, 2007).
86. Rapaport, *Friendly Fire*, 76.
87. David Makovsky, "Deterrence and the Burden of Israeli Moderates," Washington Institute for Near East Policy, August 3, 2006, http://www.washingtoninstitute.org/policy-analysis/view/deterrence-and-the-burden-of-israeli-moderates.
88. Harel and Issacharoff, *Spider Webs*, 40; Daniel Byman, *A High Price: The Triumphs and Failures of Israeli Counterterrorism* (Oxford: Oxford University Press, 2011), 240–41.
89. Harel and Issacharoff, *Spider Webs*, 40–41; Charles D. Freilich, *Zion's Dilemmas: How Israel Makes National Security Policy* (Ithaca, N.Y.: Cornell University Press, 2012), 145–46.
90. "Security Council Endorses Secretary-General's Conclusion on Israeli Withdrawal from Lebanon as of 16 June," Press Release (United Nations Security Council, June 18, 2000), http://www.un.org/press/en/2000/20000618.sc6878.doc.html.
91. Rapaport, *Friendly Fire*, 69.
92. Ibid.; Yair Evron, "Deterrence and Its Limitations," in *The Second Lebanese War: Strategic Aspects*, ed. Shlomo Brom and Meir Elran (Tel Aviv: Institute for National Security Studies, 2007), 38.
93. Sobelman, *New Rules of the Game*.
94. Syria and Lebanon never demarcated their mutual border, and Syria still refuses to do so.
95. Sneh, interview; Shai Feldman, "Deterrence and the Israel-Hezbollah War—Summer 2006," in *Deterrence in the Twenty-First Century: Proceedings*, ed. Anthony C. Cain (Maxwell AFB, Ala.: Air University Press, 2010), 279–90; Evron, "Deterrence and Its Limitations."
96. Lieberman, *Reconceptualizing Deterrence*, 205.
97. Norton, *Hezbollah*, chap. 6; Sobelman, *New Rules of the Game*, 107–9.
98. Oded Lowenheim and Gadi Heimann, "Revenge in International Politics," *Security Studies* 17, no. 4 (2008): 715.
99. Danna Harman, "Barak Warns Syria, Lebanon," *Jerusalem Post*, May 25, 2000.
100. Eliyahu Winograd, "Partial Report: The Inquiry Commission to Examine the Events of the Military Campaign in Lebanon 2006" [in Hebrew] (State of Israel, Tel Aviv, April 2007), 39, author's translation.
101. Harel and Issacharoff, *Spider Webs*, 116–18.
102. Amos Harel and Avi Issacharoff, *34 Days: Israel, Hezbollah, and the War in Lebanon* (New York: Palgrave Macmillan, 2008), 161.
103. Sobelman, *New Rules of the Game*, 46–48; Feldman, "Deterrence and the Israel-Hezbollah War," 284.

104. Byman, *High Price*, 244.
105. "Interview with Israel PM Barak on NBC News Meet the Press," Israel Ministry of Foreign Affairs, October 8, 2000, http://mfa.gov.il/MFA/PressRoom/2000/Pages/Interview%20with%20Israel%20PM%20Barak%20on%20NBC%20News%20Meet%20th.aspx.
106. Hassan A. Barari and Hahi A. M. Akho-Rashida, "The Pragmatic and the Radical: Syria and Iran and War by Proxy," in *Israel and Hizbollah: An Asymmetric Conflict in Historical and Comparative Perspective*, ed. Clive Jones and Sergio Catignani (New York: Routledge, 2010), 116.
107. Ibid., 117.
108. Harris, "Lebanon's Roller Coaster Ride," 64–67.
109. Geukjian, "Political Instability and Conflict," 524.
110. Nicholas Blanford, *Killing Mr. Lebanon: The Assassination of Rafik Hariri and Its Impact on the Middle East* (London: I. B. Tauris, 2006), 128–73.
111. Norton, *Hezbollah*, chap. 6; Harris, "Lebanon's Roller Coaster Ride," 71–72.
112. Theodor Hanf and Nawaf Salam, eds., *Lebanon in Limbo: Postwar Society and State in an Uncertain Regional Environment* (Baden-Baden: Nomos, 2003); Dib, *Warlords and Merchants*, 173–208; Gebara, "Reconstruction Survey."
113. Norton, *Hezbollah*, chap. 6.
114. Ibid.
115. Oren Barak, "Towards a Representative Military? The Transformation of the Lebanese Officer Corps since 1945," *Middle East Journal* 60, no. 1 (2006): 75–93.
116. Harel and Issacharoff, *Spider Webs*, 118.
117. Rapaport, *Friendly Fire*, 25.
118. Harel and Issacharoff, *Spider Webs*, 162.
119. Feldman, "Deterrence and the Israel-Hezbollah War," 286.
120. Rapaport, *Friendly Fire*, 19.
121. Dima Adamsky, "From Israel with Deterrence: Strategic Culture, Intra-War Coercion and Brute Force," *Security Studies* 26, no. 1 (2017): 169–70.
122. Byman, *High Price*, 244.
123. "Hizbullah Attacks Along Israel's Northern Border May 2000–June 2006," Israel Ministry of Foreign Affairs, June 1, 2006, http://mfa.gov.il/MFA/ForeignPolicy/Terrorism/Hizbullah/Pages/Incidents%20along%20Israel-Lebanon%20border%20since%20May%202000.aspx.
124. Harel and Issacharoff, *Spider Webs*, 141–44; Eliahu Winograd, "Final Report: The Inquiry Commission to Examine the Events of the Military Campaign in Lebanon 2006" [in Hebrew] (State of Israel, Tel Aviv, January 30, 2008), 48.
125. Winograd, "Final Report," 48.
126. Feldman, "Deterrence and the Israel-Hezbollah War," 285–86.
127. "Israel-Hizbullah Conflict: Victims of Rocket Attacks and IDF Casualties," Israel Ministry of Foreign Affairs, July 12, 2006, http://www.mfa.gov.il/mfa/foreignpolicy/terrorism/hizbullah/pages/israel-hizbullah%20conflict-%20victims%20of%20rocket%20attacks%20and%20idf%20casualties%20july-aug%202006.aspx.
128. Estimation of casualties and damage varies greatly. For some, see Associated Press, "Mideast War, by the Numbers," *Washington Post*, August 17, 2006, sec. World,

http://www.washingtonpost.com/wp-dyn/content/article/2006/08/17/AR
2006081700909.html; *Why They Died: Civilian Casualties in Lebanon During
the 2006 War* (New York: Human Rights Watch, September 2007), https://
www.hrw.org/sites/default/files/reports/lebanon0907.pdf; "Israel/Lebanon—
Deliberate Destruction or 'Collateral Damage?' Israeli Attacks on Civilian
Infrastructure," Amnesty International, August 23, 2006, http://www.refworld
.org/docid/4517a71c4.html.
129. Some lower-ranked commanders in the Northern Command were not that convinced. See Gal Hirsch, *War Story, Love Story* [in Hebrew] (Tel Aviv: Miskal, 2009).
130. Ofer Shelah and Yoav Limor, *Captives in Lebanon* [in Hebrew] (Tel Aviv: Yedioth Ahronoth, 2007), 45.
131. Rapaport, *Friendly Fire*, 27.
132. Giora Romm, "A Test of Rival Strategies: Two Ships Passing in the Night," in *The Second Lebanon War: Strategic Perspectives*, ed. Shlomo Brom and Meir Elran (Tel Aviv: Institute for National Security Studies, 2007), 50.
133. Ehud Olmert, interview by Raviv Drucker, *Hamakor*, Channel 10, Israeli TV, May 5, 2015.
134. See, e.g., Jonathan D. Caverley, *Democratic Militarism: Voting, Wealth, and War* (Cambridge: Cambridge University Press, 2014), 245–46; Harel and Issacharoff, *34 Days*, 81–82.
135. Harel and Issacharoff, *34 Days*, 79–81, quote on 80.
136. Ibid., 91–92.
137. Evron, "Deterrence and Its Limitations," 39; Olmert, interview.
138. Evron, "Deterrence and Its Limitations," 92–93.
139. Shelah and Limor, *Captives in Lebanon*, 62.
140. Feldman, "Deterrence and the Israel-Hezbollah War," 287.
141. Shelah and Limor, *Captives in Lebanon*, 62.
142. Lowenheim and Heimann, "Revenge in International Politics," 711–12.
143. Freilich, *Zion's Dilemmas*, 203–13.
144. Ibid.
145. Dag Henriksen, "Deterrence by Default? Israel's Military Strategy in the 2006 War against Hizballah," *Journal of Strategic Studies* 35, no. 1 (2012): 95.
146. Shelah and Limor, *Captives in Lebanon*, 45.
147. Romm, "Test of Rival Strategies," 50.
148. Shelah and Limor, *Captives in Lebanon*, 57.
149. Harel and Issacharoff, *34 Days*, 84–85.
150. Harel and Issacharoff, *34 Days*; Rapaport, *Friendly Fire*; Shelah and Limor, *Captives in Lebanon*.
151. Winograd, "Final Report."
152. "Israel-Hizbullah Conflict."
153. Shelah and Limor, *Captives in Lebanon*, 89.
154. Ibid.
155. Harel and Issacharoff, *34 Days*, 89.
156. Rapaport, *Friendly Fire*, 271.

157. Ibid.
158. Ibid., 20. See also Harel and Issacharoff, *34 Days*, 76.
159. Rapaport, *Friendly Fire*, 27.
160. Ibid., 18.
161. Ibid., 28.
162. Harel and Issacharoff, *34 Days*, 192.
163. Gil Murciano, "A Matter of Honor: A Review of Israeli Decision Making During the Second Lebanon War" (International Centre for the Study of Radicalisation and Political Violence, London, March 2011), 6, http://icsr.info/wp-content/uploads/2012/10/1304694112ICSR_AtkinPaperSeries_GilMurciano.pdf.
164. Makovsky, "Deterrence and the Burden of Israeli Moderates."
165. Yaakov Katz, "Security and Defense: The Fly on the Spider Web?," *Jerusalem Post*, July 1, 2011.
166. Winograd, "Partial Report," 87.
167. Shelah and Limor, *Captives in Lebanon*, 266.
168. Rapaport, *Friendly Fire*, 259–60; Lowenheim and Heimann, "Revenge in International Politics," 709.
169. Shelah and Limor, *Captives in Lebanon*, 186.
170. Harel and Issacharoff, *Spider Webs*, 191.
171. Rapaport, *Friendly Fire*, 191–93.
172. Byman, *High Price*, 252.
173. As cited in Amir Lupovici, *The Power of Deterrence: Emotions, Identity, and American and Israeli Wars of Resolve* (New York: Cambridge University Press, 2016), 143.
174. Evron, "Deterrence and Its Limitations," 46.
175. Freilich, *Zion's Dilemmas*, 203–4.
176. Winograd, "Final Report."
177. Feldman, "Deterrence and the Israel-Hezbollah War," 287.
178. Sneh, interview.
179. Gabriel Siboni, analyst, interview with author Boaz Atzili, July 2010, Tel Aviv, Israel.
180. "Israel Warns Hizbullah War Would Invite Destruction," *Ynetnews*, October 3, 2008, http://www.ynetnews.com/articles/0,7340,L-3604893,00.html.
181. Jean-Loup Samaan, "The Dahya Concept and Israeli Military Posture vis-à-vis Hezbollah since 2006," *Comparative Strategy* 32, no. 2 (2013): 146–59; Caverley, *Democratic Militarism*, 247.
182. Giora Eiland, "The Third Lebanon War: Target Lebanon," *Strategic Assessment* 11, no. 2 (2008): 9–17; Gabriel Siboni, "War and Victory," *Military and Strategic Affairs* 1, no. 3 (December 2009): 39–49.
183. Amos Yadlin, "How Israel Created Deterrence in the Second Lebanon War," *Ynetnews*, May 22, 2015, http://www.ynetnews.com/articles/0,7340,L-4660200,00.html.
184. Eiland, "The Third Lebanon War," 10.
185. Boaz Atzili, interview with retired senior IDF general, Herzliya, Israel, June 2013.
186. Yadlin, "How Israel Created Deterrence."

187. Daniel Sobelman, "Learning to Deter: Deterrence Failure and Success in the Israel-Hezbollah Conflict, 2006–16," *International Security* 41, no. 3 (Winter 2016): 177.
188. Quoted in ibid.
189. Quoted in ibid., 178.
190. Richard Ned Lebow and Janice Gross Stein, "Rational Deterrence Theory: I Think, Therefore I Deter," *World Politics* 41, no. 2 (1989): 208–24; Robert Jervis, "Deterrence Theory Revisited," *World Politics* 31, no. 2 (1979): 289–324.
191. Sobelman, "Learning to Deter."
192. "6 Killed in Terror Attack on Israeli Tourists in Bulgaria," Israel Ministry of Foreign Affairs, July 18, 2012, http://mfa.gov.il/MFA/ForeignPolicy/Terrorism/Palestinian/Pages/Terror_attack_Israeli_tourists_Bulgaria_18-Jul-2012.aspx; Nicholas Kulish and Eric Schmitt, "Hezbollah Is Blamed for Attack on Israeli Tourists in Bulgaria," *New York Times*, July 19, 2012, http://www.nytimes.com/2012/07/20/world/europe/explosion-on-bulgaria-tour-bus-kills-at-least-five-israelis.html; Reuters, "Israeli Tourist Terror: Seven Killed in Bus Bomb Attack in Bulgaria," *RT*, July 18, 2012, https://www.rt.com/news/israeli-tourists-bus-explosion-498/.
193. "Nasrallah: We Wouldn't Have Snatched Soldiers If We Thought It Would Spark War," *Haaretz*, August 27, 2006, http://www.haaretz.com/news/nasrallah-we-wouldn-t-have-snatched-soldiers-if-we-thought-it-would-spark-war-1.199556; Maoz, *Defending the Holy Land*.
194. Sobelman, "Learning to Deter," 184.
195. Anthony Shadid and Alia Ibrahim, "Bombing Kills Top Figure in Hezbollah," *Washington Post*, February 13, 2008, http://www.washingtonpost.com/wp-dyn/content/article/2008/02/13/AR2008021300494.html.
196. As suggested by Lieberman, *Reconceptualizing Deterrence*, and by Sobelman, "Learning to Deter."
197. See, e.g., Marisa Sullivan, *Hezbollah in Syria*, Middle East Security Report 19 (Washington, D.C.: Institute for the Study of War, April 2014), http://www.understandingwar.org/report/hezbollah-syria; Chafic Choucair, *Hezbollah in Syria: Gains, Losses and Changes* (Mecca: Al Jazeera Centre for Studies, June 1, 2016), http://studies.aljazeera.net/en/reports/2016/06/hezbollah-syria-gains-losses-160601093443171.html.
198. "Israel's Next War With Hezbollah Will Be Worse Than the Last," *Stratfor*, November 23, 2016, https://www.stratfor.com/analysis/israels-next-war-hezbollah-will-be-worse-last.
199. Michael Young, "Hezbollah's Other War," *New York Times Magazine*, August 4, 2006, See http://www.nytimes.com/2006/08/04/magazine/04lebanon.html.
200. Harris, "Lebanon's Roller Coaster Ride," 74.
201. Eyal Zisser, "Hizbollah in Lebanon: Between Tehran and Beirut, Between the Struggle with Israel, and the Struggle for Lebanon," in *Lebanon: Liberation, Conflict, and Crisis*, ed. Barry M. Rubin (New York: Palgrave Macmillan, 2009).
202. Anthony H. Cordsman, *Lessons of the 2006 Israeli-Hezbollah War*, Significant Issues Series (Washington, D.C.: Center for Strategic and International Studies, 2007).

203. Jean-Loup Samaan, *From War to Deterrence? Israel-Hezbollah Conflict since 2006* (Carlisle: Strategic Studies Institute, U.S. Army War College, May 2014), 27–29.
204. Zisser, "Hizbollah in Lebanon."

7. Triadic Coercion Beyond the Arab-Israeli Conflict

1. Sumit Ganguly, *Conflict Unending: India-Pakistan Tensions since 1947* (New York: Columbia University Press, 2001), 15–30.
2. For a thorough review, see Ganguly, *Conflict Unending*.
3. Walter C. Ladwig, "A Cold Start for Hot Wars? The Indian Army's New Limited War Doctrine," *International Security* 32, no. 3 (2007): 159.
4. Stephen H. Cohen and Sunil Dasgupta, *Arming Without Aiming: India's Military Modernization* (Washington, D.C.: Brookings Institution Press, 2010), 1–28.
5. Ibid., 2–10.
6. Zafar Iqbal Cheema, "The Strategic Context of the Kargil Conflict: A Pakistani Perspective," in *Asymmetric Warfare in South Asia*, ed. Peter R. Lavoy (Cambridge: Cambridge University Press, 2009), 41–63.
7. Stephen Tankel, *Storming the World Stage: The Story of Lashkar-e-Taiba* (Oxford: Oxford University Press, 2008), 50.
8. Ibid., 174–76.
9. Victoria Schofield, *Kashmir in Conflict: India, Pakistan and the Unending War* (New York: I. B. Tauris, 2003), 147–51.
10. Paul Staniland, *Networks of Rebellion: Explaining Insurgent Cohesion and Collapse* (Ithaca, N.Y.: Cornell University Press, 2015), 81–84; Tankel, *Storming the World Stage*, 50–51.
11. Staniland, *Networks of Rebellion*, 84–88.
12. Tankel, *Storming the World Stage*, 211–12.
13. Sumit Ganguly and Michael R. Kraig, "The 2001–2002 Indo-Pakistani Crisis: Exposing the Limits of Coercive Diplomacy," *Security Studies* 14, no. 2 (2005): 196; Tankel, *Storming the World Stage*, 183–88, 203–4.
14. Ladwig, "Cold Start for Hot Wars?," 159–60.
15. Cheema, "Strategic Context of the Kargil Conflict"; Ashley J. Tellis, C. Christine Fair, and Jamison Jo Medby, *Limited Conflicts under the Nuclear Umbrella: Indian and Pakistani Lessons from the Kargil Crisis* (Santa Monica, Calif.: RAND Corporation, 2001).
16. Ladwig, "A Cold Start for Hot Wars?," 160; Tankel, *Storming the World Stage*, 62.
17. Patrick Bratton, "Signals and Orchestration: India's Use of Compellence in the 2001–02 Crisis," *Strategic Analysis* 34, no. 4 (2010): 596; Ganguly and Kraig, "The 2001–2002 Indo-Pakistani Crisis," 298.
18. Ladwig, "Cold Start for Hot Wars?," 160–63; Ganguly and Kraig (in "The 2001–2002 Indo-Pakistani Crisis," 297–98) cite only five hundred thousand mobilized troops.
19. Bratton, "Signals and Orchestration," 598.
20. Ganguly and Kraig, "The 2001–2002 Indo-Pakistani Crisis," 303–6.

21. Tankel, *Storming the World Stage*, 66, chap. 6.
22. Quoted in Ganguly and Kraig, "The 2001–2002 Indo-Pakistani Crisis," 306.
23. Bratton, "Signals and Orchestration," 594.
24. Shashank Joshi, "India's Military Instrument: A Doctrine Stillborn," *Journal of Strategic Studies* 36, no. 4 (2013): 514–15; Ladwig, "Cold Start for Hot Wars?," 160–63.
25. Joshi, "India's Military Instrument."
26. Ladwig, "Cold Start for Hot Wars?," 158.
27. Joshi, "India's Military Instrument," 515.
28. Ladwig, "Cold Start for Hot Wars?," 163–67; Joshi, "India's Military Instrument," 515–19.
29. Ladwig, "Cold Start for Hot Wars?," 176, 190; Joshi, "India's Military Instrument," 521; Cohen and Dasgupta, *Arming Without Aiming*, 53.
30. Angela Rabasa et al., *The Lessons of Mumbai* (Santa Monica, Calif.: RAND Corporation, 2009).
31. Nirupama Subramanian, "McCain Warns Pakistan of Indian Air Strikes," *The Hindu*, December 7, 2008, http://www.thehindu.com/todays-paper/McCain-warns-Pakistan-of-Indian-air-strikes/article15356246.ece.
32. Tankel, *Storming the World Stage*, chap. 6.
33. Ravi Agrawal, "Could India and Pakistan Go to War?," CNN, September 29, 2016, http://www.cnn.com/2016/09/21/asia/india-pakistan-kashmir-conflict/.
34. "Kashmir Attack: India Launches Strikes against Militants," *BBC News*, September 30, 2016, http://www.bbc.com/news/world-asia-37504308.
35. David B. Carter, "The Compellence Dilemma: International Disputes with Violent Groups," *International Studies Quarterly*, no. 59 (2015): 461–76.
36. International Institute for Strategic Studies, "Armed Forces Personnel, Total," in *The Military Balance*, World Bank Open Data, accessed March 20, 2017, http://data.worldbank.org/indicator/MS.MIL.TOTL.P1?start=2013.
37. Stockholm International Peace Research Institute (SIPRI), "SIPRI Military Expenditure Database," *SIPRI Databases*, 2016, https://www.sipri.org/databases/milex.
38. Niaz Murtaza, "Over-Burdened Society, Over-Politicised State: Understanding Pakistan's Struggles with Governance," *Asian Journal of Social Science* 40, no. 3 (2012): 321–41; Lawrence Ziring, "Weak State, Failed State, Garrison State," in *South Asia's Weak States: Unpretending Regional Insecurity Predicament*, ed. T. V. Paul (Stanford, Calif.: Stanford University Press, 2010), 170–94.
39. "Prime Ministers," National Assembly of Pakistan, September 30, 2017, http://www.na.gov.pk/en/priminister_list.php.
40. T. V. Paul, "State Capacity and South Asia's Perennial Insecurity Problems," in *South Asia's Weak States: Understanding Regional Insecurity Predicament*, ed. T. V. Paul (Stanford, Calif.: Stanford University Press, 2010), 3–4.
41. Institute for Economics & Peace, *Global Terrorism Index 2015: Measuring and Understanding the Impact of Terrorism* (Sydney: IEP, 2015), http://economicsandpeace.org/wp-content/uploads/2015/11/Global-Terrorism-Index-2015.pdf.

42. National Consortium for the Study of Terrorism and Responses to Terrorism (START), "Global Terrorism Database from 1970 to 2016," 2017, https://www.start.umd.edu/gtd.
43. In 2005 the index was called "Failed States Index." See http://fsi.fundforpeace.org.
44. Tankel, *Storming the World Stage*, 257–69.
45. Rabasa et al., *Lessons of Mumbai*, 15–16.
46. Carter, "Compellence Dilemma," 474.
47. Hamit Bozarslan, "Kurds and the Turkish State," in *Cambridge History of Turkey*, vol. 4, *Turkey in the Modern World* (Cambridge: Cambridge University Press, 2008), 334.
48. Mesut Yegen, "'Prospective Turks' or 'Pseudo-Citizens:' Kurds in Turkey," *Middle East Journal* 63, no. 4 (2009): 600–605.
49. Mustafa Cosar Unal, *Counterterrorism In Turkey: Policy Choices and Policy Effects Toward the Kurdistan Workers' Party (PKK)* (New York: Routledge, 2012), 11–13.
50. Galia Lindenstrauss, "Turkey, the Kurds, and Turkey's Incursion into Iraq: The Effects of Securitization and Desecuritization Processes," in *Nonstate Actors in Interstate Conflicts*, ed. Dan Miodownik and Oren Barak (Philadelphia: University of Pennsylvania Press, 2014), 128, 130.
51. Ibid., 131.
52. Ibid., 133.
53. Quoted in David McDowall, *A Modern History of the Kurds* (London: I. B. Tauris, 2004), 433.
54. Feroz Ahmad, *Making of Modern Turkey* (London: Routledge, 1993), 3–4.
55. Umit Cizre, "Disentangling the Threads of Civil-Military Relations in Turkey: Promises and Perils," *Mediterranean Quarterly* 22, no. 2 (2011): 71.
56. Taner Demirel, "Lessons of Military Regimes and Democracy: The Turkish Case in a Comparative Perspective," *Armed Forces & Society* 31, no. 2 (2005): 245–71; Erik J. Zurcher, *Turkey: A Modern History* (London: I. B. Tauris, 2004).
57. Cengiz Gunes, *The Kurdish National Movement in Turkey* (New York: Routledge, 2012), 104.
58. Nicole Watts, *Activists in Office: Kurdish Politics and Protests* (Seattle: University of Washington Press, 2010), xv.
59. Hamit Bozarslan, "Human Rights and the Kurdish Issue in Turkey: 1984–1999," *Human Rights Review* 3, no. 1 (March 2001): 48; Bilgin Ayata and Deniz Yukseker, "A Belated Awakening: National and International Responses to the Internal Displacement of Kurds in Turkey," *New Perspectives on Turkey* 32 (2005): 5–42.
60. Ali L. Karaosmanoglu, "The Evolution of the National Security Culture and the Military of Turkey," *Journal of International Affairs* 54, no. 1 (Fall 2000): 201–2, 204.
61. Mustafa Aydin, "Determinants of Turkish Foreign Policy: Changing Patterns and Conjunctures During the Cold War," *Middle Eastern Studies* 36, no. 1 (2000): 103.
62. Ibid., 103, 125–26.
63. Sabri Sayari, "Turkish Foreign Policy in the Post-Cold War Era: The Challenges of Multi-Regionalism," *Journal of International Affairs* 54, no. 1 (2000): 169–70.

64. Nimet Beriker-Atiyas, "The Kurdish Conflict in Turkey: Issues, Parties, and Prospects," *Security Dialogue* 28, no. 4 (1997): 441.
65. Sayari, "Turkish Foreign Policy," 169–82; Ian O. Lesser, "Turkey in a Changing Security Environment," *Journal of International Affairs* 54, no. 1 (2000): 183–98.
66. Seban Kardas, "Turkey: Redrawing the Middle East Map or Building Sandcastles?," *Middle East Policy* 17, no. 1 (Spring 2010): 115.
67. Piotr Zaleswki, "How Turkey Went From 'Zero Problems' to Zero Friends," *Foreign Policy*, August 22, 2013, http://foreignpolicy.com/2013/08/22/how-turkey-went-from-zero-problems-to-zero-friends/.
68. Beriker-Atiyas, "Kurdish Conflict in Turkey," 441–42.
69. Christopher Phillips, "Turkey and Syria," in *Turkey's Global Strategy*, ed. Nicholas Kitchen (London: London School of Economics Reports, 2011), 36, http://www.lse.ac.uk/ideas/Assets/Documents/reports/LSE-IDEAS-Turkeys-Global-Strategy.pdf; Hasan Turunc, "Turkey and Iraq," in *Turkey's Global Strategy* (London: London School of Economics Reports, 2011), 40–42; Kemal Kirisci, "The Transformation of Turkish Foreign Policy: The Rise of the Trading State," *New Perspectives on Turkey* 40 (2009): 29–57.
70. Bayram Balci, "The Syrian Dilemma: Turkey's Response to the Crisis," Carnegie Endowment for International Peace, February 10, 2012, http://carnegieendowment.org/2012/02/10/syrian-dilemma-turkey-s-response-to-crisis#.
71. Lesser, "Turkey in a Changing Security Environment," 191.
72. "A New and Bitter Brew in the Middle East," *Economist*, October 8, 1998, http://www.economist.com/node/167759.
73. David Romano, "Turkish and Iranian Efforts to Deter Kurdish Insurgent Attack," in *Deterring Terrorism: Theory and Practice*, ed. Andreas Wenger and Alex Wilner (Stanford, Calif.: Stanford University Press, 2012), 235.
74. Phillips, "Turkey and Syria," 34; Sayari, "Turkish Foreign Policy in the Post–Cold War Era," 171–72; Lesser, "Turkey in a Changing Security Environment," 185, 192.
75. Romano, "Turkish and Iranian Efforts to Deter Kurdish Insurgent Attack," 235; Keren E. Fraiman, "Understanding Weak States and State Sponsors: The Case for Base State Coercion," in *Coercion: The Power to Hurt in International Politics*, ed. Kelly M. Greenhill and Peter Krause (New York: Oxford University Press, 2018), 129–32.
76. Nihat Ali Özcan and Özgür Özdamar, "Uneasy Neighbors: Turkish-Iranian Relations since the 1979 Islamic Revolution," *Middle East Policy* 17, no. 3 (Fall 2010): 106.
77. Elliot Hentov, "Turkey and Iran," in *Turkey's Global Strategy*, ed. Nicholas Kitchen (London: London School of Economics Reports, 2011), 29, http://www.lse.ac.uk/ideas/Assets/Documents/reports/LSE-IDEAS-Turkeys-Global-Strategy.pdf.
78. Robert Olson, "Turkey, Iran and Syria: Triadal Rapprochement," *Kurdish Life* 11 (Summer 1994): 6–7.
79. Özcan and Özdamar, "Uneasy Neighbors," 110–11.
80. Bill Park, "Turkey, the US and the KRG: Moving Parts and the Geopolitical Realities," *Insight Turkey* 14, no. 3 (2012): 118.

81. Daren Butler, "Turkey May Act with Iran against PKK Main Base in Northern Iraq," Al Arabiya News, September 16, 2011, https://www.alarabiya.net/articles/2011/09/16/167211.html.
82. Lesser, "Turkey in a Changing Security Environment," 191.
83. Ibid., 185–86.
84. William Hale, *Turkey, the US and Iraq* (London: Saqi, 2007).
85. Sayari, "Turkish Foreign Policy," 171.
86. Hale, *Turkey, the US and Iraq*.
87. Ibid.
88. Turunc, "Turkey and Iraq," 43; Stephen J. Flanagan and Samuel Brannen, *Turkey's Evolving Dynamics: Strategic Choices for U.S.-Turkey Relations*, U.S.-Turkey Strategic Initiative Final Report (Washington, D.C.: Center for Strategic & International Studies, March 2009), 41.
89. Ertan Efegil, "Turkey's New Approaches toward the PKK, Iraqi Kurds and the Kurdish Question," *Insight Turkey* 10, no. 3 (2008): 59.
90. Ibid., 58–59.
91. Flanagan and Brannen, *Turkey's Evolving Dynamics*, 41.
92. Kirisci, "The Transformation of Turkish Foreign Policy," 30–31; Tom Ruys, "Quo Vadit Jus Ad Bellum?: A Legal Analysis of Turkey's Military Operations Against the PKK in Northern Iraq," *Melbourne Journal of International Law* 9, no. 2 (2008): 334–64.
93. U.S. Department of State, "Agreement Between the United States of America and the Republic of Iraq on the Withdrawal of United States Forces from Iraq and the Organization of Their Activities During Their Temporary Presence in Iraq," November 17, 2008, https://www.state.gov/documents/organization/122074.pdf.
94. Abigail Fielding-Smith, "Turkey Finds a Gateway to Iraq," *Financial Times*, April 14, 2010, https://www.ft.com/content/4e027bc0-47e6-11df-b998-00144feab49a.
95. Park, "Turkey, the US and the KRG," 109.
96. Umit Cizre, "Leadership Gone Awry: Recep Tayyip Erdoğan and Two Turkish Elections," *Middle East Report* 276 (Fall 2015), http://www.merip.org/mer/mer276/leadership-gone-awry.
97. Berkay Mandiraci, "Turkey's PKK Conflict: The Death Toll," International Crisis Group, July 20, 2016, http://blog.crisisgroup.org/europe-central-asia/2016/07/20/turkey-s-pkk-conflict-the-rising-toll/.
98. Ryan Gingeras, "Ottoman Ghosts: Imperial Memories in Turkey and Syria," *Foreign Affairs*, October 6, 2016, https://www.foreignaffairs.com/articles/turkey/2016-10-06/ottoman-ghosts.
99. Fred Haley Lawson, "Syria's Mutating Civil War and Its Impact on Turkey, Iraq and Iran," *International Affairs* 90, no. 6 (2014): 1357.
100. Burak Bekdil, "Turkey: 'Zero Problems with Neighbors'" (Gatestone Institute International Policy Council, April 6, 2015), https://www.gatestoneinstitute.org/5471/turkey-zero-problems-neighbors.

Conclusion

1. Richard Ned Lebow and Janice Gross Stein, "Rational Deterrence Theory: I Think, Therefore I Deter," *World Politics* 41, no. 2 (1989): 224.
2. See, for example, Jack L. Snyder, *The Soviet Strategic Culture: Implications for Limited Nuclear Operations* (Santa Monica, Calif.: RAND Corporation, September 1977), http://www.dtic.mil/dtic/tr/fulltext/u2/a046124.pdf; Colin S. Gray, "National Style in Strategy: The American Example," *International Security* 6, no. 2 (1981): 21–47; Shu Guang Zhang, *Deterrence and Strategic Culture: Chinese-American Confrontations, 1949–1958* (Ithaca, N.Y.: Cornell University Press, 1992).
3. Almog Ben-Zachry, Gili Cohen, and Jacky Coury, "A Rocket from Gaza Fell on Sderot: The IDF Attacked More than Twenty Targets in the North of the Strip," [in Hebrew], *Haaretz*, August 22, 2016.

Bibliography

Abdel-Malek, Anouar. *Egypt: Military Society: The Army Regime, the Left, and Social Change under Nasser.* New York: Random House, 1968.

Abrahms, Max. "What Terrorists Really Want: Terrorist Motives and Counterterrorism Strategy." *International Security* 32, no. 4 (2008): 78–105.

Abu Toameh, Khaled. "Talking at Cross Purposes." *Jerusalem Post*, January 31, 2003.

Adamsky, Dima. *The Culture of Military Innovation: The Impact of Cultural Factors on the Revolution in Military Affairs in Russia, the US, and Israel.* Stanford, Calif.: Stanford University Press, 2010.

———."From Israel with Deterrence: Strategic Culture, Intra-War Coercion and Brute Force." *Security Studies* 26, no. 1 (2017): 157–84.

Adler, Emanuel. "Complex Deterrence in the Asymmetric-Warfare Era." In *Complex Deterrence: Strategy in the Global Age*, edited by James J. Wirtz, Patrick M. Morgan, and T. V. Paul, 85–108. Chicago: University of Chicago Press, 2009.

Adwan, Charles. "Corruption in Reconstruction: The Cost of National Consensus in Post-War Lebanon." Center for International Private Enterprise, Washington, D.C., December 1, 2004.

Agrami, Ashraf al-. "National Unity: The Need to Reconsider." *Al-Ayyam*, January 13, 2003.

Agrawal, Ravi. "Could India and Pakistan Go to War?" CNN, September 29, 2016. http://www.cnn.com/2016/09/21/asia/india-pakistan-kashmir-conflict/.

Ahmad, Feroz. *Making of Modern Turkey.* London: Routledge, 1993.

Ahren, Raphael. "Rabin Formally Opposed a Palestinian State More Than a Year after White House Handshake, Letter from 1994 Shows." *Times of Israel*, December 31, 2012. http://www.timesofisrael.com/rabin-formally-opposed-a-palestinian-state-more-than-a-year-after-white-house-handshake-letter-from-1994-shows/.

Ahronheim, Anna. "Liberman: Ties Between Israel, Arab States, 'More Crucial for Them Than Us.'" *Jerusalem Post*, April 28, 2017. http://www.jpost.com/Magazine/Liberman-Its-not-about-us-and-Gaza-489139.

"Al-Aqsa Commander: No One Can Unilaterally End De-Escalation." *Financial Times*, April 28, 2005.

Alimi, Eitan Y. "Contextualizing Political Terrorism: A Collective Action Perspective for Understanding the Tanzim." *Studies in Conflict & Terrorism* 29, no. 3 (2006): 263–83.

Aljuni, Salem. "The Palestinian Economy and the Second Intifada." *Journal of Palestine Studies* 32, no. 3 (2003): 64–73.

Almog, Doron. "Cumulative Deterrence and the War on Terrorism." *Parameters* 34, no. 4 (2004): 4–19.

Alon, Gideon, and Akiva Eldar. "Opposition Demands Probe of Gilad's 'Erroneous' Evaluations." *Haaretz*, June 11, 2004.

Alon, Hanon. *Countering Palestinian Terrorism in Israel: Toward a Policy Analysis of Countermeasures*. International Security and Arms Control. Santa Monica, Calif.: RAND Corporation, 1980.

Amnesty International. *Amnesty International Report 1996*. London: Amnesty International, January 1996.

———. *Amnesty International Report 1997*. London: Amnesty International, June 1997.

———. *Amnesty International Report 1998*. London: Amnesty International, January 1998.

———. *Amnesty International Report 1999*. London: Amnesty International, June 1999.

———. *Amnesty International Report 2000*. London: Amnesty International, June 2000.

———. *Amnesty International Report 2001*. London: Amnesty International, June 2001.

———. *Amnesty International Report 2005*. London: Amnesty International, January 2006.

———. *Broken Lives—One Year of Intifada: Israel/Occupied Territories/Palestinian Authority*. London: Amnesty International UK, 2001.

Amos, John W. *Palestinian Resistance: Organization of a Nationalist Movement*. New York: Pergamon Press, 1980.

Andoni, Lamis. "Palestinian Islamist Group Signals Shift in Strategy." *Christian Science Monitor*, September 13, 1994.

Arian, Asher. "Israeli Public Opinion on National Security 2001." Memorandum no. 60. Jaffee Center for Strategic Studies, Tel Aviv University, August 2001.

Art, Robert J., and Kelly M. Greenhill. "Coercion: An Analytical Overview." In *Coercion: The Power to Hurt in International Politics*, edited by Kelly M. Greenhill and Peter Krause, 3–32. New York: Oxford University Press, 2018.

Ashton, Nigel J. "Pulling the Strings: King Hussein's Role During the Crisis of 1970 in Jordan." *International History Review* 28, no. 1 (2006): 94–118.

Associated Press. "Mideast War, by the Numbers." *Washington Post*, August 17, 2006. http://www.washingtonpost.com/wp-dyn/content/article/2006/08/17/AR2006081700909.html.

Atzili, Boaz. *Good Fences Bad Neighbors: Border Fixity and International Conflict*. Chicago: University of Chicago Press, 2012.

———. "State Weakness and 'Vacuum of Power' in Lebanon." *Studies in Conflict & Terrorism* 33, no. 8 (2010): 757–82.
Atzili, Boaz, and Wendy Pearlman. "Triadic Deterrence: Coercing Strength, Beaten by Weakness." *Security Studies* 21 (2012): 301–35.
Avi-Hai, Avraham. *Ben Gurion, State Builder: Principles and Pragmatism, 1948–1963*. Jerusalem: Israel Universities Press, 1974.
Ayata, Bilgin, and Deniz Yukseker. "A Belated Awakening: National and International Responses to the Internal Displacement of Kurds in Turkey." *New Perspectives on Turkey* 32 (2005): 5–42.
Aydin, Mustafa. "Determinants of Turkish Foreign Policy: Changing Patterns and Conjunctures During the Cold War." *Middle Eastern Studies* 36, no. 1 (2000): 103–39.
Bailey, Clinton. *Jordan's Palestinian Challenge, 1948–1983: A Political History*. Boulder, Colo.: Westview Press, 1984.
Balci, Bayram. "The Syrian Dilemma: Turkey's Response to the Crisis." Carnegie Endowment for International Peace, February 10, 2012. http://carnegieendowment.org/2012/02/10/syrian-dilemma-turkey-s-response-to-crisis#.
Bar, Shmuel. "Deterrence of Palestinian Terrorism." In *Deterring Terrorism: Theory and Practice*, edited by Andreas Wenger and Alex Wilner, 205–27. Stanford, Calif.: Stanford University Press, 2012.
———. "Deterring Terrorists: What Israel Has Learned." *Policy Review*, no. 149 (2008): 29.
Barak, Oren. *The Lebanese Army: A National Institution in a Divided Society*. Albany: State University of New York Press, 2009.
———. "Towards a Representative Military? The Transformation of the Lebanese Officer Corps since 1945." *Middle East Journal* 60, no. 1 (2006): 75–93.
Barari, Hassan A., and Hahi A. M. Akho-Rashida. "The Pragmatic and the Radical: Syria and Iran and War by Proxy." In *Israel and Hizbollah: An Asymmetric Conflict in Historical and Comparative Perspective*, edited by Clive Jones and Sergio Catignani, 109–23. New York: Routledge, 2010.
Barghouti, Mustafa. "Posteuphoria in Palestine." *Journal of Palestine Studies* 25, no. 4 (1996): 87–96.
Bar-Haim, Sara. "The Palestine Liberation Army: Stooge or Actor?" In *The Palestinians and the Middle East Conflict: Studies in Their History, Sociology and Politics*, edited by Gabriel Ben-Dor, 173–92. Ramat Gan: Turtledove Publishing, 1978.
Bar-Joseph, Uri. "Introduction." In *Israel's National Security Towards the 21st Century*, edited by Uri Bar-Joseph, 1–12. London: Frank Cass, 2001.
———, ed. *Israel's National Security Towards the 21st Century*. London: Frank Cass, 2001.
———. "Variations on a Theme: The Conceptualization of Deterrence in Israeli Strategic Thinking." *Security Studies* 7, no. 3 (March 1, 1998): 145–81.
Barnett, Michael N. *Confronting the Costs of War: Military Power, State, and Society in Egypt and Israel*. Princeton, N.J.: Princeton University Press, 1992.
Bar-On, Mordechai. *The Gates of Gaza: Israel's Road to Suez and Back, 1955–1957*. New York: St. Martin's Press, 1995.
———. *Moshe Dayan: Israel's Controversial Hero*. New Haven, Conn.: Yale University Press, 2012.

Bar-Siman-Tov, Yaacov. *Linkage Politics in the Middle East: Syria Between Domestic and External Conflict, 1961–1970*. Boulder, Colo.: Westview Press, 1983.

Batatu, Hanna. *Syria's Peasantry, the Descendants of Its Lesser Rural Notables, and Their Politics*. Princeton, N.J.: Princeton University Press, 1999.

Beattie, Kirk J. *Egypt During the Nasser Years: Ideology, Politics, and Civil Society*. Boulder, Colo.: Westview Press, 1994.

Beaumont, Peter. "Rockets Fired into Southern Israel from Egypt's Sinai." *Guardian*, February 20, 2017.

Bekdil, Burak. "Turkey: 'Zero Problems with Neighbors.'" Gatestone Institute International Policy Council, April 6, 2015. https://www.gatestoneinstitute.org/5471/turkey-zero-problems-neighbors.

Ben Meir, Yehuda. *Civil-Military Relations in Israel*. New York: Columbia University Press, 1995.

Ben-Horin, Yoav, and Barry Posen. *Israel's Strategic Doctrine*. Santa Monica, Calif.: RAND Corporation, 1981. http://www.rand.org/pubs/reports/R2845.html.

Benn, Aluf. "The Selling of the Summit." *Haaretz*, July 27, 2001.

Bennet, James. "A People Adrift, Part I: In Chaos, Palestinians Struggle for a Way Out." *New York Times*, July 15, 2004.

Ben-Tzur, Abraham, ed. "The Syrian Ba'ath Party and Israel: Documents from the Internal Party Publications." In *Explicit Proof of Artificial Creation of Tension along the Israeli Border by Syrian Authorities and the Inter-Arab Command for Purely Inner Syrian Purposes*. Givat Haviva: Center for Arabic and Afro-Asian Studies, 1968.

Ben-Zachry, Almog, Gili Cohen, and Jacky Coury. "A Rocket from Gaza Fell on Sderot: The IDF Attacked More Than Twenty Targets in the North of the Strip." [In Hebrew]. *Haaretz*, August 22, 2016.

Berger, Thomas. "Norms, Identity, and National Security in Germany and Japan." In *The Culture of National Security: Norms and Identity in World Politics*, edited by Peter J. Katzenstein, 317–56. New York: Columbia University Press, 1996.

Beriker-Atiyas, Nimet. "The Kurdish Conflict in Turkey: Issues, Parties, and Prospects." *Security Dialogue* 28, no. 4 (1997): 439–52.

Betts, Richard K. "The Soft Underbelly of American Primacy: Tactical Advantages of Terror." *Political Science Quarterly* 117, no. 1 (2002): 19–36.

Bigman, Akiva. "Bogie Yaalon's Post-Modern IDF." *MIDA*, October 12, 2014. http://mida.org.il/2014/10/12/bogie-yaalons-post-modern-idf/.

Binder, Leonard, ed. *Politics in Lebanon*. New York: Wiley, 1966.

Bishara, Azmi. "Beyond Belief." *Al-Ahram Weekly*, July 25–31, 2002. http://www.fikrwanaqd.net/site/topics/article.asp?cu_no=1&item_no=331&version=1&template_id=273&parent_id=29.

Black, Ian. "'Israeli Attack' on Sudanese Arms Factory Offers Glimpse of Secret War." *Guardian*, October 25, 2012. https://www.theguardian.com/world/2012/oct/25/israeli-sudanese-factory-secret-war.

Blanford, Nicholas. *Killing Mr. Lebanon: The Assassination of Rafik Hariri and Its Impact on the Middle East*. London: I. B. Tauris, 2006.

Blechman, Barry M. "The Consequences of the Israeli Reprisals: An Assessment." PhD diss., Georgetown University, 1971.

"Blind Restraint." *Jerusalem Post*, November 15, 2000.

Bluhm, Michael. "Finance Ministry Puts Public Debt at $42 Billion." *Daily Star*, January 31, 2008.

Booth, William, and Hazem Balousha. "Amnesty International: Hamas Guilty of Torture, Summary Executions." *Washington Post*, May 27, 2015.

Bozarslan, Hamit. "Human Rights and the Kurdish Issue in Turkey: 1984–1999." *Human Rights Review* 3, no. 1 (March 2001): 45–54.

———. "Kurds and the Turkish State." In *Cambridge History of Turkey*. Vol. 4, *Turkey in the Modern World* 4, 333–56. Cambridge: Cambridge University Press, 2008.

Braizat, Musa S. *The Jordanian-Palestinian Relationship: The Bankruptcy of the Confederal Idea*. London: British Academic Press, 1998.

Bratton, Patrick. "Signals and Orchestration: India's Use of Compellence in the 2001–02 Crisis." *Strategic Analysis* 34, no. 4 (2010): 594–610.

Brodie, Bernard. "Implications for Military Policy." In *The Absolute Weapon: Atomic Power and World Order*, edited by Bernard Brodie, 21–69. New York: Harcourt, Brace and Company, 1946.

Brom, Shlomo. "The Withdrawal from Southern Lebanon: One Year Later." *Strategic Assessment* 4, no. 2 (August 2001). http://www.inss.org.il/publication/the-withdrawal-from-southern-lebanon-one-year-later/.

Brown, David. *The State and Ethnic Politics in Southeast Asia*. New York: Routledge, 1994.

Brown, Nathan J. "The Hamas-Fatah Conflict: Shallow but Wide." *Fletcher Forum of World Affairs* 34, no. 2 (Summer 2010): 35–49.

Brownlee, Jason. *Authoritarianism in an Age of Democratization*. New York: Cambridge University Press, 2007.

Brynen, Rex. "The Neopatrimonial Dimension of Palestinian Politics." *Journal of Palestine Studies* 25, no. 1 (1995): 23–36.

Bucaille, Laetitia. *Gaza: The Violence of Peace*. [In French]. Paris: Presses de Science Po, 1998.

Burgrová, Helena. "The Security Question in the Post-Mubarak Egypt: The Security Void in Sinai." *Obrana a Strategie*, no. 1 (2014): 65–75. http://www.obranaastrategie.cz/cs/aktualni-cislo-1-2014/clanky/the-security-question-in-the-post-mubarak-egypt.html#.WtTv4NPwaqA.

Burns, Eedson Louis Millard (E.L.M.). *Between Arab and Israeli*. London: G. G. Harrap, 1962.

Butler, Daren. "Turkey May Act with Iran Against PKK Main Base in Northern Iraq." Al Arabiya News. September 16, 2011. https://www.alarabiya.net/articles/2011/09/16/167211.html.

Byman, Daniel. "Curious Victory: Explaining Israel's Suppression of the Second Intifada." Terrorism and Political Violence 24, no. 5 (2012): 825–52.

———. *Deadly Connections: States That Sponsor Terrorism*. Cambridge: Cambridge University Press, 2005.

———. "Friends Like These: Counterinsurgency and the War on Terrorism." *International Security* 31, no. 2 (2006): 79–115.

———. *A High Price: The Triumphs and Failures of Israeli Counterterrorism*. Oxford: Oxford University Press, 2011.

Byman, Daniel, and Khaled Elgindy. "The Deepening Chaos in Sinai." *National Interest* 127 (October 2013): 43–55.
Cammett, Melani Claire. *Compassionate Communalism: Welfare and Sectarianism in Lebanon.* Ithaca, N.Y.: Cornell University Press, 2014.
Carmi, Na'ama. "Oslo: Before and after: The Status of Human Rights in the Occupied Territories." Information Sheet. Jerusalem: B'Tselem, May 1999.
Carter, David B. "The Compellence Dilemma: International Disputes with Violent Groups." *International Studies Quarterly*, no. 59 (2015): 461–76.
Caspit, Ben. "The Army Will Decide and Approve." *Maariv*, September 13, 2002. Foreign Broadcast Information Service (FBIS) Daily Reports.
——. "Israel Is Not a Country with an Army, but an Army with an Attached Country." *Maariv*, September 6, 2002. FBIS Daily Reports.
——. "Israel-Egypt Anti-Terrorism Cooperation at Zenith." Al-Monitor, May 23, 2014. http://www.al-monitor.com/pulse/originals/2014/05/israel-egypt-security-cooperation-netanyahu-livni-nuclear.html.
Catignani, Sergio. "Israeli Counter-Insurgency Strategy and the Quest for Security in the Israeli-Lebanese Conflict Arena." In *Israel and Hizbollah: An Asymmetric Conflict in Historical and Comparative Perspective*, edited by Clive Jones and Sergio Catignani, 76–88. New York: Routledge, 2010.
——. "The Strategic Impasse in Low-Intensity Conflicts: The Gap Between Israeli Counter-Insurgency Strategy and Tactics During the Al-Aqsa Intifada." *Journal of Strategic Studies* 28, no. 1 (2005): 57–75.
Caverley, Jonathan D. *Democratic Militarism: Voting, Wealth, and War.* Cambridge: Cambridge University Press, 2014.
Center for Palestine Research and Studies. "Public Opinion Poll No. 22," March 29, 1996, http://www.pcpsr.org/sites/default/files/cprs%20poll%2022.pdf.
Center of the Storm: A Case Study of Human Rights Abuses in Hebron District. New York: Human Rights Watch, April 1, 2001.
Cheema, Zafar Iqbal. "The Strategic Context of the Kargil Conflict: A Pakistani Perspective." In *Asymmetric Warfare in South Asia*, edited by Peter R. Lavoy, 41–63. Cambridge: Cambridge University Press, 2009.
Choucair, Chafic. *Hezbollah in Syria: Gains, Losses and Changes.* Mecca: Al Jazeera Centre for Studies, June 1, 2016. http://studies.aljazeera.net/en/reports/2016/06/hezbollah-syria-gains-losses-160601093443171.html.
"Chronology." *Journal of Palestine Studies* 30, no. 2 (Winter 2001).
"Chronology: 16 May–15 August 1994." *Journal of Palestine Studies* 24, no. 1 (1994): 152–74.
Civilian Pawns: Laws of War Violations and the Use of Weapons on the Israeli-Lebanese Border. New York: Human Rights Watch, May 1996.
Cizre, Umit. "Disentangling the Threads of Civil-Military Relations in Turkey: Promises and Perils." *Mediterranean Quarterly* 22, no. 2 (2011): 57–75.
——. "Leadership Gone Awry: Recep Tayyip Erdoğan and Two Turkish Elections." *Middle East Report* 276 (Fall 2015). http://www.merip.org/mer/mer276/leadership-gone-awry.

Clarke, Colin P. "How Salafism's Rise Threatens Gaza: What It Means for Hamas and Israel." *Foreign Affairs*, October 11, 2017. https://www.foreignaffairs.com/articles/israel/2017-10-11/how-salafisms-rise-threatens-gaza.

Cleveland, William L. *A History of the Middle East*. Boulder, Colo.: Westview Press, 1994.

"Clinton Telephones His 'Bridging Proposals' to Barak and Arafat." *Mideast Mirror*, November 15, 2000.

Cobban, Helena. *The Palestinian Liberation Organisation: People, Power, and Politics*. Cambridge: Cambridge University Press, 1984.

Cohen, Eliot A., Michael Eisenstadt, and Andrew J. Bacevich. *Knives, Tanks, and Missiles: Israel's Security Revolution*. Washington, D.C.: Washington Institute for Near East Policy, 1988.

Cohen, Gili, and Reuters. "Defense Minister: Sinai Militants Will Strike Again, but Iron Dome Will Keep South Israel Safe." *Haaretz*, August 13, 2013. http://www.haaretz.com/israel-news/.premium-1.541259.

Cohen, Stephen H., and Sunil Dasgupta. *Arming Without Aiming: India's Military Modernization*. Washington, D.C.: Brookings Institution Press, 2010.

Cohen, Stuart A. *Israel and Its Army: From Cohesion to Confusion*. London: Routledge, 2008.

Cook, Steven A. *Ruling but Not Governing: The Military and Political Development in Egypt, Algeria, and Turkey*. Baltimore, Md.: Johns Hopkins University Press, 2007.

Cordsman, Anthony H. *Lessons of the 2006 Israeli-Hezbollah War*. Significant Issues Series. Washington, D.C.: Center for Strategic and International Studies, 2007.

Coser, Lewis A. *The Functions of Social Conflict*. Glencoe, Ill.: Free Press, 1956.

Cox, Gary W., and Kenneth A. Shepsle. "Majority Cycling and Agenda Manipulation: Richard McKelvey's Contributions and Legacy." In *Positive Changes in Political Science: The Legacy of Richard McKelvey's Most Influential Writings*, edited by John H. Aldrich, James E. Alt, and Arthur Lupia, 19–40. Ann Arbor: University of Michigan Press, 2007.

Craig, Dylan. "Developing a Comparative Perspective on the Use of Nonstates in War." *African Security* 4, no. 3 (2011): 171–94.

Cramer, Holly, Tim Harper, Samantha Moog, and Eric Spioch. "Special Feature: Terrorism in Sinai." Middle East Institute, n.d. http://www.mei.edu/sinai-terrorism.

Crenshaw, Martha. "Coercive Diplomacy and the Response to Terrorism." In *The United States and Coercive Diplomacy*, edited by Robert Art and Patrick Cronin, 314–35. Washington, D.C.: U.S. Institute of Peace Press, 2003.

Dan, Uri. "Know Thine Enemy." *Jerusalem Post*, November 9, 2000.

Dann, Uriel. *King Hussein and the Challenge of Arab Radicalism: Jordan, 1955–1967*. New York: Oxford University Press, 1989.

David, Steven R. "Explaining Third World Alignment." *World Politics* 43, no. 2 (1991): 233–56.

Davis, Paul K., and Brian M. Jenkins. *Deterrence & Influence in Counterterrorism: A Component in the War on Al Qaeda*. Santa Monica, Calif.: RAND, 2002. http://www.dtic.mil/dtic/tr/fulltext/u2/a409007.pdf.

Dawisha, A. I. *Egypt in the Arab World: The Elements of Foreign Policy*. New York: John Wiley, 1976.

Day, Arthur R. *East Bank/West Bank: Jordan and the Prospects for Peace*. New York: Council on Foreign Relations, 1986.

"Dayan Comment." Jerusalem Domestic Service, December 30, 1968. In Reports regarding raid on Beirut Airport, Israel, H5. FBIS Daily Reports.

Dayan, Moshe. *Diary of the Sinai Campaign*. New York: Harper & Row, 1966.

———. "Military Operations in Peacetime." [In Hebrew]. *Maarachot* 118–19 (1959).

Deeb, Lara. *An Enchanted Modern: Gender and Public Piety in Shi'i Lebanon*. Princeton, N.J.: Princeton University Press, 2006.

Dekmejian, R. Hrair. *Egypt under Nasir: A Study in Political Dynamics*. Albany: State University of New York Press, 1971.

Demirel, Taner. "Lessons of Military Regimes and Democracy: The Turkish Case in a Comparative Perspective." *Armed Forces & Society* 31, no. 2 (2005): 245–71.

Dessouki, Ali E. Hillal, and Adel al-Labban. "Arms Race, Defense Expenditures and Development: The Egyptian Case 1952–1973." In *The Conflict with Israel in Arab Politics and Society*, edited by Ian Lustick, 115–27. New York: Garland, 1994.

Devenport, Mark. "Feelings Run High at the UN." *BBC News*, October 4, 2000. http://news.bbc.co.uk/2/hi/middle_east/955223.stm.

Devlin, John F. "The Baath Party: Rise and Metamorphosis." *American Historical Review* 96, no. 5 (1991): 1396–1407.

Dib, Kamal. *Warlords and Merchants: The Lebanese Business and Political Establishment*. Reading, UK: Ithaca Press, 2004.

Dishon, Daniel, ed. *Middle East Record*. Vol. 4, *1968*. Jerusalem: Israel Universities Press, 1973.

———, ed. *Middle East Record*. Vol. 5, *1969–1970*. Jerusalem: Israel Universities Press, 1977.

Diwan, Ishac, and Radwan A. Shaban, eds. *Development under Adversity: The Palestinian Economy in Transition*. Washington, D.C.: World Bank and Palestine Economic Policy Research Institute, 1999.

Dowty, Alan. *Israel/Palestine*. 3rd ed. Cambridge: Polity, 2012.

Drucker, Raviv, and Ofer Shelah. *Boomerang: The Failure of Leadership in the Second Intifada* [In Hebrew]. Jerusalem: Keter, 2005.

Drysdale, Alasdair, and Raymond A. Hinnebusch. *Syria and the Middle East Peace Process*. New York: Council of Foreign Relations, 1991.

Dugan, Laura, and Erica Chenoweth. "Moving Beyond Deterrence: The Effectiveness of Raising the Expected Utility of Abstaining from Terrorism in Israel." *American Sociological Review* 77, no. 4 (2012): 597–624.

Efegil, Ertan. "Turkey's New Approaches Toward the PKK, Iraqi Kurds and the Kurdish Question." *Insight Turkey* 10, no. 3 (2008): 53–73.

Eglash, Ruth. "As ISIS Roils Neighboring Sinai, Israel Keeps This Border Highway Empty." *Washington Post*, November 14, 2016.

"Egypt Declares State of Emergency in Sinai." *Al Jazeera*, October 25, 2014. http://www.aljazeera.com/news/middleeast/2014/10/egypt-declares-state-emergency-sinai-2014102422836500878.html.

"Egypt: Roadmap to Repression: No End in Sight to Human Rights Violations." Amnesty International, January 23, 2014. https://www.amnesty.org/en/documents/MDE12/005/2014/en/.

"Egypt Security Watch" (Infographic). Tahrir Institute for Middle East Policy, November 16, 2015. http://timep.org/esw/infographics/.

"Egyptians Tear Down Israeli Flag as Hundreds Storm Cairo Embassy." *Haaretz*, September 9, 2011. http://www.haaretz.com/israel-news/egyptians-tear-down-israeli-flag-as-hundreds-storm-cairo-embassy-1.383568.

"Egypt's Lawless Peninsula." *Al Jazeera*, August 14, 2013. http://www.aljazeera.com/programmes/insidestory/2013/08/20138146027683120.html.

"Egypt's Security: Threat and Response." Tahrir Institute for Middle East Policy, October 27, 2014. http://timep.org/commentary/egypts-security-threat-response/.

Eiland, Giora. "The Third Lebanon War: Target Lebanon." *Strategic Assessment* 11, no. 2 (2008): 9–17.

Eldar, Akiva. "Military Intelligence Presented Erroneous Assumption on Palestinians." *Haaretz*, June 10, 2004.

El-Din, Amr Nasr. "And Then There Was Sinai." Carnegie Endowment for International Peace, July 11, 2013. http://carnegieendowment.org/sada/52366.

El-Hokayem, Emile. "Hizballah and Syria: Outgrowing the Proxy Relationships." *Washington Quarterly* 30, no. 2 (2007): 35–52.

El-Husseini, Rola. *Pax Syriana: Elite Politics in Postwar Lebanon.* Syracuse, N.Y.: Syracuse University Press, 2012.

El-Khazen, Farid. *The Breakdown of the State in Lebanon, 1967–1976.* Cambridge, Mass.: Harvard University Press, 2000.

Elran, Meir. "The Civilian Front in the Second Lebanon War." In *The Second Lebanon War: Strategic Perspectives*, edited by Meir Elran and Shlomo Brom, 101–18. Tel Aviv: Institute for National Security Studies, 2007.

Elster, Jon. *Alchemies of the Mind: Rationality and the Emotions.* New York: Cambridge University Press, 1999.

Enderlin, Charles. *Shattered Dreams: The Failure of the Peace Process in the Middle East, 1995–2002.* New York: Other Press, 2003.

Erased In A Moment: Suicide Bombing Attacks Against Israeli Civilians. New York: Human Rights Watch, October 2002.

"Eshkol Addresses Knesset in Beirut Operation." Jerusalem Domestic Service, December 31, 1968. FBIS Daily Reports.

"Eshkol Statement." Jerusalem Domestic Service, December 29, 1968. In Reports regarding raid on Beirut Airport, Israel, H3. FBIS Daily Reports.

Evangelista, Matthew. *Innovation and the Arms Race: How the United States and the Soviet Union Develop New Military Technologies.* Ithaca, N.Y.: Cornell University Press, 1988.

Evron, Yair. "Deterrence and Its Limitations." In *The Second Lebanese War: Strategic Aspects*, edited by Shlomo Brom and Meir Elran, 35–49. Tel Aviv: Institute for National Security Studies, 2007.

"Excessive Force: Human Rights Violations during IDF Actions in Area A." Jerusalem: B'Tselem, December 2001. https://www.btselem.org/download/200112_excessive_force_eng.pdf.

"Factbox: Key Violent Incidents in Sinai since 2004." *Egypt Independent*, May 21, 2013. http://www.egyptindependent.com/news/factbox-key-violent-incidents-sinai-2004.

Faour, Muhammad A. "Religion, Demography, and Politics in Lebanon." *Middle Eastern Studies* 43, no. 6 (2007): 909–21.

Farsakh, Leila. "Under Siege: Closure, Separation and the Palestinian Economy." *Middle East Report* 217 (Winter 2000): 22–25.

"Fatalities Before Operation 'Cast Lead.'" B'Tselem, n.d. http://www.btselem.org/statistics/fatalities/before-cast-lead/by-date-of-event.

"Fateh Al-Tanzim Leader in West Bank Marwan Al-Barghuthi Interviewed on Intifadah." *Al-Majallah*, October 29, 2000. FBIS Daily Reports.

"Fateh Can Be Rescued from Itself." *Mideast Mirror*, October 25, 2004.

Fearon, James D., and David D. Laitin. "Ethnicity, Insurgency, and Civil War." *American Political Science Review* 97, no. 1 (2003): 75–90.

Feldman, Ilana. *Governing Gaza: Bureaucracy, Authority, and the Work of Rule, 1917–1967*. Durham, N.C.: Duke University Press, 2008.

———. *Police Encounters: Security and Surveillance in Gaza under Egyptian Rule*. Stanford, Calif.: Stanford University Press, 2015.

Feldman, Shai. "Deterrence and the Israel-Hezbollah War—Summer 2006." In *Deterrence in the Twenty-First Century: Proceedings*, edited by Anthony C. Cain, 279–90. Maxwell AFB, Ala.: Air University Press, 2010.

Fielding-Smith, Abigail. "Turkey Finds a Gateway to Iraq." *Financial Times*, April 14, 2010. https://www.ft.com/content/4e027bc0-47e6-11df-b998-00144feab49a.

Filiu, Jean-Pierre, and John King. *Gaza: A History*. New York: Oxford University Press, 2014.

Fisher-Ilan, Allyn. "Israel Shoots down Rocket Targeting Resort City Eilat." Reuters, August 12, 2013.

Flanagan, Stephen J., and Samuel Brannen. *Turkey's Evolving Dynamics: Strategic Choices for U.S.-Turkey Relations*. U.S.-Turkey Strategic Initiative Final Report. Washington, D.C.: Center for Strategic & International Studies, March 2009.

"For the Record: Interview with Yezid Sayigh." *Palestine Report*, March 7, 2001.

Fraiman, Keren E. "Understanding Weak States and State Sponsors: The Case for Base State Coercion." In *Coercion: The Power to Hurt in International Politics*, edited by Kelly M. Greenhill and Peter Krause, 117–37. New York: Oxford University Press, 2018.

Freedman, Lawrence. *Deterrence*. Cambridge: Polity Press, 2004.

Freilich, Charles D. *Zion's Dilemmas: How Israel Makes National Security Policy*. Ithaca, N.Y.: Cornell University Press, 2012.

Friedman, Thomas L. "Foreign Affairs; Arafat's War." *New York Times*, October 13, 2000.

Fruchter-Ronen, Iris. "Black September: The 1970–71 Events and Their Impact on the Formation of Jordanian National Identity." *Civil Wars* 10, no. 3 (2008): 244–60.

Fuller, Graham E., and Rend Rahim Francke. *The Arab Shi'a: The Forgotten Muslims*. Basingstoke: St. Martin's Press, 1999.

Gandolfo, Luisa. *Palestinians in Jordan: The Politics of Identity*. New York: I. B. Tauris, 2012.

Ganguly, Sumit. *Conflict Unending: India-Pakistan Tensions since 1947*. New York: Columbia University Press, 2001.

Ganguly, Sumit, and Michael R. Kraig. "The 2001–2002 Indo-Pakistani Crisis: Exposing the Limits of Coercive Diplomacy." *Security Studies* 14, no. 2 (2005): 290–324.

Ganor, Boaz. *The Counter-Terrorism Puzzle: A Guide for Decision Makers*. New Brunswick, N.J.: Transaction Publishers, 2005.

——. "Israel, Hamas, and Fatah." In *Democracy and Counterterrorism: Lessons from the Past*, edited by Robert J. Art and Louise Richardson, 261–304. Washington, D.C.: U.S. Institute of Peace Press, 2007.

Gaspard, Toufic K. *A Political Economy of Lebanon, 1948–2002: The Limits of Laissez-Faire*. Leiden: Brill, 2004.

Gates, Carolyn. *The Merchant Republic of Lebanon: Rise of an Open Economy*. London: I. B. Tauris, 1998.

Gebara, Khalil. "Reconstruction Survey: The Political Economy of Corruption in Post-War Lebanon." Beirut: Lebanese Transparency Association, 2007.

Gellman, Barton. "If It's Lights Out for Israeli Synagogue, Beirut Must Go Dark Too." *Washington Post*, April 15, 1996.

——. "Raids Draw Wide Praise In Israel; Lebanon Operation Boosts Peres' Image." *Washington Post*, April 14, 1996.

George, Alexander. "The Need for Influence Theory and Actor-Specific Behavioral Models of Adversaries." *Comparative Strategy* 22, no. 5 (2003): 463–87.

George, Alexander L., and Richard Smoke. *Deterrence in American Foreign Policy: Theory and Practice*. New York: Columbia University Press, 1974.

Geukjian, Ohannes. "Political Instability and Conflict after the Syrian Withdrawal from Lebanon." *Middle East Journal* 68, no. 4 (2014): 521–45.

Gibler, Douglas M. "Outside-In: The Effects of External Threat on State Centralization." *Journal of Conflict Resolution* 54, no. 4 (August 2010): 519–42.

Gilbert, Nina. "Mofaz Warns of Conflict Following Summit Failure." *Jerusalem Post*, July 26, 2000.

Ginbar, Yuval. "Routine Torture: Interrogation Methods of the General Security Service." Jerusalem, B'Tselem, February 1998. http://www.btselem.org/publications/summaries/199802_routine_torture.

Gingeras, Ryan. "Ottoman Ghosts: Imperial Memories in Turkey and Syria." *Foreign Affairs*, October 6, 2016. https://www.foreignaffairs.com/articles/turkey/2016-10-06/ottoman-ghosts.

Golani, Moti. *Israel in Search of a War: The Sinai Campaign, 1955–1956*. Brighton: Sussex Academic Press, 1998.

Gold, Zack. "Egypt's War on Terrorism." Carnegie Endowment for International Peace, May 22, 2014. http://carnegieendowment.org/sada/?fa=55670.

——. "Security in the Sinai: Present and Future." ICCT Research Paper, The Hague, International Centre for Counter-Terrorism, March 2014. http://www.icct.nl/download/file/ICCT-Gold-Security-In-The-Sinai-March-2014.pdf.

———. "Sinai Security: Opportunities for Unlikely Cooperation Among Egypt, Israel, and Hamas." Saban Center Analysis Paper, no. 30, Brookings Institution, Washington, D.C., , 2013.

"Golda Meir's Knesset Remarks." Jerusalem Domestic Service, April 10, 1973. In Reportage on Beirut Attack Continues, Israel, H1. FBIS Daily Reports.

Goldenberg, Suzanne. "Barak Rushes to Blame Unyielding Arafat." *Guardian*, July 26, 2000.

Gray, Colin S. *Modern Strategy*. Oxford: Oxford University Press, 1999.

———. "National Style in Strategy: The American Example." *International Security* 6, no. 2 (1981): 21–47.

———. "Out of the Wilderness: Prime Time for Strategic Culture." *Comparative Strategy* 26, no. 1 (2007): 1–20.

"Great Majority: Apply More Power; Rise to Netanyahu." *Hatzofe*, October 13, 2000.

Greenway, H.D.S. "Israel's Aim: A Buffer Zone Free of Palestinians." *Washington Post*, March 16, 1978.

Grynkewich, Alexus G. "Welfare as Warfare: How Violent Non-State Groups Use Social Services to Attack the State." *Studies in Conflict & Terrorism* 31, no. 4 (2008): 350–70.

Gunes, Cengiz. *The Kurdish National Movement in Turkey*. New York: Routledge, 2012.

Gunning, Jeroen. *Hamas in Politics: Democracy, Religion, Violence*. New York: Columbia University Press, 2008.

———. "Peace with Hamas? The Transforming Potential of Political Participation." *International Affairs* 80, no. 2 (2004): 233–55.

Haddad, Bassam. *Business Networks in Syria: The Political Economy of Authoritarianism*. Stanford, Calif.: Stanford University Press, 2012.

Haddad, Simon. "The Origins of Popular Support for Lebanon's Hezbollah." *Studies in Conflict & Terrorism* 29, no. 1 (2006): 21–34.

Haddad, Toufic. "Overcoming the Culture of Petitions: Critiquing the Role and Influence of Palestinian 'Secular, National, Democratic' Forces." *Between the Lines* 11, no. 14 (March 2002): 30–36.

Hafez, Mohammed. "Palestinian Violent Events Database." Monterey, Calif.: Naval Postgraduate School, 2004–2006.

Hale, William. *Turkey, the US and Iraq*. London: Saqi, 2007.

Hamad, Ghazi A. "The Islamist Catch-22." *Palestine Report*, December 13, 2000.

———. "The Relationship Between Hamas and the Palestinian National Authority (PNA): The Conflictual Past and the Unknown Future." In *Palestinian Perspectives*, edited by Wolfgang Freund, 175–202. Frankfurt am Main: Peter Lang, 1999.

Hanf, Theodor, and Nawaf Salam, eds. *Lebanon in Limbo: Postwar Society and State in an Uncertain Regional Environment*. Baden-Baden: Nomos, 2003.

Harakabi, Yehoshafat. *Fedayeen Action and Arab Strategy*. Adelphi Papers, no. 53 London: Institute for Strategic Studies, December 1968.

Harb, Ashgan. "Gas Pipeline in Sinai Bombed for 15th Time since Revolution Started." *Egypt Independent*, October 4, 2015. http://www.egyptindependent.com/news/gas-pipeline-sinai-bombed-15th-time-revolution-started.

Harb, Mona, and Reinoud Leenders. "Know Thy Enemy: Hizbullah, 'Terrorism' and the Politics of Perception." *Third World Quarterly* 26, no. 1 (2005): 173–97.

Harel, Amos. "Not Mutual Trust, Just Interests." *Haaretz*, April 28, 2000.

Harel, Amos, and Avi Issacharoff. "Israel-Sinai Border Attack Thwarted, but Ominous Signs Loom Ahead." *Haaretz*, August 6, 2012. http://www.haaretz.com/blogs/east-side-story/israel-sinai-border-attack-thwarted-but-ominous-signs-loom-ahead-1.456350.

———. *The Seventh War*. [In Hebrew]. Tel Aviv: Miskal, 2004.

———. *Spider Webs*. [In Hebrew]. Tel Aviv: Miskal, 2008.

———. *34 Days: Israel, Hezbollah, and the War in Lebanon*. New York: Palgrave Macmillan, 2008.

Harik, Judith Palmer. *Hezbollah: The Changing Face of Terrorism*. New York: I. B. Tauris, 2004.

Harman, Danna. "Barak Warns Syria, Lebanon." *Jerusalem Post*, May 25, 2000.

Harris, William. "Lebanon's Roller Coaster Ride." In *Lebanon: Liberation, Conflict, and Crisis*, edited by Barry M. Rubin, 63–82. New York: Palgrave Macmillan, 2009.

Hass, Amira. "Don't Shoot till You Can See They're over the Age of 12." *Haaretz*, November 20, 2000.

———. *Drinking the Sea at Gaza: Days and Nights in a Land under Siege*. Translated by Elana Wesley and Maxine Kaufman-Lacusta. New York: Henry Holt, 1999.

———. "Gaza Workers and the Palestinian Authority." *Middle East Report* 194 (August 1995): 25–26.

———. "Israel's Closure Policy: An Ineffective Strategy of Containment and Repression." *Journal of Palestine Studies* 31, no. 3 (2002): 5–20.

———. "Operation Destroy the Data." *Haaretz*, April 24, 2002.

Hassan, Ahmed Mohamed, and Yusri Mohamed. "At Least 23 Egyptian Soldiers Killed in Deadliest Sinai Attack in Years." Reuters, July 7, 2017. https://www.reuters.com/article/us-philippines-quake-idUSKBN1AR0EJ.

Haugbolle, Sune. *The Alliance Between Iran, Syria and Hizbollah and Its Implications for the Political Development in Lebanon and the Middle East*. Copenhagen: Danish Institute for International Studies, 2006.

Haughton, Jonathan. "An Assessment of the Tax System in Lebanon." Suffolk University, Boston, 2004.

Heller, Mark A. "Implications of the Withdrawal from Lebanon for Israeli-Palestinian Relations." *Strategic Assessment* 3, no. 1 (June 2000). http://www.inss.org.il/publication/implications-of-the-withdrawal-from-lebanon-for-israeli-palestinian-relations/.

Hendrix, Cullen S. "Measuring State Capacity: Theoretical and Empirical Implications for the Study of Civil Conflict." *Journal of Peace Research* 47, no. 3 (2010): 273–85.

Henriksen, Dag. "Deterrence by Default? Israel's Military Strategy in the 2006 War against Hizballah." *Journal of Strategic Studies* 35, no. 1 (2012): 95–120.

Hentov, Elliot. "Turkey and Iran." In *Turkey's Global Strategy*, edited by Nicholas Kitchen, 28–33. London: London School of Economics Reports, 2011. http://www.lse.ac.uk/ideas/Assets/Documents/reports/LSE-IDEAS-Turkeys-Global-Strategy.pdf.

Herbst, Jeffrey Ira. *States and Power in Africa: Comparative Lessons in Authority and Control.* Princeton, N.J.: Princeton University Press, 2000.

Hermann, Tamar. *The Israeli Peace Movement: A Shattered Dream.* New York: Cambridge University Press, 2009.

Herzog, Michael. "The Next Battle in the Israel-Hezbollah War Is Unfolding in Southern Syria." *Business Insider*, March 5, 2015. http://www.businessinsider.com/the-next-battle-in-the-israel-hezbollah-war-is-unfolding-in-southern-syria-2015-3.

———. "The Palestinian Intifada (Part I): Palestinian Lessons and Prospects." *Policywatch.* Washington, D.C.: Washington Institute for Near East Policy, September 29, 2004.

Heydemann, Steven. *Authoritarianism in Syria: Institutions and Social Conflict, 1946–1970.* Ithaca, N.Y.: Cornell University Press, 1999.

Hilal, Jamil. *The Palestinian Political Order after Oslo: A Critical Analytical Study.* [In Arabic]. Ramallah, West Bank: Muwatin, 1998.

Hinnebusch, Raymond A. *Authoritarian Power and State Formation in Ba'thist Syria: Army, Party, and Peasant.* Boulder, Colo.: Westview Press, 1990.

———. "The Foreign Policy of Syria." In *The Foreign Policies of Middle East States: Between Agency and Structure*, edited by Anoushiravan Ehteshami and Raymond A. Hinnebusch. Boulder, Colo.: Lynne Rienner, 2002.

———. *The International Politics of the Middle East.* New York: Palgrave, 2003.

———. "Revisionist Dreams, Realist Strategies: The Foreign Policy of Syria." In *The Foreign Policies of Arab States*, edited by Ali E. Hillal Dessouki and Bahgat Korany, 283–322. Boulder, Colo.: Westview Press, 1991.

———. *Syria: Revolution from Above.* London: Routledge, 2002.

Hirsch, Gal. "From "Cast Lead" to "Other Way": The Development of the Campaign in the Central Command, 2000–2003." [In Hebrew]. *Maarachot* 393 (February 2004).

———. *War Story, Love Story.* [In Hebrew]. Tel Aviv: Miskal, 2009.

"Hizbullah Attacks along Israel's Northern Border May 2000–June 2006." Israel Ministry of Foreign Affairs, June 1, 2006. http://mfa.gov.il/MFA/ForeignPolicy/Terrorism/Hizbullah/Pages/Incidents%20along%20Israel-Lebanon%20border%20since%20May%202000.aspx.

Hockstader, Lee. "Israel Sets Out Charges Arafat Supported Terror." *Washington Post*, May 6, 2002.

Holmes, Amy Austin. "There Are Weeks When Decades Happen: Structure and Strategy in the Egyptian Revolution." *Mobilization* 17, no. 4 (2012): 391–410.

Holsti, Kalevi. *The State, War and the State of War.* Cambridge: Cambridge University Press, 1996.

Homan, Richard L. "Israelis Launch Attack into Lebanon." *Washington Post*, March 15, 1978.

Hroub, Khaled. *Hamas: Political Thought and Practice.* Washington, D.C.: Institute for Palestine Studies, 2000.

———. "The Hamas Movement Between the Palestinian Authority and Israel: From the Triangle of Forces to the Hammer and Anvil." [In Arabic]. *Majallat Al-Dirasat Al-Filastiniyah* 18 (Spring 1994): 30–34.

Hudson, Michael C. *The Precarious Republic: Political Modernization in Lebanon.* Boulder, Colo.: Westview Press, 1985.
Human Rights Watch. *World Report 1997.* New York: HRW, 1998.
———. *World Report 1998.* New York: HRW, 1999.
———. *World Report 1999.* New York: HRW, 2000.
———. *World Report 2005.* New York: HRW, 2006.
Hutchison, Elmo H. *Violent Truce: A Military Observer Looks at the Arab-Israeli Conflict 1951–1955.* New York: Devin-Adair, 1956.
Huth, Paul, and Bruce Russett. "What Makes Deterrence Work? Cases from 1900 to 1980." *World Politics* 36, no. 4 (1984): 496–526.
"Illusions of Restraint: Human Rights Violations During the Events in the Occupied Territories 29 September–2 December 2000." Jerusalem: B'Tselem, December 2000.
"Implementation of the Fourth Geneva Convention in the Occupied Palestinian Territories: History of a Multilateral Process (1997–2001)." *International Review of the Red Cross*, no. 847 (September 30, 2002): 661–98.
Inbar, Efraim. "The 'No Choice War' Debate in Israel." *Journal of Strategic Studies* 12, no. 1 (1989): 22–37.
Inbar, Efraim, and Shmuel Sandler. "Israel's Deterrence Strategy Revisited." *Security Studies* 3, no. 2 (Winter 1993/94): 330–58.
Inbar, Efraim, and Eitan Shamir. "'Mowing the Grass:' Israel's Strategy for Protracted Intractable Conflict." *Journal of Strategic Studies* 37, no. 1 (2014): 65–90.
"Index of CPRS Polls." Palestinian Center for Policy and Survey Research, August 2, 2013. http://www.pcpsr.org/en/node/151.
Institute for Economics & Peace. "Global Terrorism Index 2015: Measuring and Understanding the Impact of Terrorism." Sydney: IEP, 2015. http://economicsandpeace.org/wp-content/uploads/2015/11/Global-Terrorism-Index-2015.pdf.
International Institute for Strategic Studies. "Armed Forces Personnel, Total." In *The Military Balance.* World Bank Open Data. Accessed March 20, 2017. http://data.worldbank.org/indicator/MS.MIL.TOTL.P1?start=2013.
———. "Hamas Coup in Gaza: Fundamental Shift in Palestinian Politics." *Strategic Comments* 13, no. 5 (June 2007).
Interview by author Boaz Atzili with former high-ranking military intelligence officer, Herzliya, June 2010.
Interview by author Boaz Atzili with retired senior IDF officer, Tel Aviv, July 2010.
Interview by author Boaz Atzili with a senior Israeli decision-maker, Tel Aviv, June 2010.
Interview by author Wendy Pearlman with analyst, Gaza City, July 2005.
"Interview with Israel PM Barak on NBC News Meet the Press." Israel Ministry of Foreign Affairs, October 8, 2000. http://mfa.gov.il/MFA/PressRoom/2000/Pages/Interview%20with%20Israel%20PM%20Barak%20on%20NBC%20News%20Meet%20th.aspx.
"The Intifada in Figures: Statistics on Israel's Violations of Human Rights in the Occupied Palestinian Territories, September 28, 2000–September 28, 2003." Gaza: Al-Mezan Center for Human Rights, 2003.

"IPS Forum: The Tunnel Crisis." *Journal of Palestine Studies* 26, no. 2 (Winter 1997): 95–101.

Isacoff, Jonathan B. "Between Militarism and Moderation in Israel: Constructing Security in Historical Perspective." In *Redefining Security in the Middle East*, edited by Tami Amanda Jacoby and Brent E. Sasley, 41–61. Manchester: Manchester University Press, 2002.

———. *Writing the Arab-Israeli Conflict: Pragmatism and Historical Inquiry*. Lanham, Md.: Lexington Books, 2006.

"ISIS Claims Rocket Attack on Israel." *Jerusalem Post*, April 10, 2017.

"Israel and the Occupied Territories: Under the Rubble: House Demolition and Destruction of Land and Property." Amnesty International, May 18, 2004. https://www.amnesty.org/en/documents/MDE15/033/2004/en/.

Israel Defense Forces. "IDF Strategy" Document: *Deterring Terror, How Israel Confronts the Next Generation of Threats*. Translated by Susan Rosenberg. Belfer Center Special Report. Cambridge, Mass.: Belfer Center, August 2016. http://www.belfercenter.org/sites/default/files/legacy/files/IDF%20doctrine%20translation%20-%20web%20final2.pdf.

"Israel Force Crosses Border with Jordan." Jerusalem Domestic Service, November 13, 1966. FBIS Daily Reports.

"Israel Hits Palestinian 'Camp' in Syria." *BBC News*, October 5, 2003. http://news.bbc.co.uk/2/hi/middle_east/3165394.stm.

"Israel Warns Hizbullah War Would Invite Destruction." *Ynetnews*, October 3, 2008. http://www.ynetnews.com/articles/0,7340,L-3604893,00.html.

"Israel-Egypt Cooperation Surpasses Expectation." *Middle East Monitor*, January 28, 2015. https://www.middleeastmonitor.com/news/middle-east/16624-israeli-tv-israeli-egyptian-cooperation-surpasses-expectation.

"Israel-Hizbullah Conflict: Victims of Rocket Attacks and IDF Casualties." Israel Ministry of Foreign Affairs, July 12, 2006. http://www.mfa.gov.il/mfa/foreignpolicy/terrorism/hizbullah/pages/israel-hizbullah%20conflict-%20victims%20of%20rocket%20attacks%20and%20idf%20casualties%20july-aug%202006.aspx.

"Israeli Army Officers Criticize IDF's 'Policy of Restraint,' 'Weakness.'" *Maariv*. November 27, 2000.

"Israeli Chief of Staff on Terrorism, Security." Jerusalem Domestic Service, August 2, 1985. FBIS Daily Reports.

"Israeli Settlers Decide to Drop Restraint, Stage Anti-Palestinian Protests." *BBC News*, November 6, 2000.

"Israel/Lebanon—Deliberate Destruction or 'Collateral Damage?' Israeli Attacks on Civilian Infrastructure." Amnesty International, August 23, 2006. http://www.refworld.org/docid/4517a71c4.html.

"Israel's Mufaz—Cabinet Rejected 'Dozens' of IDF Plans Against Palestinians." *Hatzofe*, November 24, 2000. FBIS Daily Reports.

"Israel's Next War With Hezbollah Will Be Worse Than the Last." *Stratfor*, November 23, 2016. https://www.stratfor.com/analysis/israels-next-war-hezbollah-will-be-worse-last.

Issacharoff, Avi. "The Egyptian Revolution Has Created a Vacuum in Sinai." *Haaretz*, August 19, 2011. http://www.haaretz.com/blogs/2.244/the-egyptian-revolution-has-created-a-vacuum-in-sinai-1.379438.

Jaber, Hala. *Hezbollah: Born with a Vengeance*. New York: Columbia University Press, 1997.

Jacoby, Jeff. "Would Rabin Have Pulled the Plug on a 'Peace Process' That Failed?" *Boston Globe*, October 22, 2015. https://www.bostonglobe.com/opinion/2015/10/22/would-rabin-have-pulled-plug-peace-process-that-failed/fgHF1Y8bkh7leSbtgHfleL/story.html.

Jarbawi, Ali. "Critical Reflections on One Year of the Intifada." *Between the Lines* 1, no. 12 (October 2001): 9–14.

Jarbawi, Ali, and Wendy Pearlman. "Struggle in a Post-Charisma Transition: Rethinking Palestinian Politics after Arafat." *Journal of Palestine Studies* 36, no. 4 (2007): 6–21.

Jerusalem Media and Communication Centre. "Public Opinion Poll," February 1996. http://www.jmcc.org/documentsandmaps.aspx?id=498.

———. "Public Opinion Poll," August 1996. http://www.jmcc.org/documentsandmaps.aspx?id=495.

———. "Public Opinion Poll No. 17," October 1996. http://www.jmcc.org/documentsandmaps.aspx?id=494.

———. "Public Opinion Poll No. 37," June 2000. http://www.jmcc.org/documentsandmaps.aspx?id=463.

———. "Public Opinion Poll No. 51," June 2004. http://www.jmcc.org/documentsandmaps.aspx?id=449.

Jervis, Robert. "Deterrence Theory Revisited." *World Politics* 31, no. 2 (1979): 289–324.

———. *Perception and Misperception in International Politics*. Princeton, N.J.: Princeton University Press, 1976.

Jervis, Robert, Richard Ned Lebow, and Janice Gross Stein. *Psychology and Deterrence*. Baltimore, Md.: Johns Hopkins University Press, 1985.

Johnston, Alastair Iain. "Cultural Realism and Strategy in Maoist China." In *The Culture of National Security: Norms and Identity in World Politics*, edited by Peter J. Katzenstein, 216–68. New York: Columbia University Press, 1996.

———. "Thinking about Strategic Culture." *International Security* 19, no. 4 (1995): 32–64.

Joshi, Shashank. "India's Military Instrument: A Doctrine Stillborn." *Journal of Strategic Studies* 36, no. 4 (2013): 512–40.

Karaosmanoglu, Ali L. "The Evolution of the National Security Culture and the Military of Turkey." *Journal of International Affairs* 54, no. 1 (Fall 2000): 199–216.

Kardas, Seban. "Turkey: Redrawing the Middle East Map or Building Sandcastles?" *Middle East Policy* 17, no. 1 (Spring 2010): 115–36.

Karmon, Ely. "Arafat's Strategy—Lebanonization and Entanglement." Herzliya, Israel: International Institute for Counter-Terrorism, November 16, 2000. https://www.ict.org.il/Article.aspx?ID=794.

Karsh, Efraim. "Arafat's Grand Strategy." *Middle East Quarterly* 11, no. 2 (Spring 2004): 1–9.

———. *Arafat's War: The Man and His Battle for Israeli Conquest.* New York: Grove Press, 2007.

"Kashmir Attack: India Launches Strikes against Militants." *BBC News*, September 30, 2016. http://www.bbc.com/news/world-asia-37504308.

Katz, Yaakov. "Security and Defense: The Fly on the Spider Web?" *Jerusalem Post*, July 1, 2011.

Katzenstein, Peter J., ed. *The Culture of National Security: Norms and Identity in World Politics.* New York: Columbia University Press, 1996.

Keinon, Herb, and Yaakov Lappin. "2 Israelis Injured by Cross-Border Fire from Syria." *Jerusalem Post*, August 27, 2014. http://www.jpost.com/Middle-East/Syrian-mortar-falls-in-northern-Golan-Heights-lightly-injuring-one-372526.

Kerr, Malcolm H. "Hafiz Asad and the Changing Patterns of Syrian Politics." *International Journal* 28, no. 4 (1973): 689–706.

Kessel, Jerrold. "250,000 Flee from Israel's Onslaught; Scores of Lebanese Civilians Dead and Hundreds Injured in Three-Day Attack." *Guardian*, July 29, 1993.

———. "Israel Takes Its Revenge On Hizbullah." *Guardian*, July 27, 1993.

Khalaf, Salah (Abu Iyad), with Eric Rouleau. *My Home, My Land: A Narrative of the Palestinian Struggle.* Translated by Linda Butler Koseoglu. New York: Times Books, 1981.

Khalaf, Samir. *Civil and Uncivil Violence in Lebanon: A History of the Internationalization of Communal Conflict.* New York: Columbia University Press, 2002.

———. *Lebanon's Predicament.* New York: Columbia University Press, 1987.

Khalidi, Walid. *Conflict and Violence in Lebanon: Confrontation in the Middle East.* Cambridge, Mass.: Harvard University Press, 1983.

Khatib, Ghassan. "A Bloody Peace Process?" *Palestine Report*, October 4, 1996.

Khouri, Fred J. "Friction and Conflict on the Israeli-Syrian Front." *Middle East Journal* 17, no. 1/2 (1963): 14–34.

———. "The Policy of Retaliation in Arab-Israeli Relations." *Middle East Journal* 20, no. 4 (1966): 435–55.

Khoury, Jack. "Israeli Jets Attack Near Damascus, Syria Confirms; 'Hezbollah Arms Targeted.'" *Haaretz*, November 30, 2016. http://www.haaretz.com/israel-news/1.756132.

Khoury, Jack, and Gilli Cohen. "Egyptian Officials: Israeli Drone Strikes Sinai Rocket-Launching Site, Kills Five." *Haaretz*, August 11, 2013. http://www.haaretz.com/israel-news/.premium-1.540699.

Kier, Elizabeth. *Imagining War: French and British Military Doctrine Between the Wars.* Princeton, N.J.: Princeton University Press, 1997.

Kilcullen, David. *Counterinsurgency.* New York: Oxford University Press, 2010.

Kimmerling, Baruch, and Joel S. Migdal. *The Palestinian People: History.* Cambridge, Mass.: Harvard University Press, 2003.

Kirisci, Kemal. "The Transformation of Turkish Foreign Policy: The Rise of the Trading State." *New Perspectives on Turkey* 40 (2009): 29–57.

Kirkpatrick, David D. "Militant Group in Egypt Vows Loyalty to ISIS." *New York Times*, November 10, 2014. http://www.nytimes.com/2014/11/11/world/middleeast/egyptian-militant-group-pledges-loyalty-to-isis.html?_r=0.

Kisirwani, Maroun, and William M. Parle. "Assessing the Impact of the Post Civil War Period on the Lebanese Bureaucracy: A View from Inside." *Journal of Asian and African Studies* 22, no. 1 (1987): 17–32.

Klein, Menachem. "The 'Tranquil Decade' Re-Examined: Arab-Israeli Relations During the Years 1957–67." In *Israel: The First Hundred Years*. Vol. 2, *From War to Peace?*, edited by Efraim Karsh, 68–82. London: Routledge, 2000.

Knopf, Jeffrey W. "The Fourth Wave in Deterrence Research." *Contemporary Security Policy* 31, no. 1 (2010): 1–33.

Kober, Avi. "The Intellectual and Modern Focus in Israeli Military Thinking as Reflected in *Ma'arachot* Articles, 1948–2000." *Armed Forces & Society* 30, no. 1 (2003): 141–60.

———. "A Paradigm in Crisis? Israel's Doctrine of Military Decision." *Israel Affairs* 2, no. 1 (1995): 188–211.

———. "What Happened to Israeli Military Thought?" *Journal of Strategic Studies* 34, no. 5 (2011): 707–32.

Kovac, Nikola, and Trista Guertin. "Armed Groups in the Sinai Peninsula." Civil-Military Fusion Centre, February 2013. http://www.operationspaix.net/DATA/DOCUMENT/7805~v~Armed_Groups_in_the_Sinai_Peninsula.pdf.

Krasner, Stephen D. "Talking Tough to Pakistan: How to End Islamabad's Defiance." *Foreign Affairs* 91, no. 1 (February 2012): 87–96.

Krauthammer, Charles. "Arafat's Strategy." *Washington Post*, October 20, 2000.

Kulish, Nicholas, and Eric Schmitt. "Hezbollah Is Blamed for Attack on Israeli Tourists in Bulgaria." *New York Times*, July 19, 2012. http://www.nytimes.com/2012/07/20/world/europe/explosion-on-bulgaria-tour-bus-kills-at-least-five-israelis.html.

Kupchan, Charles. *How Enemies Become Friends: The Sources of Stable Peace*. Princeton, N.J.: Princeton University Press, 2010.

Kuperman, Ranan D. "The Impact of Internal Politics on Israel's Reprisal Policy During the 1950s." *Journal of Strategic Studies* 24, no. 1 (2001): 1–28.

Labaki, Boutros. "The Balance of Power Between Sects and the Making of Internal Conflict in Lebanon." [In Arabic]. *Al-Waqia* 5–6 (1983).

Ladwig, Walter C. "A Cold Start for Hot Wars? The Indian Army's New Limited War Doctrine." *International Security* 32, no. 3 (2007): 158–90.

Lake, David A. "Rational Extremism: Understanding Terrorism in the Twenty-First Century." *Dialogue IO* 1, no. 1 (2002): 15–29.

Lantis, Jeffrey S. "Strategic Culture and Tailored Deterrence: Bridging the Gap Between Theory and Practice." *Contemporary Security Policy* 30, no. 3 (2009): 467–85.

Lappin, Yaakov, Khaled Abu Toameh, and Lahav Harkov. "Gaza Will Pay a 'Heavy Price' for Rocket Fire, Says Ya'alon." *Jerusalem Post*, May 28, 2015.

Laqueur, Walter. *The Road to Jerusalem: The Origins of the Arab-Israeli Conflict, 1967*. New York: Macmillan, 1968.

Laub, Zachary. "Security in Egypt's Sinai Peninsula." Council of Foreign Relations, December 11, 2013. https://www.cfr.org/backgrounder/security-egypts-sinai-peninsula.

Lawson, Fred Haley. *Global Security Watch—Syria*. Santa Barbara, Calif.: Praeger, 2013.

———. "Syria's Mutating Civil War and Its Impact on Turkey, Iraq and Iran." *International Affairs* 90, no. 6 (2014): 1351–65.

———. *Why Syria Goes to War: Thirty Years of Confrontation*. Ithaca, N.Y.: Cornell University Press, 1996.

"Lebanon." United Nations Relief and Works Agency, July 1, 2014. http://www.unrwa.org/where-we-work/lebanon.

Lebow, Richard Ned, and Janice Gross Stein. "Rational Deterrence Theory: I Think, Therefore I Deter." *World Politics* 41, no. 2 (1989): 208–24.

Lefkovits, Etgar, and Margot Dudkevitch. "1,500 Protest in Capital against 'Restraint.'" *Jerusalem Post*, November 15, 2000.

Lesch, David. "Syria: Playing with Fire." In *The 1967 Arab-Israeli War: Origins and Consequences*, edited by Avi Shlaim and William Roger Louis, 79–98. New York: Cambridge University Press, 2012.

Lesser, Ian O. "Turkey in a Changing Security Environment." *Journal of International Affairs* 54, no. 1 (2000): 183–98.

Levin, Andrea. "The Media's Tunnel Vision." *Middle East Quarterly* 3, no. 4 (1996): 3–9.

Levite, Ariel. *Offense and Defense in Israeli Military Doctrine*. Boulder, Colo.: Westview Press, 1989.

Levi, Yosi. "Shit Bet: Fears Mounting about Jewish Underground." *Maariv*, November 15, 2000.

Lieber, Dov. "Egypt Foreign Minister Makes a Rare Visit for Netanyahu Meet." *Times of Israel*, July 10, 2016. http://www.timesofisrael.com/egyptian-foreign-minister-to-visit-tel-aviv-for-netanyahu-meeting/.

Lieberman, Elli. *Reconceptualizing Deterrence: Nudging Toward Rationality in Middle East Rivalries*. London: Routledge, 2013.

Limor, Yoav. "IDF Battalion Commanders Are Sharply Criticizing the Policy of Restraint." *Maariv*, November 27, 2000.

———. "If the Palestinians Will Conduct Battles—We Will Respond in a Harsh Manner." *Maariv*, July 18, 1997.

Lindenstrauss, Galia. "Turkey, the Kurds, and Turkey's Incursion into Iraq: The Effects of Securitization and Desecuritization Processes." In *Nonstate Actors in Interstate Conflicts*, edited by Dan Miodownik and Oren Barak, 125–39. Philadelphia: University of Pennsylvania Press, 2014.

Lindsey, Ursula. "The Cult of Sisi." *New York Times*, September 12, 2013. http://latitude.blogs.nytimes.com/2013/09/12/the-cult-of-sisi/.

Lischer, Sarah Kenyon. *Dangerous Sanctuaries: Refugee Camps, Civil War, and the Dilemmas of Humanitarian Aid*. Ithaca, N.Y.: Cornell University Press, 2005.

Little, Tom. *Modern Egypt*. London: Ernest Benn, 1967.

Lomsky-Feder, Edna, and Eyal Ben-Ari. *The Military and Militarism in Israeli Society*. Albany: State University of New York Press, 1999.

Longhurst, Kerry. "The Concept of Strategic Culture." In *Military Sociology: The Richness of a Discipline*, edited by Gerhard Kümmel, Andreas Prüfert, and Astrid Albrecht-Heide, 301–10. Baden-Baden: Nomos, 2000.

Love, Kennett. *Suez: The Twice-Fought War: A History*. New York: McGraw-Hill, 1969.

Lowenheim, Oded, and Gadi Heimann. "Revenge in International Politics." *Security Studies* 17, no. 4 (2008): 685–724.

Lupovici, Amir. "The Emerging Fourth Wave of Deterrence Theory—Toward a New Research Agenda." *International Studies Quarterly* 54, no. 3 (2010): 705–32.

———. *The Power of Deterrence: Emotions, Identity, and American and Israeli Wars of Resolve*. New York: Cambridge University Press, 2016.

Luttwak, Edward, and Dan Horowitz. *The Israeli Army*. London: Harper & Row, 1975.

Mabro, Robert. *The Egyptian Economy, 1952–1972*. Oxford: Clarendon Press, 1974.

MacAskill, Ewen. "We Must Destroy Palestinian Threat, Army Chief Says." *Guardian*, August 26, 2002. https://www.theguardian.com/world/2002/aug/27/israel.

Mahnken, Thomas G. *Technology and the American Way of War*. New York: Columbia University Press, 2008.

Makdisi, Ussama Samir. *The Culture of Sectarianism: Community, History, and Violence in Nineteenth-Century Ottoman Lebanon*. Berkeley: University of California Press, 2000.

Makovsky, David. "Deterrence and the Burden of Israeli Moderates." Washington Institute for Near East Policy, August 3, 2006. http://www.washingtoninstitute.org/policy-analysis/view/deterrence-and-the-burden-of-israeli-moderates.

Maktabi, Rania. "The Lebanese Census of 1932 Revisited: Who Are the Lebanese?" *British Journal of Middle Eastern Studies* 26, no. 2 (1999): 219–41.

Malka, Amos. "Israel and Asymmetrical Deterrence." *Comparative Strategy* 27, no. 1 (2008): 1–19.

Malley, Robert, and Hussein Agha. "Camp David: The Tragedy of Errors." *New York Review of Books*, August 9, 2001.

Mandiraci, Berkay. "Turkey's PKK Conflict: The Death Toll." International Crisis Group, July 20, 2016. http://blog.crisisgroup.org/europe-central-asia/2016/07/20/turkey-s-pkk-conflict-the-rising-toll/.

Mann, Joseph. "The Syrian Neo-Ba'th Regime and the Kingdom of Saudi Arabia, 1966–70." *Middle Eastern Studies* 42, no. 5 (2006): 761–76.

Mann, Michael. *The Sources of Social Power*. Vol. 2, *The Rise of Classes and Nation-States, 1760–1914*. 2nd ed. Cambridge: Cambridge University Press, 2012.

Mansfield, Peter. *Nasser's Egypt*. Baltimore, Md.: Penguin Books, 1965.

Maoz, Moshe. *Asad: The Sphinx of Damascus: A Political Biography*. New York: Weidenfeld & Nicholson, 1988.

———. *Syria and Israel: From War to Peacemaking*. Oxford: Oxford University Press, 1995.

Maoz, Moshe, and Avner Yaniv, eds. *Syria under Assad: Domestic Constraints and Regional Risks*. New York: St. Martin's Press, 1986.

Maoz, Zeev. "Arab Nonstate Aggression and Israeli Limited Uses of Force" Dataset. *The Quantitative History of the Arab-Israeli Conflict*, 2008. http://vanity.dss.ucdavis.edu/~maoz/quanthist.htm.

———. *Defending the Holy Land: A Critical Analysis of Israel's Security & Foreign Policy.* Ann Arbor: University of Michigan Press, 2006.

Maoz, Zeev, and Ben D. Mor. *Bound by Struggle: The Strategic Evolution of Enduring International Rivalries.* Ann Arbor: University of Michigan Press, 2002.

March, James G., and Johan P. Olsen. *Democratic Governance.* New York: Free Press, 1995.

———. *Rediscovering Institutions: The Organizational Basis of Politics.* New York: Free Press, 1989.

Marcus, Yoel. "Dr. Cease-Fire and Mr. Terror." *Haaretz,* June 12, 2001.

Mastanduno, Michael, David A. Lake, and G. John Ikenberry. "Toward a Realist Theory of State Action." *International Studies Quarterly* 33, no. 4 (1989): 457–74.

Mattar, Mohammad F. "On Corruption." In *Options for Lebanon,* edited by Nawaf Salam, 173–208. London: I. B. Tauris, 2004.

Mazrui, Ali Al'Amin, and Christophe Wondji, eds. *Africa since 1935.* Berkeley: University of California Press, 1993.

McAdam, Doug, Sidney G. Tarrow, and Charles Tilly. *Dynamics of Contention.* Cambridge: Cambridge University Press, 2001.

McDowall, David. *A Modern History of the Kurds.* London: I. B. Tauris, 2004.

McLaurin, R. D. "Lebanon and Its Army: Past, Present, and Future." In *The Emergence of a New Lebanon: Fantasy or Reality,* edited by Edward E. Azar, 79–114. New York: Praeger, 1984.

McManus, Allison. "The Battle for Egypt's Sinai." Tahrir Institute for Middle East Policy, December 5, 2014. http://timep.org/commentary/battle-egypts-sinai/.

"Meeting of the Senior Staff of the Ministry of Foreign Affairs (Tel Aviv, 2 February 1953)." In *Documents on the Foreign Policy of Israel,* edited by Yemima Rosenthal. Jerusalem: Israel State Archives, 1995.

Meital, Yoram. *Peace in Tatters: Israel, Palestine, and the Middle East.* Boulder, Colo.: Lynne Rienner, 2006.

Merari, Ariel, and Shlomo Elad. *The International Dimension of Palestinian Terrorism.* Jerusalem: Jerusalem Post Press, 1986.

Middle East Watch. *Syria Unmasked: The Suppression of Human Rights by the Asad Regime.* New Haven, Conn.: Yale University Press, 1991.

Migdal, Joel S. *Strong Societies and Weak States: State-Society Relations and State Capabilities in the Third World.* Princeton, N.J.: Princeton University Press, 1988.

Miller, Benjamin. "The Concept of Security: Should It Be Redefined?" In *Israel's National Security Towards the 21st Century,* edited by Uri Bar-Joseph, 13–42. London: Routledge, 2001.

Miller, Paul D. "How to Exercise U.S. Leverage over Pakistan." *Washington Quarterly* 35, no. 4 (2012): 37–52.

Minter, William. *Apartheid's Contras: An Inquiry into the Roots of War in Angola and Mozambique.* Johannesburg: Witwatersrand University Press, 1994.

Mishal, Shaul, and Avraham Sela. *The Palestinian Hamas: Vision, Violence, and Coexistence.* New York: Columbia University Press, 2006.

"Misuse of Weapons on the Part of Palestinian Security Force Personnel, 2001." [In Arabic]. Ramallah, West Bank: PICCR, 2002.

Morgan, Patrick M. *Deterrence Now.* Cambridge: Cambridge University Press, 2003.

Morris, Benny. *The Birth of the Palestinian Refugee Problem, 1947–1949*. Cambridge: Cambridge University Press, 1989.

———. *Israel's Border Wars, 1949–1956: Arab Infiltration, Israeli Retaliation, and the Countdown to the Suez War*. Oxford: Clarendon Press, 1993.

Murciano, Gil. "A Matter of Honor: A Review of Israeli Decision Making During the Second Lebanon War." International Centre for the Study of Radicalisation and Political Violence, London, March 2011. http://icsr.info/wp-content/uploads/2012/10/1304694112ICSR_AtkinPaperSeries_GilMurciano.pdf.

Murtaza, Niaz. "Over-Burdened Society, Over-Politicised State: Understanding Pakistan's Struggles with Governance." *Asian Journal of Social Science* 40, no. 3 (2012): 321–41.

Nagl, John A. *Counterinsurgency Lessons from Malaya and Vietnam: Learning to Eat Soup with a Knife*. Westport, Conn.: Praeger, 2002.

Nahas, Charbel. "Emigration." [In French]. *Le Commerce Du Levant*, October 2007, 32–38.

———. "Emigration (2)." [In French]. *Le Commerce Du Levant*, November 2007, 42–44.

Naim, Mona, and Joe Stork. "Interview with Mahmoud Darwish: 'My Opposition to the Terms of the Accord Is a Measure of My Attachment to Real Peace.'" *Middle East Report* 194/195 (July/August 1995).

Nasr, Salim. "Roots of the Shi'i Movement." *MERIP Reports* 133 (May/June 1985): 10–16.

"Nasrallah: We Wouldn't Have Snatched Soldiers If We Thought It Would Spark War." *Haaretz*, August 27, 2006. http://www.haaretz.com/news/nasrallah-we-wouldn-t-have-snatched-soldiers-if-we-thought-it-would-spark-war-1.199556.

National Consortium for the Study of Terrorism and Responses to Terrorism (START). "Global Terrorism Database from 1970 to 2016." 2017. https://www.start.umd.edu/gtd.

"The Nature and Extent of Palestinian Terrorism, 2006." Israel Ministry of Foreign Affairs, March 1, 2007. http://www.mfa.gov.il/mfa/foreignpolicy/terrorism/palestinian/pages/palestinian%20terrorism%202006.aspx.

Naveh, Shimon. "The Cult of the Offensive Preemption and Future Challenges for Israeli Operational Thought." *Israel Affairs* 2, no. 1 (1995): 168–98.

Nevo, Joseph. *King Abdallah and Palestine: A Territorial Ambition*. London: Macmillan, 1996.

"A New and Bitter Brew in the Middle East." *Economist*. October 8, 1998. http://www.economist.com/node/167759.

Nolen, Stephanie. "Arafat Moves to Consolidate Renewed Support." *Palestine Report*, October 4, 1996.

Norton, Augustus Richard. *Hezbollah: A Short History*. Princeton, N.J.: Princeton University Press, 2007.

———. "The Return of Egypt's Deep State." *Current History* 112, no. 758 (2013): 338–44.

Norton, Augustus Richard, and Jillian Schwedler. "(In)security Zones in South Lebanon." *Journal of Palestine Studies* 23, no. 1 (1993): 61–79.

O'Brien, Patrick Karl. *The Revolution in Egypt's Economic System: From Private Enterprise to Socialism, 1952–1965*. New York: Oxford University Press, 1966.

Olmert, Ehud. Interview by Raviv Drucker. *Hamakor*, Channel 10, Israeli TV, May 5, 2015.

Olmert, Yossi. "Arabs Read Prudence As Weakness." *Jerusalem Post*, October 17, 2000.

———. "Arafat's Little Game of Cease-Fires." *Jerusalem Post*, June 10, 2001.

Olson, Robert. "Turkey, Iran and Syria: Triadal Rapprochement." *Kurdish Life* 11 (Summer 1994): 6–7.

O'Neill, Bard. *Armed Struggle in Palestine: A Political-Military Analysis*. Boulder, Colo.: Westview Press, 1978.

Oniss, Juan de. "Syria Said to Tell Guerrillas to Quit Villages Near Heights." *New York Times*, January 24, 1973.

Oren, Michael B. "Escalation to Suez: The Egypt-Israel Border War, 1949–56." *Journal of Contemporary History* 24, no. 2 (1989): 347–73.

———. *Origins of the Second Arab-Israel War: Egypt, Israel and the Great Powers 1952–56*. London: Frank Cass, 1992.

———. *Six Days of War: June 1967 and the Making of the Modern Middle East*. New York: Oxford University Press, 2002.

O'Sullivan, Arieh. "How Far Can Our War for Peace Go?" *Jerusalem Post*, October 10, 2000.

Owen, Edward, and Şevket Pamuk. *A History of Middle East Economies in the Twentieth Century*. Cambridge, Mass.: Harvard University Press, 1999.

Owen, Roger. *State, Power and Politics in the Making of the Modern Middle East*. 3rd ed. London: Routledge, 2004.

Ozanne, Julian, and Mark Nicholson. "Israel Steps up Attacks on South Lebanon." *Financial Times*, July 28, 1993.

Özcan, Nihat Ali, and Özgür Özdamar. "Uneasy Neighbors: Turkish-Iranian Relations since the 1979 Islamic Revolution." *Middle East Policy* 17, no. 3 (Fall 2010): 101–17.

Palestinian Academic Society for the Study of International Affairs. *Annual Report 1996*. Jerusalem: PASSIA, 1997.

Palestinian Human Rights Monitoring Group (PHRMG). "Gaza in Turmoil: The Power Struggle within the Palestinian Authority." *The Monitor* 8, no. 1 (May 2005).

———. "The 'Intra'fada: The Chaos of Weapons—an Analysis of Internal Palestinian Violence." *The Monitor* 7, no. 1 (April 2004).

———. "Overkill: Israeli Bombardment and Destruction of Palestinian Civilian Homes and Infrastructure." *The Monitor* 5, no. 1 (February 2001).

Pape, Robert A. "The Strategic Logic of Suicide Terrorism." *American Political Science Review* 97, no. 3 (2003): 343–61.

Park, Bill. "Turkey, the US and the KRG: Moving Parts and the Geopolitical Realities." *Insight Turkey* 14, no. 3 (2012): 109–24.

Parsons, Nigel Craig. *The Politics of the Palestinian Authority: From Oslo to Al-Aqsa*. New York: Routledge, 2005.

Paul, T. V. "Complex Deterrence: An Introduction." In *Complex Deterrence: Strategy in the Global Age*, edited by T. V. Paul, Patrick M. Morgan, and James J. Wirtz, 1–27. Chicago: University of Chicago Press, 2009.

———. "State Capacity and South Asia's Perennial Insecurity Problems." In *South Asia's Weak States: Understanding Regional Insecurity Predicament*, edited by T. V. Paul, 3–30. Stanford, Calif.: Stanford University Press, 2010.

"'Peaceful Intifada' Will Go on." *Mideast Mirror*, November 2, 2000. FBIS Daily Reports.

Pearlman, Wendy. "Competing for Lebanon's Diaspora: Transnationalism and Domestic Struggles in a Weak State." *International Migration Review* 48, no. 1 (Spring 2014): 34–75.

———. "The Palestinian National Movement." In *The 1967 Arab-Israeli War: Origins and Consequences*, edited by Avi Shlaim and William Roger Louis, 126–48. New York: Cambridge University Press, 2012.

———. "Palestinians and the Arab Spring." In *Civil Resistance and the Arab Spring*, edited by Adam Roberts, Timothy Garton Ash, and Michael Willis, 116–40. Oxford: Oxford University Press, 2015.

———. "Spoiling Inside and Out: Internal Political Contestation and the Middle East Peace Process." *International Security* 33, no. 3 (Winter 2008): 79–109.

———. *Violence, Nonviolence, and the Palestinian National Movement*. Cambridge: Cambridge University Press, 2011.

Pedahzur, Ami. *The Israeli Secret Services and the Struggle Against Terrorism*. New York: Columbia University Press, 2009.

Pedatzur, Reuven. "More Than a Million Bullets." *Haaretz*, June 29, 2004.

Pelcovits, Nathan Albert. *The Long Armistice: UN Peacekeeping and the Arab-Israeli Conflict, 1948–1960*. Boulder, Colo.: Westview Press, 1993.

Peri, Yoram. *Between Battles and Ballots: Israeli Military in Politics*. New York: Cambridge University Press, 1985.

———. *Generals in the Cabinet Room: How the Military Shapes Israeli Policy*. Washington, D.C.: United States Institute of Peace, 2006.

———. *The Israeli Military and Israel's Palestinian Policy: From Oslo to the Al Aqsa Intifada*. Peaceworks, no. 47. Washington, D.C.: United States Institute of Peace, 2002.

Perthes, Volker. *The Political Economy of Syria under Asad*. London: I. B. Tauris, 1995.

———. *Syria under Bashar Al-Asad: Modernisation and the Limits of Change*. Oxford: Oxford University Press, 2004.

Peters, Anne Mariel, and Pete W. Moore. "Beyond Boom and Bust: External Rents, Durable Authoritarianism, and Institutional Adaptation in the Hashemite Kingdom of Jourdan." *Studies in Comparative International Development* 44, no. 3 (2009): 264–65.

Petran, Tabitha. *The Struggle over Lebanon*. New York: Monthly Review Press, 1987.

Petrelli, Niccolò. "Deterring Insurgents: Culture, Adaptation and the Evolution of Israeli Counterinsurgency, 1987–2005." *Journal of Strategic Studies* 36, no. 5 (2013): 666–91.

Pfeffer, Anshel. "Coordinated Attacks in South Kill 8." *Haaretz*, August 19, 2011. http://www.haaretz.com/coordinated-attacks-in-south-israel-kill-8-1.379428.

Phillips, Christopher. "Turkey and Syria." In *Turkey's Global Strategy,* edited by Nicholas Kitchen, 34–39. London: London School of Economics Reports, 2011. http://

www.lse.ac.uk/ideas/Assets/Documents/reports/LSE-IDEAS-Turkeys-Global-Strategy.pdf.

Piazza, James A. "Incubators of Terror: Do Failed and Failing States Promote Transnational Terrorism?" *International Studies Quarterly* 52, no. 3 (2008): 469–88.

Picard, Elizabeth. *Lebanon: A Shattered Country: Myths and Realities of the Wars in Lebanon*. New York: Holmes & Meier, 1996.

Pillar, Paul R. *Terrorism and U.S. Foreign Policy*. Washington, D.C.: Brookings Institution Press, 2001.

"Playing with Fire on the Temple Mount: Use of Lethal and Excessive Force by the Israel Police Force" Case Study No. 7, Jerusalem: B'Tselem, December 1996. http://www.btselem.org/publications/summaries/199612_playing_with_fire.

"Policy of Destruction: House Demolitions and Destruction of Agricultural Land in the Gaza Strip." Jerusalem: B'Tselem, February 2002.

"Press Briefing by Colonel Daniel Reisner—Head of the International Law Branch of the IDF Legal Division." Israel Ministry of Foreign Affairs, November 15, 2000. http://mfa.gov.il/MFA/PressRoom/2000/Pages/Press%20Briefing%20by%20Colonel%20Daniel%20Reisner-%20Head%20of.aspx.

"Press Conference with Acting Foreign Minister Ben-Ami." Israel Ministry of Foreign Affairs, October 1, 2000. http://mfa.gov.il/MFA/ForeignPolicy/MFADocuments/Yearbook13/Pages/171%20%20Press%20conference%20with%20Acting%20Foreign%20Minister.aspx.

Pressman, Jeremy. "The Second Intifada: An Early Look at the Background and Causes of Israeli-Palestinian Conflict." *Journal of Conflict Resolution* 22, no. 2 (2003): 114–41.

———. "Visions in Collision: What Happened at Camp David and Taba?" *International Security* 28, no. 2 (2003): 5–43.

Priestland, Jane, ed. *Records of Jordan 1919–1965*. 14 vols. Cambridge: Cambridge Archive Editions, 1996.

"Prime Ministers." National Assembly of Pakistan, September 30, 2017. http://www.na.gov.pk/en/priminister_list.php.

Prunier, Gérard. *Africa's World War: Congo, the Rwandan Genocide, and the Making of a Continental Catastrophe*. New York: Oxford University Press, 2009.

Prusher, Ilene R. "Palestinians Talk of a New Intifadah." *Christian Science Monitor*, August 19, 1996.

Purkitt, Helen. "Dealing with Terrorism: Deterrence and the Search for an Alternative Model." In *Conflict in World Society: A New Perspective on International Relations*, edited by Michael Banks and John W. Burton, 161–73. New York: St. Martin's Press, 1984.

"Question of the Violation of Human Rights in the Occupied Arab Territories, Including Palestine: Report of the Human Rights Inquiry Commission Established pursuant to Commission Resolution S 5/1 of 19 October 2000." United Nations Economic and Social Council Commission on Human Rights (UN-ECOSOC), March 16, 2001.

Quinlivan, James T. "Coup-Proofing: Its Practice and Consequences in the Middle East." *International Security* 24, no. 2 (1999): 131–65.

Rabasa, Angela, Robert D. Blackwill, Peter Chalk, Kim Cragin, Christine C. Fair, Brian A. Jackson, Brian Michael Jenkins, Seth G. Jones, Nathaniel Stestak, and Ashley J. Tellis. *The Lessons of Mumbai*. Santa Monica, Calif.: RAND Corporation, 2009.

Rabbani, Mouin. "Negotiating Over the Clinton Plan." Press Information Note, no. 43. *Middle East Report*, January 6, 2001. http://www.merip.org/mero/mero010601.

——. "Palestinian Authority, Israeli Rule: From Transitional to Permanent Arrangement." *Middle East Report* 201 (1996): 2–22.

Rabinovich, Itamar. "A New Israeli Policy on Syria: Should Israel Threaten Intervention?" *Order from Chaos* (blog). Brookings Institution, February 13, 2015. http://www.brookings.edu/blogs/order-from-chaos/posts/2015/02/13-new-israeli-policy-on-syria-rabinovich.

——. *Syria under the Ba'th, 1963–66: The Army-Party Symbiosis*. Jerusalem: Israel Universities Press, 1972.

——. *The View from Damascus: State, Political Community and Foreign Relations in Modern and Contemporary Syria*. London: Vallentine Mitchell, 2008.

——. *Waging Peace: Israel and the Arabs, 1948–2003*. Princeton, N.J.: Princeton University Press, 2004.

Rapaport, Amir. *Friendly Fire*. [In Hebrew]. Tel Aviv: Maariv, 2007.

Rasler, Karen. "Internationalized Civil War: A Dynamic Analysis of the Syrian Intervention in Lebanon." *Journal of Conflict Resolution* 27, no. 3 (1983): 421–56.

Rathmell, Andrew. *Secret War in the Middle East: The Covert Struggle for Syria, 1949–1961*. London: I. B. Tauris, 1995.

Ravid, Barak. "Netanyahu Says Israel to Determine If Syrian Mortar Fire Was Intentional." *Haaretz*, November 12, 2012. http://www.haaretz.com/israel-news/netanyahu-says-israel-to-determine-if-syrian-mortar-fire-was-intentional.premium-1.477228.

Razing Rafah: Mass Demolitions in the Gaza Strip. New York: Human Rights Watch, October 2004.

"Reasons for Action." Jerusalem Domestic Service, December 28, 1968. In Reports regarding raid on Beirut Airport, Israel, H2. FBIS Daily Reports.

Regular, Arnon. "Palestinian Inquiry Blames Yasser Arafat for Anarchy." *Haaretz*, August 10, 2004.

Reno, William. *Warlord Politics and African States*. Boulder, Colo.: Lynne Rienner, 1998.

"Report of the Secretary-General Prepared Pursuant to General Assembly Resolution ES-10/10." United Nations, July 30, 2002. https://unispal.un.org/DPA/DPR/unispal.nsf/0/FD7BDE7666E04F5C85256C08004E63ED.

Reuters. "Israeli Tourist Terror: Seven Killed in Bus Bomb Attack in Bulgaria." *RT*, July 18, 2012. https://www.rt.com/news/israeli-tourists-bus-explosion-498/.

Richards, Alan, and John Waterbury. *A Political Economy of the Middle East*. 2nd ed. Boulder, Colo.: Westview Press, 1996.

Romano, David. "Turkish and Iranian Efforts to Deter Kurdish Insurgent Attack." In *Deterring Terrorism: Theory and Practice*, edited by Andreas Wenger and Alex Wilner, 228–50. Stanford, Calif.: Stanford University Press, 2012.

Romm, Giora. "A Test of Rival Strategies: Two Ships Passing in the Night." In *The Second Lebanon War: Strategic Perspectives*, edited by Shlomo Brom and Meir Elran, 49–60. Tel Aviv: Institute for National Security Studies, 2007.

Rose, David. "The Gaza Bombshell." *Vanity Fair*, April 2008.

Ross, Dennis. *The Missing Peace: The Inside Story of the Fight for Middle East Peace*. New York: Farrar, Straus and Giroux, 2004.

Roy, Sara M. "Palestinian Society and Economy: The Continued Denial of Possibility." *Journal of Palestine Studies* 30, no. 4 (2001): 5–20.

———. "The Transformation of Islamist NGOs in Palestine." *Middle East Report* 214 (Spring 2000): 24–26.

———. "Why Peace Failed: An Oslo Autopsy." In *Failing Peace: Gaza and the Palestinian-Israeli Conflict*. London: Pluto, 2007.

Rubin, Barry M. "The Future of Palestinian Politics: Factions, Frictions and Functions." *Middle East Review of International Affairs* 4, no. 3 (September 2000). http://www.rubincenter.org/2000/09/rubin-2000-09-07/.

Ruys, Tom. "Quo Vadit Jus Ad Bellum?: A Legal Analysis of Turkey's Military Operations Against the PKK in Northern Iraq." *Melbourne Journal of International Law* 9, no. 2 (2008): 334–64.

Saadi, Yazan al-. "Palestinian Reconciliation: A History of Documents." *Al-Akhbar*, April 28, 2014. http://english.al-akhbar.com/node/19580.

Sabry, Mohannad. "By Military or Militants, Society Is the Casualty in Sinai." Tahrir Institute for Middle East Policy, July 24, 2014. http://timep.org/esw/articles-analysis/military-militants-society-casualty-sinai/.

Said, Edward. *Peace and Its Discontents: Gaza-Jericho, 1993–1995*. New York: Vintage, 1995.

———. "The Tragedy Deepens." *Al-Ahram Weekly*, December 7, 2000.

Saideman, Stephen M., and Marie-Joëlle Zahar. "Causing Security, Reducing Fear: Deterring Intra-State Violence and Assuring Government Restraint." In *Intra-State Conflict, Governments And Security: Dilemmas Of Deterrence And Assurance*, edited by Stephen M. Saideman and Marie-Joelle Zahar, 1–19. London: Routledge, 2008.

Salama, Vivian. "What's Behind the Wave of Terror in the Sinai." *Atlantic*, November 22, 2013. http://www.theatlantic.com/international/archive/2013/11/whats-behind-the-wave-of-terror-in-the-sinai/281751/.

Salehyan, Idean. Rebels Without Borders: Transnational Insurgencies in World Politics. Ithaca, N.Y.: Cornell University Press, 2009.

———. "Transnational Rebels: Neighboring States as Sanctuary for Rebel Groups." *World Politics* 59, no. 2 (2007): 217–42.

Salibi, Kamal. *The Modern History of Jordan*. London: I. B. Tauris, 1993.

Samaan, Jean-Loup. "The Dahya Concept and Israeli Military Posture vis-à-vis Hezbollah since 2006." *Comparative Strategy* 32, no. 2 (2013): 146–59.

———. *From War to Deterrence? Israel-Hezbollah Conflict since 2006*. Carlisle: Strategic Studies Institute, U.S. Army War College, May 2014.

Samii, Abbas William. "A Stable Structure on Shifting Sands: Assessing the Hizbullah-Iran-Syria Relationship." *Middle East Journal* 62, no. 1 (2008): 32–53.

Samuels, David. "In a Ruined Country." *Atlantic*, September 2005.

Sanger, David E., and Mark Mazzetti. "Israel Struck Syrian Nuclear Project, Analysts Say." *New York Times*, October 14, 2017. http://www.nytimes.com/2007/10/14/washington/14weapons.html.

Sayari, Sabri. "Turkish Foreign Policy in the Post-Cold War Era: The Challenges of Multi-Regionalism." *Journal of International Affairs* 54, no. 1 (2000): 169–82.

Sayigh, Rosemary. *The Palestinians: From Peasants to Revolutionaries*. New York: Zed Books, 2007.

Sayigh, Yezid. "Above the State: The Officers' Republic in Egypt." Carnegie Papers, Carnegie Endowment for International Peace, Washington, D.C., August 2012. http://carnegieendowment.org/files/officers_republic1.pdf.

———. "Arafat and the Anatomy of a Revolt." *Survival* 43, no. 3 (September 2001): 47–60.

———. *Armed Struggle and the Search for State: The Palestinian National Movement, 1949–1993*. Oxford: Oxford University Press, 1997.

———. "Escalation or Containment? Egypt and the Palestine Liberation Army, 1964–67." *International Journal of Middle East Studies* 30, no. 1 (1998): 97–116.

———. "Palestine—Where To?" Presented at the PASSIA Roundtable Meeting and Discussion, Jerusalem, July 9, 2002. http://passia.org/meetings/54?year=2002.

———. "Turning Defeat into Opportunity: The Palestinian Guerrillas after the June 1967 War." *Middle East Journal* 46, no. 2 (1992): 244–65.

Schelling, Thomas C. *Arms and Influence*. New Haven, Conn.: Yale University Press, 1966.

———. *The Strategy of Conflict*. Cambridge, Mass.: Harvard University Press, 1960.

Schiff, Zeev. *A History of the Israeli Army, 1874 to the Present*. New York: Macmillan, 1985.

Schofield, Victoria. *Kashmir in Conflict: India, Pakistan and the Unending War*. New York: I. B. Tauris, 2003.

Schultz, Kenneth A. "The Enforcement Problem in Coercive Bargaining: Interstate Conflict over Rebel Support in Civil Wars." *International Organization* 64, no. 2 (2010): 281–312.

Schweitzer, Yoram. "Egypt's War in the Sinai Peninsula: A Struggle That Goes Beyond Egypt." *INSS Insight*, Institute for National Security Studies, February 3, 2015. http://www.inss.org.il/publication/egypts-war-in-the-sinai-peninsula-a-struggle-that-goes-beyond-egypt/.

Schweitzer, Yoram, and Ofir Winter. "Egypt's War on Terrorism in the Sinai Peninsula: Alliance with Tribes, Partnership with Israel?" *INSS Insight*, Institute for National Security Studies, June 15, 2017. http://www.inss.org.il/publication/egypts-war-terrorism-sinai-peninsula-alliance-tribes-partnership-israel/.

Seale, Patrick. *The Struggle for Syria: A Study of Post-War Arab Politics 1945–1958*. New Haven, Conn.: Yale University Press, 1987.

Seale, Patrick, and Maureen McConville. *Assad of Syria: The Struggle for the Middle East*. London: I. B. Tauris, 1988.

Seay, Angela, and Patricia Toye, eds. *Israel: Boundary Disputes with Arab Neighbours, 1946–1964*. 10 vols. Cambridge: Cambridge Archive Editions, 1995.

Sebag, Ronen. "Lebanon: The Intifada's False Premise." *Middle East Quarterly* 9, no. 2 (Spring 2002): 13–21.

"Security Council Endorses Secretary-General's Conclusion on Israeli Withdrawal from Lebanon as of 16 June." Press Release. United Nations Security Council, June 18, 2000. http://www.un.org/press/en/2000/20000618.sc6878.doc.html.

Segev, Tom. *1967: Israel, the War, and the Year That Transformed the Middle East*. Translated by Jessica Cohen. New York: Metropolitan Books, 2007.

Seitz, Charmaine. "Coming of Age: HAMAS's Rise to Prominence in the Post-Oslo Era." In *The Struggle for Sovereignty: Palestine and Israel, 1993–2005*, edited by Joel Beinin and Rebecca L. Stein, 112–29. Stanford, Calif.: Stanford University Press, 2006.

Sela, Avraham. *The Decline of the Arab-Israeli Conflict: Middle East Politics and the Quest for Regional Order*. Albany: State University of New York Press, 1998.

Seymour, Martin. "The Dynamics of Power in Syria since the Break with Egypt." *Middle Eastern Studies* 6, no. 1 (1970): 35–47.

Shackle, Samira. "Unprecedented Security Cooperation Between Egypt and Israel in the Sinai." *Middle East Monitor*, January 27, 2014. https://www.middleeastmonitor.com/20140127-unprecedented-security-cooperation-between-egypt-and-israel-in-the-sinai/.

Shadid, Anthony. "Syrian Elite to Fight Protests to 'the End.'" *New York Times*, May 10, 2011. http://www.nytimes.com/2011/05/11/world/middleeast/11makhlouf.html.

Shadid, Anthony, and Alia Ibrahim. "Bombing Kills Top Figure in Hezbollah." *Washington Post*, February 13, 2008. http://www.washingtonpost.com/wp-dyn/content/article/2008/02/13/AR2008021300494.html.

Shaery-Eisenlohr, Roschanack. *Shi'ite Lebanon: Transnational Religion and the Making of National Identities*. New York: Columbia University Press, 2008.

Sharon, Ariel, and David Chanoff. *Warrior: An Autobiography*. 2nd ed. New York: Simon & Schuster, 2001.

Sharvit, Keren, Arie W. Kruglanski, Mo Wang, Xiaoyan Chen, Lauren M. Boyatzi, Boaz Ganor, and Eitan Azani. "The Effects of Israeli Use of Coercive and Conciliatory Tactics on Palestinian's Use of Terrorist Tactics: 2000–2006." *Dynamics of Asymmetric Conflict* 6, no. 1–3 (2013): 22–44.

Shelah, Ofer, and Yoav Limor. *Captives in Lebanon*. [In Hebrew]. Tel Aviv: Yedioth Ahronoth, 2007.

Shemesh, Moshe. *Arab Politics, Palestinian Nationalism and the Six Day War: The Crystallization of Arab Strategy and Nasir's Descent to War, 1957–1967*. Brighton: Sussex Academic Press, 2008.

———. "The Fida'iyyun Organization's Contribution to the Descent to the Six-Day War." *Israel Studies* 11, no. 1 (2006): 1–34.

———. "The IDF Raid on Samu': The Turning-Point in Jordan's Relations with Israel and the West Bank Palestinians." *Israel Studies* 7, no. 1 (2002): 139–67.

Sherwood, Harriet. "Thirteen Killed as Israeli Troops Open Fire on Nakba Day Border Protests." *Guardian*, May 15, 2011. http://www.theguardian.com/world/2011/may/15/israeli-troops-kill-eight-nakba-protests.

Shikaki, Khalil. "Palestinians Divided." *Foreign Affairs* 81, no. 1 (2002): 89–105.

Shimshoni, Jonathan. *Israel and Conventional Deterrence: Border Warfare from 1953 to 1970*. Ithaca, N.Y.: Cornell University Press, 1988.

Shlaim, Avi. "Conflicting Approaches to Israel's Relations with the Arabs: Ben Gurion and Sharett, 1953–1956." *Middle East Journal* 37, no. 2 (1983): 180–201.

———. *The Iron Wall: Israel and the Arab World.* New York: W.W. Norton, 2001.

———. *Israel and Palestine: Reappraisals, Revisions, Refutations.* Brooklyn, N.Y.: Verso, 2010.

———. "Jordan: Walking the Tight Rope." In *The 1967 Arab-Israeli War: Origins and Consequences,* edited by Avi Shlaim and William Roger Louis, 99–125. New York: Cambridge University Press, 2012.

———. *Lion of Jordan: The Life of King Hussein in War and Peace.* New York: Knopf, 2009.

Shlaim, Avi, and William Roger Louis, eds. *The 1967 Arab-Israeli War: Origins and Consequences.* New York: Cambridge University Press, 2012.

Sibilla, Chris. "Jordan's Black September, 1970." *Moments in U.S. Diplomatic History.* July 8, 2015. Association for Diplomatic Studies and Training. http://adst.org/2015/07/jordans-black-september-1970/.

Siboni, Gabi, and Ram Ben-Barak. "The Sinai Peninsula Threat Development and Response Concept." Saban Center Analysis Paper, no. 31. Brookings Institution, Washington, D.C., 2014.

Siboni, Gabriel. Interview with author Boaz Atzili. Tel Aviv, Israel, July 2010.

———. "War and Victory." *Military and Strategic Affairs* 1, no. 3 (December 2009): 39–49.

Sil, Rudra, and Peter J. Katzenstein. *Beyond Paradigms: Analytic Eclecticism in the Study of World Politics.* Basingstoke: Palgrave Macmillan, 2010.

"Sinai Residents Complain of Violations by Egypt Army." *Al-Monitor,* May 7, 2014. http://www.al-monitor.com/pulse/originals/2014/05/egypt-sinai-war-on-terror-civilians.html.

Sirriyeh, Hussain. "The Emergence of Hizbollah and the Beginning of Resistance, 1982–85." In *Israel and Hizbollah: An Asymmetric Conflict in Historical and Comparative Perspective,* edited by Clive Jones and Sergio Catignani, 39–48. New York: Routledge, 2010.

"6 Killed in Terror Attack on Israeli Tourists in Bulgaria," Israel Ministry of Foreign Affairs, July 18, 2012. http://mfa.gov.il/MFA/ForeignPolicy/Terrorism/Palestinian/Pages/Terror_attack_Israeli_tourists_Bulgaria_18-Jul-2012.aspx.

Skocpol, Theda. *States and Social Revolutions: A Comparative Analysis of France, Russia, and China.* Cambridge: Cambridge University Press, 1979.

Slonim, Ori. "The Hamas and Terror: An Alternative Explanation for the Use of Violence." *Strategic Assessment* 2, no. 3 (December 1999). http://www.inss.org.il/publication/the-hamas-and-terror-an-alternative-explanation-for-the-use-of-violence/.

Smelser, Neil J., and Faith Mitchell, eds. *Discouraging Terrorism: Some Implications of 9/11.* Washington, D.C.: National Academies Press, 2002.

Smith, Terence. "Explanation in Tel Aviv; Brennan Urges Minimum Wage Rise." *New York Times,* April 11, 1973.

———. "Scores of Israeli Planes Strike 10 Guerrilla Bases in a Reprisal for Munich." *New York Times,* September 9, 1972.

Smyth, Phillip. "Israel Is the New Front in the Syrian War." *Foreign Policy,* January 28, 2015. https://foreignpolicy.com/2015/01/28/israel-is-the-new-front-in-the-syrian-war/.

Sneh, Moshe. Interview with author Boaz Atzili. Netanya, Israel, July 19, 2010.
Snyder, Glenn Herald. *Deterrence and Defense: Toward a Theory of National Security*. Princeton, N.J.: Princeton University Press, 1961.
Snyder, Jack L. *The Soviet Strategic Culture: Implications for Limited Nuclear Operations*. Santa Monica, Calif.: RAND Corporation, September 1977. http://www.dtic.mil/dtic/tr/fulltext/u2/a046124.pdf.
Sobelman, Daniel. "Hizbollah: From Terror to Resistance." In *Israel and Hizbollah: An Asymmetric Conflict in Historical and Comparative Perspective*, edited by Clive Jones and Sergio Catignani, 49–66. New York: Routledge, 2010.
——. "Learning to Deter: Deterrence Failure and Success in the Israel-Hezbollah Conflict, 2006–16." *International Security* 41, no. 3 (Winter 2016): 151–96.
——. *New Rules of the Game: Israel and Hizbollah after the Withdrawal from Lebanon*. Tel Aviv: Jaffee Center for Strategic Studies, 2004.
Soifer, Hillel, and Matthias vom Hau. "Unpacking the Strength of the State: The Utility of State Infrastructural Power." *Studies in Comparative International Development* 43, no. 3–4 (2008): 219–30.
Sondhaus, Lawrence. *Strategic Culture and Ways of War*. London: Routledge, 2006.
Sontag, Deborah. "And Yet So Far: A Special Report: Quest for Mideast Peace: How and Why It Failed." *New York Times*, July 26, 2001.
"Special Briefing: Attacks Against Security Forces Continue in Egypt's North Sinai." Tahrir Institute for Middle East Policy, September 11, 2017. https://timep.org/special-reports/special-briefing-attacks-against-security-forces-continue-in-egypts-north-sinai/.
"Special Report: How Cairo Is Taking the Fight to Sinai Militants." Reuters, February 5, 2015. http://www.reuters.com/article/2015/02/05/us-egypt-sinai-militants-specialreport-idUSKBN0L80XM20150205.
Staniland, Paul. *Networks of Rebellion: Explaining Insurgent Cohesion and Collapse*. Ithaca, N.Y.: Cornell University Press, 2015.
Starr, Joyce R. "Lebanon's Economy: The Costs of Protracted Violence." In *The Emergence of a New Lebanon: Fantasy or Reality?*, edited by Edward E. Azar, 69–78. New York: Praeger, 1984.
"Statement by Israel Ambassador Lancry to 10th Emergency Session of the UN General Assembly," October 18, 2000. http://mfa.gov.il/MFA/InternatlOrgs/Speeches/Pages/Statement%20by%20Israel%20Ambassador%20Lancry%20to%2010th%20Emer.aspx.
"Statistics on Palestinians in the Custody of the Israeli Security Forces." B'Tselem, August 9, 2017. http://www.btselem.org/statistics/detainees_and_prisoners.
Steele, Jonathan. "How Yarmouk Refugee Camp Became the Worst Place in Syria." *Guardian*, March 5, 2015. http://www.theguardian.com/news/2015/mar/05/how-yarmouk-refugee-camp-became-worst-place-syria.
Stein, Janice Gross. "Rational Deterrence Against 'Irrational' Adversaries? No Common Knowledge." In *Complex Deterrence: Strategy in the Global Age*, edited by T. V. Paul, Patrick M. Morgan, and James J. Wirtz, 58–82. Chicago: University of Chicago Press, 2009.

Stern, Moran. "The Reality of Israel-Egypt Relations." *MenaSource* (blog). Atlantic Council, October 28, 2016. http://www.atlanticcouncil.org/blogs/menasource/the-reality-of-israel-egypt-relations.

Stewart, Megan. "Civil War as State-Making: Strategic Governance in Civil War." *International Organization* 72, no. 1 (Winter 2018): 205–26.

Stock, Ernest. *Israel on the Road to Sinai, 1949–1956: With a Sequel on the Six-Day War, 1967.* Ithaca, N.Y.: Cornell University Press, 1967.

Stockholm International Peace Research Institute (SIPRI). "SIPRI Military Expenditure Database." *SIPRI Databases*, 2016. https://www.sipri.org/databases/milex.

Strategic Assessment Initiative. *Planning Considerations for International Involvement in the Palestinian Security Sector.* Washington, D.C.: Strategic Assessment Initiative, July 2005. http://www.strategicassessments.org/ontherecord/saipublications/SAI-Planning_Considerations_for_International_Involvement_July_2005.pdf. Accessed August 19, 2007.

Subramanian, Nirupama. "McCain Warns Pakistan of Indian Air Strikes." *The Hindu*, December 7, 2008. http://www.thehindu.com/todays-paper/McCain-warns-Pakistan-of-Indian-air-strikes/article15356246.ece.

Sullivan, Marisa. *Hezbollah in Syria*. Middle East Security Report 19. Washington, D.C.: Institute for the Study of War, April 2014. http://www.understandingwar.org/report/hezbollah-syria.

Swisher, Clayton E. *The Truth about Camp David: The Untold Story about the Collapse of the Middle East Peace Process.* New York: Nation Books, 2004.

"Syria under Bashar (I): Foreign Policy Challenges." Middle East Report, no. 24. Brussels: International Crisis Group, February 11, 2004.

Syrian Centre for Policy Research. "Alienation and Violence: Impact of the Syria Crisis Report 2014," March 15, 2015. http://www.unrwa.org/resources/reports/alienation-and-violence-impact-syria-crisis-2014.

Tal, David. "The 1956 Sinai War: A Watershed in the History of the Arab-Israeli Conflict." In *Reassessing Suez 1956: New Perspectives on the Crisis and Its Aftermath*, edited by Simon C. Smith, 133–47. Aldershot: Ashgate, 2008.

Tamari, Dov. "Offense or Defense: Do We Have a Choice?" [In Hebrew]. *Maarachot* 289–290: (October 1983): 5–11.

Tamari, Dov, and Meir Califi. "The IDF's Operational Concept." [In Hebrew]. *Maarachot* 423 (2009): 26–41.

Tankel, Stephen. *Storming the World Stage: The Story of Lashkar-e-Taiba.* Oxford: Oxford University Press, 2008.

Tellis, Ashley J., C. Christine Fair, and Jamison Jo Medby. *Limited Conflicts under the Nuclear Umbrella: Indian and Pakistani Lessons from the Kargil Crisis.* Santa Monica, Calif.: RAND Corporation, 2001.

Tessler, Mark A. *A History of the Israeli-Palestinian Conflict.* Bloomington: Indiana University Press, 1994.

"Text of Bush's Address." CNN, September 11, 2001. Accessed October 26, 2015. http://edition.cnn.com/2001/US/09/11/bush.speech.text/.

Thies, Cameron G. "War, Rivalry, and State Building in Latin America." *American Journal of Political Science* 49, no. 3 (2005): 451–65.

"A Time to Deter." *Jerusalem Post*, November 10, 2000.

Tisdall, Simon. "Syrian President Admits Military Setbacks, in First Public Speech for a Year." *Guardian*, July 26, 2015. http://www.theguardian.com/world/2015/jul/26/syrian-president-public-speech-bashar-al-assad.

Traboulsi, Fawwaz. *A History of Modern Lebanon*. 2nd ed. London: Pluto Press, 2012.

Trager, Robert F., and Dessislava P. Zagorcheva. "Deterring Terrorism: It Can Be Done." *International Security* 30, no. 3 (2005): 87–123.

"Trigger Happy: Unjustified Shooting and Violation of the Open-Fire Regulations During the Al-Aqsa Intifada." Jerusalem: B'Tselem, March 2002.

Turki, Fawaz. *The Disinherited: Journal of a Palestinian Exile*. New York: Monthly Review Press, 1972.

Turunc, Hasan. "Turkey and Iraq." In *Turkey's Global Strategy*, edited by Nicholas Kitchen, 40–44. London: London School of Economics Reports, 2011.

Tzur, Nadir. "The Test of Consciousness: The Crisis of Meanings in the IDF and Israeli Society and Their Exposure in the Second Lebanon War." [In Hebrew]. *Military and Strategy* [2, no. 2 (2010). http://heb.inss.org.il/uploadimages/Import/(FILE)1286797368.pdf.

UN Department of Public Information. *Yearbook of the United Nations, 1955*. New York: UN Department of Public Information, 1956.

Unal, Mustafa Cosar. *Counterterrorism in Turkey: Policy Choices and Policy Effects Toward the Kurdistan Workers' Party (PKK)*. New York: Routledge, 2012.

"Under the Guise of Security: Routing the Separation Barrier to Enable Israeli Settlement Expansion in the West Bank." Jerusalem: B'Tselem, December 2005.

United Nations DESA/Population Division. "World Population Prospects 2017." Accessed April 14, 2018, https://esa.un.org/unpd/wpp/Download/Standard/Population.

U.S. Army. *Insurgencies and Countering Insurgencies*. Washington, D.C.: Department of the Army, May 2014. https://fas.org/irp/doddir/army/fm3-24.pdf.

U.S. Census Bureau. "International Programs: Country Rank." Accessed November 11, 2015. http://www.census.gov/population/international/data/countryrank/rank.php.

U.S. Department of Defense. *Strategic Deterrence Joint Operating Concept, Version 1.0*. Offutt Air Force Base, Nebraska: U.S. Strategic Command, February 2004.

U.S. Department of State. "Agreement Between the United States of America and the Republic of Iraq on the Withdrawal of United States Forces from Iraq and the Organization of Their Activities During Their Temporary Presence in Iraq," November 17, 2008. https://www.state.gov/documents/organization/122074.pdf.

——. "Chapter 3: State Sponsors of Terrorism." *Country Reports on Terrorism, 2008*. April 30, 2009. http://www.state.gov/j/ct/rls/crt/2008/122436.htm.

Usher, Graham. "Closures, Cantons and the Palestinian Covenant." *Middle East Report* 199 (Summer 1996): 33–37.

——. *Dispatches from Palestine: The Rise and Fall of the Oslo Peace Process*. London: Pluto Press, 1999.

———. "Facing Defeat: The Intifada Two Years On." *Journal of Palestine Studies* 32, no. 2 (2003): 21–40.
———. "Fatah's Tanzim: Origins and Politics." *Middle East Report* 217 (Winter 2000): 6–7.
———. "Hamas Seeks a Place at the Table." *Middle East International*, no. 476 (May 13, 1994): 17–18.
———. *Palestine in Crisis: The Struggle for Peace and Political Independence after Oslo.* Transnational Institute Series. London: Pluto Press, 1995.
———. "Picture of War." *Middle East International*, no. 535 (October 4, 1996): 3–5.
———. "Resistance and Negotiations." *News from Within* 12, no. 10 (November 1996): 7–9.
Van Creveld, Martin. *The Land of Blood and Honey: The Rise of Modern Israel.* New York: Thomas Dunne Books, 2010.
———. *The Sword and the Olive: A Critical History of the Israeli Defense Force.* New York: Public Affairs, 1998.
Van Dam, Nikolaos. *The Struggle for Power in Syria: Politics and Society under Asad and the Ba'th Party.* 4th ed. London: I. B. Tauris, 2011.
Van Evera, Stephen. "The Cult of the Offensive and the Origins of the First World War." *International Security* 9, no. 1 (1984): 58–107.
Vardi, Gil-li. "'Pounding Their Feet:' Israeli Military Culture as Reflected in Early IDF Combat History." *Journal of Strategic Studies* 31, no. 2 (2008): 295–324.
Vatikiotis, P. J. *The Egyptian Army in Politics: Pattern for New Nations?* Bloomington: Indiana University Press, 1961.
———. *The History of Egypt.* 2nd ed. Baltimore, Md.: Johns Hopkins University Press, 1980.
———. *The History of Modern Egypt: From Muhammad Ali to Mubarak.* 4th ed. Baltimore, Md.: Johns Hopkins University Press, 1991.
———. *Nasser and His Generation.* New York: St. Martin's Press, 1978.
"W. Eytan (Tel Aviv) to the Israel Missions Abroad. 9 April 1951." In *Documents on the Foreign Policy of Israel*, edited by Yemima Rosenthal. Jerusalem: Israel State Archives, 1995.
Wasserstein, Bernard. *Israelis and Palestinians: Why Do They Fight? Can They Stop?* 2nd ed. New Haven, Conn.: Yale University Press, 2004.
Watanabe, Lisa. "Sinai Peninsula—from Buffer Zone to Battlefield." CSS Analysis in Security Policy. Center for Security Studies, February 2015. http://www.css.ethz.ch/publications/pdfs/CSSAnalyse168-EN.pdf.
Waterbury, John. *The Egypt of Nasser and Sadat: The Political Economy of Two Regimes.* Princeton, N.J.: Princeton University Press, 1983.
Watts, Nicole. *Activists in Office: Kurdish Politics and Protests.* Seattle: University of Washington Press, 2010.
Weber, Max. "Politics as a Vocation." In *From Max Weber: Essays in Sociology*, edited by Hans Heinrich Gerth and C. Wright Mills, 77–128. New York: Oxford University Press, 1958.
Wedeen, Lisa. *Ambiguities of Domination: Politics, Rhetoric, and Symbols in Contemporary Syria.* Chicago: University of Chicago Press, 1999.

Weinberger, Naomi Joy. *Syrian Intervention in Lebanon: The 1975–76 Civil War.* New York: Oxford University Press, 1986.

Wenger, Andreas, and Alex Wilner, eds. *Deterring Terrorism: Theory and Practice.* Stanford, Calif.: Stanford University Press, 2012.

"West Bank Closure Count and Analysis." Jerusalem: United Nations Office for the Coordination of Humanitarian Affairs, January 2006. https://www.ochaopt.org/content/west-bank-closure-count-and-analysis-january-2006.

Wheelock, Keith. *Nasser's New Egypt: A Critical Analysis.* New York: Praeger, 1960.

"Who Governs the West Bank? Palestinian Administration under Israeli Occupation." Middle East Report, no. 32. Amman/Brussels: International Crisis Group, September 28, 2004.

Why They Died: Civilian Casualties in Lebanon During the 2006 War. New York: Human Rights Watch, September 2007. https://www.hrw.org/sites/default/files/reports/lebanon0907.pdf.

Williams, Dan. "Israel Didn't Target Iranian General in Strike: Source." Reuters, January 20, 2015. http://www.reuters.com/article/2015/01/20/us-mideast-crisis-israel-syria-idUSKBN0KT1HQ20150120.

Wilner, Alex. "Deterring the Undeterrable: Coercion, Denial, and Delegitimization in Counterterrorism." *Journal of Strategic Studies* 34, no. 1 (2011): 3–37.

Winograd, Eliyahu. "Final Report: The Inquiry Commission to Examine the Events of the Military Campaign in Lebanon 2006." [In Hebrew]. State of Israel, Tel Aviv, January 30, 2008.

——. "Partial Report: The Inquiry Commission to Examine the Events of the Military Campaign in Lebanon 2006." [In Hebrew]. State of Israel, Tel Aviv, April 2007.

Withnall, Adam. "Israel Launches Attack on Syria with Air Strikes in Response to Death." *Independent*, June 23, 2014. http://www.independent.co.uk/news/world/middle-east/israel-launches-attack-on-syria-with-air-strikes-in-response-to-death-of-golan-heights-teenager-9556153.html.

World Bank. *Fifteen Months—Intifada, Closures, and Palestinian Economic Crisis: An Assessment.* Washington, D.C.: World Bank Group, March 2002. http://documents.worldbank.org/curated/en/394371468049795957/Fifteen-months-Intifada-closures-and-Palestinian-economic-crisis-an-assessment.

——. *West Bank and Gaza Update: One Year of Intifada, Closures and Palestinian Economic Crisis.* West Bank and Gaza Strip: World Bank Group, November 2001.

Worth, Robert F. "Lawless Sinai Shows Risks Rising in Fractured Egypt." *New York Times*, August 10, 2013. http://www.nytimes.com/2013/08/11/world/middleeast/lawless-sinai-shows-risks-rising-in-fractured-egypt.html.

Yaari, Ehud. *Egypt and the Fedayeen, 1953–1956.* [In Hebrew]. Givat Haviva: Center for Arabic and Afro-Asian Studies, 1975.

——. *Strike Terror: The Story of Fatah.* Translated by Esther Yaari. New York: Sabra Books, 1970.

Yaari, Ehud, and Normand St. Pierre. "Sinai: The New Frontier of Conflict?" Washington Institute, November 20, 2011. http://www.washingtoninstitute.org/policy-analysis/view/sinai-the-new-frontier-of-conflict.

Yaari, Ehud, Aaron Zelin, and Matthew Levitt. "Israel's Evolving Terrorist Threats from Sinai to Syria." Washington Institute for Near East Policy, 2014. http://www.washingtoninstitute.org/policy-analysis/view/israels-evolving-terrorist-threats-from-sinai-to-syria.

Yadlin, Amos. "How Israel Created Deterrence in the Second Lebanon War," May 22, 2015. http://www.ynetnews.com/articles/0,7340,L-4660200,00.html.

Yaniv, Avner. *Deterrence Without the Bomb: The Politics of Israeli Strategy*. Lexington, Mass.: Lexington Books, 1987.

Yegen, Mesut. "'Prospective Turks' or 'Pseudo-Citizens:' Kurds in Turkey." *Middle East Journal* 63, no. 4 (2009): 600–605.

Yom, Sean. *From Resilience to Revolution: How Foreign Interventions Destabilize the Middle East*. New York: Columbia University Press, 2016.

Yossef, Amr. "Securing the Sinai." *Foreign Affairs*, September 28, 2011. https://www.foreignaffairs.com/articles/middle-east/2011-09-28/securing-sinai.

Young, Michael. "Hezbollah's Other War." *New York Times Magazine*, August 4, 2006. See http://www.nytimes.com/2006/08/04/magazine/04lebanon.html.

Zaleswki, Piotr. "How Turkey Went From 'Zero Problems' to Zero Friends." *Foreign Policy*, August 22, 2013. http://foreignpolicy.com/2013/08/22/how-turkey-went-from-zero-problems-to-zero-friends/.

Zerubavel, Yael. *Recovered Roots: Collective Memory and the Making of Israeli National Tradition*. Chicago: University of Chicago Press, 1997.

Zhang, Shu Guang. *Deterrence and Strategic Culture: Chinese-American Confrontations, 1949–1958*. Ithaca, N.Y.: Cornell University Press, 1992.

Ziadeh, Radwan. *Power and Policy in Syria: Intelligence Services, Foreign Relations and Democracy in the Modern Middle East*. London: I. B. Tauris, 2011.

Zilberstein, Ronit. "Sinai Is Becoming a Terrorist Launching Pad, Netanyahu Says." *Israel Hayom*, April 5, 2012. http://www.israelhayom.com/site/newsletter_article.php?id=3832.

Ziring, Lawrence. "Weak State, Failed State, Garrison State." In *South Asia's Weak States: Unpretending Regional Insecurity Predicament*, edited by T. V. Paul, 170–94. Stanford, Calif.: Stanford University Press, 2010.

Zisser, Eyal. *Asad's Legacy: Syria in Transition*. New York: New York University Press, 2001.

——. *Commanding Syria: Bashar Al-Asad and the First Years in Power*. London: I. B. Tauris, 2007.

——. "Hizbollah in Lebanon: Between Tehran and Beirut, Between the Struggle with Israel, and the Struggle for Lebanon." In *Lebanon: Liberation, Conflict, and Crisis*, edited by Barry M. Rubin, 155–76. New York: Palgrave Macmillan, 2009.

——. "Hizbollah: The Battle over Lebanon." *Military and Strategic Affairs* 1, no. 2 (October 2009): 47–59.

Zurcher, Erik J. *Turkey: A Modern History*. London: I. B. Tauris, 2004.

Index

Page numbers in italics refer to figures and tables.

Abbas, Mahmoud, 168–70
Abdullah (king of Jordan), 42, 195
Abu Nidal organization, 120–21
Adamsky, Dima, 49, 51
Adana Agreement, 233
ADLs. *See* Armistice Demarcation Lines
airplanes, 121, 182–83
AKP. *See* Justice and Development Party
Amal, 122, 204
AMB. *See* al-Aqsa Martyrs Brigade
"Amos *vs.* Amos" controversy, 158
"analytical eclecticism," 3
ANM. *See* Arab Nationalist Movement
Ansar Al-Islam, 179–80
Ansar Bait al-Maqdis, 89
anti-intellectualism, 24, 26, 57, 202–4
appropriateness. *See* logic of appropriateness
al-Aqsa Martyrs Brigades (AMB), 163–66, *164–65*, 168
al-Aqsa Mosque, 143, 148–49

Arab League, 44, 83, 97
Arab Nationalist Movement (ANM), 82–83
Arab Summit 1964, 83
Arafat, Yasser, 82; Assad, H., and, 121–22; Camp David II and, 132, 147–48, 162; Israeli perceived defiance of, 149–50; Israeli perceived distrust of, 134–35, 167, 173; Netanyahu and, 143–44; PA and, 134–35, 138–39; Second Intifada and, 158, 160–61; U.S. and, 132, 141, 147–48, 162. *See also* Fatah; Hamas; Oslo Agreement; Palestine Liberation Organization
armistice, 29; Egypt-Israel Armistice Agreement, 23, 59, 65–66, 96, 245; Mixed Armistice Commissions, 30, 63–64, 68, 73–74, 263n45
Armistice Demarcation Lines (ADLs), 23, 35, 59, 73–74
al-Assad, Bashar, 123–28, 189, 196

al-Assad, Hafez, 96, 104–5, 115; Arafat and, 121–22; Ba'ath Party and, 104–5, 111; economic policy and, 112–14, 117; Jadid against, 106–11; Lebanon and, 120–21; nonstate actors and, 128, 245; PKK and, 233–34; Turkey and, 233–34, 240. *See also* Fatah; Jordan; Palestinians

assassinations, 43, 136, 143, 146, 196, 213

Aswan Dam, 78

Atzili, Boaz, 268*n*157

Ayyash, Yahya, 138, 141

Ba'ath Military Organizational Bureau, 104

Ba'ath Party, 43, 95, 102, 128, 245–46; Assad, H., and, 104–5, 111; divisions within, 103–4; escalation and, 107; Regional Command of, 103, 106, 108–9; UAR and, 100–101

Baghdad Pact, 75

Bailey, Clinton, 44

Bandung conference, 75–76

Bangladesh (East Pakistan), 221

Barak, Ehud, 146–48, 152–54; against Arafat, 158, 160–61; against Hezbollah, 188, 190, 195; on Lebanese withdrawal by Israel, 192, 194; Syria and, 190, 195–96; on toughness image, 157; on 2006 War, 212. *See also* Second Intifada

Barghouti, Marwan, 140, 158, 162

Bar-Siman-Tov, Yaacov, 107

Barzani, Masoud, 236

"basic security" (*bitachon bsisi*), 28

Batatu, Hanna, 113–14, 116, 120

Beilin, Yossi, 188

Belfer Center, 268*n*161

Ben-Ami, Shlomo, 151, 154

Ben-Gurion, David, 27, 31, 33–34, 38, 73, 97

Beriker-Atiyas, Nimet, 232

Berri, Nabih, 204

bilateral cooperation, 62; Egypt regime strength and, 85–92, 275*n*173

bilateral strategies, 4

bitachon bsisi ("basic security"), 28

bitachon shotef ("current security"), 28

Black September. *See* Jordan

Border Police (Border Corps), 30–31, 263*n*47

Brannen, Samuel, 237

Bratton, Patrick, 225

brute force, 4, 53, 92, 166

Burns, Representative E. L. M., 35, 64, 71

bus attacks and bombings, 69, 89, 120, 137, 263*n*46

Bush, George W., 1, 167

Byman, Daniel, 5–6, 8, 128, 135

Camp David, 160–62

Camp David II, 132, 147–48, 162, 171–72

capability, 50, 53, 188, 209, 227

Carter, David, 13, 227–29, 255*n*2

Caspit, Ben, 152–53, 155, 157, 160

ceasefire, 167, 221

"Cedar Revolution," 196–97

Chamoun, Camille, 179

chapter synopses, 242–49

Chehab, Fuad, 178

Christopher, Warren, 189

civil war: in Jordan, 47; in Lebanon, 119, 179–80, 186; in Libya, 87; in Pakistan, 221; in Turkey, 236

Clinton, Bill, 143, 147

coercive leverage, 150–51

Cohen, Stephen, 220

Cold Start, 225–26, 229

Cold War, 99, 220, 232

compellence, 5–6

compellence, transitive, 255*n*2

"compellence dilemma," 13, 255n2
complex deterrence, 17, 250
Conference of the Nonaligned Movement, 75–76
"consciousness operations," 54–55, 268n161. *See also* enemy consciousness
constructivist sensitivity, 3
Contra rebels, in Nicaragua, 2
contributions: extensions and, 249–52; implications and, 17–18
cooperative host, 7–8, *8*, 11–12, 24, 244; Jordan as, 46–47; Lebanon as, 182, 185, 247; 1949–1956, *39*; 1956–1990, *41*; PA and, 132, 138; Rabin Doctrine and, 52–53, 105; regime capacity and, 9
Cordsman, Anthony, 214
Coser, Lewis, 14
counterproductive coercion, 6, 7
coup d'état: in Iraq, 43; in Jordan, 43; neo-Ba'ath, 106
cross-border smuggling, 29, 87–89, 277n201
"cult of offensive," 29; in Israel, 20, 24–25, 35, 57–58, 262n29
cumulative deterrence, 28, 54–55
"current security" (*bitachon shotef*), 28

Dahiya, Lebanon, 201, 209–10
"Dahiya Doctrine," 210
Dahlan, Mohammed, 157
Dasgupta, Sunil, 220
David, Steven, 10, 18
Davutoglu, Ahmet, 232
Dayan, Moshe, 33–36, 71, 77, 183
"decision tree," 7–9, *8*, 11–12, 38–39, *41*, 47, 55, 69, 243
Defense of the Land operational plan, 194, 205
defiant host, 7, 24, *39*, 40, *41*, 42; outcomes of, *8*, 11; Rabin Doctrine and, 52–53. *See also* Egypt; Palestinian Authority; Syria
Dekmejian, R. Hrair, 80, 84
demilitarized zone (DMZ), 96–97
deterrence, 15; complex, 17, 250; "consciousness operations" and, 54–55; cumulative, 28, 54–55; by denial, 4; extended, 50–51; general, 28; Hezbollah and, 192–93, 203–5, 209–13, 215; IDF on, 50–53, 198; indirect, 5; "internalized," 61; in Israeli decision-making, 52; in Israeli triadic coercion, after 1990, 51–52, 56–57; from Lebanese withdrawal by Israel, 192, 215; logic of, 4–5, 199; "mowing the grass" as, 53, 170, 286n157; PA and, 145, 156, 246–47; peace through, 155–56; pride of, 155; by punishment, 4–6; in strategic culture ideas, Lebanon, 202–4; from Suez War, 60; "tailored," 52; in 2006 War, 203–5, 209–10
deterrence theory, 14
Deuxième Bureau, 97–98
diplomatic pressure, 121
DMZ. *See* demilitarized zone
doctrines, 49, 210; Cold Start, 225–26, 229; Sundarji Doctrine, 223. *See also* Rabin Doctrine
drones, armed, 90
Drucker, Raviv, 150

East Pakistan (Bangladesh), 221
economics: Assad, H., and, 112–14, 117; in Egypt since 1949, 67; in Lebanon, 178–79; Nasser and, 72; nonstate actors' restriction, 1956–1979 and, 81; PA and, 138–39; in Pakistan, 227; Second Intifada and, 149–50; Syrian border friction foundations, 1949–1962, and, 98;

Syrian triadic conflicts since 2000 and, 127
Egypt, 90, 92, 94; ADLs and, 23; credible threats to, 61; insurgency and, 88–89, 91; Morsi in, 87–88, 91; 1949–1956, 63–65, *64*; after 1967 War, 84, 93; Syria and, 100, 103, 105–6. *See also* Gaza Strip; Nasser, Gamal Abdel; Sinai peninsula; el-Sisi, Abdel Fattah
Egypt-Israel Armistice Agreement (1949), 23, 59, 65–66, 96, 245
Egypt regime strength, 20–21, 93–95; bilateral cooperation and, 85–92, 275*n*173; nonstate actors, 1954–1956, and, 71–78; nonstate actors' restriction, 1956–1979, and, 78–85. *See also* Nasser, Gamal Abdel
Egypt regime weakness: Gaza Strip and, 69–71; Naguib and, 67–68; nonstate autonomy, 1949–1954, 65–71; Palestine Border Guard and, 70; RCC and, 66–71; retaliation raids and, 68–69; strike and, 67
Egypt since 1949: attacks on, 59–60, *60*, 68–69; bilateral collaboration with, 62; discontent in, 66; economics in, 67; invasion of, 62; Israel's triadic conflict with, first period, 61, 92; Israel's triadic conflict with, second period, 62, 92; Israel's triadic conflict with, third period, 62, 92–93; Israel's triadic conflict with, fourth period, 62, 93–94; reforms in, 66–67; UNTSO and, 63; after uprising, 62. *See also* Suez War
Eiland, Giora, 210–11
Eisenkott, Gadi, 207–8, 210
Elad, Shlomo, 182
Elevated Waters operational plan, 197, 205
enemy consciousness, 247; in Israeli triadic coercion, after 1990, 54–55, 268*n*159; Second Intifada and, 159–60, 168; in strategic culture ideas, Lebanon, 207–9; in strategic culture ideas, PA, 159–60
Erdoğan, Recep Tayyip, 232, 235, 237–39
Eshkol, Levy, 105, 107, 183
Evron, Yair, 209
extended deterrence, 50–51

"Failed State Index," 208*n*43
Farouk (king of Egypt), 66, 92
Fatah (Palestine Liberation Movement), 45, 82; Abbas and, 168–69; First Intifada and, 139–40; in Jordan, 106–7; in Lebanon, 182, 184; nonstate actors' restriction, 1956–1979, and, 83–84; origin of, 44; suicide attacks by, 163; as "Syrian puppet organization," 105; in Syrian regime capacity, 1970–2000, 115–16, 119–20; in Syria under, 1963–1970, 101–7
Fedayeen (Egyptian army contingent), 76–77, 81–82, 245
fedayeen (Palestinian guerrilla fighters), 44, 46–47, 102–5, 108, 117; in Syrian regime capacity, 1970–2000, 110, 115–18. *See also* Fatah; Palestine Liberation Organization
Feldman, Ilana, 65, 82
Feldman, Shai, 198
Fernandes, George, 220
First Intifada, 139–40, *142*
"Four Mothers, The," 190
"Fragile States Index," 208*n*43, 228
Fraiman, Keren, 6, 255*n*2
Freedman, Lawrence, 61
Free Officers' Movement, 66, 68–69, 92
Friedman, Thomas, 160
Friendly Fire: How We Failed Ourselves in the Second Lebanon War (Rapaport), 209

Ganor, Boaz, 137
Gantz, Benni, 212
Gaza Strip, 23, 59; Egypt regime weakness and, 69–71; Israeli raids into, 63–64, *64*; Nasser and, 74–75; Operation Cast Lead, 50; Operation Pillar of Defense, 50; Operation Protective Edge, 50; retaliation raids into, 68–69; wars against, 170; withdrawal from, 133
general deterrence, 28
General Federation of Egyptian Trade Unions, 80
General Staff Intelligence Division, 144
Gilad, Amos, 158
Golan Heights (Golan): annexation of, 114–15; Hezbollah and, 196; Mt. Dov/Sheba Farms as, 193; occupation of, 108; Syrian regime capacity, 1970–2000, and, 110, 114–18; Syrian triadic conflicts since 2000 and, 125–26
Gold, Zack, 91
Goldstein, Baruch, 137, 141
Gray, Colin, 15
Great Britain, 23; Jordan and, 42–43
Gulf War, 130, 235

Habbash, George, 82
Haddad, Wadi, 82
Hafez, Mustapha, 70
al-Hafiz, Amin, 105
Halutz, Dan, 200, 203–6, 210
Hamas, 133–34, 253–54; elections 2006 and, 169; kidnapping by, 202–3; Oslo Agreement and, 140; PA and, 137, 139–42, 162–63; public opinion and, 140–41; Qassam rockets from, 168; suicide attacks and bombings by, 141, 162–63, *164*–65, 289*n*61. *See also* Arafat, Yasser; Gaza Strip
Haqqani, Hussein, 225

Harel, Amos, 90, 207
Harel, Yitzhak, 206–7
Hariri, Rafik, 186, 196, 213
Harris, William, 214
Hashemite Kingdom of Jordan, 42–43
Hass, Amira, 166
Henrikson, Dag, 202
Hezbollah, 50–51, 96, 125; agency of, 185–86; Barak against, 188, 190, 195; decision-making about, 175–76, 248; deterrence and, 192–93, 203–5, 209–13, 215; founding of, 185; Golan and, 196; Iran and, 185; kidnapping by, 199; Lebanon 1985–2000 and, 181, 185–89; leverages and, 247; restraint of, 212–13; rockets from, 186–87, 201; "rules of the game" with, 193; Syrian regime capacity, 1970–2000, and, 122–23; Syrian triadic conflicts since 2000 and, 126–27; triadic coercion and, 194–95, 253
Hinnebusch, Raymond, 101, 111–12, 114
Hizb-ul-Mujahideen, 222
Horowitz, Dan, 35
host states, 1, 3, 4, 5, *8*, 21–22. *See also* Egypt; India; Lebanon; Palestinian National Authority; Syria; Turkey
host states predisposition, 7, *8*, 11–12; Israeli triadic coercion, 1956–1990 and, *39*, 40, *41*, 42; Rabin Doctrine and, 40, *41*, 42
Hourani, Albert, 125
Hudson, Michael, 177
Human Rights Watch, 163
Hussein (king of Jordan), 43–46, 110
Hussein, Saddam, 155, 235–36
Hutchison, E. H., 63–64

Ice Breaker operational plan, 197–98, 200, 205
IDF. *See* Israel Defense Forces

INDEX [355]

IDF Northern Command, 304n129
"IDF Strategy" document, 50–52, 54–55, 253
improvised explosive device, 190
Inbar, Efraim, 53
India, 21; Cold Start from, 225–26, 229; decision-making in, 220–21; lessons from, 239–41; map of, *220*; Mumbai attacks in, 226, 228–29; Operation Parakram from, 224–25, 229, 240, 249, 307n18; Parliament House attack in, 224; partition of, 219; strategic culture of, 220–21, 248–49; Sundarji Doctrine of, 223; triadic coercion and, 221, 224–25, 228–29, 239–40, 249. *See also* Kashmir
indirect deterrence, 5
infiltrations, into Israel, 245, 263n40, 278n1; border lands and, 31; Border Police and, 30–31, 263n47; motivations for, 29; nonviolence of, 29; Palmach and, 33; responses of, 30–38, *32*, *37*; retaliation raids against, 31–36, *32*, 263n44; Suez War and, 63–64; violence of, 29–30, *30*
infrastructural power, 10
instrumental utility. *See* intrinsic utility/instrumental utility
insurgency, 13; counterinsurgency, 49, 54, 223; Egypt and, 88–89, 91; scholarship on, 17–18, 250
intelligence, 222; Mossad, 26, 40, 200; on PA, 144–45; Shin Bet, 26, 89, 138, 154
"internalized deterrence," 61
International Crisis Group, 124
Inter-Services Intelligence (ISI), 222–25, 228
interstate balance of power, *8*; Rabin Doctrine and, *41*

interstate dynamics, 7–9, *8*, 13–14
intifada, 74–75; First Intifada, 139–40, 142. *See also* Second Intifada
intrastate dynamics, 7–9, *8*
intrinsic utility/instrumental utility, 3, 131, 252; in Israeli triadic coercion, after 1990, 51–52; in strategic culture ideas, Lebanon, 193–94, 202–4; in strategic culture ideas, PA, 155–56, 176
Iran, 122; Hezbollah and, 185; Turkey and, *230*, 230–31, 234–35
Iran-Iraq War, 234
Iraq, 21, 81, 99, 109; coup d'état in, 43; Hussein, S., of, 155, 235–36; Iran-Iraq War, 234; ISIS, 85, 238, 253; map of, *230*; military of, 75; regime weakness of, 236–38; Turkey and, *230*, 235–39; U.S. and, 130, 237
Iron Dome antiballistic missile system, 89–90
ISI. *See* Inter-Services Intelligence
ISIS. *See* Islamic State in Iraq and Syria
Islamic Jihad, 133–34; Oslo Agreement and, 140; rockets from, 171; suicide attacks by, 164–65, 169
Islamic State in Iraq and Syria (ISIS), 85, 238, 253
Israel, 38, *39*, 40, *41*, 42; ADLs for, 23; assassinations by, 136; "civil-military partnership" in, 25; "cult of offensive" in, 20, 24–25, 35, 57–58, 262n29; defense of, 89–90; Egypt since 1949 attacks and, 59–60, *60*; Likud government of, 120, 132; Ministry of Foreign Affairs in, 25, 31; "national security triangle" of, 27–28; perceived vulnerability of, 27, 55; politicians in, 24; Sinai peninsula attack in, 89; statehood of, 23; strategic culture of, 168–71; strategic

[356] INDEX

rationality of, 90–91; Suez War and, 20; UN resolution against, 34; war inevitability in, 27. *See also specific topics*

Israel Defense Forces (IDF), 25–26; against communities, 33–34; correlation related to, 36, *37*, 265*n*84; on deterrence, 50–53, 198; extrajudicial killings by, 166; failures of, 32–36, *37*; "IDF Strategy" document, 50–52, 54–55, 253; against Lebanese withdrawal by Israel, 190–91; leverages from, 51; "national security triangle" of, 27–28; "New Operational Concept" of, 195; nonstate actors and, 48; operational concept of, 48–50; Palestinian fatalities and, 31, *32*, 34, 36, *37*, 286*n*7; Qibya attack by, 34; readiness of, 33; on Second Intifada, 146, 157; against states, 34–35, 38; TOHAD of, 49; Unit 101 of, 33–35, 38, 73, 264*n*58

Israeli decision-making processes, 25, 172; anti-intellectualism in, 24, 26, 57, 202–4; blitzkrieg in, 27–28, 48; decentralization of, 26–27; deterrence in, 52; goal in, 37–38; military in, 29; security and, 26

Israeli-Egypt cooperation, 93–94; regime strength and, 90–92

Israeli intelligence agency (Mossad), 26, 40, 200

Israeli internal security service (Shin Bet), 26, 89, 138, 154

Israeli National Security Council, 26

Israeli strategic culture, 23–24, 57, 244–45; decision-making of, 25–27, 172; Second Intifada and, 173–74; summation of, 28–29

Israeli triadic coercion, 1949–1956, *39*, 244. *See also* Egypt; Syria

Israeli triadic coercion, 1956–1990, 24, 38, 244, 247; host state predisposition and, *39*, 40, *41*, 42; outcomes of, *41*, 42

Israeli triadic coercion, after 1990, 24–25; deterrence in, 51–52, 56–57; enemy consciousness in, 54–55, 268*n*159; intrinsic utility/instrumental utility in, 51–52; logic of appropriateness, 55–56, 244–45; nuance lack in, 52–54, 56–57; strategic thinking shift and, 48–51. *See also* Lebanon; Palestinian National Authority

Issacharoff, Avi, 90, 204–5, 207

Iyad, Abu, 75

Jadid, Salah, 106–11
Jaish-e Mohammed (JeM), 223–27
Jamaat-i-Islami, 222
Jammu, 219, 221–22
Jammu and Kashmir Liberation Front (JKLF), 222
JeM. *See* Jaish-e Mohammed
Jerusalem Media and Communication Centre (JMCC), 289*n*61
Jibril, Ahmed, 115–16
JKLF. *See* Jammu and Kashmir Liberation Front
JMCC. *See* Jerusalem Media and Communication Centre
Johnston, Alastair Iain, 161
Jordan, regime strength of: Abdullah of, 42, 195; ADLs and, 23; civil war in, 47; as cooperative host, 46–47; coup d'état in, 43; Fatah in, 106–7; Great Britain and, 42–43; King Hussein of, 43–46, 110; 1948 War and, 42; PFLP and, 47; PLO and, 47; Rabin Doctrine and, 42–48, 52–53; retaliation raids against, 32–33; Syria

compared to, 40; Syrian attack by, 110; West Bank and, 42–43
"July War" (2006), 199
Justice and Development Party (AKP), 231–32, 238

Kabila, Joseph, 13
Kargil War of 1999, 223–25
Kashmir: ceasefire in, 221; division of, 219; JeM and, 226–27; JKLF, 222; Maharaja of, 219; map of, *220*; 1947–1948 war in, 221; 1965 war in, 221; 1987 conflict in, 221–22; nonstate actors in, 219; rigged elections in, 221–22; Simla Accord and, 221–22; triadic coercion in, 219
Kemal, Mustafa, 231
kidnapping, 136, 199, 202–3, 206
Klein, Menachem, 40, 244, 265*n*90
Knopf, Jeffrey, 5
Kurdistan Regional Government (KRG), 235–37
Kurdistan Workers' Party (PKK), 2, 21, 229, 232, 238; Assad, H., and, 233–34; cost of, 230; decision-making related to, 248–49; embargo and, 236–37; formation of, 230; Iran and, 234–35; regional support of, 230–31
Kurds, 229, 235–36

Labor Party, 132, 135–36, 146
Lahoud, Emil, 196
land and water rights, 96–97
Laqueur, Walter, 79
Lashkar-e-Taiba (LeT), 222, 224–26
Lawrence of Arabia, 13
Lebanese Civil War, 119, 179; Syria and, 180, 186
Lebanese withdrawal by Israel, 176, 198; deterrence from, 192, 215; IDF against, 190–91; Nasrallah on, 191–92, 207–9; Palestinians and, 146–47, 156–57; public opinion on, 190–92, 215; strategic culture and, 193–94; by Syria, 196–97; UN on, 193, 196–97; Ya'alon and, 192, 194–95
Lebanon, 21; ADLs and, 23; airplanes and, 182–83; Ansar Al-Islam against, 179–80; Assad, H., and, 120–21; Cairo Agreement for, 183–84; Christians in, 177; civil war in, 119, 179–80, 186; confessional political system of, 177; consensus in, 182; as cooperative host, 182, 185, 247; Dahiya, 201, 209–10; decision-making about, 175–76, 199, 304*n*129; demonstrations in, 183; deterrence and, 175; economics in, 178–79; elites in, 178; Fatah in, 182, 184; Hezbollah 1985–2000 and, 181, 185–91; infrastructure and, 175; leverages in, 186–89, 194, 247; military budget of, 179; 1977–1978 invasions of, 120; nonstate actors and, 181–82; "Pax Syriana" in, 186–87; PFLP and, 182–83; PLO 1949–1985 and, 182–85; power in, 180; Rabin Doctrine and, 184–85, 187, 215; reform in, 178; refugees in, 180–81; regime and, 176–77; regime capacity of, 178–80, 204–5, 247; "Second Lebanon War," 199; Shia in, 177, 181, 185, 201; siege in, 185; SLA, 180, 191; state weakness of, 176–84, 253; strategic culture ideas, 202–9; Syria border with, 302*n*94; Syria compared to, 40, 47; Syrian regime capacity, 1970–2000, and, 119–21, 186; Taif Agreement and, 180, 186, 213; territory sovereignty of, 180, 197, 206; triadic coercion with, 176, 185–87, 194–95, 197–98, 199–209;

[358] INDEX

2006 War with, 199–209, 304n129; UNIFIL in, 184–85
Lebow, Richard Ned, 212, 242
Lesh, David, 102
LeT. *See* Lashkar-e-Taiba
leverages approach (*torat hamanofim*): Hezbollah and, 247; from IDF, 51; in Lebanon, 186–89, 194, 198, 205, 247; in Second Intifada, 150–51
Levi, Moshe, 118
Liberation Rally, 67
Liberman, Avigdor, 91
Libya, 87
Lieberman, Elli, 61
Likud government, 120, 132
Limor, Yoav, 204, 208
Lipkin-Shahak, Amnon, 145, 157
logic of appropriateness, 15–16, 105; Israeli triadic coercion, after 1990, 55–56, 244–45; in strategic culture ideas, Lebanon, 205–7; in strategic culture ideas, PA, 131, 160–61, 172
logic of consequences, 16, 160, 252–53
logic of deterrence, 4–5, 199
Lupovici, Amir, 15
Luttwak, Edward, 35

Maale Akrabim (Negev) bus attack, 69, 263n46
Maharaja of Kashmir, 219
Makhluf, Rami, 125
Makleff, Mordechai, 97
Makovsky, David, 192
Malka, Amos, 158, 170, 191
Mandate: of Palestine, 23; of Transjordan, 42
Mann, Michael, 10
Mansfield, Peter, 67, 77
Maoz, Moshe, 99
Maoz, Zeev, 59–61, *60*, 278n1; data from, 29–30, *30, 32, 37*, 59–61, *60*,

263n44; on Hezbollah, 188–89; on PA, 150
March, James, 15–16
McAdam, Doug, 10
McCain, John, 226
Mecca Agreement, 169
Meir, Golda, 184
Merari, Ariel, 182
Meridor, Dan, 155
Military Committee, 101
Mixed Armistice Commissions, 30, 63–64, 68, 73–74, 263n45
Mofaz, Shaul, 146, 151, 157, 193
morale, 32
Morris, Benny, 29, 61, 74
Morsi, Mohammed, 87–88, 91
Mossad (Israeli intelligence agency), 26, 40, 200
Mt. Dov/Sheba Farms, 193
Mozambique, 13
Mubarak, Hosni, 85–87, 93, 245
Mughniyah, Imad, 213
mukhtars (village leaders), 65
Mumbai attacks (India), 226, 228–29
Musharraf, Pervez, 224
Muslim Brotherhood, 67, 88, 113; Nasser and, 71–73, 84

Naguib, Mohammed, 67–68, 71
Nasrallah, Hassan, 213–14; on Lebanese withdrawal by Israel, 191–92, 207–9
Nasser, Gamal Abdel, 19, 43, 61, 68, 79, 245; consolidation by, 62; death of, 111; demands for, 75; economics and, 72; Fedayeen and, 76–77, 81–82, 245; Gaza Strip demonstrations and, 74–75; *intifada* and, 74–75; legitimacy of, 73, 92–93; militancy for, 75–76; Muslim Brotherhood and, 71–73, 84; popularity of, 81, 84; regime capacity and, 72–73; regional politics and,

75–76; retaliation raid against, 73–74, 76; Soviet weapons for, 77–78; "spider web" speech of, 207–9; Suez Canal and, 78, 244; Suez War and, 245; Syria and, 100, 103. *See also* nonstate actors' restriction, 1956–1979

National Command, of Ba'ath Party, 103

nationalism, 121–22

"national security triangle," 27–28

National Union, 79–80

Naveh, Shimon, 49

Netanyahu, Benjamin, 91, 212; Arafat and, 143–44; election of, 143

"New Operational Concept," 195

Nicaragua, 2

Nir, Shmuel, 54

nonstate actors, 4, 11–12; Assad, H., and, 128, 245; Egypt regime strength, 1954–1956, and, 71–78; IDF and, 48; in Kashmir, 219; Lebanon and, 181–82; punishment and, 5; in Sinai peninsula, 86–87

nonstate actors' restriction, 1956–1979: ANM and, 82–83; coercer state in, 78–79; economics and, 81; Egypt regime strength and, 78–85; Fatah and, 83–84; Fedayeen and, 81–82; leverages and, 82; National Union and, 79–80; PLA and, 83; reforms and, 80–81, 92–93; regime capacity and, 79–80, 80–81; Sadat and, 84–85; Suez War in, 79

nonstate host, PA as, 133–35

nuance lack: in Israeli triadic coercion, after 1990, 52–54, 56–57; in strategic culture ideas, Lebanon, 204–5; in strategic culture ideas, PA, 156–60

Ocalan, Abdullah, 233, 240

Ofir, Gabi, 145

Olmert, Ehud, 200–201, 206

Olmert, Yossi, 156

Olsen, Johan, 15–16

"omnibalancing," 18

O'Neill, Bard, 116

"ontological security," 15

Operation Accountability, 187–89, 198

Operation Cast Lead, 50

Operation Defensive Shield, 166–68

Operation Eagle, 87

Operation Euphrates Shield, 238

Operation Grapes of Wrath, 187–89, 198

Operation Hammer, 236

Operation Kinneret, 100

Operation Parakram, 224–25, 229, 240, 249, 307n18

Operation Peace of Galilee, 185

Operation Pillar of Defense, 50

Operation Protective Edge, 50

Operation Sinai, 87–88

Operation Theory Research Institute (OTRI), 159, 267n145

Operation Webs of Steel, 208–9

Oren, Michael, 63

Oslo Agreement: Hamas and, 140; Netanyahu against, 143–44; PA and, 122, 130, 133–34, 161–62, 171, 246; Palestinian fatalities and, 133, 286n7

Oslo II (Taba Agreement), 136, 154

OTRI. *See* Operation Theory Research Institute

Ottoman Empire, 232. *See also* Lebanon

Owen, Roger, 79

PA. *See* Palestinian National Authority

Pakistan, 21; civil war in, 221; coercion in, 255n4; economics in, 227; ISI and, 224–25; JeM in, 223–25; JKLF and, 222; Kargil War of 1999, 223–25; LeT in, 222, 224–25; regime capability in, 227; regime capacity of, 227–29;

regime weakness of, 227–29, 240; standoff with, 226; Taliban in, 1–2, 228; terrorists within, 227–28; triadic coercion and, 224–25, 228–29; U.S. and, 1–2, 155n4

Palestine Border Guard, 70, 82

Palestine Liberation Movement. *See* Fatah

Palestine Liberation Organization (PLO), 44, 47, 83, 103, 215; Assad, H., and, 115–16, 119; Likud government against, 120; Operation Peace of Galilee against, 185; recognition of, 130, 133, 183–84; as state-within-a-state, 180–81

Palestinian guerrilla fighters. *See* fedayeen

Palestinian Liberation Army (PLA), 83, 109, 115, 119, 130

Palestinian National Authority (Palestinian Authority) (PA), 19, 21, 51, 149–50; Arafat and, 134–35, 138–39; Camp David II and, 147–48, 171–72; ceasefires and, 167; closure of, 136, 138–39; cohesion in, 139–40; decision-making in, 151–54; defiance of, 146; deterrence and, 145, 156, 246–47; distinction of, 130–31; economics and, 138–39; elections in, 169; external leadership and, 140; Hamas and, 137, 139–42, 162–63; as host regime, 131, 134; before institutional development, 137–38; intelligence on, 144–45; Labor Party and, 132, 135–36, 141; Lebanese withdrawal by Israel and, 146–47; logic of appropriateness and, 131, 160–61; as nonstate host, 133–35; Oslo Agreement and, 122, 130, 133–34, 161–62, 171, 246; peace dividends for, 136; periods and, 131; predispositions of, 130, 138, 144; public opinion and, 134, 140–41, 143–44; regime capacity of, 138, 172–73; socioeconomics and, 138–39; without statehood, 134; strategic culture ideas in, 131, 154–61; suicide attacks by, *164*; territory sovereignty of, 136–37; triadic coercion and, 131, 141–43, 145, 165–68, 172; tunnel clashes and, 143–45; violence reduction and, *142*, 142–43; as weak regime, 131, 135–38, 161–62, 165–68, 171. *See also* Fatah; Second Intifada

Palestinians, 29; confidence of, 157; fatalities and, 31, *32*, 34, 36, *37*, 286n7; national movement of, 82; public opinion of, 289n61; resentment of, 66; schism among, 169–70; for suicide attacks, 163. *See also* Fatah; Palestinian National Authority

Palmach, 33

Paratroop Battalion 202, 35

Parliament House attack, 224

Party of Democratic Union (PYD), 238

Patriotic Union of Kurdistan (PUK), 236

Paul, T. V., 227

"Pax Syriana," 186–87

peace, 136, 254; through deterrence, 155–56

Peace Administration, 152–53

Pedahzur, Ami, 268n159

Peres, Shimon, 135, 203

Peretz, Amir, 200–201

Peri, Yoram, 25, 150–51

Perthes, Volker, 105, 123–24

PFLP. *See* Popular Front for the Liberation of Palestine

Pillar, Paul, 7–8

PKK. *See* Kurdistan Workers' Party

PLA. *See* Palestinian Liberation Army

"plausibility probe," 19
PLO. *See* Palestine Liberation Organization
policy implications, 18, 239–40
Popular Front for the Liberation of Palestine (PFLP), 47, 115–16, 163, 164
predispositions, 130, 138, 144. *See also* host states predisposition
propaganda, 43, 55
public opinion, 289n61; Hamas and, 140–41; on Lebanese withdrawal by Israel, 190–92, 215; of nationalist movements, 82–83; PA and, 134, 140–41, 143–44
PUK. *See* Patriotic Union of Kurdistan
PYD. *See* Party of Democratic Union

al-Qaeda, 1, 85, 87, 223, 227–28
Qassam rockets, 168
Qibya attack, 34
Qutri faction, of Ba'ath Party, 103

Rabbini, Nouin, 144
Rabin, Yitzhak, 35–36, 301n60; assassination of, 143; on PA, 135; on Syria, 105, 107
Rabin Doctrine, 39, 247, 265n90; Barak and, 195–96; cooperative host and, 52–53, 105; host states predisposition and, 40, 41, 42; Jordan and, 42–48, 52–53; Lebanon and, 184–85, 187, 215; Syria and, 105, 245
Rabinovich, Itamar, 125–26
Rapaport, Amir, 192, 198, 209
RCC. *See* Revolutionary Command Council
realist international relations theory, 117–18
reforms: in Egypt since 1949, 66–67; in Lebanon, 178; nonstate actors' restriction, 1956–1979 and, 80–81, 92–93; in Syria under Ba'ath, 1963–1970, 102–3
refugees, 71, 95; Barak and, 148; barrier and, 277n201; civil resistance of, 125; in Lebanon, 180–81; from 1948 War, 29, 42, 63; from 1967 War, 46; "War of the Camps" and, 121
regime, 8–9; Lebanon and, 176–77
regime capacity, 9–10, 12, 14, 25, 80–81, 250; of Egypt, 62, 72; of Lebanon, 178–80, 204–5, 247; Nasser and, 72–73; nonstate actors' restriction, 1956–1979 and, 79–80; of PA, 138, 172–73; of Pakistan, 227–29; in regime strength, 10–11, 257n29; of Syria, 91, 102–3, 113–14; in Syrian regime capacity, 1970–2000, 113–14. *See also* Syrian regime capacity, 1970–2000
regime coercion, 152–53, 242, 249–50; counterproductive, 6, 7; in Pakistan, 255n4; regime strength and, 14–15. *See also* triadic coercion; *specific topics*
regime cohesion: description of, 9–10; Egypt and, 72–74, 79–80, 82, 91–92; Hashemite challenges to, 42–43; infiltrations and, 71; Lebanon and, 176–78, 186, 200–201, 215; Operation Sinai and, 88; PA and, 130–31, 136, 139–40, 142–43, 165, 172; Pakistan and, 226, 228–29, 240; of RCC, 66–68; regime assets and, 14–15; of Syria, 95–96, 98–99, 102, 105–6, 108–23, 128; Turkey and, 230, 234, 237–38. *See also* regime capacity
regime strength, 12–13, 18, 240–41, 243, 250; from coercion, 14–15; cohesion in, 9–10; in "decision tree," 8–9; Israeli-Egypt cooperation and, 90–92; Rabin Doctrine, Jordan, and,

[362] INDEX

52–53; regime capacity in, 10–11, 257n29; from Suez War, 92–93, 245; in Syria, 20–21, 114–19; in Syrian regime capacity, 1970–2000, 114–19. *See also* Egypt regime strength

regime weakness: of Iraq, 236–38; of Pakistan, 227–29, 240; strategic culture and, 161–68, *164–65*; of Syria, 95–96, 99, 102–6, 124–29. *See also* Egypt regime weakness

Regional Command, of Ba'ath Party, 103, 106, 108–9

reprisal raids. *See* retaliation raids

research methodology, 18–19

retaliation raids, *32*, 36, 63–65, *64*, 263n44; directives for, 34; into Gaza Strip, 68–69; against Jordan, 32–33; against Nasser, 73–74, 76; Paratroop Battalion 202 for, 35

Revolutionary Command Council (RCC), 66–71

Rhodesia, 13

rockets, 168, 171, 186–87

Ross, Dennis, 146, 187, 189

Rwanda, 13

Sadat, Anwar, 84–85

al-Sadr, Musa, 181

Sa'iqa (Thunderbolt), 109–11, 115

Salafism, 170–71

Salehyan, Idean, 1

Salibi, Kamal, 42–43

Samu' raid, 44–46

Sarraj, Abd al-Hamid, 98

Saudi Arabia, 84

Sayigh, Yezid, 70, 83, 115, 157, 162

SCAF. *See* Supreme Council of the Armed Forces

Seale, Patrick, 99–100, 103, 106, 117–18

Second Intifada (2000–2004), 51–52, 154, 158, 172; aggressive coercion in, 152–53; Camp David and, 160–62; coercive leverage in, 150–51; enemy consciousness and, 159–60, 168; fatalities in, 149; Hamas in, 162–63; IDF on, 146, 157; Israeli strategic culture and, 173–74; PA and, 149–50; Peace Administration in, 152–53; Temple Mount/al-Aqsa Mosque and, 148–49; triadic coercion and, 151

"Second Lebanon War" (2006), 199

Segev, Tom, 105

Seko, Mubutu Sese, 13

Shalev, Arie, 48–49

Shalit, Gilad, 202–3

Shamir, Eitan, 53

Sharett, Moshe, 31–32, 34, 36, 69

Sharon, Ariel, 33, 35, 74, 148, 154, 169

Sharqawi, Abdullah, 65

Sheba Farms, 193, 195, 212

Shelah, Ofer, 150, 204, 208

Shemesh, Moshe, 45

Shia, 177, 181, 185, 201. *See also* Hezbollah

Shimshoni, Jonathan, 6, 61, 74

Shin Bet (Israeli internal security service), 26, 89, 138, 154

Shishakli, Adib, 98–99

Shlaim, Avi, 45, 47

Shoukry, Sameh, 91

Shuqayri, Ahmed, 83

Siboni, Gabriel, 210–11, 268n157

siege mentality, 49, 55

Simla Accord, 221–22

Sinai Bedouin tribes, 93–94

Sinai militants, 85–86

Sinai peninsula, 85, 93–94; Ansar Bait al-Maqdis, 89; attack from, 89; "buffer zone" in, 88–89; insurgency in, 88–89; lawlessness of, 87; nonstate actors in, 86–87; Operation Eagle

into, 87; Operation Sinai in, 87–88; SCAF in, 87
Singh, Manmohan, 226
Siniora, Fouad, 197, 213–14
el-Sisi, Abdel Fattah, 88, 245
SLA. *See* South Lebanon Army
Slonim, Ori, 141–42
smuggling, cross-border, 29, 87–89, 277*n*201
Smyth, Phillip, 127
Sneh, Ephraim, 191, 210
socioeconomics, 98; PA and, 138–39
South Africa, 13
South Lebanon Army (SLA), 180, 191
Soviet weapons, 77–78
state sponsors, 8
Stein, Janice Gross, 212, 242
Strategic Assessment Initiative, 165
strategic culture, 3, 18, 218, 251; Abbas and, 168–70; attention to, 16–17; definition of, 15; of India, 220–21, 248–49; institutions and, 16; of Israel, 168–71; policy implications and, 18, 239–40; regime schism and, 169–70; regime weakness and, 161–68, *164–65*; triadic coercion and, 243–44, 252–54; of Turkey, 233–34, 248–49; in 2006 War, 199–209, 216, 247–48
strategic culture decision-making processes, 10, 251; in India, 220–21; in Israel about Hezbollah, 175–76, 248; about Lebanon, 175–76, 199, 304*n*129; after 1967 War, 48–49; in PA, 151–54; PKK related to, 248–49; recommendations for, 252–54; in Turkey, 231–32; in 2006 War, 199–202, 216. *See also* Israeli decision-making
strategic culture ideas, Israel, 27–28

strategic culture ideas, Israel regarding Lebanon: enemy consciousness in, 207–9; intrinsic utility/instrumental utility in, 193–94, 202–4; logic of appropriateness in, 205–7; nuance lack in, 204–5
strategic culture ideas, Israel regarding the PA, 154; enemy consciousness in, 159–60; intrinsic utility/instrumental utility in, 155–56, 176; logic of appropriateness in, 131, 160–61; nuance lack in, 156–60
strategic rationality, 90–91
Sudan, 2
Suez Canal, 78, 244
Suez War. *See* War of 1956
suicide attacks, 163, *164–65*, 169
suicide bombings, 141, 162–63, 289*n*61
Sundarji Doctrine, 223
Supreme Council of the Armed Forces (SCAF), 87
Suwydani, Ahmed, 104
Swisher, Clayton, 148
Syria, 278*n*1; ADLs and, 23; Barak and, 190, 195–96; border friction foundations, 1949–1962, 96–101; cohesion of, 240; DMZ and, 96–97; Egypt and, 100, 103, 105–6; ISIS, 85, 238, 253; Jordan compared to, 40; leadership in, 196; Lebanese Civil War and, 180, 186; Lebanese withdrawal by, 196–97; Lebanon border with, 302*n*94; Lebanon compared to, 40, 47; map of, *230*; Nasser and, 100, 103; 1948 War and, 98; 1967 War and, 107–8; "Pax Syriana," 186–87; Rabin Doctrine and, 105, 245; Rabin on, 105, 107; regime capacity of, 91, 102–3, 113–14; regime strength in, 20–21,

114–19; regime weakness of, 95–96, 99, 102–6, 124–29; triadic coercion in, 95–96; Turkey and, 233, 238–39, 248–49; U.S. and, 119, 121, 124, 196. *See also* al-Assad, Bashar; al-Assad, Hafez; Hezbollah

Syrian border friction foundations, 1949–1962: Baʻath Party and, 100–105; class conflict and, 98; coup d'état in, 98–99; defiance of, 99; Deuxième Bureau and, 97–98; Egypt and, 100; interstate competition over, 99–100; land and water rights in, 96–97; neo-Baʻath coup d'état, 106; regime weakness of, 99; socioeconomics and, 98; UAR and, 100–101

"Syrian puppet organization," 105

Syrian regime capacity, 1970–2000: Abu Nidal organization and, 120–21; diplomatic pressure in, 121; Emergency Law in, 113; Fatah in, 115–16, 119–20; fedayeen control in, 115–16; GDP and, 113–14; Golan and, 110, 114–18; Hezbollah and, 122–23; Israel agreement and, 122–23; Jordan attack and, 110; Lebanon and, 119–21, 186; military buildup and, 114; Muslim Brotherhood in, 113; nationalism in, 121–22; realist international relations theory and, 117–18; regime capacity in, 113–14; regime strength in, 114–19; surveillance and, 112–13; terrorism and, 121; triadic coercion and, 118–19

"Syrian syndrome," 105

Syrian triadic conflicts since 2000: Assad, B., and, 123–24; economics and, 127; Golan and, 125–27; Hezbollah and, 126–27; International Crisis Group and, 124; Israeli fatalities in, 126; regime weakness in, 124–29; terrorism and, 124–25; "two-edged sword" in, 128

Syria under Baʻath, 1963–1970: Baʻath Party in, 101–9, 128, 245–46; escalation from, 107; Fatah in, 101–7; Jadid and, 106–11; neo-Baʻath coup d'état in, 106; 1967 War and, 107–8; reforms in, 102–3; regime weakness in, 102–6

Taba Agreement (Oslo II), 136, 154
Taba conference (2001), 154
Taif Agreement (1989), 180, 186, 213
"tailored deterrence," 52
Tal, Israel, 48
Taliban, 1–2, 228
Tankel, Stephen, 222
Tanzim, 140, 167
Tarrow, Sidney, 10
Tellis, Ashley, 225
Temple Mount/al-Aqsa Mosque, 143, 148–49
territory sovereignty: of Lebanon, 180, 197, 206; of PA, 136–37
terrorism, 121, 124–25. *See also specific topics*
Tessler, Mark, 103
"Third Lebanon War, The: Target Lebanon" (Eiland), 210–11
Thunderbolt (Saʻiqa), 109–11, 115
Tilly, Charles, 10
Training and Doctrine Division (TOHAD), 49
transitive compellence, 255n2
"Treaty of Brotherhood, Cooperation, and Coordination" (1991), 187
triadic coercion, 3, 218, 242; brute force in, 4; causes and, 13–17; compellence in, 5–6; counterproductive, 6, 7; definition of, 3; deterrence by punishment in, 4–6; indirect deterrence in, 5; outcomes of, 6–12,

7, *8*, 243; prevalence of, 1–2; regime strengths and, 9–12, 18; sources of, 243; strategic culture and, 243–44; strategy of, 2; in 2006 War, 198–209, 216; after 2006 War, 209–14, 216–17. *See also specific topics*
triadic conflicts, 250–52
tunnel crisis/clashes (1996), 132, 143–45
Turkey, 218; AKP in, 231–32, 238; Assad, H., and, 233–34, 240; civil war in, 236; Cold War and, 232; decision-making in, 231–32; Iran and, *230*, 230–31, 234–35; Iraq and, *230*, 235–39; KRG in, 235–37; Kurds in, 229–30, 235–36; lessons from, 239–41; map of, *230*; military in, 231–33; Ottoman Empire and, 232; PKK in, 2, 21, 229–38, 248–49; PUK in, 236; PYD and, 238; strategic culture of, 233–34, 248–49; Syria and, 233, 238–39, 248–49; triadic coercion and, 231, 234–36, 239, 249; U.S. and, 237
Turkey-Iran Commission on Security Cooperation, 235
TWA airplanes, 121
2006 War. *See* War of 2006

UAR. *See* United Arab Republic
UN. *See* United Nations
UNIFIL. *See* United Nations Interim Force in Lebanon
Unit 101, 33–35, 38, 73, 264*n*58
United Arab Republic (UAR), 100–101
United Nations (UN), 23; on Lebanese withdrawal by Israel, 193, 196–97; Security Council, 34, 76–77, 193, 263*n*46
United Nations Interim Force in Lebanon (UNIFIL), 184–85

United Nations Truce Supervision Organization (UNTSO), 63, 263*n*45
United States (U.S.): Arafat and, 132, 141, 147–48, 162; Aswan Dam and, 78; Baghdad Pact from, 75; Camp David from, 160–62; Camp David II from, 132, 147–48, 162, 171–72; Iraq and, 130, 237; Operation Grapes of Wrath and, 188; Pakistan and, 1–2, 155*n*4; Qibya and, 34; Syria and, 119, 121, 124, 196; and War of 2006, 200–201
UNTSO. *See* United Nations Truce Supervision Organization
U.S. *See* United States

Van Evera, Stephen, 262*n*29
Vardi, Gil-li, 26, 29
Vatikiotis, P. J., 78, 80
village leaders (*mukhtars*), 65

Wachsman, Nachson, 136–38
"war model" of counterterrorism, 268*n*159
War of 1948, 27, 32; demobilization after, 33; Gaza Strip in, 63; Israeli's statehood and, 23; Jordan and, 42; refugees from, 29, 42; Syria and, 98; West Bank and, 42
War of 1956 (Suez War), 20, 24, 59; coercer in, 78–79; deterrence from, 60; documents and, 64; Israeli infiltrations and, 63–64; Nasser and, 245; regime strength from, 92–93, 245; triadic coercion after, 38, 40, 60–62, 92, 245
War of 1967, 46; decision-making after, 48–49; Egypt after, 84, 93; Syria and, 107–8
War of 2006, 176; anti-intellectualism in, 202–4; Barak on, 212; Bint Jbail and,

208–9; decision-making in, 199–202, 216; deterrence in, 203–5, 209–13; fatalities in, 203–4; with Lebanon, 199–209, 304n129; residential areas in, 201–2, 209; strategic culture ideas, Lebanon, in, 202–9, 216, 247–48; strategic culture in, 199–209, 216, 247–48; target in, 210–11; triadic coercion in, 198–209, 216; triadic coercion since, 209–14, 216–17
War of Attrition (1967–1970), 84, 93
War of the Camps, 121
water rights, 96–97
weak regime: PA as, 131, 135–38, 161–62, 165–68, 171; RCC as, 68–71; regime capacity of, 12
Weber, Max, 10
Weizman, Ezer, 184
West Bank, 156–57; Jordan and, 42–43; 1948 War and, 42; Qibya attack in, 34; Samu' raid in, 44–46

Wheelock, Keith, 68
white minority governments, 13
Winograd Commission, 194, 203, 209–10
withdrawal: from Gaza Strip, 133. *See also* Lebanese withdrawal by Israel
World War I, 262n29

Ya'alon, Moshe, 49, 147, 149–50; on Iron Dome, 89–90; Lebanese withdrawal by Israel and, 192, 194–95; Second Intifada and, 158–59
Yaari, Ehud, 64, 72
Yadlin, Amos, 210–12
Yaniv, Avner, 59–61

Zaire, 13
Zambia, 13
Zimbabwe, 13

GPSR Authorized Representative: Easy Access System Europe, Mustamäe tee
50, 10621 Tallinn, Estonia, gpsr.requests@easproject.com

www.ingramcontent.com/pod-product-compliance
Lightning Source LLC
Chambersburg PA
CBHW021930290426
44108CB00012B/790